essays

for J. M. B.

essays

method, content, conscience

Fred L. Bergmann
DePauw University

WM. C. BROWN COMPANY PUBLISHERS
Dubuque, Iowa

ACKNOWLEDGMENTS

Mortimer J. Adler, "How to Mark a Book." *Saturday Review of Literature*, July 6, 1940. Copyright © 1940 The Saturday Review Company, Inc.; renewed 1967 Saturday Review, Inc. Reprinted by permission of the author.

Russell Baker, "Pop Art." The New York *Times,* April 23, 1963. Copyright © 1963 by The New York Times Company. Reprinted by permission.

James Baldwin, "The Discovery of What It Means to be an American." Reprinted from *Nobody Knows My Name* by James Baldwin. Copyright © 1954, 1956, 1958, 1959, 1960, 1961 by James Baldwin and used by permission of the publisher, The Dial Press, Inc.

Marston Bates, "Black, White, Colored." Copyright © 1968 by Marston Bates. Reprinted by arrangement with Walker and Company, New York.

Robert Benchley, "What College Did to Me." From *Inside Benchley* by Robert Benchley. Copyright, 1927 by Harper & Brothers; renewed, 1955 by Gertrude D. Benchley.

Vance Bourjaily, "Hemingway on Trial, Judge Baker Presiding." *New York Times Book Review,* April 27, 1969. Copyright © 1969 by The New York Times Company. Reprinted by permission of Russell & Volkening, Inc.

Earl H. Brill, "Sex is Dead!" *The Christian Century,* August 3, 1966. Copyright © by The Christian Century Foundation. Reprinted by permission.

Van Wyck Brooks, "Thoreau at Walden." From the book *The Flowering of New England* by Van Wyck Brooks. Copyright, 1936, 1952 by Van Wyck Brooks. Renewal, ©, 1964 by Gladys Brooks. Reprinted by permission of the publishers.

Grace Brown, "The One-Egg Cake." From *Expository Writing* by Mervin Curl. Revised edition copyright 1931 by Mervin James Curl. Reprinted by permission of the publishers, Houghton Mifflin Company.

Art Buchwald, "I Don't Know" and "Confrontation Is Something a Professor Must Face Up To." Copyright © 1969 by The Washington Post Company. Used by permission of the author.

Rachel Carson, "The Gray Beginnings." From *The Sea Around Us* by Rachel L. Carson. Copyright 1950, 1951 by Rachel L. Carson. Reprinted by permission of Oxford University Press, Inc.

Eldridge Cleaver, "The Blood Lust." From *Soul on Ice* by Eldridge Cleaver. Copyright © 1968 by Eldridge Cleaver. Used with permission of McGraw-Hill Book Company.

Samuel L. Clemens, "The Boys' Ambition." From *Life on the Mississippi* by Samuel L. Clemens. Reprinted by permission of Harper and Row, Publishers.

Logan Clendening, "Reproduction and Sex." From *The Human Body* by Logan Clendening. Copyright 1927, 1930, 1937, 1945 by Alfred A. Knopf, Inc. Reprinted by permission.

Henry Steele Commager, "Is the World Safer for Anything?" *Saturday Review,* November 9, 1968. Copyright © 1968 Saturday Review, Inc. Reprinted by permission of the author.

Sir Geoffrev Crowther, "English and American Education." *The Atlantic,* April, 1960. Copyright © 1960 by The Atlantic Monthly Company, Boston, Mass. Reprinted with permission.

e.e. cummings, "i & selfdiscovery." Reprinted by permission of the publishers from e.e. cummings, *i: Six Nonlectures.* Cambridge, Mass.: Harvard University Press, Copyright, 1953, by E.E. Cummings. Poetry copyright 1925, 1935, 1954, by E.E. Cummings; copyright 1963 by Marion Morehouse Cummings; copyright 1926 by Horace Liveright. Reprinted from *Poems, 1923-1954* by permission of Harcourt, Brace & World, Inc.

Clarence Day, "Hens and Grammarians." Copyright 1936 and renewed 1964 by Katherine B. Day. Reprinted from *After All* by Clarence Day, by permission of Alfred A. Knopf, Inc.

Lord Dunsany, "A Moral Little Tale." From *Fifty-One Tales* by Lord Dunsany. Copyright © 1915 by Little, Brown and Company.

Albert Einstein, "E=mc²." From *Out of My Later Years* by Albert Einstein. Copyright 1950 by the Philosophical Library, Inc. Reprinted by permission of the publisher.

Herbert Gold, "The Age of Happy Problems." Reprinted from *The Age of Happy Problems* by Herbert Gold. Copyright © 1952,

1954, 1957, 1958, 1960, 1961, 1962 by Herbert Gold and used by permission of the publisher, The Dial Press, Inc.

Harvey Goldberg and William Appleman Williams, "The Heart of Radicalism." From Harvey Goldberg, ed., *American Radicals.* Copyright © 1957 by Monthly Review, Inc. Reprinted by permission of the publisher.

LeRoi Jones, "Expressive Language." From *Home: Social Essays* by LeRoi Jones. Reprinted by permission of William Morrow and Company, Inc. Copyright © 1963, 1966 by LeRoi Jones.

Kenneth Keniston, "The Cult of the Present." From *The Uncommitted: Alienated Youth in American Society,* copyright © 1962, 1965 by Kenneth Keniston. Reprinted by permission of Harcourt, Brace & World, Inc.

Irving Kristol, "What's Bugging the Students?" *The Atlantic,* November, 1965. Copyright © 1965, by The Atlantic Monthly Company, Boston, Mass. Reprinted with permission.

Joseph Wood Krutch, "Life, Liberty, and the Pursuit of Welfare." *Saturday Evening Post,* July 15, 1961. Reprinted by permission of the author.

Lauriat Lane, Jr., "Why *Huckleberry Finn* is a Great World Novel." *College English,* October, 1955. Reprinted with the permission of the National Council of Teachers of English and Lauriat Lane, Jr.

John Lear, "Spinning the Thread of Life." *Saturday Review,* April 5, 1969. Copyright © 1969 Saturday Review, Inc. Photographs by O.L. Miller, Jr., and Barbara R. Beatty, Biology Division, Oak Ridge National Laboratory. Reprinted by permission.

Abraham Lincoln, "Address at Gettysburg," 1863.

William McCord, "We Ask the Wrong Questions about Crime." *The New York Times Magazine,* November 21, 1965. Copyright © 1965 by The New York Times Company. Reprinted by permission.

Marshall McLuhan, Classroom Without Walls." From *Explorations in Communication,* edited by Edmund Carpenter and Marshall McLuhan. Reprinted by permission of the Beacon Press, copyright © 1960 by Beacon Press.

Don McNeill, "Autumn in the Haight: Where Has Love Gone?" *The Village Voice,* November 30, 1967. Reprinted by permission of *The Village Voice.* Copyrighted by The Village Voice, Inc., 1967.

Roger D. Masters, "What in Marx Speaks to Today's Young Iconoclasts?" *Saturday Review,* April 5, 1969. Copyright © 1969 by Saturday Review, Inc. Reprinted by permission of the author.

Wright Morris, "The Function of Style: Ernest Hemingway." From *The Territory Ahead* by Wright Morris. Copyright © 1957 by the Macmillan Company; copyright © 1957, 1958 by Wright Morris. Reprinted by permission of the author.

Allan Morrison, "The White Power Structure." From *The White Problem in America* by the Editors of *Ebony.* Copyright © 1965, 1966 by Johnson Publishing Company, Inc. Originally published in *Ebony,* August, 1965. Reprinted by permission of the publisher.

The Editors of *Newsweek,* "The Great Truffle Snuffle." From *Newsweek,* February 24, 1969. Copyright Newsweek, Inc., 1969. Reprinted by permission.

George Orwell, "Shooting an Elephant." From *Shooting an Elephant and Other Essays* by George Orwell. Copyright, 1945, 1946, 1949, 1950 by Sonia Brownell Orwell. Reprinted by permission of Harcourt, Brace & World, Inc., and Secker & Warburg, Ltd.

Francis Parkman, "The Black Hills." From *The Oregon Trail,* 1849.

Henry S. Resnik, "How Hermann Hesse Speaks to the College Generation." Copyright © 1969 by Henry S. Resnik. Reprinted by permission of Cyrilly Abels.

Kenneth Rexroth, "Uncle Tom's Cabin." *Saturday Review,* January 11, 1969. Copyright © 1969 Saturday Review, Inc. Reprinted by permission of the author.

Leo Rosten, "The Joys of Yiddish." *Harper's Magazine,* October, 1968. Copyright © by Leo Rosten. Reprinted by permission of the author.

George Santayana, "Patriotism." "Patriotism" is reprinted with the permission of Charles Scribner's Sons from *Little Essays* by George Santayana.

Arthur M. Schlesinger, "Our Ten Contributions to Civilization." *The Atlantic,* March, 1959. Copyright © 1959, by The Atlantic Monthly Company, Boston, Mass. Reprinted by permission of Mrs. Elizabeth B. Schlesinger.

Charles M. Schulz, "A Comic Strip Has to Grow." *Saturday Review,* April 12, 1969. Copyright © 1969 Saturday Review, Inc. Reprinted by permission of the author.

Jonathan Swift, "A Modest Proposal," 1729.

Thomas S. Szasz, "What Psychiatry Can and Cannot Do." Copyright © 1964, by Harper's Magazine, Inc. Reprinted from the February, 1964, issue of *Harper's Magazine* by permission of the author.

Henry David Thoreau, from *Walden,* 1854.

Alexis de Tocqueville, "The Restless Spirit of the Americans." From *Democracy in America,* 1838.

The New Yorker, "In Search of a Future." Notes and Comments in *The New Yorker,* March 22, 1969. Copyright © 1969 The New Yorker Magazine, Inc. Reprinted by permission of the publisher.

Dylan Thomas, "Holiday Memory." From Dylan Thomas, *Quite Early One Morning.* Copyright 1954 by New Directions Publishing Corporation. Reprinted by permission of New Directions Publishing Corporation and of J.M. Dent and Sons, Ltd.

The Editors of *Time,* "The Plight of the U.S. Patient." *Time,* February 21, 1969. Reprinted by permission from *Time,* The Weekly News Magazine. Copyright, Time, Inc., 1969.

Harvey Wheeler, "Bringing Science Under Law." From *The Center Magazine,* March, 1969, a publication of The Center for the Study of Democratic Institutions.

E.B. White, "Walden—June 1939." From *One Man's Meat* by E.B. White. Copyright 1939 by E.B. White.

George Wiswell, "Why Men Fall in Love." *Esquire,* March, 1955. Copyright © 1955 by Esquire Magazine. Reprinted by permission.

CONTENTS

PART II: SOME TYPES OF ESSAYS

PREFACE

The subtitle of this collection—*Method, Content, Conscience*—illuminates the criteria employed by the editor in making the selections. Method is the vehicle of the essayist: what means did he use to best advance his ideas? Nine different modes of development are illustrated in the essays which follow. What the essayist has to say to today's readers—the Content of the subtitle—and his point of view—his "Conscience"—are what makes the essays worth reading and studying. A great variety of subjects relating to the world in which we live will be found in the selections, along with a great variety in points of view. Taken together, the method, the content, and the conscience of the writer supply stimulation for both thought and writing.

The individual essays in Part I, which deals with methods of essay development, are followed by questions and problems which may stimulate thinking and discussion, by suggestions for the student's own writing, and by (in most instances) a list of related readings. The suggestions for further reading are given in short form as they are not intended to serve as bibliographies for the essays but merely as guides which may lead the interested student to related readings in the library. How much use the student and the teacher will want to make of these appendixes to the essays must be an individual matter; the essays will speak for themselves both as examples of careful prose composition and as vehicles for the communication of ideas.

F.L.B.

INTRODUCTION

WHAT IS THE ESSAY?

Dr. Johnson's *Dictionary*, 1755:
1. Attempt, endeavour
2. A loose sally of the mind; an irregular indigested piece; not a regular and orderly composition
3. A trial; an experiment

The Oxford Universal Dictionary, 3d ed. rev., 1955:
2. An attempt, endeavour 1598
3. (obs.) A first attempt in learning or practice—1734; a first draft—1793
4. A short composition on any particular subject; orig. "an irregular undigested piece" (J), but now said of a finished treatise 1597

Webster's Third New International Dictionary, 1961
1a. an effort made to do or perform: Attempt, Endeavor
 b. the result or product of the effort to do or perform something
2a. an analytic, interpretative, or critical literary composition usu. much shorter and less systematic and formal than a dissertation or thesis and usu. dealing with its subject from a limited often personal point of view (persuasion is more starkly and simply the purpose of the essay than of fiction or poetry, since the essay deals always with an idea—Katharine F. Gerould).
 b. something resembling or suggesting such a composition esp. in its presentation of an extended analytic, interpretative, or critical view of something

The Random House Dictionary of the English Language, 1966
1. a short literary composition on a particular theme or subject, usually in prose and generally analytic, speculative, or interpretative
2. an effort to perform or accomplish something; attempt
4. *Obs.* a tentative effort; trial; assay.

The American Heritage Dictionary of the English Language, 1969
2. A testing or trial of the value or nature of a thing . . .
3. A short literary composition on a single subject, usually presenting the personal views of the author

When Michel de Montaigne poured forth his thoughts and ideas on paper between the years 1571 and 1580, he was making *essais*, trials, attempts to present his thoughts, ideas, and something of his personality for his readers; for, he said, "It is myself that I portray."

In doing so he gave the name to a whole body of writing which stretches from classical times to the present and which has changed over the years to mean much more than Dr. Samuel Johnson's definition of 1755 would suggest: "attempt, endeavour . . . a loose sally of the mind; an irregular indigested piece; not a regular and orderly composition." So great, in fact, has the change been that a recent definition will not even limit the species to prose: "a short literary composition on a particular theme or subject, usually in prose and generally analytic, speculative, or interpretative" (*The Random House Dictionary of the English Language,* 1966).

We shall be safe enough today, however, to limit the essay to prose composition, to indicate its essential brevity (shorter than a novel, shorter than a book), and to suggest that its content is analytic, interpretative, speculative, or critical, frequently from a personal point of view. Its tone may vary from the very light to the deeply serious; its presentation is generally artistic. In other words, the essay is a short composition in which the author presents an idea or series of ideas, generally worthwhile ones, in finished prose form.

Because the term *essay* is so all-inclusive, it has become traditional to classify essays by type. So wide is the range of subjects and methods, however, that few students of the essay today are likely to agree entirely on what the classification should be. One convenient device, however, is to classify essays according to style. In England in the sixteenth and seventeenth centuries four distinct styles of essay writing came into use: the *grand* style, the *utilitarian* style, the *euphuistic* style, and the *familiar* style. The grand style was the style of Cicero's essays, its chief characteristics being fullness (*copia*), passion and intensity, vast use of authority, solemnity and dignity of movement, and heavy use of rhetorical ornamentation: parallelism, antithesis, paradox, repetition, and so on. This style makes use of elaborate sentence structure and suggests prose written for purposes of oratory. Milton's prose, as in the *Areopagitica,* is an example from the period, as is Ruskin's in the nineteenth century. The utilitarian style is a reaction to the grand style—actually an attack upon it. It is called utilitarian because the object is to convey ideas as briefly and as literally as possible. Bacon's brief aphoristic style serves as an example from the period, as DeFoe's does for the next age and Charles Lamb's for the nineteenth century. Its hallmarks are simplicity, directness, and lack of concern for art for art's sake. The euphuistic style, named for a sixteenth-century prose work by John Lyly, is, on the contrary, the height of ornateness. The attempt is only vaguely utilitarian; the chief purpose of the euphuistic style is to present "beautiful" prose. At its worst this style hardly presents beautiful prose; with its clutter of alliteration, antitheses, parallelism, and every sort of literary figure, not to speak of a plethora of word plays, quotations from the classics, and references to (un)natural history, it makes tedious reading today. But in the sixteenth century euphuism did focus the attention of readers on style, did make the English style-conscious. The fourth style of the period, the familiar style, returns to the personal approach of Montaigne; an example is Isaac Walton's *The Compleat Angler.*

Modern essay style comes most directly from the utilitarian and the familiar styles, although of course the grand and the euphuistic styles have left their mark. But the classification of essays has greatly expanded through the years. Classification is sometimes done by modes—for example, definition, classification, argument—and sometimes by types—e.g., biographical, satirical, reviews. Sometimes subject is used as the basis for classification—essays dealing with ideas, essays dealing with writing, essays dealing with the arts (or any other subject). Or the subject may be more explicitly the basis— essays on democracy, on education, on religion, on technology. Sometimes method is the key to classification—using reasoning, explaining through description, using the narrative method. The methods of classification are legion, and any one method is likely to be as good as any other. What is important is to use a method of classification which will help the student both to understand the writer's purpose and method and to provide him with useful models for study as he works to perfect his own writing. Such a method is attempted in this collection.

RHETORICAL MODES OF THE ESSAY

The first group of essays in this collection is presented according to modes or styles. The modes selected are definition, comparison and contrast, cause and effect, classification and analysis, argument and persuasion, explanation and process, example, description, and narration. Other methods—for example, analogy—might have been included. But it must be borne in mind that the methods overlap; that an essay is rarely developed entirely according to one method, and to include all methods would confront the reader with an overwhelming number of examples. The methods chosen for this book are considered to be the most useful to the college student of writing, and the essays selected to illustrate these modes are developed *primarily* according to the indicated mode. The reader should not, however, expect to find the distinctions among the various modes always clear-cut; it is not a matter of black or white but of the methods the author of the individual essay selected in order to present his subject effectively.

In addition to these methods of essay development, the book includes in Part II a group of essays classified by types or kinds: literary, book review, autobiographical and biographical, satirical and humorous, and reporting. In these essays the reader will note a variety of methods of development and may determine that some methods are particularly suited to certain types of essays. Careful analysis of the essays grouped by types will be of value to the student who is attempting to improve his own writing.

Some of these types are distinguished from other types by their content. Literary essays, book reviews, and autobiographical and biographical essays obviously depend on their subject for their classification by type. This is not to say, of course, that method and manner are not important to them; book reviewers, for example, generally employ the method of revelation of the book's contents and the manner of the critic. Literary essays vary greatly in method and manner; there is wide divergence between the essay written for high school students of literature and that written for such a scholarly journal as *PMLA,* which presents essays of little interest to the general reading public but addresses itself rather to specialists. The method of biographical and autobiographical essays is generally that of chronology, although the manner varies widely from writer to writer. The hallmark of the familiar, or personal, essay is the author's manner; it is virtually impossible to find a standardized method for these essays except in a collection of them by the same writer. So varied, in fact, is the familiar or personal essay that its methods are employed in virtually all essays except those of the most formal type. Logan Clendening's essay on human reproduction, reprinted in this book under explanation and process, is a happy example of the familiar technique. Because the manner of the familiar essay has been so widely adapted to other modes and types of the essay, no special category is assigned to it in this volume. E.C. Benson, a British master of the familiar essay, once said of the form, "The important thing is that [it] should possess what may be called atmosphere and personality." Surely any essay except the most formal aspires to these qualities.

Satirical and humorous essays, on the other hand, show considerable similarity of manner from writer to writer; the careful selection of facts or traits of character, the bending of those facts or traits, the willful exaggeration, the ironic tone are standard characteristics. Likewise reporting, as with the book review, reveals both a typical method and a typical manner. The different characteristics of these types of essays will be enlarged upon in the prefaces to the examples given in this book.

THE ESSAY TODAY

The essay today differs very greatly from the essay of past centuries, just as the present-day novel differs from that of the eighteenth century. Both the essay and the novel have grown and have changed considerably through the years, as man's world, his ideas, and the limits of his knowledge have expanded and changed. One important characteristic of the essay is that it is not a static form as, for example, the conventional sonnet is likely to be; it is, rather, a reflection of its time. The essayist is always trying to say something of relevance to his contemporaries. To accomplish this aim he employs a greatly expanded variety of modes and types—such a variety, in fact, that it is now virtually impossible, as we have seen, to make an all-inclusive definition of the form. But basic to the essay is still the original idea of a person trying, *essaying,* to express personal views. One can, of course, draw distinctions between such forms as the short biography and the book review, between a study of urban social problems and an analysis of Chaucer's narrative methods, between a report on the use of drugs today and a satirical piece on student activism in political life. And yet one would soon find that the categories overlap in structure, method, manner, and objective. Thus today the term *essay* is a convenient one to include a vast variety of prose types which differ from other prose forms—the novel, for example, or the objective report—mainly in length, in expression of personal views, and in content, dealing, as it does, with things readily at hand rather than creating new things as the writer of fiction does.

Yet even when contrasting the essay and fiction one is not differentiating adequately. Clarence Day creates his grammarians, Don McNeill his hippies. For many readers Rachel Carson actually creates the sea. And who wishes to check the veracity of Mark Twain's stories of his boyhood, or the facts in Robert Benchley's humorous pieces? The essay today is indeed a broad form. It is more profitably read, studied, analyzed as an individual piece of writing than forced, as a literary kind, into a narrow mold.

WRITING ESSAYS

To write an essay is to record reaction to and interpretation of experience. The essay may merely record that reaction or interpretation; it may explain it; it may analyze it; it may argue against it; it may attempt to persuade others to accept a like reaction or interpretation. In any event, the essay communicates. And as communication is inextricably bound to communal life (hermits are generally not good essayists), the reading of essays, the study of essays, and the practice of writing essays are part and parcel of education. In fact, much of the reading of the college student is made up of essays, and most of what he writes will be in essay form.

To write an essay is, furthermore, to differentiate between the mere communication of facts and the presentation of a point of view, an analysis, or an interpretation of facts and ideas. The newspaper article traditionally records facts; the essay indulges in mental play with facts and ideas. When one communicates by way of the article, he provides grist for someone else's mill; when one communicates by way of the essay, he supplies the meal.

To practice writing the essay is, then, to experiment with the communication of ideas. Such practice is a more fundamental approach to living—but not a more valuable one—than is the practice of fiction. Most students do not practice essay writing in order to become writers of essays; rather, they practice to become better communicators—of themselves, their ideas, their analyses and interpretations of facts—and so to make a personal rather than an impersonal place for themselves in the world.

Necessary to the practice of writing essays is the practice of reading them. By studying the methods which are available, the styles which may be employed, the types which may be used to communicate, the practicer learns how to communicate. The student must know the main point, the "thesis," of the essay he reads. He should know the device or devices the author has used to establish his thesis—definition, explanation, argument, description, and so on. It will be well for the student to determine whether the writer has used an objective or a subjective approach, a mental or an emotional appeal, or both; and he should know why one approach was used rather than, or more than, another. He must study the author's style in order to determine if it is an effective one for the kind of subject the author is dealing with. Finally, he should criticize all of these factors in order to determine their relative effectiveness in the particular essay and in essays of like subject. By careful reading, by detailed analysis, by thoughtful evaluation of essays the student goes a long way toward improving the communication of his own ideas. The purpose of this book is to provide a collection of essays which will further that aim.

PART I

METHODS
OF
ESSAY
DEVELOPMENT

TO EXPLAIN

When the writer of an essay tells how something is done or how to do something, he uses the method of explanation or process in developing his essay. In some of the essays which follow, Mortimer J. Adler explains how to read a book, Grace Brown gives the process of producing a one-egg cake, Rachel Carson gives an explanation of how the young planet Earth acquired an ocean, and Logan Clendening outlines the process of reproduction. To give an explanation or clarify a process is one of the most common forms of exposition. It is the basis of much of the teaching the student receives from the earliest grades through college.

The most important consideration in developing an essay by explanation or process is logical order. For clarity and ease of comprehension the reader must have the first step first, the last step last, with all intermediate steps in proper sequence. This is not to say, of course, that such essays are merely outlines—although it is true that this is one of the easiest kinds of essays to outline. Note, for example, the difference between a recipe for a cake in any standard cookbook and Grace Brown's essay on the one-egg cake. Description, narration, example, analysis often play an important part in essays developed by this method. After all, the explanation must be both clear and interesting. Many of us never read a cookbook recipe, but any of us will read Grace Brown's essay with pleasure.

Just as explanation is the basis of much of the teaching you receive, so also is the explanatory essay one of the commonest kinds of writing you will be called upon to do. Reading the following essays will give you insight into the methods which may be employed in making adequate and readable explanations of processes. The essays under many of the other headings in this book are also basically explanations. To define is to explain meaning. To compare and contrast, to classify and analyze, to give examples, to describe—all these are to explain. One uses causes or effects, or both, to explain, just as one argues to explain and explains to persuade. To explain, then, is implicit in most methods of essay development. This particular category, however, contains essays which are different from "explanations" of the meaning of democracy or the nature of poetry; the writers tell how to do something or how something happened. Sometimes, of course, the writer goes beyond the explanation of a process, as Logan Clendening does when he analyzes the emotion *love.* Here is an excellent example of a writer who uses more than one method in developing his essay.

HOW TO MARK A BOOK

Mortimer J. Adler

You know you have to read "between the lines" to get the most out of anything. I want to persuade you to do something equally important in the course of your reading. I want to persuade you to "write between the lines." Unless you do, you are not likely to do the most efficient kind of reading. 1

I contend, quite bluntly, that marking up a book is not an act of mutilation but of love. 2

You shouldn't mark up a book which isn't yours. Librarians (or your friends) who lend you books expect you to keep them clean, and you should. If you decide that I am right about the usefulness of marking books, you will have to buy them. Most of the world's great books are available today, in reprint editions, at less than a dollar. 3

There are two ways in which one can own a book. The first is the property right you establish by paying for it, just as you pay for clothes and furniture. But this act of purchase is only the prelude to possession. Full ownership comes only when you have made it a part of yourself, and the best way to make yourself a part of it is by writing in it. An illustration may make the point clear. You buy a beefsteak and transfer it from the butcher's ice-box to your own. But you do not own the beefsteak in the most important sense until you consume it and get it into your bloodstream. I am arguing that books, too, must be absorbed in your bloodstream to do you any good. 4

Confusion about what it means to *own* a book leads people to a false reverence for paper, binding, and type—a respect for the physical thing—the craft of the printer rather than the genius of the author. They forget that it is possible for a man to acquire the idea, to possess the beauty, which a great book contains, without staking his claim by pasting his bookplate inside the cover. Having a fine library doesn't prove that its owner has a mind enriched by books; it proves nothing more than the he, his father, or his wife, was rich enough to buy them. 5

There are three kinds of book owners. The first has all the standard sets and best-sellers—unread, untouched. (This deluded individual owns woodpulp and ink, not books.) The second has a great many

---

Throughout this book the paragraphs of the essays are numbered in the right margin of the page, the number appearing at the center of the paragraph. Occasionally blocks of very short paragraphs, as when conversation is being reported, are considered, for the sake of simplicity, as a single unit and are so marked.

books—a few of them read through, most of them dipped into, but all of them as clean and shiny as the day they were bought. (This person would probably like to make books his own, but is restrained by a false respect for their physical appearance.) The third has a few 6
books or many—every one of them dog-eared and dilapidated, shaken and loosened by continual use, marked and scribbled in from front to back. (This man owns books.)

Is it false respect, you may ask, to preserve intact and unblemished a beautifully printed book, an elegantly bound edition? Of course not. I'd no more scribble all over the first edition of *Paradise Lost* than I'd give my baby a set of crayons and an original Rem- 7
brandt! I wouldn't mark up a painting or a statue. Its soul, so to speak, is inseparable from its body. And the beauty of a rare edition or of a richly manufactured volume is like that of a painting or a statue.

But the soul of a book *can* be separated from its body. A book is more like the score of a piece of music than it is like a painting. No great musician confuses a symphony with the printed sheets of music. Arturo Toscanini reveres Brahms, but Toscanini's score of the C-minor Symphony is so thoroughly marked up that no one but the maestro himself can read it. The reason why a great conductor makes 8
notations on his musical scores—marks them up again and again each time he returns to study them—is the reason why you should mark up your books. If your respect for magnificent binding or typography gets in the way, buy yourself a cheap edition and pay your respects to the author.

Why is marking up a book indispensable to reading it? First, it keeps you awake. (And I don't mean merely conscious; I mean wide awake.) In the second place, reading, if it is active, is thinking, and thinking tends to express itself in words, spoken or written. The 9
marked book is usually the thought-through book. Finally, writing helps you remember the thoughts you had, or the thoughts the author expressed. Let me develop these three points.

If reading is to accomplish anything more than passing time, it must be active. You can't let your eyes glide across the lines of a book and come up with an understanding of what you have read. Now an ordinary piece of light fiction, like say, *Gone with the Wind*, doesn't require the most active kind of reading. The books you read for pleasure can be read in a state of relaxation, and nothing is lost. 10
But a great book, rich in ideas and beauty, a book that raises and tries to answer great fundamental questions, demands the most active reading of which you are capable. You don't absorb the ideas of

John Dewey the way you absorb the crooning of Mr. Vallee. You have to reach for them. That you cannot do while you're asleep.

If, when you've finished reading a book, the pages are filled with your notes, you know that you read actively. The most famous *active* reader of great books I know is President Hutchins, of the University of Chicago. He also has the hardest schedule of business activities of any man I know. He invariably reads with a pencil, and sometimes, when he picks up a book and pencil in the evening, he finds himself, instead of making intelligent notes, drawing what he calls "caviar factories" on the margins. When that happens, he puts the book down. He knows he's too tired to read, and he's just wasting time.

But, you may ask, why is writing necessary? Well, the physical act of writing, with your own hand, brings words and sentences more sharply before your mind and preserves them better in your memory. To set down your reaction to important words and sentences you have read, and the questions they have raised in your mind, is to preserve those reactions and sharpen those questions.

Even if you wrote on a scratch pad, and threw the paper away when you had finished writing, your grasp of the book would be surer. But you don't have to throw the paper away. The margins (top and bottom, as well as side), the end-papers, the very space between the lines, are all available. They aren't sacred. And, best of all, your marks and notes become an integral part of the book and stay there forever. You can pick up the book the following week or year, and there are all your points of agreement, disagreement, doubt, and inquiry. It's like resuming an interrupted conversation with the advantage of being able to pick up where you left off.

And that is exactly what reading a book should be: a conversation between you and the author. Presumably he knows more about the subject than you do; naturally, you'll have the proper humility as you approach him. But don't let anybody tell you that a reader is supposed to be solely on the receiving end. Understanding is a two-way operation; learning doesn't consist in being an empty receptacle. The learner has to question himself and question the teacher. He even has to argue with the teacher, once he understands what the teacher is saying. And marking a book is literally an expression of your differences, or agreements of opinion, with the author.

There are all kinds of devices for marking a book intelligently and fruitfully. Here's the way I do it:

1. Underlining: Of major points, of important or forceful statements.

2. Vertical lines at the margin: To emphasize a statement already underlined.

3. Star, asterisk, or other doo-dad at the margin: To be used sparingly, to emphasize the ten or twenty most important statements in the book. (You may want to fold the bottom corner of each page on which you use such marks. It won't hurt the sturdy paper on which most modern books are printed, and you will be able to take the book off the shelf at any time and, by opening it at the folded-corner page, refresh your recollection of the book.)

4. Numbers in the margin: To indicate the sequence of points the author makes in developing a single argument.   15

5. Numbers of other pages in the margin: To indicate where else in the book the author made points relevant to the point marked; to tie up the ideas in a book, which, though they may be separated by many pages, belong together.

6. Circling of key words or phrases.

7. Writing in the margin, or at the top or bottom of the page, for the sake of: Recording questions (and perhaps answers) which a passage raised in your mind; reducing a complicated discussion to a simple statement; recording the sequence of major points right through the book. I use the end-papers at the back of the book to make a personal index of the author's points in the order of their appearance.

The front end-papers are, to me, the most important. Some people reserve them for a fancy bookplate. I reserve them for fancy thinking. After I have finished reading the book and making my personal index on the back end-papers, I turn to the front and try to   16 outline the book, not page by page, or point by point (I've already done that at the back), but as an integrated structure, with a basic unity and an order of parts. This outline is, to me, the measure of my understanding of the work.

If you're a die-hard anti-book-marker, you may object that the margins, the space between the lines, and the end-papers don't give you room enough. All right. How about using a scratch pad slightly smaller than the page-size of the book—so that the edges of the   17 sheets won't protrude? Make your index, outlines, and even your notes on the pad, and then insert these sheets permanently inside the front and back covers of the book.

Or, you may say that this business of marking books is going to slow up your reading. It probably will. That's one of the reasons for doing it. Most of us have been taken in by the notion that speed of reading is a measure of our intelligence. There is no such thing as the right speed for intelligent reading. Some things should be read quickly and effortlessly, and some should be read slowly and even laboriously. The sign of intelligence in reading is the ability to read different things differently according to their worth. In the case of good 18 books, the point is not to see how many of them you can get through, but rather how many can get through you—how many you can make your own. A few friends are better than a thousand acquaintances. If this be your aim, as it should be, you will not be impatient if it takes more time and effort to read a great book than it does a newspaper.

You may have one final objection to marking books. You can't lend them to your friends because nobody else can read them without being distracted by your notes. Furthermore, you won't want to 19 lend them because a marked copy is a kind of intellectual diary, and lending it is almost like giving your mind away.

If your friend wishes to read your *Plutarch's Lives,* "Shakespeare," or *The Federalist Papers,* tell him, gently but firmly, to buy 20 a copy. You will lend him your car or your coat—but your books are as much a part of you as your head or your heart.

QUESTIONS AND PROBLEMS

1. What is the tone of the essay? What is Adler's manner of approaching the reader? How does he address the reader?
2. This essay is basically an explanation of a process; but, as with almost all essays, it is more than this.
   a. Where does the explanation of the process begin?
   b. In par. 3 two other devices are used. What are they?
   c. What is the method of development in par. 6?
3. What is the effect of the use of statements in parentheses in par. 6? Would the statements be as effective without the parentheses?
4. Comment on the structure of the passage which is made up of pars. 9, 10, 11, and 12. Is it a useful structure? If it is effective, what makes it so?
5. Of the three objections one may have to marking books (pars. 17-19), which is the most serious? Why?

SUGGESTIONS FOR WRITING

1. Find out all you can about new methods of learning speed-reading. Write an explanation of such a method.
2. Write an essay entitled "How to Kill a Book."
3. Write an essay on a book which has become "absorbed in your bloodstream" (par. 4). Tell how that book became a part of you.
4. Write an essay in which you classify types of readers, or write one on types of college readers. Make use of examples.
5. Write a narrative about how you came to buy your first book (other than a textbook).

6. Write an essay in differentiation among books to *keep*, books to *lend*, and books to *throw away*.

SUGGESTIONS FOR FURTHER READING

Mortimer J. Adler, *How to Read a Book* (Simon and Schuster)
Robert B. Downs, *The Power of Books* (Syracuse)
Clifton Fadiman, *A Lifetime Reading Plan* (World; Avon)
Helen E. Haines, *Living with Books*, 2nd ed. (Columbia)
John Passmore, *Reading and Remembering* (Cambridge)

THE GRAY BEGINNINGS

Rachel L. Carson

And the earth was without form, and void; and darkness was upon the face of the deep.

GENESIS

Beginnings are apt to be shadowy, and so it is with the beginnings of that great mother of life, the sea. Many people have debated how and when the earth got its ocean, and it is not surprising that their explanations do not always agree. For the plain and inescapable truth is that no one was there to see, and in the absence of eyewitness accounts there is bound to be a certain amount of disagreement. So if I tell here the story of how the young planet Earth acquired an ocean, it must be a story pieced together from many sources and containing whole chapters the details of which we can only imagine. The story is founded on the testimony of the earth's most ancient rocks, which were young when the earth was young; on other evidence written on the face of the earth's satellite, the moon; and on hints contained in the history of the sun and the whole universe of star-filled space. For although no man was there to witness this cosmic birth, the stars and the moon and the rocks were there, and, indeed, had much to do with the fact that there is an ocean.   1

The events of which I write must have occurred somewhat more than 2 billion years ago. As nearly as science can tell that is the approximate age of the earth, and the ocean must be very nearly as old. It is possible now to discover the age of the rocks that compose the crust of the earth by measuring the rate of decay of the radioactive materials they contain. The oldest rocks found anywhere on   2 earth—in Manitoba—are about 2.3 billion years old. Allowing 100 million years or so for the cooling of the earth's materials to form a rocky crust, we arrive at the supposition that the tempestuous and violent events connected with our planet's birth occurred nearly 2½ billion years ago. But this is only a minimum estimate, for rocks indicating an even greater age may be found at any time.

The new earth, freshly torn from its parent sun, was a ball of whirling gases, intensely hot, rushing through the black spaces of the universe on a path and at a speed controlled by immense forces. Gradually the ball of flaming gases cooled. The gases began to liquefy, and Earth became a molten mass. The materials of this mass eventually became sorted out in a definite pattern: the heaviest in   3 the center, the less heavy surrounding them, and the least heavy forming the outer rim. This is the pattern which persists today—a central sphere of molten iron, very nearly as hot as it was 2 billion years ago, an intermediate sphere of semiplastic basalt, and a hard outer shell, relatively quite thin and composed of solid basalt and granite.

The outer shell of the young earth must have been a good many millions of years changing from the liquid to the solid state, and it is believed that, before this change was completed, an event of the greatest importance took place—the formation of the moon. The next time you stand on a beach at night, watching the moon's bright path across the water, and conscious of the moon-drawn tides, re-   4
member that the moon itself may have been born of a great tidal wave of earthly substance, torn off into space. And remember that if the moon was formed in this fashion, the event may have had much to do with shaping the ocean basins and the continents as we know them.

There were tides in the new earth, long before there was an ocean. In response to the pull of the sun the molten liquids of the earth's whole surface rose in tides that rolled unhindered around the globe and only gradually slackened and diminished as the earthly shell cooled, congealed, and hardened. Those who believe that the moon is a child of earth say that during an early stage of the earth's development something happened that caused this rolling, viscid tide to gather speed and momentum and to rise to unimaginable heights. Apparently the force that created these greatest tides the earth has ever known was the force of resonance, for at this time the period of   5
the solar tides had come to approach, then equal, the period of the free oscillation of the liquid earth. And so every sun tide was given increased momentum by the push of the earth's oscillation, and each of the twice-daily tides was larger than the one before it. Physicists have calculated that, after 500 years of monstrous, steadily increasing tides, those on the side toward the sun became too high for stability, and a great wave was torn away and hurled into space. But immediately, of course, the newly created satellite became subject to physical laws that sent it spinning in an orbit of its own about the earth.

There are reasons for believing that this event took place after the earth's crust had become slightly hardened, instead of during its partly liquid state. There is to this day a great scar on the surface of the globe. This scar or depression holds the Pacific Ocean. According to some geophysicists, the floor of the Pacific is composed of basalt, the substance of the earth's middle layer, while all other oceans are floored with a thin layer of granite. We immediately wonder what   6 became of the Pacific's granite covering and the most convenient assumption is that it was torn away when the moon was formed. There is supporting evidence. The mean density of the moon is much less than that of the earth (3.3 compared with 5.5), suggesting that the moon took away none of the earth's heavy iron core, but that it is composed only of the granite and some of the basalt of the outer layers.

The birth of the moon probably helped shape other regions of the world ocean besides the Pacific. When part of the crust was torn away, strains must have been set up in the remaining granite envelope. Perhaps the granite mass cracked open on the side opposite the moon scar. Perhaps, as the earth spun on its axis and rushed on its orbit through space, the cracks widened and the masses of granite began to drift apart, moving over a tarry, slowly hardening layer of   7
basalt. Gradually the outer portions of the basalt layer became solid and the wandering continents came to rest, frozen into place with oceans between them. In spite of theories to the contrary, the weight of geologic evidence seems to be that the locations of the major ocean basins and the major continental land masses are today much the same as they have been since a very early period of the earth's history.

But this is to anticipate the story, for when the moon was born there was no ocean. The gradually cooling earth was enveloped in heavy layers of cloud, which contained much of the water of the new planet. For a long time its surface was so hot that no moisture could fall without immediately being reconverted to steam. This dense, perpetually renewed cloud covering must have been thick enough   8
that no rays of sunlight could penetrate it. And so the rough outlines of the continents and the empty ocean basins were sculptured out of the surface of the earth in darkness, in a Stygian world of heated rock and swirling clouds and gloom.

As soon as the earth's crust cooled enough, the rains began to fall. Never have there been such rains since that time. They fell continuously, day and night, days passing into months, into years,   9
into centuries. They poured into the waiting ocean basins, or, falling upon the continental masses, drained away to become sea.

That primeval ocean, growing in bulk as the rains slowly filled its basins, must have been only faintly salt. But the falling rains were the symbol of the dissolution of the continents. From the moment the rains began to fall, the lands began to be worn away and carried to   10
the sea. It is an endless, inexorable process that has never stopped— the dissolving of the rocks, the leaching out of their contained miner-

als, the carrying of the rock fragments and dissolved minerals to the ocean. And over the eons of time, the sea has grown ever more bitter with the salt of the continents.

In what manner the sea produced the mysterious and wonderful stuff called protoplasm we cannot say. In its warm, dimly lit waters the unknown conditions of temperature and pressure and saltiness must have been the critical ones for the creation of life from non-life.   11 At any rate they produced the result that neither the alchemists with their crucibles nor modern scientists in their laboratories have been able to achieve.

Before the first living cell was created, there may have been many trials and failures. It seems probable that, within the warm saltiness of the primeval sea, certain organic substances were fashioned from carbon dioxide, sulphur, phosphorus, potassium, and calcium. Per-   12 haps these were transition steps from which the complex molecules of protoplasm arose—molecules that somehow acquired the ability to reproduce themselves and begin the endless stream of life. But at present no one is wise enough to be sure.

Those first living things may have been simple microorganisms rather like some of the bacteria we know today—mysterious border-line forms that were not quite plants, not quite animals, barely over the intangible line that separates the non-living from the living. It is doubtful that this first life possessed the substance chlorophyll, with which plants in sunlight transform lifeless chemicals into the living   13 stuff of their tissues. Little sunshine could enter their dim world, penetrating the cloud banks from which fell the endless rains. Prob-ably the sea's first children lived on the organic substances then present in the ocean waters, or, like the iron and sulphur bacteria that exist today, lived directly on inorganic food.

All the while the cloud cover was thinning, the darkness of the nights alternated with palely illumined days, and finally the sun for the first time shone through upon the sea. By this time some of the living things that floated in the sea must have developed the magic of   14 chlorophyll. Now they were able to take the carbon dioxide of the air and the water of the sea and of these elements, in sunlight, build the organic substances they needed for life. So the first true plants came into being.

Another group of organisms, lacking the chlorophyll but needing organic food, found they could make a way of life for themselves by devouring the plants. So the first animals arose, and from that day to   15 this, every animal in the world has followed the habit it learned in the ancient seas and depends, directly or through complex food chains, on the plants for food and life.

As the years passed, and the centuries, and the millions of years, the stream of life grew more and more complex. From simple, one-celled creatures, others that were aggregations of specialized cells arose, and then creatures with organs for feeding, digesting, breathing, reproducing. Sponges grew on the rocky bottom of the sea's edge and coral animals built their habitations in warm, clear waters.   16 Jellyfish swam and drifted in the sea. Worms evolved, and starfish, and hard-shelled creatures with many-jointed legs. The plants, too, progressed, from the microscopic algae to branched and curiously fruiting seaweeds that swayed with the tides and were plucked from the coastal rocks by the surf and cast adrift.

During all this time the continents had no life. There was little to induce living things to come ashore, forsaking their all-providing, all-embracing mother sea. The lands must have been bleak and hostile beyond the power of words to describe. Imagine a whole continent of naked rock, across which no covering mantle of green had been   17 drawn—a continent without soil, for there were no land plants to aid in its formation and bind it to the rocks with their roots. Imagine a land of stone, a silent land, except for the sound of the rains and winds that swept across it. For there was no living voice, and nothing moved over its surface except the shadows of the clouds.

Meanwhile, the gradual cooling of the planet, which had first given the earth its hard granite crust, was progressing into its deeper layers; and as the interior slowly cooled and contracted, it drew away   18 from the outer shell. This shell, accommodating itself to the shrinking sphere within it, fell into folds and wrinkles—the earth's first mountain ranges.

Geologists tell us that there must have been at least two periods of mountain building (often called "revolutions") in that dim period, so long ago that the rocks have no record of it, so long ago that the mountains themselves have long since been worn away. Then there   19 came a third great period of upheaval and readjustment of the earth's crust, about a billion years ago, but of all its majestic mountains the only reminders today are the Laurentian hills of eastern Canada, and a great shield of granite over the flat country around Hudson Bay.

The epochs of mountain building only served to speed up the processes of erosion by which the continents were worn down and their crumbling rock and contained minerals returned to the sea. The uplifted masses of the mountains were prey to the bitter cold of the

upper atmosphere and under the attacks of frost and snow and ice   20
the rocks cracked and crumbled away. The rains beat with greater
violence upon the slopes of the hills and carried away the substance
of the mountains in torrential streams. There was still no plant covering to modify and resist the power of the rains.

And in the sea, life continued to evolve. The earliest forms have
left no fossils by which we can identify them. Probably they were
softbodied, with no hard parts that could be preserved. Then, too,
the rock layers formed in those early days have since been so altered   21
by enormous heat and pressure, under the foldings of the earth's
crust, that any fossils they might have contained would have been
destroyed.

For the past 500 million years, however, the rocks have preserved
the fossil record. By the dawn of the Cambrian period, when the
history of living things was first inscribed on rock pages, life in the
sea had progressed so far that all the main groups of backboneless or
invertebrate animals had been developed. But there were no animals
with backbones, no insects or spiders, and still no plant or animal
had been evolved that was capable of venturing onto the forbidding   22
land. So for more than three-fourths of geologic time the continents
were desolate and uninhabited, while the sea prepared the life that
was later to invade them and make them habitable. Meanwhile, with
violent tremblings of the earth and with the fire and smoke of roaring volcanoes, mountains rose and wore away, glaciers moved to and
fro over the earth, and the sea crept over the continents and again
receded.

It was not until Silurian time, some 350 million years ago, that
the first pioneer of land life crept out on the shore. It was an arthro-
pod, one of the great tribe that later produced crabs and lobsters and
insects. It must have been something like a modern scorpion, but,   23
unlike its descendants, it never wholly severed the ties that united it
to the sea. It lived a strange life, half-terrestrial, half-aquatic, something like that of the ghost crabs that speed along the beaches today,
now and then dashing into the surf to moisten their gills.

Fish, tapered of body and stream-molded by the press of running
waters, were evolving in Silurian rivers. In times of drought, in the
drying pools and lagoons, the shortage of oxygen forced them to   24
develop swim bladders for the storage of air. One form developed an
air-breathing lung and by its aid could live buried in the mud for long
periods.

It is very doubtful that the animals alone would have succeeded
in colonizing the land, for only the plants had the power to bring

about the first amelioration of its harsh conditions. They helped make soil of the crumbling rocks, they held back the soil from the rains that would have swept it away, and little by little they softened and subdued the bare rock, the lifeless desert. We know very little about the first land plants, but they must have been closely related to some of the larger seaweeds that had learned to live in the coastal shadows, developing strengthened stems and grasping, rootlike hold-fasts to resist the drag and pull of the waves. Perhaps it was in some coastal lowlands, periodically drained and flooded, that some such plants found it possible to survive, though separated from the sea. This also seems to have taken place in the Silurian period.

The mountains that had been thrown up by the Laurentian revo-lution gradually wore away, and as the sediments were washed from their summits and deposited on the lowlands, great areas of the continents sank under the load. The seas crept out of their basins and spread over the lands. Life fared well and was exceedingly abundant in those shallow, sunlit seas. But with the later retreat of the ocean water into the deeper basins, many creatures must have been left stranded in shallow, landlocked bays. Some of these animals found means to survive on land. The lakes, the shores of the rivers, and the coastal swamps of those days were the testing grounds in which plants and animals either became adapted to the new conditions or perished.

As the lands rose and the seas receded, a strange fishlike creature emerged on the land, and over the thousands of years its fins became legs, and instead of gills it developed lungs. In the Devonian sand-stone this first amphibian left its footprint.

On land and sea the stream of life poured on. New forms evolved; some old ones declined and disappeared. On land the mosses and the ferns and the seed plants developed. The reptiles for a time domi-nated the earth, gigantic, grotesque, and terrifying. Birds learned to live and move in the ocean of air. The first small mammals lurked inconspicuously in hidden crannies of the earth as though in fear of the reptiles.

When they went ashore the animals that took up a land life carried with them a part of the sea in their bodies, a heritage which they passed on to their children and which even today links each land animal with its origin in the ancient sea. Fish, amphibian, and reptile, warm-blooded bird and mammal—each of us carries in our veins a salty stream in which the elements sodium, potassium, and calcium are combined in almost the same proportions as in sea water. This is our inheritance from the day, untold millions of years ago,

25

26

27

28

when a remote ancestor, having progressed from the one-celled to the many-celled stage, first developed a circulatory system in which the   29 fluid was merely the water of the sea. In the same way, our lime-hardened skeletons are a heritage from the calcium-rich ocean of Cambrian time. Even the protoplasm that streams within each cell of our bodies has the chemical structure impressed upon all living matter when the first simple creatures were brought forth in the ancient sea. And as life itself began in the sea, so each of us begins his individual life in a miniature ocean within his mother's womb, and in the stages of his embryonic development repeats the steps by which his race evolved, from gill-breathing inhabitants of a water world to creatures able to live on land.

Some of the land animals later returned to the ocean. After perhaps 50 million years of land life, a number of reptiles entered the sea in Mesozoic time. They were huge and formidable creatures. Some had oarlike limbs by which they rowed through the water; some were web-footed, with long, serpentine necks. These grotesque monsters disappeared millions of years ago, but we remember them   30 when we come upon a large sea turtle swimming many miles at sea, its barnacle-encrusted shell eloquent of its marine life. Much later, perhaps no more than 50 million years ago, some of the mammals, too, abandoned a land life for the ocean. Their descendants are the sea lions, sea elephants, and whales of today.

Among the land mammals there was a race of creatures that took to an arboreal existence. Their hands underwent remarkable development, becoming skilled in manipulating and examining objects, and along with this skill came a superior brain power that compensated for what these comparatively small mammals lacked in strength. At   31 last, perhaps somewhere in the vast interior of Asia, they descended from the trees and became again terrestrial. The past million years have seen their transformation into beings with the body and brain and the mystical spirit of man.

Eventually man, too, found his way back to the sea. Standing on its shores, he must have looked out upon it with wonder and curiosity, compounded with an unconscious recognition of his lineage. He could not physically re-enter the ocean as the seals and whales had   32 done. But over the centuries, with all the skill and ingenuity and reasoning powers of his mind, he has sought to explore and investigate even its most remote parts, so that he might re-enter it mentally and imaginatively.

He fashioned boats to venture out on its surface. Later he found ways to descend to the shallow parts of its floor, carrying with him the air that, as a land mammal long unaccustomed to aquatic life, he needed to breathe. Moving in fascination over the deep sea he could not enter, he found ways to probe its depths, he let down nets to capture its life, he invented mechanical eyes and ears that could re-create for his senses a world long lost, but a world that, in the deepest part of his subconscious mind, he had never wholly forgotten. 33

And yet he has returned to his mother sea only on her own terms. He cannot control or change the ocean as, in his brief tenancy of earth, he has subdued and plundered the continents. In the artificial world of his cities and towns, he often forgets the true nature of his planet and the long vistas of its history, in which the existence of the race of men has occupied a mere moment of time. The sense of all these things comes to him most clearly in the course of a long ocean voyage, when he watches day after day the receding rim of the 34 horizon, ridged and furrowed by waves; when at night he becomes aware of the earth's rotation as the stars pass overhead; or when, alone in this world of water and sky, he feels the loneliness of his earth in space. And then, as never on land, he knows the truth that his world is a water world, a planet dominated by its covering mantle of ocean, in which the continents are but transient intrusions of land above the surface of the all-encircling sea.

QUESTIONS AND PROBLEMS

1. Miss Carson explains the beginnings of "Mother Sea" by what might be called process analysis. How is this analysis organized?
2. The author admits that "there is bound to be a certain amount of disagreement" in the explanation she gives for the beginning of the ocean.
   a. What does the title of this essay mean?
   b. What is the basis of disagreement?
   c. How does she qualify the facts she presents?
3. The strong and varied rhythms of Miss Carson's sentences suggest a poetic quality in her prose. Choose four or five sentences in which you find this poetic quality particularly evident. Defend your choices.
4. Miss Carson begins her essay with a quotation from Genesis: "And the earth was without form, and void; and darkness was upon the face of the deep."
   a. Is the quotation appropriate in light of the Biblical accounts of creation?
   b. Discuss the Biblical "six days" of creation in light of Miss Carson's account of the creation of the earth in pars. 2, 3, and 4.
   c. The Biblical account continues: "And God said, 'Let the waters bring forth abundantly the moving creature that hath life, and fowl that may fly above the earth in the open firmament of heaven.'" Can this passage be explained in terms of Miss Carson's account of the beginnings of life in pars. 11, 12, and 13?

5. In spite of the fact that this is a scientific explanation of a process for laymen, does Miss Carson add an air of mystery and wonder to it? Find an example in par. 10. Are there other examples in the essay?
6. Miss Carson explains her larger process by breaking it into a series of sub-processes, one of which explains the formation of the moon. What are the other subprocesses she explains?
7. Miss Carson always keeps her lay readership in mind. Cite several examples which indicate that she is not writing for a group of fellow scientists.
8. The table of contents of this book will indicate the eight other methods of essay development which are explained and illustrated. What other methods does Miss Carson make use of in addition to explanation of a process? Give an example of each one you find.
9. In reference to Miss Carson's statement that some scientists believe the moon to be "a child of earth" (par. 5), comment on recent findings based on materials brought from the moon by our astronauts.
10. In the essay there is use of such words as "freshly torn," "pull," "helped shape," "torn away." How do the images evoked by these words relate to the subject and the tone of the essay?

SUGGESTIONS FOR WRITING

1. Write an explanation of one of the recent experiments in underwater living.
2. If you have ever lived on the seashore or visited the shore for a period of time, write a piece explaining how you discovered the meaning of the sea.
3. Write a researched account of Pleistocene glaciation.
4. Write an essay on the accuracy of the observations on sailing the seas which Coleridge, who had never been at sea, gives in *The Rime of the Ancient Mariner*.
5. Write an explanation of the moon's crust or of the moon's formation based upon reports of scientists who have studied the moon rocks which have been brought to earth by the astronauts.
6. If you have had experience in a hurricane or tornado, write an explanatory essay on what it is and what causes it.
7. Explain the protective devices against radiation, temperature, etc., required in space vehicles.
8. Write for a layman audience an explanation of ocean tides.

SUGGESTIONS FOR FURTHER READING

Irving Adler, *How Life Began* (New American Library)
Willard Bascom, *Waves and Beaches: The Dynamics of the Ocean Surface* (Doubleday)
William Beebe, *Half Mile Down* (Harcourt, Brace & World)
Peter J. Brancazio and A.G.W. Cajeron, eds., *The Origin and Evolution of Atmospheres and Oceans* (Wiley)
Rachel Carson, *The Edge of the Sea* (Oxford)
Joseph Conrad, *The Mirror of the Sea* (Doubleday-Page)
Reginald Daly, *Our Mobile Earth* (Scribner)
Charles Darwin, *The Diary of the Voyage of H.M.S. Beagle*, ed. Nora Barlow (Cambridge)
George Gamow, *Creation of the Universe* (Viking)

Charles C. Gillispie, *Genesis and Geology: The Decades Before Darwin* (Harper)
Karl Heim, *Christian Faith and Natural Science* (Harper)
Thor Heyerdahl, *Kon-Tiki* (Rand McNally)
H.A. Marmer, *The Sea* (Appleton-Century)
Herman Melville, *Moby-Dick* (various publishers)
Hans Pettersson, *The Ocean Floor* (Yale)
Lionel A. Walford, *The Living Resources of the Sea* (Ronald)
Alfred Russell Wallace, *Island Life* (Macmillan)
C.M. Yonge, *The Sea Shore* (Collins)

THE ONE-EGG CAKE
Grace Brown

The one-egg cake is not one of those haughty, high-bred confec-
tions that must have the refinement of thrice-bolted flour and
dry-whipped whites of eggs, that cannot allow a rude foot to cross
the kitchen floor while they grandly bake, lest their sensitive, poised
delicacy swoon from shock. The one-egg cake is sturdy, stocky, humble. It asks for only the simplest of materials, and shrinks not from
hastiness in the handling. It evolved, like the hoof of the horse or the
wing of the bird, in answer to a natural need; or in answer to two   1
natural needs: that of the impecunious, for dessert; and that of the
busy housewife, for time. It is indigenous anywhere. It would undoubtedly be edible to the last crumb if, flour lacking, it were made
of hominy grits or bran and shorts. But in spite of its modesty, it
may easily attain to the distinction of the cake in Katherine Mansfield's story: "And God said: 'Let there be cake.' And there was
cake. And God saw that it was good."

Its implements are such as any igloo might keep on the kitchen
shelf: *one* mixing bowl, *one* cup, *one* tablespoon, *one* teaspoon, *one*
sheet of waxed paper, *one* baking pan. Its *one* regret is that it must
occasionally deviate in material from the absolute unity which is its   2
ideal. But its method of procedure wastes not one movement. Anyone who wishes to attempt this adventure toward perfect unity
should proceed as follows.

Into the one mixing bowl sift an indeterminate quantity of
flour—any kind of flour. From this measure two cupsful onto the
waxed paper and return the remainder to wherever it came from.
Measure one cup (the same cup) of sugar into the bowl. Add to it six
tablespoons of soft shortening. If you have a good eye for quantity,
guess at it and put in *one* six-tablespoon lump. Cream them together
with one clean right hand—after first oiling the baking pan with it,
and thus saving one washing. Next break the one egg—the egg of the
title role—into the bowl and beat briskly with the tablespoon into
the creamed sugar and shortening. Into the cup (the same cup) meas-   3
ure two-thirds of a cup of milk. Pour one-third into the bowl and
shake in half the measured flour. Beat the mixture briskly. Into the
remaining flour measure three teaspoons of baking powder. Shake
the flour and baking powder into the sifter held over the bowl and
sift them in. Pour in the rest of the milk. Beat again in a lively
manner. Flavor with one teaspoon (the same teaspoon) of vanilla or
one teaspoon of cinnamon or one square of melted chocolate. Pour it

into the oiled pan and bake it in one oven. If no oven is handy, use one pressure cooker. If it is served to *one* husband, *one* daughter, and *one* son, it will disappear in *one* meal.

QUESTIONS AND PROBLEMS

1. Can you construct a typical cookbook recipe from Grace Brown's essay? Try it. Has she omitted any ingredient or any step in the process?
2. What is the essential difference between the cookbook recipe and this author's essay? Are there other differences? Which would you rather read? Which would you rather use in cooking?
3. Who was Katherine Mansfield? From which story is the quotation in par. 1 taken?
4. Is the comparison in par. 1 between the one-egg cake and the hoof of the horse or the wing of the bird an apt one? In making this comparison, what tone is Grace Brown setting?
5. What is your assessment of the diction of this essay? How does the quality of the prose differ from that of Rachel Carson's in "The Gray Beginnings"? Is there a reason for this difference?

SUGGESTIONS FOR WRITING

1. "How to" explanations are supposed to be foolproof. Try to write a foolproof explanation of how to tie a bow tie or how to make a baked Alaska. Begin with an outline (your "recipe"). Then try to write a piece which will give as much pleasure as Grace Brown's does.
2. Utilitarian prose and literary prose are two different kinds. Yet any utilitarian subject may be improved by adding a literary flavor. Make an attempt to give more than a utilitarian explanation of one of the following:
   a. How to paint a house
   b. How to buy a book
   c. How to make a dormitory room a room to live in
   d. How to catch a man (or a woman)
   e. How to determine the quality of a restaurant
   f. How to start a riot.

A COMIC STRIP HAS TO GROW
Charles M. Schulz

Drawing a daily comic strip is not unlike having an English theme hanging over your head every day for the rest of your life. I was never very good at writing those English themes in high school, and I usually put them off until the last minute. The only thing that saves me in trying to keep up with a comic strip schedule is the fact that it is quite a bit more enjoyable.   **1**

I am really a comic strip fanatic and always have been. When I was growing up in St. Paul, Minnesota, we subscribed to both local newspapers and always made sure that we went to the drugstore on Saturday night to buy the Minneapolis Sunday papers so that we would be able to read every comic published in the area. At that time I was a great fan of Buck Rogers, Popeye, and Skippy.   **2**

After high school I had a job delivering packages around the downtown St. Paul area, and I used to enjoy walking by the windows of the St. Paul *Pioneer Press* and watching the Sunday comics as they came rolling off the presses. It was my dream, of course, that one day my own comic strip would be included.   **3**

Almost twenty years have gone by since I first began drawing Charlie Brown and Snoopy, and I find that I still enjoy drawing them as much as I ever did, but, strangely enough, one of my greatest joys is gaining an extra week on the schedule. I have walked away from the post office many times with a tremendous feeling of joy, knowing that I have mailed in six strips that I thought were really good and that I have gained a week on that oppressive schedule.   **4**

During these twenty years I have had the opportunity to observe what makes a good comic strip. I am convinced that the ones that have survived and maintained a high degree of quality are those which have a format that allows the creator room to express every idea that comes to him. A comic strip should have a very broad keyboard and should certainly not be a one- or two-note affair. If you are going to survive, you simply have to make use of every thought and every experience which have come to you.   **5**

A comic strip also has to grow. The only way you can stay ahead of your imitators is to search out new territories. Also, what is funny in a comic strip today will not necessarily be funny the following week. A good example of this is the character of Snoopy. The mere fact that we could read Snoopy's thoughts was funny in itself when *Peanuts* first began. Now, of course, it is the content of those thoughts that is important, and as he progresses in his imagination to new personalities, some of the things which he orginally did as an ordinary dog would no longer be funny. Snoopy's personality in the strip has to be watched very carefully, for it can get away from me. Control over such a character requires a certain degree of common sense. I also believe that a comic strip, like a novel, should introduce the reader to new areas of thought and endeavor; these areas should be treated in an authentic manner. I never draw about anything unless I feel that I have a better than average knowledge of my subject. This does not mean that I am an expert on Beethoven, kite-flying, or psychiatry, but it means that as a creative person I have the ability to skim the surface of such subjects and use just what I need.

Many times people come up to me and tell me how much they appreciate the philosophy of *Peanuts*. This never fails to confuse me, for I really do not know what this philosophy is. It has always seemed to me that the strip has a rather bitter feeling to it, and it certainly deals in defeat. It has given me the opportunity to express many of my own thoughts about life and people. It is my own opinion that it is absolutely necessary for each one of us to strive to gain emotional maturity. Unless a person becomes mature in all things, he will always have fears and anxieties plaguing him. It is interesting to put these adult fears and anxieties into the conversations of the children in *Peanuts*. The passage of time is an area that will almost always show up a person's immaturity. Children have a strange attitude toward time, for they do not have the patience to wait for days to pass. They want what they want immediately, and adults who are incapable of learning to wait for things will find themselves in all sorts of trouble.

It is also immature not to be able to realize that things that are going to happen in the future are quite often inevitable. If children are allowed to do so they will put off almost anything merely because it is in the future; of course, adults will do the same.

I am asked quite frequently to attempt to analyze each of the characters in the strip, but I find myself incapable of doing this. I really cannot talk about Charlie Brown, Linus, or Lucy as individuals. I can draw them, and I can think of things for them to do, but I do not talk well about them.

One thing that does interest me, however, is the set of offstage characters I have gradually accumulated. A reader once wrote to me and gave a fairly good description of what he thought Peppermint Patty's father must be like. This offstage parent refers to his daughter as a "rare gem" and apparently tolerates her tomboyishness quite

well. The reader speculated that her father has either divorced his
wife or perhaps she has died. I have treated Charlie Brown's father in   10
a fair amount of detail, because I have let it be known that he is very
receptive to his son's impromptu visits to the barber shop. Most of
this is autobiographical, for my dad always greeted me cordially
when I would drop in at his barber shop, and I used to go there and
sit and read the newspapers and magazines until he closed his shop in
the evening. He also never objected if I rang the NO SALE button on
the cash register and removed a nickel for a candy bar.

Linus's mother seems to be the peculiar one. As Charlie Brown
once remarked, "I am beginning to understand why you drag that
blanket around." She seems to be obsessed with his doing well in   11
school and tries to spur him on by sneaking notes into his lunch
which read, "Study hard today. Your father and I are very proud of
you and want you to get a good education."

Some of the offstage characters reach a point where they could
never be drawn. I think the little redheaded girl is a lot like the inside
of Snoopy's doghouse. Each of us can imagine what she must look   12
like much better than I could ever draw her, and I am sure that every
reader sees a different doghouse interior and would be a little disappointed if I were to attempt to draw it in detail.

Linus's beloved Miss Othmar, his teacher, is a rather strange person, and I have tried to do much with her through the conversation
of Linus. I have experimented with a two-level story line at times. I
have tried to show Linus's view of what is happening at school, but
then show what actually was occurring. I have done this to bring out   13
a truth I have observed, and this is that children see more than we
think they do but at the same time almost never seem to know what
is going on. This is an interesting paradox, and one with which adults
should try to acquaint themselves if they are going to deal well with
children.

I am very proud of the comic strip medium and am never
ashamed to admit that I draw a comic strip. I do not regard it as
great art, but I have always felt it is certainly on the level with other
entertainment mediums which are part of the so-called "popular
arts." In many ways, I do not think we have realized the potential of
the comic strip, but sometimes I feel it is too late. Many regard the
comic page as a necessary evil and a nuisance, but it is there and it
helps sell newspapers. With a little more tolerance and with a little   14
more dedication on the part of those who create the comics, perhaps
we could do better. I look back upon great features such as *Out Our
Way,* and I feel that perhaps we can never recapture some of that

glory. I really shudder when I read a description of a new feature about to be launched by some newspaper syndicate and they refer to it as "off-beat." It is time we have some new features which are "on-beat" and which are about real people doing real things.

QUESTIONS AND PROBLEMS

1. In reference to Schulz's requirements for a good comic strip (par. 5), rate some comic strips you know other than *Peanuts*.
2. Are comic strips art? If so, what kind of art? Discuss the value of the comic strip as education and as entertainment.
3. How does the creator of a comic strip achieve reader-participation? Cite examples from *Peanuts* and/or from other comic strips.
4. If you are a reader of comic strips and are told to read "something worthwhile" instead, what would your reply be?
5. Is the comic strip "pop art"? Explain the meaning of the term.
6. What would be the value of having new "on-beat" comic strips (see final paragraph of essay)? If possible, make specific suggestions.

SUGGESTIONS FOR WRITING

1. Write a "profile" on Charles M. Schulz or another popular creator of a comic strip.
2. Give a step-by-step explanation of how a comic strip is drawn and printed.
3. Explain how comic-strip techniques can be used to advantage in education.
4. Watch a number of television cartoon programs for children. Draw conclusions.
5. Find a real-life Linus with a "security blanket." Write a character sketch.

SUGGESTIONS FOR FURTHER READING

Jules Feiffer, *Great Comic Book Heroes* (Dial)
Robert L. Short, *The Gospel According to Peanuts* (John Knox)
David M. White and Robert H. Abel, *Funnies* (Free Press)
Allen Willette, *These Top Cartoonists Tell How They Create America's Favorite Comics* (Allied Publications)

REPRODUCTION AND SEX
Logan Clendening

To reproduce a new and distinct human body requires the cooperation of two other matured human bodies, differing slightly in   1
structure from one another and known technically among biologists
as male and female.

On the whole it seems rather a clumsy arrangement. It is difficult
to discover any unusual perspicacity on the part of deity in such a
scheme. It does not, moreover, appear to be an inescapable rule of
biology. A unicellular organism regularly reproduces another individual by the simple expedient of dividing into two. Even much higher   2
up in the structural tree such animals as the seaworm, *Planaria
maculata,* are able to reproduce or at least regenerate after being
divided either horizontally or vertically, each half regenerating a
head, a tail, or another eye as the occasion demands.

Among vertebrates, of course, such things do not happen at all.
Among vertebrates the absence of the necessity for male parents is
found only in research laboratories and the Gospel according to St.
Luke. Jacques Loeb was able to fertilize with chemical salts the eggs
of a female frog, so that adult living frogs resulted. The explanation
of this, as advanced by competent biologists, is that to fertilization
there are two elements. When the sperm, as the male element of
reproduction is called, enters the female element, the ovum, it brings
first its contribution of nuclear chromosomes and secondly a chemi-   3
cal change somewhat as if it were a catalyst. Previous to fertilization
the egg membrane is very impervious to any salts in the medium
surrounding it. The entrance of the sperm seems to allow certain salts
to enter the egg cytoplasm. It is these salts, rather than the union of
the chromosomes of sperm and ovum, that initiate the rapid growth
and multiplication of the germinating cells. By changing the chemical
content of the solution in which the frog and sea urchin eggs were
kept, Loeb could instigate a development unquestionably, but one
never imitated in nature.

Nature seems certain, however, that the plan of having two parents is a success. And we must try to explain or understand the
advantages which her experience has taught her. One reason suggests
itself immediately. In a wild state the danger to any animal's life is
constant and imminent. If the destinies of the unborn individual   4
were invested in one animal and that animal killed, the next generation, so far as that unit was concerned, would be completely wiped

out. As it is, the male can guard the female, bear the brunt of any attack, even be destroyed, without affecting the unborn at all.

The great advantage of bisexual parentage, however, lies in the enormous possiblity of variation. A single individual reproducing passes over to its offspring only its own somatic characteristics. A terrific monotony would result. But with bisexual parentage the male element, the sperm, as well as the female element, the ovum, bears all the possibilities of all its ancestors in its chromosomes. These divergent strains joining are bound to result in fresh and new combinations which furnish a constant set of variations, upon which natural selection can fasten.   5

Mammals, to which class the order of primates, including the species man, belongs, are distinguished by the facts that during the early stages of development the offspring is harboured inside the body of the female in an organ called the womb or uterus, and that after it is extruded from the mother's body, the mother nourishes it by elaborating a nutritious fluid, milk, in certain glands, the breasts or mammæ. This general plan has been much praised and is supposed to represent a great improvement over other methods of reproduction in the animal kingdom and a particular solicitation towards man and especially woman on the part of that force external to ourselves   6
which makes for righteousness. I am not sure that such praise is entirely deserved. The most sensible arrangement, I submit, is that developed in another branch of the tree of evolution—the birds, reptiles, and fishes. If I were picking out the animal mothers which seem to have had the advantage of the greatest amount of foresight on the part of that force external to ourselves which makes for righteousness, I should most unquestionably give my vote to an egg-laying order. The hen, it seems to me, has it all over the woman in this respect.

The hen is able to extrude the fertilized egg from her body with no more discomfort than arises from the writing of a sonnet.* From prevalent complaints on the subject which reach me from time to time I deduce that this is a distinct advantage over the human manœuvre. Nor is this virtuosity of the hen's attended with any

---

*I wrote this ten years ago purely on the basis of personal observation. All the hens I ever saw lay an egg did so with the same painless ease that I have indicated. But nothing in this world seems to be perfected and I was informed soon after this sentence was first seen in print that hens frequently have to be assisted, at least in the delivery of their first egg, by the farmer's wife, who greases her finger and inserts it in the cloaca, divulsing it. Hens have even been known to die without this aid. However, the experience is comparatively rare and confined to the first delivery, so for all practical purposes my comparison stands.

decompensating lack of efficiency in the product. Her egg after extrusion is endowed with the ability to develop and produce an individual quite as complex as any human prototype: its liver when put
under the microscope has cells and structure as intricate and praise-
worthy as the liver of the infant daughter of a congressman. Its eye
can hardly be distinguished from a human eye; it has retina, iris, rods   7
and cones, sclera—all the same, all equally perfect. It is true that
there are more creases in the brain of the human infant than in the
brain of the chick, but in rebuttal it can be advanced that there are
more feathers on the chick, and whether one is more important than
the other is distinctly debatable. Plainly, however, argument is useless: the human female is a mammal and not a bird, and there is no
way to change her methods of reproduction. But equally plainly,
however superior we may feel about other instances of omnipotent
grace so far as our structure and function are concerned, there is no
use in assuming an air of false pride and pre-eminence over the hen in
the special matter of our divergent modes of reproduction.

Platitudinous as these statements may seem and indeed are, they
nevertheless are, and always have been, fraught with a deep significance to the human race, particularly on the basis of such social
problems as are usually encompassed by the term "the Woman Question." The position of woman, the equality or inequality of the
sexes, woman's place in the sun, the double standard of morals,
about all of which young dramatists and sociologists have perspired
for so many æons, are at bottom biological problems, and not social
or moral or economic problems at all. At times this is faintly recognized and even mildly mentioned; in most discussions of the subject,   8
however, the biology and psychology of sex are treated as if they did
not exist. But from the time when the morning stars sang together
and until the period when the last representatives of animal life on
the chilly remains of this planet are crawling along the shores of the
still faintly warm rivulets at the equator, males will look at the
phenomena of existence from one view-point and females from another. And that is one of the things I always tell my young candi-
dates for ordination when they are sent to me for advice.

Instances are on every hand, but I will choose one of a totally
impersonal nature from a volume of fiction—*The Painted Veil,* by W.
Somerset Maugham. For purposes of experiment I have set a large
number of women, fairly representative as to intelligence, to the   9
perusal of a highly significant passage in this not otherwise notable
book. I have directed their particular attention to a scene in which a
woman has a very important conversation with a man.

The opening chapter of the novel depicts a bedchamber in the home of a British Government bacteriologist stationed in China. The time is early afternoon. His wife is entertaining her clandestine lover, who happens to be lieutenant-governor of the province. Their seance 10 is interrupted by hearing someone trying to turn the knob of the door to the room. It is noted that the lieutenant-governor hastily attempts to put on his shoes. The intruder, however, goes away and the lovers convince themselves that it was merely a servant.

The next day the woman's husband discloses the fact that he himself was the intruder and that he thus assured himself of positive knowledge of the intrigue. The woman admits it frankly and says that if she is divorced, her lover will divorce his own wife and marry her. At this the husband is highly amused. His amusement provokes her to the most positive reiteration of faith in her lover. Whereupon the husband announces that he has been ordered to an inland city where cholera is raging; if he takes her with him, it means very probable death for both. If he goes alone, it means very probable death for him. He generously proposes that if her lover will make a 11 statement in writing to the effect that when she becomes a widow, the lover will divorce his own wife and marry her, the husband will go to the cholera-infested city alone. If the lover refuses, she must either go with her husband into the danger zone or submit to divorce under conditions amounting to disgrace. Certain of the loyalty of her lover, she goes to interview him. It is this interview to which I have directed the attention of my female friends.

The lover, of course, upon hearing the terms of the proposal, is thoroughly upset, fumbles round in a very inglorious manner, and finally flatly refuses. The woman sits before him aghast, with true astonishment. She has believed every one of his professions. He points out to her gravely and carefully how such a proceeding would jeopardize all his chances of advancement in the Civil Service, and that even on the chance that he did all this and married her, they would be ruined and penniless. She replies merely by saying: "But you said you loved me and would do anything for me." He acknowledges this, submits it was a justifiable overstatement under the circumstances, and hurries on to show that his wife is a perfectly inno- 12 cent party and should not be required to suffer for their misdeeds. She replies merely by saying: "But you made me believe you loved me and promised to do anything for me." He turns from this to bring into her focus his children; he reminds her that she has no children to consider; his children require his care and also have a reasonable right to be protected from a legacy of disgrace. She merely repeats monotonously: "Why did you make me believe you really were mad about me?" So he has to reply shamefacedly that probably that is the kind of person he is. She then wants to know whether he is willing to allow her to go to her death. And he takes her in his arms and kisses her and says, in effect, that he is afraid he is willing to do just that.

Every woman to whom I have submitted this document has without exception applied exactly the same word to the lover. He is a *"cad."* This, of course, is a female word, carrying with its use all the force and despotism of a shibboleth. The truth being that whether or   13
not there is any word for him, the man is, under duress, exhibiting the quintessence of the male view-point. He is doing exactly what all wives, all safe women, all vested authority, have planned through all the ages that he should do.

It is because the women to whom I have submitted this problem fail so totally to grasp these elementary truths that I venture to elaborate the theme at such length. Let us get down to fundamentals. What is the female view-point? The female view-point is dependent upon an instinctive inner knowledge of the role the female plays in the process of reproduction. The female knows perfectly well that she must attract a male mate. She also knows that after she has attracted one, if she accepts him and submits to him, the legitimate result of the adventure for her will be pregnancy. During that period of pregnancy and even more so during labour and the period of the   14
puerperium she knows that she will be helpless and relatively defenceless, that she will require guardianship, protection, and service. She will depend upon the male to furnish these. Therefore she will instinctively make perfectly sure of such things before she submits herself to him. In a state of nature among lower animals this is accomplished in many subtle ways. In a state of civilization the females from the earliest time have ranged Church, State, home, and Rotary on their side in order to compel its assurance. If some foolish one like the lady in my fable chooses to disregard these plain guide-posts, she has, if she comes to grief, only herself to blame.

The male, in fact, has no such preoccupations as beset the female. He has no period of pregnancy in contemplation. He has no puerperium or feeding of the young to consider. He is scourged by another inexorable law of nature—the urge for reproduction, the will to live. He is expressly made to roam over the earth impregnating as many females as he possibly can. It is the deepest instinct in his heart, except the instinct for self-preservation. It is the deepest desire of nature, or, if you prefer the term, the deepest desire of God. It is simply silly to pretend that it is not, or to try to control it by moral admonitions. The only thing that can control him is the common sense of the female. The sense to lead him to the altar or the justice   15 court, the sense to use the means her old mothers fashioned for her to bind him with hoops of steel. And he, too, uses wiles. He will bow his neck to matrimony only if that is the only way out. He wonders all the rest of his life why he did it. He never submits tamely. He promises to love her for ever if she will accede to him. He lies, he coaxes, he fawns in order to accomplish his purpose. And after it is accomplished he is alertly ready for the next candidate, and to remind him of the means he used to accomplish it or to call him names for using them is as unworldly as to rebuke the flowers for blooming or the bees for visiting them.

And all these things, I think, I should tell to everyone's daughter.   16 Except for the sly fact that she knows them already.

Of course, in a state of civilization certain modifications are imposed upon biologic laws. But the fundamentals remain. Love is a trick of nature—a trick to carry out her insatiable lust for reproduction. For Schopenhauer, you know, was right—the only God you can discern in nature is a "will to live."* I go into my garden—the shrubs, the flowers, and even more energetically the dandelions are reproducing as fast as ever they can. In my pool the little gold-fish are making new little gold-fish until the water swarms with them. Why? I haven't the slightest idea. At least I do not know the ultimate reason—the general scheme. Why they do it—the immediate impulse—is, I have no doubt, just as sweet and as irresistible to the gold-fish as to the boy   17 and girl over the garden gate. Love is concocted of its unbearable ecstasy and its poignant sweetness because in no other way can the crafty old schemer, nature, carry out her purpose. The boy thinks it a specially dispensed miracle that he should be born in the same village with the one girl who is completely desirable. The poor dear does not know that he would have found one no matter where he was born. It is nature's way of getting her world populated. If either the boy or the girl realized the stifling responsibilities they were assuming, the last representative of the human race would ere long be sitting by the empty shores of the eternal ocean.

But they do not know, and society has wisely built up another trick, called marriage, because it found out that such things were necessary if nature's purposes were to be adequately fulfilled. The

---

*A great physicist with whom I was once discussing this eternally fascinating question said: "My idea of the nature of God is energy." I am inclined to think his definition is more comprehensive. But in the world of living creatures it amounts to will.

boy and girl enter this state two utterly unfamiliar elements. They enter it in a state of delirious ecstasy. They enter it because it seems to be the one way to carry out their most cherished and most selfish objects. Is it any wonder they so often find that instead of a paradise it is a prison? Is it any wonder that they find the two strange elements unassimilable? Is it any wonder that after a time they find themselves pulling to get asunder? They went in, as every human creature goes into everything, he to please himself, she to please herself. After marriage, in most instances, they each continue to try 18 to please the one person they most wish to gratify—himself or herself. These two objects may conflict. And by that time there are the children to be considered. And the hoarse chuckle of Mother Nature and of Mother Church is heard in the wings. No, the wonder is that in so many instances it turns out well at all. For sometimes in spite of all the cynics and all the natural philosophers it does do that. Sometimes by some curious alchemy it becomes that very state which the marriage service so wistfully describes, "like unto the mystical union that is between Christ and His Church." How I do not know. Some union of purpose and of thought, some strange anabolism of human spirits, some mystical method by which two people can work out their separate destinies, yet work them out together.

QUESTIONS AND PROBLEMS

1. The warfare between men and women is, from the point of view of this essay, what kind of warfare?
2. Dr. Clendening's style in this essay is personal and informal.
   a. At what point in the essay is the reader first made aware of this fact?
   b. Is the style suitable to the subject? Why or why not?
   c. Is any flippancy involved? If so, cite examples.
3. How does the outline of William Somerset Maugham's *The Painted Veil* further the subject of the essay?
4. Dr. Clendening characterizes both love and marriage as tricks of nature (pars. 17-18). Why does he call them tricks?
5. Do you agree with the author's definition of love in par. 17? What definition would you give?
6. Comment on Dr. Clendening's insistence on the element of selfishness in marriage. Do you think his is a fair statement of the matter? Why or why not?
7. Explain the terms *vertebrates*, *"the Woman Question,"* *somatic characteristics.*

SUGGESTIONS FOR WRITING

1. Write an essay in definition of love.
2. Write an explanation of asexual reproduction, including specific examples.
3. Describe the process a student goes through in getting a date.

4. Investigate study habits of assorted students in the college library. Write either a serious or a humorous report on your findings.
5. Explain the use of one of the newer pieces of scientific equipment which may be found in a college laboratory.
6. Write an explanation of how the human brain functions.
7. Describe in detail a psychological experiment.
8. Describe a manufacturing process with which you are familiar.
9. Write a familiar essay on the warfare between men and women.
10. Following Dr. Clendening's use of a literary example in this essay, choose a work of literature which concerns itself with a motivating force in man. Explain in an essay.

SUGGESTIONS FOR FURTHER READING

Aristotle, *Generation of Animals* (Harvard)

Remy de Gourmont, *The Natural Philosophy of Love,* tr. Ezra Pound (Collier)

Sigmund Freud, *Three Essays on Sexuality* (Avon)

José Ortega y Gasset, *On Love* (Meridian)

Group for the Advancement of Psychiatry, *Sex and the College Student* (Atheneum)

D.H. Lawrence, *Sex, Literature, and Censorship* (Viking; Twayne)

Floyd M. Martinson, *Marriage and the American Ideal* (Dodd, Mead)

TO DEVELOP BY EXAMPLE

One of the most frequently heard expressions in the classroom is "For example–." In explaining a subject, nothing is more useful and effective than a concrete example. The teacher uses the device of example to make abstract ideas concrete and interesting, for examples appeal to the student's own experience. So it is with the essayist, who is, for his specific purpose, a teacher. He knows that nothing will make his meaning more immediately evident than one or more well-chosen examples. Examples give concrete meaning to abstract ideas, clarify definitions, and provide precise meanings for generalizations.

If in maintaining that much formal education is not a necessary ingredient for the achieving of commanding success in life one cites the example of Abraham Lincoln, he is both proving his point and clarifying his statement. If one explains that the term *personification* in literary style means the endowing of an inanimate object with the attributes of life, he immediately clarifies the statement, and makes it more interesting, by quoting some such line as Carl Sandburg, "The fog comes in on little cat feet." D.G. Rossetti, in "The Blessed Damozel," gives precision to the color of his subject's hair by stating, "Her hair that lay along her back / Was yellow like ripe corn."

It is important, of course, that the example be relevant to the subject and that, furthermore, it not be a generalization itself. If one is proving the thesis that certain television programs have an unwholesome effect on the developing personalities of children, it is not very helpful to say, "There is a great deal of shooting on television." The helpful specific example would point out what kind of shooting, by what kind of people, on what kind of program or even on what specific programs. The examples used, furthermore, must be typical rather than exceptional.

An essay developed through the use of example will usually not be limited to a single instance. To explain the term "Pop Art" one would not, surely, limit himself to a single work—or even to the works of a single artist. The range of examples will be determined by the topic itself and must be sufficiently inclusive to clarify and make precise the meaning of the topic. Note the number of examples used by Thomas S. Szasz, in one of the following essays, to clarify his argument against paternalistic psychiatry. Indeed, Dr. Szasz's essay is an excellent illustration of use of the extended example. By employing the typical case method, he adds, by giving example after example, increasingly more weight to his argument.

E = MC²

Albert Einstein

In order to understand the law of the equivalence of mass and energy, we must go back to two conservation or "balance" principles which, independent of each other, held a high place in pre-relativity physics. These were the principle of the conservation of energy and   1
the principle of the conservation of mass. The first of these, advanced by Leibnitz as long ago as the seventeenth century, was developed in the nineteenth century essentially as a corollary of a principle of mechanics.

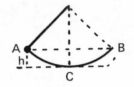

Drawing after Dr. Einstein's original

Consider, for example, a pendulum whose mass swings back and forth between the points A and B. At these points the mass m is higher by the amount h than it is at C, the lowest point of the path (see drawing). At C, on the other hand, the lifting height has disappeared and instead of it the mass has a velocity v. It is as though the lifting height could be converted entirely into velocity, and vice   2
versa. The exact relation would be expressed as $mgh = \frac{m}{2}v^2$, with g representing the accleration of gravity. What is interesting here is that this relation is independent of both the length of the pendulum and the form of the path through which the mass moves.

The significance is that something remains constant throughout the process, and that something is energy. At A and at B it is an energy of position, or "potential" energy; at C it is an energy of motion, or "kinetic" energy. If this concept is correct, then the sum $mgh + m\frac{v^2}{2}$ must have the same value for any position of the pen-   3
dulum, if h is understood to represent the height above C, and v the velocity at that point in the pendulum's path. And such is found to be actually the case. The generalization of this principle gives us the law of the conservation of mechanical energy. But what happens when friction stops the pendulum?

The answer to that was found in the study of heat phenomena. This study, based on the assumption that heat is an indestructible substance which flows from a warmer to a colder object, seemed to give us a principle of the "conservation of heat." On the other hand, from time immemorial it has been known that heat could be produced by friction, as in the fire-making drills of the Indians. The physicists were for long unable to account for this kind of heat "production." Their difficulties were overcome only when it was successfully established that, for any given amount of heat produced by friction, an exactly proportional amount of energy had to be expended. Thus did we arrive at a principle of the "equivalence of work and heat." With our pendulum, for example, mechanical energy is gradually converted by friction into heat.

    4

In such fashion the principles of the conservation of mechanical and thermal energies were merged into one. The physicists were thereupon persuaded that the conservation principle could be further extended to take in chemical and electromagnetic processes—in short, could be applied to all fields. It appeared that in our physical system there was a sum total of energies that remained constant through all changes that might occur.

    5

Now for the principle of the conservation of mass. Mass is defined by the resistance that a body opposes to its acceleration (inert mass). It is also measured by the weight of the body (heavy mass). That these two radically different definitions lead to the same value for the mass of a body is, in itself, an astonishing fact. According to the principle—namely, that masses remain unchanged under any physical or chemical changes—the mass appeared to be the essential (because unvarying) quality of matter. Heating, melting, vaporization, or combining into chemical compounds would not change the total mass.

    6

Physicists accepted this principle up to a few decades ago. But it proved inadequate in the face of the special theory of relativity. It was therefore merged with the energy principle—just as, about 60 years before, the principle of the conservation of mechanical energy had been combined with the principle of the conservation of heat. We might say that the principle of the conservation of energy, having previously swallowed up that of the conservation of heat, now proceeded to swallow that of the conservation of mass—and holds the field alone.

    7

It is customary to express the equivalence of mass and energy (though somewhat inexactly) by the formula $E = mc^2$, in which c represents the velocity of light, about 186,000 miles per second. E is the energy that is contained in a stationary body; m is its mass. The energy that belongs to the mass m is equal to this mass, multiplied by the square of the enormous speed of light—which is to say, a vast amount of energy for every unit of mass.　8

But if every gram of material contains this tremendous energy, why did it go so long unnoticed? The answer is simple enough: so long as none of the energy is given off externally, it cannot be observed. It is as though a man who is fabulously rich should never spend or give away a cent; no one could tell how rich he was.　9

Now we can reverse the relation and say that an increase of E in the amount of energy must be accompanied by an increase of $\frac{E}{c^2}$ in the mass. I can easily supply energy to the mass—for instance, if I heat it by 10 degrees. So why not measure the mass increase, or weight increase, connected with this change? The trouble here is that in the mass increase the enormous factor c^2 occurs in the denominator of the fraction. In such a case the increase is too small to be measured directly; even with the most sensitive balance.　10

For a mass increase to be measurable, the change of energy per mass unit must be enormously large. We know of only one sphere in which such amounts of energy per mass unit are released: namely, radioactive disintegration. Schematically, the process goes like this: An atom of the mass M splits into two atoms of the mass M' and M", which separate with tremendous kinetic energy. If we imagine these two masses as brought to rest—that is, if we take this energy of motion from them—then, considered together, they are essentially poorer in energy than was the original atom. According to the equivalence principle, the mass sum M' + M" of the disintegration products must also be somewhat smaller than the original mass M of the disintegrating atom—in contradiction to the old principle of the conservation of mass. The relative difference of the two is on the order of 1/10 of one percent.　11

Now, we cannot actually weigh the atoms individually. However, there are indirect methods for measuring their weights exactly. We can likewise determine the kinetic energies that are transferred to the disintegration products M' and M". Thus it has become possible to test and confirm the equivalence formula. Also, the law permits us to calculate in advance, from precisely determined atom weights, just how much energy will be released with any atom disintegration we have in mind. The law says nothing, of course, as to whether—or how—the disintegration reaction can be brought about.　12

What takes place can be illustrated with the help of our rich man. The atom M is a rich miser who, during his life, gives away no money (*energy*). But in his will he bequeaths his fortune to his sons M' and M'', on condition that they give to the community a small amount, less than one thousandth of the whole estate (*energy or mass*). The sons together have somewhat less than the father had (*the mass sum M' + M'' is somewhat smaller than the mass M of the radioactive atom*). But the part given to the community, though relatively small, is still so enormously large (*considered as kinetic energy*) that it brings with it a great threat of evil. Averting that threat has become the most urgent problem of our time. 13

QUESTIONS AND PROBLEMS

1. Who was Leibnitz? What major impact did he make upon social thought?
2. Explain in your own terms the formula $E=mc^2$ (par. 8). What is the name of the device Einstein uses in par. 9 to explain why the vast amount of energy in every gram of material went so long unnoticed?
3. Einstein repeats the device in the last paragraph. Is it effectively used? For what kind of readership do you think the essay was written?
4. Einstein deals in this essay with energy.
   a. What is the dictionary defintion?
   b. In what way does he expand upon the definition?
   c. Is he interested in its connotative or its denotative meaning?
5. Discuss the impact of $E=mc^2$ on the modern world.

SUGGESTIONS FOR WRITING

1. Using a basic diagram, illustrate a law of physics or explain an experiment in chemistry.
2. Write an explanation of how something works—television, a carburetor, a barometer.
3. Write a paper in definition of *energy*. Use examples or analogies to clarify your definition.
4. Write a research paper on the theory of relativity, or write a paper on new findings since Einstein first proposed his theory.
5. Write a character sketch of the ideal scientist, making use of examples.
6. What does the term "philosophy of science" mean? Write an essay in explanation of the term.

SUGGESTIONS FOR FURTHER READING

Arthur Bawden, *Matter and Energy: The Fundamentals of Physical Science* (Holt, Rinehart & Winston)
Germaine Beiser and Arthur Beiser, *Physics for Everybody* (Dutton)
C.D. Broad, *Scientific Thought* (Humanities; Littlefield)
Ludwig Buchner, *Force and Matter* (Truth)

Albert Einstein, *The Meaning of Relativity* (Princeton); *Philosopher Scientist*, 2
    vols. (Harper)
Harry Messel and S.T. Butler, eds., *Introduction to Modern Physics* (St. Martins)
Rudolph E. Peierls, *Laws of Nature* (Scribner)
P.A. Schlipp, ed., *Albert Einstein: Philosopher Scientist*, 2 vols. (Harper)
Leonard de Vries, *Book of the Atom*, tr. E.G. Breeze (Macmillan)

POP ART
Russell Baker

The big news in American culture these days is "pop art." Many culture insiders believe it may be a bigger craze than folk singing before the summer is out, and no wonder.   1

The highly publicized exhibition which opened here the other day at the Gallery of Modern Art demonstrated that "pop art" is not only more fun than anything since the Keystone Kops, but also an exhilarating tonic for the ego. A lot of people who have been standing around modern art galleries for years feeling scared and bourgeois are going to go away from this show convinced that almost anybody can be an artist.   2

For example, consider the effect on the viewer of Jim Dine's brooding black study, "Shovel With Long Handle." What Jim did was to take a canvas seven feet long and cover it with black paint. He then took a coalshovel seven feet long and covered that with black paint. Then, he attached the shovel to the canvas!   3

The viewer's first response is: "I could do that if I had some canvas, a shovel and black paint." He realizes only gradually that it is not so simple as that. The effect of "Shovel With Long Handle," he senses, is dependent upon its subtle relationship to two other Dine works in the same room.   4

These are "Black Backroom"—a sink stuck on canvas on which a good bit of black paint has been indiscriminately smeared around—and "Black Window." "Black Window," as its title suggests, is a black window—sill, sash, frame and glass—to which several pieces of hardware are audaciously attached to the top. These include an axe, pliers, a wrench, a can opener, an egg beater and a carving knife.   5

In a different vein, there is George Brecht's "Stool." Brecht has taken a stool and placed a bag of oranges on it. The gallery has arranged matters so that the viewer comes to "Stool" immediately after the emotional shock of Claes Oldenburg's "Pants." "Pants" is an oversize pair of bright blue men's trousers made of sailcloth and hung on an outsized clothes hanger.   6

One moves, confused and shaken, from "Pants" to the cool serenity of "Stool," with its bag of oranges, and finds himself subtly led to reminiscences about oranges he has seen on stools in other times, other places.   7

The viewer moves with continuing pleasure through a constant series of surprises. Here, for example, is "Starchief," by Robert Watts. It is a green dashboard from a Pontiac Starchief. Plugged into   8 an electrical outlet, it makes monotonous noises while its odometer clicks off the miles at a rate which indicates the thing is supposed to be moving at 300 miles per hour.

And here is Robert Rauschenberg's "Black Market," a big rectangle of canvas on which the artist has placed a bedspring, a 1959 Ohio license plate, four metal-jacketed notebooks on which the public may express itself, and a one-way street sign with a dog leash dangling from the arrow tip.   9

The leash leads to a box on the floor containing a green comb, several yellow pencils, some inking pads and stamps, and the car repair bill of one C.V. West for brake work by the Temple Motor Company of Alexandria, Va., last Tuesday. The bill was for $53.60. Among the public expressions recorded in the notebooks this weekend was one stating, "Rauschenberg, you are mad."   10

In an essay for the exhibit program, Alan R. Solomon takes a very somber view of all this, arguing that it has something to do with the fact that modern man "sees himself in his art . . . as a disrupted, contorted victim of the modern cataclysm, torn by forces of a magnitude beyond his comprehension, a grim figure, full of despair and anguish, entirely without hope."   11

This may be so, but if it is why does the visitor leave the exhibition feeling relaxes, pleased and full of interior giggles?   12

If "pop art" catches on with the public, as it very well may, American cellars this summer will be the scene of more welding and sawing and hammering and soldering than at any time since the do-it-yourself craze subsided. And it won't be contorted victims of cataclysm stripping the hardware stores, but a bunch of optimists pursuing the will-o-the-wisp of art.   13

QUESTIONS AND PROBLEMS

1. How does the author set the tone for his essay in the opening paragraphs? What is that tone?
2. Does he give any indication in this essay that he is treating his subject with a degree of seriousness?
3. Comment on the author's descriptions of pop art items in the exhibition. Can the pieces be clearly "seen" by the reader?
4. This review was written for a newspaper. What qualities of style suggest its publication in the daily press?
5. Comment in detail on the author's diction and syntax. What are the qualities which make this an effective report?

SUGGESTIONS FOR WRITING

1. Make a tour of the art gallery or museum of your college. Write an essay in which the works you see become illustrations for the thesis of your essay.

2. Write a satire on the life and works of an imaginary pop artist.
3. Explain the meaning of *theater of the absurd,* using examples to illustrate.
4. Explain the theory of nonobjective art. Include descriptions of some notable works in this field.
5. Explain the difference between traditional and contemporary music. Consult a composer or a member of your music faculty for information.
6. Explain the theories of architecture of Frank Lloyd Wright. Include descriptions of some of his constructions.
7. Make a study of the number of traditional plays produced by the drama department of your school during the past ten years as opposed to the number of contemporary plays. What trends do you find, what point can you prove?
8. Describe an art show you have attended.

SUGGESTIONS FOR FURTHER READING

John Cage, *Silence* (Wesleyan)
Joyce Cary, *Art and Reality* (Harper & Row)
Robert Corrigan, ed., *The Theatre of the Absurd* (Grove)
E.M. Forster, "Art for Art's Sake," in *Two Cheers for Democracy* (Harcourt, Brace & World)
Felix Klee, *Paul Klee* (Braziller)
John A. Kouwenhoven, *The Beer Can by the Highway* (Doubleday)
Marshall McLuhan, *Understanding Media: The Extensions of Man* (McGraw-Hill)
Piet Mondrian, *Plastic Art and Pure Plastic Art and Other Essays* (Wittenborn)
John Rublowsky and K. Heyman, *Pop Art* (Basic Books)
Frederic Taubes, *Abracadabra and Modern Art* (Dodd, Mead)

HENS AND GRAMMARIANS
Clarence Day

A bloodless but angry battle has been going on for the last hundred years between grammarians and setting hens. As the hens themselves are too busy to fight, they have not taken the trouble to meet   1
the grammarians and deal with them as they deserve, but their faithful friends and owners, the farmers, have fought the war for them.

The grammarians contend that there are no such things as setting hens. If any setting hen were to appear at a grammarian's door and   2
try to hatch eggs in his apartment, he would turn her into a sitting hen instantly.

He would point out to her that "sit" and "set" are now two different words. Originally, they both were forms of "sittan," a verb meaning "squat," which the ancient Saxons used when they squatted down on their haunches around the fire at night. Sometimes before "sittan" down they would "settan" their clubs in the corners. Ac-   3
cording to the grammarians, the ancient Saxons were quite fussy about this, and they used "settan" only in connection with an act done to something, whereas "sittan" wasn't an act they did to anything—it was just an act that they did.

Reasoning on this basis, grammarians point out that a farmer may "set" a hen if he wants to, but he mustn't then say that she is "setting," because she isn't. She is merely "sitting." Farmers argue that the purpose of language is to convey clear and accurate meanings, and a hen that is hatching eggs is doing a lot more than sitting.

Grammarians retort, "Look at Congress. When Congress is in Washington trying to hatch out some new legislation, nobody says Congress is 'setting'—we all say it is 'sitting.' " The farmer obstinately replies that hens are different. They work harder than Congress.

Extremists among the farmers have got so rebellious that they hardly use "sit" at all. When one of them wants to have a talk with his friends, he tells them to "set down and rest." Grammarians say that it's vulgar of a farmer to "set," even on a settee. The farmer complains that grammarians don't call all setters vulgar—English setters and typesetters, for instance. Why be so strict with a farmer? Grammarians will let him set a good example, or a clock, or his traps; he can also set his hand to the plow. Can't he ever set down?

No wonder these two words make trouble. You can "set" someone on to fight for you, but you must "sit" on him to stop him. After you have set a person at ease, you might think he could set at ease. But he can't.

It's not only farmers. Tailors bother grammarians too. Tailors say a coat "sets" well. If they say that to a grammarian, it makes him fell bad—or badly. (Some say one, some the other.) He tells them it may possibly "sit" well on him, but a coat cannot "set." A tailor in Bergen County, New Jersey, got so discouraged about this last year that he went out of business and became a sailor and is now setting sails.

The rule is simple enough; its never to use "set" except with an object, but unfortunately the rule isn't perfect. To the intense annoyance of grammarians, like other rules, it has to permit some exceptions. One of the largest of these is the sun. He rises grammatically enough in the morning, but he sets every night. When the grammarians surrendered on this point, which they did long ago, some of them lamely explained that their rule was all right; it still applied to everybody and everything "except heavenly bodies." Others got out of it by decreeing a special dispensation, which now appears in the dictionaries, permitting us all to use "set" when it means "sink below the horizon." Anything to avoid fighting the sun.

A few grammarians are nowadays beginning to be lenient with hens, but these soft-hearted persons are denounced by the staunch

But the sun's an exception ⸺

old standpatters. In order to please the strict ones, hens apparently   10
must either become heavenly bodies or else learn to sink below the
horizon before they can be called setting hens.

QUESTIONS AND PROBLEMS

1. How would you classify this essay as a type or kind? Explain.
2. How early in the essay is the tone set? Discuss the importance of this
   position for the kind of essay it is.
3. The underlying purpose of Clarence Day in this essay is revealed indirectly.
   a. What is that purpose?
   b. Does he communicate it clearly and successfully?
   c. Can the reader learn something of importance about language from this
      essay? If so, what?
4. On the basis of this essay, how would you characterize Day as a person?
5. What matter of importance regarding the adoption of the light and the
   serious attitude in an essay may be learned from this one?

SUGGESTIONS FOR WRITING

1. Write a report on current campus slang, using illustrations.
2. Make a comparison between the slang of your father's college days and that
   in vogue today.
3. Make a study of the argot of juvenile gangs, prisoners, or an underworld
   group.
4. If you have had experience with the people of a ghetto, report on the
   differences between their grammar and diction and that which we call
   "standard." Defend the former in terms of communication.

5. Investigate the differences between "home" and "school" grammar in any particular group of people. Illustrate.
6. Read a novel published during the "roaring 20's" or one with that period as a setting. What peculiarities of diction do you find?

SUGGESTIONS FOR FURTHER READING

Janet R. Aiken, "Good and Bad Grammar." *The American Mercury*, November, 1932.

C. Merton Babcock, *The Ordeal of American English* (Houghton Mifflin)

Henry W. Fowler, *Dictionary of Modern English Usage*, 2nd ed. rev. by E. Gowers (Oxford)

Elijah L. Jacobs, *Them Ain't Mistakes* (Windfall Press)

Raven I. McDavid, Jr., "Usage, Dialects and Functional Varieties." Prefatory essay in *The Random House Dictionary of the English Language*

Henry L. Mencken, *The American Language*, 3 vols. and 2 supplements (Knopf)

THE JOYS OF YIDDISH
Leo Rosten

I have just finished writing a long, long book.* I wrote it because there was no other way in which I could have it: a discursive lexicon of Yiddish words and phrases that (1) are part of English (*kibitzer, shlemiel, shmaltz*); (2) are rapidly becoming part of English (*megil-*   1 *la*—a long, boring account; *yenta*—a gossip; *chutzpa*—nerve, effrontery); or (3) should become part of our noble tongue, in my opinion, because there just are no English words like them (*shmoos, kvetch*— of these, more later).

Some contemporary Yiddish words are used in both England and the United States: *mish-mash, gonif, fin* (five); others are coined by, and indigenous to, Jews in the United States: *donstairsikeh* (the   2 woman who lives downstairs), *kochalayn* (a room or bungalow, in a Catskill resort, that contains "cook alone" privileges), *shmegegge* (hot air, "baloney," nonsense).

Every so often I run across the statement that *Webster's Un-abridged Dictionary* contains five hundred Yiddish words. I do not know if this is true, and I certainly doubt that anyone actually counted them. For my part, I have long been surprised by the num-ber of Yiddish words thriving in everyday English that are not in   3 *Webster's* nor in other standard dictionaries, including the imcompar-able thirteen-volumed *Oxford English Dictionary,* nor in H.L. Mencken's *The American Language,* nor in Eric Partridge's *Diction-ary of Slang and Unconventional English,* etc.

It is ironic that never in its history has Yiddish been so influen-tial—among Gentiles; among Jews, the tongue is running dry. Surely we are witnessing a revolution in the mores when a Pentagon officer describes the air bombardment encircling Haiphong as "the bagel strategy." Or when the *Wall Street Journal* headlines a story about student movements: "REVOLUTION, SHMEVOLUTION." Or when a gag lapel-button reads:

Marcel Proust

is a

Yenta

And how could we manage without such priceless coinages as *beat-nik, peacenik, no-goodnik?* Or the all-purpose device, exuberantly lifted from common Jewish practice, of flatly dismissing something by repeating it with an *sh* play preceding the first syllable; "Fat-

---

The Joys of Yiddish (McGraw-Hill).

shmat, she's happy," "Rich-shmich, he won't contribute a dime."
Who has not heard or used phrases such as these:

> Get lost. 4
> You should live so long.
> My son, the physicist.
> I need it like a hole in the head.
> All *right* already.
> It shouldn't happen to a dog.
> Okay by me.
> He knows from nothin'.
> Who *needs* it?
> From that he makes a *liv*ing?
> Do him something.
> *This* I need yet?
> Excuse the expression.
> Go fight City Hall.
> I should have such luck.
> It's a nothing of a dress.
> On him it looks good.
> Listen, *bubele* . . . ?

Or consider the Ashkenazic panoply in which insult and in-
nuendo may be arrayed. Problem: Whether to attend a concert by
your neighbor, niece, or wife's friend. The same sentence may be put
through maneuvers of matchless versatility:

(1) "*Two* tickets for her concert I should buy?" (Meaning: "I'm
having enough trouble deciding if it's worth one.")

(2) "Two *tickets* for her concert I should buy?" ("You mean to
say she isn't distributing free passes? The hall will be empty!")

(3) "Two tickets for *her* concert I should buy?" ("Did she buy 5
tickets to *my* daughter's recital?")

(4) "Two tickets for her *concert* I should buy?" ("You mean to
say they call what she does a 'concert'?!")

(5) "Two tickets for her concert *I* should buy?" ("After what she
did to me?")

(6) "Two tickets for her concert I *should* buy?" ("Are you giving
me lessons in ethics?")

(7) "Two tickets for her concert I should *buy?*" ("I wouldn't go
even if she gave me a complimentary!")

I am not for a moment suggesting that other languages lack virtuosity in the deployment of affect; but I do believe that Jews revel
in the embroidery of emotional distinctions. I also think that Jews 6

think they just *have* more moods to express than anyone else and, thinking so, they are driven to competitive exercises in linguistic dexterity.

I have always marveled at how fertile Yiddish is in what may be called the vocabulary of insight, that is, in the range and variety and nuances of words for delineating character types. Little miracles of discriminatory precision are enshrined in the subtleties of the distinction among, say, namby-pambies, like a *nebbech*, a *shlemiel*, a *dop-*   7
pess, a *nafish*, a *shmendrick*, a *shnook;* or among dreary drips: a *shlep*, a *shlump*, a *kvetch;* or among such braggarts as a *plosher*, a *fifer*, a *fonfer*, a *trombenik*, a *bluffer;* or among dolts, like a *klutz*, a *zhlub*, a *yold*, a *Chaim Yankel;* or show-offs: an *alrightnik*, a *k-nocker*, a *macher*, a *boychik*.

The sense of psychological differentiation is so acute in Yiddish that a word like, say, *paskudnyak* has no peer in any language I know for the vocal delineation of a nasty character. And Yiddish creates   8
new names with ease for new personality types: A *nudnik* being a persistent pest, a *phudnik* is a *nudnik* with a Ph.D.

Yiddish, incidentally, is not Hebrew; they are entirely different languages. A knowledge of one will not provide even a rudimentary understanding of the other. Yiddish does use the letters of the Hebrew alphabet, employs many Hebrew words, and is written, like Hebrew, from right to left, thusly: UOY EVOL I ACIREMA. But Yiddish descends from German (perhaps 80 per cent of its vocabu-   9
lary is German). Yiddish and Hebrew are as different from each other as are French and English, which also use a common alphabet and together proceed from left to right. Nor is "Yiddish," the name of a language, a synonym for "Jewish." Technically speaking, there is no language called "Jewish"; Jews do not speak "Jewish" any more than Canadians speak Canadian, or Baptists read Baptist.*

Yiddish is the Robin Hood of languages. I think it a tongue that never takes its tongue out of its cheek. Steeped in sentiment, it is sluiced with sarcasm; it favors paradox, because only paradox can do justice to the injustices of life; it excels in irony, because the only   10
way Jews could retain their sanity was to view a horrifying world with sardonic and astringent eyes. In its heart, Yiddish swings between *shmaltz* and derision.

Despite popular belief, Yiddish is not a new language (though it did not come fully into its own, building a literature of its own, until

---

*But in popular usage, even among Jews, "Jewish" *is* used as a synonym for "Yiddish." "Yiddish" comes from the German *Judisch,* which means "Jewish," as does the Yiddish word "Yiddish." Purists may frown, but the words are used interchangeably.

the mid-nineteenth century). Yiddish is actually older than the English we use today; it was born around the tenth century, when Jews from Northern France, who spoke Old French and, of course, Hebrew, migrated to towns along the Rhine, where they began to use the local German dialect. Hebrew remained untouched as the "sacred," the liturgical language—for reading Torah and Talmud, for use in prayer and in scholarly or theological discourse. 11

Yiddish took root in the ghettos, which began in walled *juderias* in Spain back in the thirteenth century.* The new parlance combined Middle High German, some Old German, remnants of Old French and Old Italian, many Hebrew names and phrases, and local dialects. The Jews wrote this German phonetically, using the letters of the Hebrew alphabet—just as, in Spain, they wrote Spanish and Arabic with Hebrew letters—from right to left. But Yiddish did not really flower until after the fifteenth century, when the Jews went to Eastern Europe—Poland, Galicia, Hungary, Romania, Russia. There the buoyant tongue picked up new locutions, adapting itself to the street and the marketplace. Yiddish became the Jews' tongue via the Jewish mother, who was denied a Hebrew education. It is often called affectionately *mama-loshen,* "the mother's tongue." 12

Professor Max Weinreich has given us an exhilarating epigram: "A language is a dialect that has an army and a navy." Yiddish, unlike Hebrew, the official language of Israel, has neither army, navy, nor governmental mandate. It has only ardent practitioners and sentimental protectors. In Israel, Yiddish has been accorded short shrift by officials and populace alike. 13

Few instruments of human speech have led so parlous a life, amidst such inhospitable neighbors, against such fierce opposition. And I know of no tongue so beset by schisms and fevers and ambivalences from within the community that gave it birth: Jewish purists derided Yiddish for its "bastard" origins and hybrid vocabulary; Hebraicists called it vulgar, "uncivilized cant"; German Jews called it a "barbarous argot," a "piggish jargon." But it remained dear to the hearts of the Jews of Eastern Europe, the Ashkenazim, who brought it to Western Europe and the United States. 14

It is worth noting that before coming to America, nearly all male adult Jews could handle at least *three* languages: Hebrew, "the sacred tongue" used in the synagogue and the mandatory "houses of study"; Yiddish, spoken at home and among Jews; and the language 15

---

*The Lateran Councils of 1179 and 1215 forbade Jews to live close to Christians, and in 1555 Paul IV ordered segregated quarters for Jews in the Papal States.

of the land in which they lived (Russian, Polish, Hungarian, etc.). My father, a workingman denied the equivalent of a high-school education in Poland, knew Yiddish, Hebrew, Polish—then learned to speak and read English quite comfortably.

As for the Jews' well-known passion for learning, we might remember that for several thousand years, while most mortals were illiterate, every Jewish male over six (unless defective) could read and write. The Jewish boy's mother would give him honey-cakes, shaped in the letters of the alphabet, before he went off to the *cheder*   16 (Hebrew school) on his first day, or when he returned, to tell him that "learning is sweet." And after the boy completed his first lesson, some parents would surreptitiously drop a coin before him. "Ah, an angel dropped that from heaven to show you how pleased God is that you learned your first lesson."

In my book I often use a story, joke, or anecdote to illustrate the meaning of a word. This is unorthodox among lexicographers, but the Jewish story (*myseh*) possesses an instructive bouquet all its own. It is at its best when it points a moral or moralizes a problem. A very   17 large part of Jewish humor is cerebral. It is, like Sholem Aleichem's, reason gone mischievous, or, like Groucho Marx's, reason gone mad. Jewish jokes drape laughter on logic—in despair.

The first riddle I ever heard, one familiar to almost every Jewish child, was propounded to me by my father:

"What is it that hangs on the wall, is green, wet—and whistles?"

I knit my brow and thought and thought, and in final perplexity said, "I give up."

"A herring," said my father.

"A *herring*?!" I echoed. "A herring doesn't hang on a wall!"

"So hang it there."   18

"But a herring isn't green!" I protested.

"Paint it."

"But a herring isn't *wet*."

"If it's just painted, it's still wet."

"But—" I sputtered, summoning all my outrage, "—*a herring doesn't whistle!*"

"Well," smiled my father. "I just put that in to make it hard."

Yiddish was my first language (I was brought to the United States when I was three) and it should be obvious, by now, that I   19 regard it with special affection. Here are some examples of individual entries in *The Joys of Yiddish:*

Shmoos (shmues shmooze shmoose)

—rhymes with "stews" and "ooze." (Hebrew: *shmuos:* "rumors," "idle talk.")

Both a verb and noun, *shmoos* (which is how I prefer to spell it) means a friendly, gossipy, heart-to-heart talk—or, to have such a talk.

"They had a little *shmoos* and settled everything."

"She *shmoosed* with her father until dinner." 20

"How about a walk and a *shmoos?*"

"There's nothing better, to get something off your chest, than a *shmoos* with a friend."

Gelett Burgess, who invented the word "blurb," once tried to get "huzzlecoo," a word he coined, used in English. "Huzzlecoo" never caught on; but it was a dead ringer for *shmoos.*

Alav ha-sholom (masculine)
Aleha ha-shalom (feminine)

-pronounced *aw-LUV ha sha-LOAM* or *AW-luv ha SHO-lem.* (The first pronunciation is Hebrew, and elegant; the second is Yiddish, and brisk.) The two Hebrew words are often pronounced as if one—*alevasholem.* The feminine form is pronounced *Ah-leh-ha ha-SHO-lem* or *sha-LOAM.*

Literally: "On him (or her) peace."

The phrase is used, automatically, when referring to someone who is dead—as, in English, one says, " . . . of blessed memory," or, "May he rest in peace." When a man says, "My Uncle Harry, *aleva-* 21 *sholem,* once said . . . ," you can be sure that Uncle Harry is dead.

As a boy, I was fascinated by the obligatory *"alevasholem,"* but puzzled to hear: "That man? A liar, a no-good, *alevasholem.*" Thus relism, wrestling with ritual, resolves ambivalence. In fact, the primary purpose of ritual is to provide a routine for the management of emotion. Routine reduces anxiety by removing choices.

It also used to please me, as a boy, to hear a patriarch utter a fearsome oath thusly: "May beets grow in his belly! God forbid." It pleased me, I say, because "God forbid" took the edge off a malediction uttered in anger—*after* the anger had been healthily expressed.

*

It was at the great Café Royale, on Second Avenue in New York City, *alevasholem,* that I first heard this classic joke:

Scene: Restaurant
Waiter: "Tea or coffee, gentlemen?"   22
First customer: "I'll have tea."
Second customer: "Me, too—and be sure the glass is clean!"
                    (Waiter exits, returns.)
Waiter: "Two teas. Which one asked for the clean glass?"

Fin (finif finiff finnif)

—pronounced to rhyme, respectively, with "tin," "lymph," "sin if." (German: *fünf*, "five.")
(1) Five.
(2) A five-dollar bill; a five-pound note.
(3) A five-year jail sentence.

"Fin" is the Anglicized and contracted form of *finif*, the Yiddish word for "five," and is widely used in colloquial English, especially by sports fans, gamblers, Broadway types, night-club habitues, and newspaper columnists who memorialize these gaudy provinces of diversion. "Fin" is so much a part of American vernacular that I do not italicize it.   23

"Fin" and *finif* were used with his customary felicity by Damon Runyon, in his stories about that after-twilight world in which lived his "more than somewhat" unforgettable guys and dolls. "Fin" appears in John O'Hara's emphatically non-Jewish dialogue, going back to the early 1930s. It is standard argot among connoisseurs of boxing, racing, dice, poker, *et alia*.

H.L. Mencken attributes "fin" to German, not Yiddish (*The American Language*); I think this wrong. The word *funf* is indubitably German; but the pronunciation *finif*, in two syllables, or *finf* (not funf) in one, is just as indubitably Yiddish. Wentworth and Flexner's excellent *Dictionary of American Slang* attributes "fin" flatly to Yiddish, as do I.

Aha!

—pronounced with a note of sudden comprehension, pleasure, or triumph.

This versatile expletive is widely used by old-fashioned Jews to signify:
(a) Comprehension: "You don't subtract but multiply? Ah*a*!"
(b) Illumination: *"Aha! That's* why they called off the party!"
(c) Surprise: "The *doctor* was wrong? Aha!"
(d) Sententious hinting: "Just ask her—and watch her expression. Aha!"

(e) Delight: "Ah-a! Then I win the bet!"

(f) Triumph: "Ah*a*!" (meaning, "So now do you admit you're wrong?")

Aha! is not to be confused with *Hoo-Ha!,* its blood cousin. Perhaps the best way to illustrate the difference is with this story:

For twenty years Mr. Sokoloff had been eating at the same restaurant on Second Avenue. On this night, as on every other, Mr. Sokoloff ordered chicken soup. The waiter set it down and started off. Mr. Sokoloff called, "Waiter!"

"Yeah?"

"Waiter, please taste this soup."

The waiter said, "Why? Twenty years you've been eating the chicken soup here, no? Have you ever had a bad plate—"

"Waiter," said Sokoloff firmly, "Taste the soup."

"Sokoloff, what's the *matter* with you?"

"Taste the *soup!*"

"All right, all right," grimaced the waiter. "I'll taste—where's the spoon?"

"Ah*a*!" cried Sokoloff.

Mazel tov!

—pronounced *MOZ-z'l,* to rhyme with "shnozzle"; *tov* is pronounced *tuv, tuff,* or *tawf.* (Hebrew: *mazal:* "luck"; *tov:* "good.")

"Congratulations!" or "Thank God!" rather than the literal meaning: "Good luck." The distinction is as important as it is subtle.

Do not say *"Mazel tov!"* to a fighter entering a ring (it suggests you are congratulating him for having made it to the arena), or a girl about to have her nose bobbed (which would mean "and about time, too!").

Say *"Mazel tov!"* to an Israeli ship captain when he first takes command: this congratulates him on his promotion; don't say *"Mazel tov!"* when the ship reaches port: this suggests you're surprised he got there.

At all Jewish celebrations—a birth, wedding, graduation, *Bar Mitzvah*—you will hear *Mazel tovs* resounding like buckshot in a tin shed.

The ancient Hebrews, like the ancient Babylonians, Egyptians, and Greeks, fiddled around with astrology. In the Bible, *mazal* referred to a planet, a contellation of the zodiac, and the word was invoked when "fate" was involved. Later, Talmudic sages sternly warned the Jews to eschew soothsaying and diviners. (Poor believing Jews had a hard time knowing what to think: the Bible, after all, talks of the "signs of heaven"—Jeremiah, for instance, and Isaiah. But the Midrash teaches: "The Holy One forbade astrology in Israel"; and it is said that God made Abraham "a prophet, not an astrologer.") The great Maimonides called astrology "a disease, not a science."

Nonetheless, Jews continued to utter *"Mazel tov!"* Soon the supernatural aspects were forgotten (just as "God be with you" became "goodbye") and *mazel* became simply "luck"; *"Mazel tov!,"* "congratulations."

*

Mournfully, Mr. Lefkowitz entered the office of his burial society. "I've come to make the funeral arrangements for my dear wife."

"Your wife?" asked the astonished secretary. "But we buried her 26 last year!"

"That was my first wife," sighed lugubrious Lefkowitz. "I'm talking about my second."

"Second? *I* didn't know you had remarried. *Mazel tov!"*

Shammes (shamus shammus)

—pronounced *SHAH-mes,* to rhyme with "promise." (Hebrew: *shamash:* "servant.")

(1) The sexton or caretaker of the synagogue; the "servant" of a congregation of worshipers. In the old country, and in the early decades of this century in America, a *shammes* had many duties beyond the janitorial. He was expected to keep the synagogue clean and warm; to repair minor damage; to see that prayer books and ceremonial objects were safely preserved. He would go around the village waking up congregation members, calling them to prayer, announcing sunset and Sabbath times (often by trumpet). He also was used to carry messages, and acted as a bailiff to the religious court. He collected synagogue dues, made funeral arrangements, and rounded up a *minyan.* He would even fill in for a cantor with a sore throat.

(2) In American slang: a detective, policeman, guard. *Shammes,* 27 in this usage, enjoys wide popularity in detective fiction and among the Irish, who spell it *shamus,* which sounds more Gaelic than Yiddish. Eric Partridge and others claim that *shamus* derives from the Irish name Seamus, and some say that since so many Irish immigrants became policemen, the name Seamus grew to be associated with police.

(3) A "private eye."

(4) A functionary on a low level; an unimportant menial. "A *shammes* in a pickle factory" is a Yiddish phrase for a low man on anyone's totem pole.

(5) Sycophant; a hanger-on. "Every movie producer has to have a *shammes.*"

(6) A "stool pigeon"; an informer.

(7) The ninth candle of the Chanukah *menorah,* used to light the others.

*

On the high Holy Days, seats in the synagogue are often sold in advance, to provide revenue for synagogue upkeep. In a small *shul* in Coney Island, a Jew without a ticket came running up to the door: "Let me in, let me in! I must see Abe Baum!"

The *shammes* barred his way. "No one gets in without a ticket!"   28

"It's an emergency! I'll come right out! It'll only take five seconds!"

"Okay," said the *shammes.* "But don't let me catch you praying!"

*

The visiting rabbi stopped in the middle of his sermon and signaled to the *shammes.* "In the second row," he whispered, "is a man sound asleep. Wake him up."   29

"That's not fair," said the *shammes.*

"What do you mean, 'not fair'?"

"You put him to sleep; you wake him up."

QUESTIONS AND PROBLEMS

1. Why does Rosten call Yiddish "the Robin Hood of languages" (par. 10)? Explain.
2. Rosten speaks of Yiddish being older than contemporary English (par. 11). What was English like in the tenth century? Find some examples.
3. Rosten makes a distinction (par. 11) between Yiddish as the common language of the Rhineland Jews and Hebrew as the "sacred" language. What differences do you find today in the English language as it is used for specialized purposes—in church, in textbooks, on the campus, at home, etc.?
4. Why in Israel today has Yiddish "been accorded short shrift by officials and populace alike" (par. 13)? Suggest some reasons.
5. Having read the examples Rosten gives from his book *The Joys of Yiddish,* clarify his statement (par. 17) that "Jewish jokes drape laughter on logic—in despair."

SUGGESTIONS FOR WRITING

1. Make a study of some foreign words which have been brought into general English usage. Write a report developed by specific example. (Such a book as Mary S. Serjeantson's *History of Foreign Words in English* will be helpful.)
2. Find words, once considered slang, which are now accepted as standard English. Develop a paper by specific example.
3. What are some specialized words which are used by students on your campus? Explain and illustrate their meaning.
4. Write an essay on "home English" vs. "school English."
5. Have you ever had difficulty in making yourself understood by a foreigner or by a person from another part of our country? If so, explain, giving examples.
6. Develop by example an essay on different terms used by the English and by Americans for the same thing: gasoline, petrol; windshield, windscreen; rest area, layby; etc.

SUGGESTIONS FOR FURTHER READING

Sarah Betsky, ed., *Onions and Cucumbers and Plums: 46 Yiddish Poems in English* (Wayne State)

Abraham N. Franzblau, *Stories from Hebrew and Yiddish Sources,* 2 vols. (Union of American Hebrew Congregations)

Isaac Goldberg, trans., *Six Plays of the Yiddish Theatre* (Bruce Humphries)

Sol Liptzin, *The Flowering of Yiddish Literature* (Yoseloff)

Leo Rosten, *The Joys of Yiddish* (McGraw-Hill)

Mary S. Serjeantson, *History of Foreign Words in English* (Barnes and Noble)

Uriel Weinreich and Beatrice Weinrich: *Say It in Yiddish* (Dover); *Yiddish Language and Folklore* (Humanities)

WHAT PSYCHIATRY CAN AND CANNOT DO

Thomas S. Szasz, M.D.

Psychiatry today is the curious position of being viewed simultaneously with too much reverence and with undue contempt. Indeed, thoughtful Americans can be roughly divided between those who dismiss all forms of psychiatric practice as worthless or harmful and those who regard it as a panacea for crime, unhappiness, political fanaticism, promiscuity, juvenile delinquency—and virtually every other moral, personal, and social ill of our time.   1

The adherents of this exaggerated faith are, I believe, the larger and certainly the more influential group in shaping contemporary social policy. It is they who beat the drums for large-scale mental-health programs and who use the prestige and the services of a massive psychiatric establishment as a shield of illusion, concealing some   2 ugly realities we would rather not face. Thus when we read in the paper that the alcoholic, the rapist, or the vandal needs or will be given "psychiatric care," we are reassured that the problem is being solved or, in any event, effectively dealt with, and we dismiss it from our minds.

I contend that we have no right to this easy absolution from responsibility. In saying this I do not, as a practicing psychiatrist, intend to belittle the help which my profession can give to some troubled individuals. We have made significant progress since the   3 pre-Freudian era when psychiatry was a purely medical and custodial enterprise. In contemporary America, much of psychiatric practice consists of psychotherapy, and much of psychiatric theory is psychological and social, rather than biological and medical.

Our refusal to recognize this difference—that is, between deviations from biological norms which we usually call "illness," and deviations from social norms which we call "mental illness" (or crime, delinquency, etc.)—has made it possible to popularize the simplistic cliches of current mental-health propaganda. One of these, for instance, is the deceptive slogan, "Mental illness is like any other illness." This is not true; psychiatric and medical problems are not fundamentally similar. In curing a disease like syphilis or pneumonia,   4 the physician benefits both the patient and society. Can the psychiatrist who "cures" a "neurosis" make the same claim? Often he cannot, for in "mental illness" we find the individual *in conflict* with those about him—his family, his friends, his employer, perhaps his whole society. Do we expect psychiatry to help the individual—or

society? If the interests of the two conflict, as they often do, the
psychiatrist can help one only by harming the other.

Let us, for example, examine the case of a man I will call Victor
Clauson. He is a junior executive with a promising future, a wife who
loves him, and two healthy children. Nevertheless he is anxious and
unhappy. He is bored with his job which he believes saps his initiative   5
and destroys his integrity; he is also dissatisfied with his wife, and
convinced he never loved her. Feeling like a slave to his company, his
wife, and his children, Clauson realizes that he has lost control over
the conduct of his life.

Is this man "sick"? And if so, what can be done about it? At
least half a dozen alternatives are open to him. He could throw
himself into his present work or change jobs or have an affair or get a
divorce. Or he could develop a psychosomatic symptom such as   6
headaches and consult a doctor. Or, as still another alternative, he
could seek out a psychotherapist. Which of these alternatives is the
right one for him? The answer is not easy.

For in fact, hard work, an affair, a divorce, a new job may all
"help" him; and so may psychotherapy. But "treatment" cannot
change his external, social situation; only he can do that. What   7
psychoanalysis (and some other therapies) *can* offer him is a better
knowledge of himself, which may enable him to make *new choices* in
the conduct of his life.

Is Clauson "mentally sick"? If we so label him, what then is he to
be cured of? Unhappiness? Indecision? The consequences of earlier   8
unwise decisions?

These are problems in living, not diseases. And by and large it is
such problems that are brought to the psychiatrist's office. To ameliorate them he offers not treatment or cure but psychological counseling. To be of any avail this process requires a consenting, cooperative
client. There is, indeed, no way to "help" an individual who does not   9
want to be a psychiatric patient. When treatment is *imposed* on a
person, inevitably he sees it as serving not his own best interests, but
the interests of those who brought him to the psychiatrist (and who
often pay him).

Take the case of an elderly widow I will call Mrs. Rachel Abelson. Her husband was a successful businessman who died five years
ago, bequeathing part of his estate of $4 million to his children and
grandchildren, part to charities, and one-third to his wife. Mrs. Abel-   10
son had always been a frugal woman, whose life revolved around her
husband. After he died, however, she changed. She began to give her

money away—to her widowed sister, to charities, and finally to distant relatives abroad.

After a few years, Mrs. Abelson's children remonstrated, urging her to treat herself better instead of wasting her money on people who had long managed by themselves. But Mrs. Abelson persisted in doing what she felt was "the right thing." Her children were wealthy; she enjoyed helping others.

Finally, the Abelson children consulted the family attorney. He was equally dismayed by the prospect that Mrs. Abelson might spend all the money she controlled in this fashion. Like the children, he reasoned that if Mr. Abelson had wanted to help his third cousin's poverty-stricken daughters in Romania, he could have done so himself; but he never did. Convinced they ought to carry out the essence of their father's intention and keep the money in the family, the Abelson children petitioned to have their mother declared mentally incompetent to manage her affairs. Thereafter Mrs. Abelson became inconsolable. Her bitter accusations and the painful scenes that resulted only convinced her children that she really was mentally abnormal. When she refused to enter a private sanitarium voluntarily, she was committed by court order. She died two years later, and her will—leaving most of her assests to distant relatives—was easily broken on psychiatric grounds.

Like thousands of other involuntary mental patients, Mrs. Abelson was given psychiatric care in the hope of changing behavior offensive to others. Indeed, what was Mrs. Abelson's illness? Spending her money unwisely? Disinheriting her sons? In effect, recourse to psychiatry provided Mrs. Abelson's children with a socially acceptable solution for their dilemma, not hers. To an appalling degree state mental hospitals perform a like function for the less affluent members of our society.

Out of all too many comparable cases, I will cite that of a man we may call Tim Kelleher, who worked steadily as a truck driver for forty years, supporting a wife and nine children. In his early sixties, Kelleher found jobs getting scarcer. Now in his late seventies, he has not worked for over a decade. Since his wife died a few years ago he has lived with one or another of his children.

For two years his daughter Kathleen, mother of four, has been caring for him. Because the old man has grown progressively senile and burdensome, Kathleen's husband wants to shift the responsibility to the other children. But they all feel they've done their share.

Mr. Kelleher's future depends on what his family decides to do with him. One of them may still be willing to take care of him, but if not, he will be committed to a state mental hospital. His case will be   16 diagnosed as a "senile psychosis" or something similar. About a third of the patients now in our mental hospitals are such "geriatric" cases. This is how psychiatry meets a purely socioeconomic need.

If Mr. Kelleher or one of his children were even moderately wealthy, they could hire a companion or nurse to care for him at home or they could place him in a private nursing home. There   17 would be no need to label him a "mental patient" and confine him to a building he will never again leave, and where he will doubtless die within a year.

But for the poor, the public mental hospital is often the only way. Such is the plight of Mrs. Anna Tarranti (this is not her real name). At thirty-two—but looking ten years older—she has just been delivered of her seventh child. Her husband is a construction worker, sporadically employed, and a heavy drinker. After each of the last   18 three babies was born, Mrs. Tarranti was so "depressed" that she had to stay in the hospital an extra week or more. Now she complains of exhaustion, cannot eat or sleep, and does not want to see her baby. At the same time she feels guilty for not being a good mother and says she ought to die.

The fact is that Mrs. Tarranti is overwhelmed. She has more children than she wants, a husband who earns only a marginal living, and religious beliefs that virtually prohibit birth control. What should she do? She knows that if she goes home, she'll soon be pregnant   19 again, a prospect she cannot tolerate. She would like to stay in the hospital, but the obstetrical ward is too busy to keep her long without a bona fide obstetrical illness.

Again, psychiatry comes to the rescue. Mrs. Tarranti's condition is diagnosed as a "postpartum depression" and she is committed to the state hospital. As in the case of Mr. Kelleher, society has found   20 no more decent solution to a human problem than involuntary confinement in a mental hospital.

In effect psychiatry has accepted the job of warehousing society's undesirables. Such, alas, has long been its role. More than a hundred years ago, the great French psychiatrist Philippe Pinel observed that "public asylums for maniacs have been regarded as places   21 of confinement for such of its members as have become dangerous to the peace of society."

Nor have we any right to comfort ourselves with the belief that in our enlightened age confinement in a mental institution is really the same as any other kind of hospitalization. For even though we show more compassion and understanding toward the insane than some of our forebears, the fact is that the person diagnosed as mentally ill is stigmatized—particularly if he has been confined in a public mental hospital. These stigmata cannot be removed by mental-health "education," for the root of the matter is our intolerance of certain kinds of behavior.   22

Most people who are considered mentally sick (especially those confined involuntarily) are so defined by their relatives, friends, employers, or perhaps the police—*not* by themselves. These people have upset the social order—by disregarding the conventions of polite society or by violating laws—so we label them "mentally ill" and punish them by commitment to a mental institution.   23

The patient knows that he is deprived of freedom because he has annoyed others, not because he is sick. And in the mental hospital he learns that until he alters his behavior, he will be segregated from society. But even if he changes and is permitted to leave, his record of confinement goes with him. And the practical consequences are more those of a prison than a hospital record. The psychological and social damage thus incurred often far outweighs the benefits of any psychiatric therapy.   24

Consider, for example, the case of a young nurse I will call Emily Silverman, who works in a general hospital in a small city. Unmarried and lonely, she worries about the future. Will she find a husband? Will she have to go on supporting herself in a job that has become drudgery? She feels depressed, sleeps poorly, loses weight. Finally, she consults an internist at the hospital and is referred to a psychiatrist. He diagnoses her trouble as a case of "depression" and prescribes "antidepressant" drugs. Emily takes the pills and vists the psychiatrist weekly, but she remains depressed and begins to think about suicide. This alarms the psychiatrist, who recommends hospitalization. Since there is no private mental hospital in the city, Emily seeks admission to the state hospital nearby. There, after a few months, she realizes that the "treatment" the hospital offers cannot help her solve her problems. She then "recovers" and is discharged.   25

From now on, Emily is no longer just a nurse; she is a nurse with a "record" of confinement in a state mental hospital. When she tries to return to her job, she will probably find it filled and that there are no openings. Indeed, as an ex-mental patient she may find it impossible to obtain any employment in nursing. This is a heavy price to pay for ignorance, yet no one warned her of the hazards involved before she decided to enter the hospital for her "depression."   26

Because the therapeutic potentialities of psychiatry are consistently exaggerated and its punitive functions minimized or even denied, a distorted relationship between psychiatry and the law has evolved in our time.   27

Years ago some people accused of serious crimes pleaded "insanity." Today they are often charged with it. Instead of receiving a brief jail sentence, a defendant may be branded "insane" and incarcerated *for life* in a psychiatric institution.   28

This is what happened, for example, to a filling-station operator I will call Joe Skulski. When he was told to move his business to make way for a new shopping center, he stubbornly resisted eviction. Finally the police were summoned. Joe greeted them with a warning shot in the air. He was taken into custody and denied bail, because the police considered his protest peculiar and thought he must be crazy. The district attorney requested a pretrial psychiatric examination of the accused. Mr. Skulski was examined, pronounced mentally unfit to stand trial, and confined in the state hospital for the criminally insane. Through it all, he pleaded for the right to be tried for his offense. Now in the mental hospital he will spend years of fruitless effort to prove that he is sane enough to stand trial. If convicted, his prison sentence would have been shorter than the term he has already served in the hospital.   29

Joe, like most patients in public mental hospitals, is a victim of social injustice. A wealthy and important man would have a chance, and the means, to rebut the charge of mental illness—as indeed happened when the government last year tried to handle the incident of General Edwin Walker in this fashion.   30

All this is not to say that our public mental hospitals serve no socially necessary purpose. They do, in fact, perform two essential—and very different—functions. On the one hand, they help *patients* recover from personal difficulties by providing them with room, board, and a medically approved escape from everyday responsibilities. On the other hand, they help *families* (and society) care for those who annoy or burden them unduly. It is important that we sort out these very different services, for unfortunately their goals are not the same. To relieve people annoyed by the eccentricities, failings, or outright meanness of so-called mentally disturbed persons requires that something be done *to* mental patients, not *for* them.   31
The aim here is to safeguard the sensibilities not of the patient, but of those he upsets. This is a moral and social, not a medical, problem. How, for example, do you weigh the right of Mr. Kelleher to spend his declining years in freedom and dignity rather than as a psychiatric

prisoner, against the right of his children to lead a "life of their own" unburdened by a senile father? Or the right of Mrs. Tarranti to repudiate overwhelming responsibilities against her husband's and children's need for the services of a full-time wife and mother? Or the right of Mrs. Abelson to give away her money to poor relatives, against her children's claim on their father's fortune?

Granting that there can often be no happy resolution to such conflicts, there is no reason to feel that we are as yet on the right road. For one thing—we still tolerate appalling inequities between our treatment of the rich and the poor. Though it may be no more 32 than a dimly grasped ideal, both medicine and law strive to treat all people equally. In psychiatry, however, we not only fail to approximate this goal in our practice; we do not even value it as an ideal.

We regard the rich and influential psychiatric patient as a self-governing, responsible client—free to decide whether or not to be a patient. But we look upon the poor and the aged patient as a ward of the state—too ignorant or too "mentally sick" to know what is best 33 for him. The paternalistic psychiatrist, as an agent of the family or the state, assumes "responsibility" for him, defines him as a "patient" against his will, and subjects him to "treatment" deemed best for him, with or without his consent.

Do we really need more of this kind of psychiatry? 34

QUESTIONS AND PROBLEMS

1. Explain how the very term *psychiatry* lulls many of us into a feeling of security.
2. Clarify the distinction between deviations from biological norms and deviations from social norms.
3. What is the one thing which psychoanalysis can do for a person?
4. What is Dr. Szasz's method of showing us the futility of the term "mentally sick" for an anxious, unhappy man like Victor Clauson (par. 8)? Is irony involved? What of Mrs. Abelson (par. 13)?
5. This essay might have been placed under the heading "To Argue and Persuade." Would that have been a more fitting label for its method of development?
6. What is the difference between helping patients and helping families or society in general? What kinds of problems are involved?
7. What is it that psychiatry *cannot* do?
8. If you have a staff psychiatrist or psychologist on your campus, find out what his chief functions are. Are student problems different from the kinds of problems Dr. Szasz discusses in this essay?

SUGGESTIONS FOR WRITING

1. Conduct a series of interviews which will supply material for an article on "The Problems Students Face." In writing it, make use of the method of extended example, the typical case method.
2. What is the present student attitude toward the "mentally sick"? Report on a sampling of student attitudes toward mental illness and psychiatry.
3. Visit a mental institution or the psychiatric ward of a hospital. Report your impressions of the care the patients are receiving.
4. To what extent does your state provide funds for the care of psychiatric patients? Make a comparison between your state and other states in this regard. Develop an argument as to the adequacy or inadequacy of such aid in your state.
5. Write a review of Dr. Sazsz's book, *Law, Liberty, and Psychiatry.*
6. Write an essay on the responsibility of society to the mentally unstable.

SUGGESTIONS FOR FURTHER READING

Erving Goffman, *Asylums* (Aldine; Doubleday)

Milton Greenblatt and Others, *From Custodial to Therapeutic Patient Care in Mental Hospitals* (Russell Sage)

Ken Kersey, *One Flew Over the Cuckoo's Nest* (Viking)

Joaquim M. Machado de Assis, *The Psychiatrist and Other Stories*, trans. W.A. Grossman and H. Caldwell (Univ. of California)

A. Strauss and Others, *Psychiatric Ideologies and Institutions* (Free Press)

Thomas S. Szasz, *Law Liberty, and Psychiatry* (Macmillan); *The Myth of Mental Illness* (Harper; Dell)

Carter C. Umbarger and Others, *College Students in a Mental Hospital (Grune & Stratton)*

TO COMPARE AND CONTRAST

As development by definition clarifies a term or an idea by setting limits about it, development by comparison and contrast clarifies by enlarging the subject, by bringing in one or more additional elements which explain the meaning of the subject by linking it to a similar element or by showing how it differs from another element. Sir Geoffrey Crowther, in a following essay, gives us a clear picture of American education by showing how it differs from British education; he elucidates the one subject by contrasting it with the other. Henry Steele Commager compares the world of 1918 with that of today to raise the provocative question, "Is the world safer for anything?" And Irving Kristol contrasts the youth of today with the mores of an older generation. In each essay comparison and/or contrast is employed to clarify the writer's meaning, to project the writer's message.

Comparison, it must be pointed out, is not analogy. The subjects used for comparison and contrast must be from comparable groups; in the very fact that they are comparable lies their value in clarifing the author's point. Analogy, on the other hand, uses fancied resemblance between two subjects of different classes or species. Analogies illuminate a subject intuitively, as in figures of speech ("How far that little candle throws his beams! / So shines a good deed in a naughty world"—Shakespeare). It usually limits itself to a single comparison of unlike elements. Essays developed by comparison and contrast, on the other hand, give an extended treatment of likenesses and differences of subjects in the same general category. Analogy may show great insight and be expressed with great beauty ("Life, like a dome of many coloured glass, / Stains the white radiance of eternity"—Shelley), but it is a limited device. Comparison and contrast dwell upon details.

Analogy is imaginative; comparison is based upon careful observation. One cannot contrast British and American educational systems without having known or studied both thoroughly. Knowledge of the subject must be so thorough that the writer is able to deal with the typical and not the atypical; he must compare objects or details which are self-evident parts of the elements

being compared. And finally, the writer uses comparison and contrast to establish or prove his point; he is not dealing with the decoration of his subject but
with building it, with making it substantial.

Sometimes the essayist, in using the devices of comparison and contrast,
dwells only upon similarities; sometimes he limits himself to differences. More
often than not, however, he presents both similarities and dissimilarities, albeit
stressing the one which advances his argument or clarifies the point of his essay.
When the writer presents both sides he has two methods of proceeding: either to
group all similarities and all differences in two major parts of the essay, or to
present similarities and/or dissimilarities of each major point as he proceeds with
his thesis. In reading the following essays you should be aware of the various
possibilities open to the author. Why did he choose the pattern which is evident
in his essay?

THE AGE OF HAPPY PROBLEMS
Herbert Gold

Recently I have had occasion to live again near my old college campus. I went into a hole-in-the-wall bakery where the proprietor recognized me after ten years. "You haven't changed a bit, son," he said, "but can you still digest my pumpernickel? The stomach gets older, no? Maybe you want something softer now—a nice little loaf I got here."   1

He had worn slightly. But for me the change was from twenty-two to thirty-two, and it is this ten-year time that I want to think about—the generation which came back from the war to finish college on the GI Bill and is now deep into its career. We are the generation which knew the Depression only through the exhilaration of the burgeoning New Deal and the stunned passion of war. I remember the bank crash because my mother wept and I said, "If we're poor now, can I wear corduroy pants?" For the most part, we   2 were taken care of and never hopelessly hunted jobs. Now some of us say we are cool, say we are beat; but most of us are allrightniks—doing okay. We are successful. In the late forties and the fifties, it was hard to know economic struggle and want—and for the most part we didn't experience these traditional elements of youth—and it was hard for the skilled and the trained not to know success. We did not doubt overmuch. We have done well. How well?

"Money money money," as Theodore Roethke says.

> I have married my hands to perpetual agitation,
> I run, I run to the whistle of money.   3
>
> Money money money
> Water water water

I should like to take a look at some of the college idealists. The lawyer, fascinated by "the philosophy of law," now uses his study to put a smooth surface on his cleverness. Cardozo and Holmes? Very interesting, but let's find that loophole. The doctor who sent flowers to the first mother whose baby he delivered now specializes in "real-estate medicine"—his practice gives him capital for buying apartment houses. The architect who sat up all night haranguing his   4 friends about Lewis Mumford and Frank Lloyd Wright now works for a mass builder who uses bulldozers to level trees and slopes, then puts up tri-level, semi-detached, twenty-year-mortgaged, fundamentally identical dormitories for commuters. He admits that his designs make no decent sense, but they do have that trivial, all-important meaning: "It's what the market wants, man. You'd rather I taught city planning for six thousand a year?"

The actor becomes a disc jockey, the composer an arranger, the painter a designer; the writer does TV scripts in that new classic formula, "happy stories about happy people with happy problems." How hard it is to be used at our best! One of the moral issues of every age has been that of finding a way for men and women to test, reach, and overreach their best energies. Society has always worked to level us. Socrates has always made it hot for the citizens in the market place. But there was usually room for the heroic—hemlock   5 not a serious deterrent—and perhaps rarely so much room on all levels as in the frontier turbulence of the nineteenth and early twentieth century in America. Hands reached out like the squirming, grasping, struggling railroad networks; the open society existed; freedom had a desperate allure for the strongly ambitious, and men stepped up to take their chances—Abraham Lincoln and William James, Mark Twain and Melville, Edison and Rockfeller and Bet-a-Million Gates.

Allowing for a glitter of nostalgia on what we imagine about the past, still something has happened to change the old, movemented, free, open American society to something persuasive, plausible, comfortable, and much less open. We are prosperous, we get what we think we want, we have a relatively stable economy without totalitar-   6 ian rule. "I'm not selling out," my friend the architect says, "I'm buying in." Without attempting a simple explanation of the causes of this age of happy problems, let us look at its consequences for the new postwar young people who should be in full action toward their ambitions and the surest, sturdiest signs of a civilization's health.

What are these personal symptoms? How is the vital individual human creature doing in his staff meetings, at his family's table, over the baby's bassinet, and with that distant secret self that he may sometimes meet at the water cooler? Well, for this man it is very hard to be exceptional. Talent apart, he has too much to do, too much on his mind, to give himself over to his best energies. Think, for example, of the writers in the advertising agencies, on TV, or in the colleges. They all wanted to write great books; they tend now to   7 prefer "competence" as an ideal to greatness. Some of them are trying, but they risk the situation of the girl in the short-story writing class: "I can't be a creative writer, I can't, because I'm still a stupid virgin." She will take up going steady, she will take up marriage; she will be mildly disappointed; she will remain as she was, but aging—"adjusted," "integrated," virgin to danger, struggle, and the main chance of love and work.

In composite, in our thirties, we of this prosperous and successful generation are still in good health and rather fast at tennis (but practicing place shots which will eliminate the need to rush the net); hair receding but still attractive to college girls, or at least recent graduates; a slight heaviness at the middle which makes us fit our   8
jackets with especial care (sullen jowls beginning, too) or, if not that, a skinnines of anxiety (etching around the mouth, dryness of lips). We go to an athletic club. We play handball in heavy shirts "to sweat it off."

The girls we marry are beautiful in wondrous ways. Savant make-up is no longer sufficient. Blemishes are scraped until the skin is pink and new; scars are grown away by cortisone injections—what reason to be marked in this world?; noses are remade, the same for   9
mother and daughter, just like heredity. Money is spent much more gracefully than in those fantastic times when silver coins were put in ears and jewels in navels.

The old truth—"we must all come from someplace"—is amended. We can create ourselves in our own image. And what is our own   10
image? The buttery face in the Pond's advertisement, the epicene face in the Marlboro publicity.

The matters that we are told to worry about—and perhaps we think we worry about them—do not really trouble us. The prospect of war is like a vague headache, no worse. The memory of war is even dimmer. A depression is something which will reduce the value of our shares in the mutual fund, make us keep the old car another   11
year. Radioactive fallout and the slow destruction of the human species through cancerous mutation—well, what is so much bother to imagine cannot really come to pass. Who lets the newspaper interfere with a good meal?

II

Still, we are not blithe spirits; birds we are not. This generation is particularly distinguished by its worry about making its wives happy, about doing right by its kids (title of a hugely popular paperbound book: *How to Play with Your Child*), about acquiring enough leisure and symbols of leisure, which it hopes to cash in for moral comfort.   1
Fortune reports a method used by salesmen to get the second room air conditioner to the couple which already has one in its bedroom. "The machine operates as expected? Fine! You sleep better with it?

So do I, that's just dandy. But, friends, let me tell you how I sleep so much better now that I know my kiddies are cool and comfy, too."

This capitalizes on the child-oriented anxiety which the class known commericially as Young Marrieds has been taught to feel by modern psychiatry. Advertisements for *McCall's*, "The Magazine of Togetherness," demonstrate Togetherness in a brilliant summer scene. The man, wearing a white skirtlike apron and a proud simper, [2] is bending to serve a steak to his wife (summer frock, spike heels), who will season it for them and for their happy gamboling children. The little boy and girl are peeking and smiling. The wife is lying in a garden chair. Togetherness consists in the husband's delighting his wife and kids by doing the cooking.

Actually, of course, most American women don't want to go this far. They are already equal with men. Women are usually too wise to define "equal" as "better than." It is not momism or any such simple psychological gimmick that tells this sad tale. The consumer culture—in which leisure is a menace to be met by anxious continual consuming—devours both the masculinity of men and the femininity [3] of women. The life of consuming requires a neuter anxiety, and to pressure to conform, to watch for our cues, to consume, makes us all the same—we are customers—only with slightly different gadgets. Women have long bought men's shirts; men are buying colognes with "that exciting musky masculine tang."

Togetherness represents a curious effort by a woman's magazine to bring men back into the American family. Togetherness does not restore to the man a part of his old-time independence. It does not even indicate that he may be the provider with an independent role defined partly by ambitions outside his family. Instead, it suggests the joys of being a helpmate, a part of the woman's full life, and battens greedily on the contemporary male's anxiety about pleasing his wife. The Togetherness theme has been a great commercial success. A full-page advertisement by that canny old American institu- [4] tion, the New York Stock Exchange, shows a photograph of a harried young man pleading with a young woman on a parlor couch. She remains unconvinced, pouting, hands gloved and folded together, as brutal as the shocked beauties in the classical halitosis or B.O. trage-dies. The caption reads: "Is the girl you want to marry reluctant to say Yes? Do you need to build character with your wife? Then just use the magic words: I'LL START A MONTHLY INVESTMENT PLAN."

It used to be thought that answering economic needs was the main purpose of man's economic efforts. Now, however, an appeal to

emotional insecurity about money—without crass financial trouble—can do good work for an advertiser. "Do you need to build character 5
with your wife?" This is whimsey with a whammy in it. Money works symbolically to stimulate, then assuage male doubts.

> She: What can the stock do for our marriage?
> He: It can help keep it sweet and jolly because when we own stock we are part-owners of the company.

In the image projected by this advertisement, the wife is prosecutor, judge, and jury. She may fall into a less exalted role, however, while her husband is downtown making the money which will go for food, clothing, shelter, and sound common stocks. That she too frets about keeping her marriage sweet and jolly is obvious. The popular media again point to trouble while pitching a new solution to her 6
problems. One of the former radio soap operas is now sponsored by Sleep-eze. Apparently almost everyone uses soap these days, but not everyone has caught on to the virtues of non-habit-forming sedatives. Want your husband to love you? This pill will help or your money back. "Ladies! Fall asleep without that unsightly twisting and turning."

It's time to mention Barbara. A tough wise creature of a girl, Barbara comes to this observation out of her marriage and love life: "Men worry too much about making the girl happy. We seem to 7
scare them out of themselves. Let them really be pleased—that's what we want most of all—and then we'll be happy. Delighted. But really."

In other words, long live primary narcissism! And secondary. And tertiary. But let us call it by an older, better name—respect for 8
the possibilities of the self. This includes the possibility of meaningful relationships with meaningful others.

III

Our wounds as a people in this time and place are not unique in kind, but the quality of difference makes this a marvelously disturbing period. The economic problem, no longer rooted in hunger for essential goods, food, housing, clothing, is an illustration of the difference. Sure, we are still busy over food—but packaged foods, lux- 1
ury foods, goodies in small cans; housing—but the right house in the right neighborhood with the right furnishings and the right mortgage; clothing—but the cap with the strap in the back, Ivy League pants, charcoal gray last year and narrow lapels this year, and male fashions changing as fast as female.

It used to be thought that, given money, relative job security, and the short work week, culture would then bloom like the gardens in the suburbs and the individual spirit would roar with the driving power of a Thunderbird getting away after a red light.   2

Who could have predicted that we would have to keep pace with a cultural assembly line in the leisure-time sweatshop? At least in the older sweatshop, you sighed, packed, and left the plant at last. Now we are forever harassed to give more, more, more. We no longer have to keep up with the Joneses; we must keep up with Clifton Fadiman. He is watching *you.* The steady pressure to consume, absorb, participate, receive, by eye, ear, mouth, and mail, involves a cruelty to intestines, blood pressure, and psyche unparalleled in history. The   3 frontiersmen could build a stockade against the Indians, but what home is safe from Gilbert Highet? We are being killed with kindness. We are being stifled with cultural and material joys. Our wardrobes are full. What we really need is a new fabric that we don't have to wrinkle, spot, wash, iron, or wear. At a beautiful moment in *Walden,* Thoreau tells how he saw a beggar walking along with all his belongings in a single sack on his back. He wanted to weep for the poor man—because he still has that sack to carry.

The old-style sweatshop crippled mainly the working people. Now there are no workers left in America; we are almost all middle class as to income and expectations. Even the cultural elite labors among the latest in hi-fi equipment, trips to Acapulco and Paris, the right books in the sewn paper editions (Elizabeth Bowen, Arnold Toynbee, Jacques Barzun—these are the cultivated ones, remember), *Fortune* and the *Reporter,* art movies and the barbecue pit and the Salzburg music festival. It is too easy to keep up with the Joneses about cars and houses, but the Robert Shaw Chorale is a *challenge.*   4 In the meantime, the man in the sweatshop is divorced or psychoanalyzed (these are perhaps remedies in a few cases); he raises adjusted children, or kills them trying; he practices Togetherness in a home with a wife who is frantic to be a woman and a nonwoman at the same time; he broods about a job which does not ask the best that he can give. But it does give security; it is a good job. (In college this same man learned about the extreme, tragic instances of desire. Great men, great books. Now he reads Evelyn Waugh.)

In his later, philosophical transmogrification, David Riesman consoles the radar-flaunting other-directeds by holding out the reward of someday being "autonomous" if they are very, very good. Same thing, brother, same thing. When he describes the autonomous personality's "intelligent" distinctions among consumer products, exercising his creative imagination by figuring out why *High Noon* is a better western than a Gene Autry, well, then, in the words of Elvis Presley:

> Ah feel so lonely,
> Ah feel so lo-oh-oh-lonely.

We're in Heartbreak Hotel where, as another singer, Yeats, put it:

> The ceremony of innocence is drowned;
> The best lack all conviction, while the worst
> Are filled with a passionate intensity.

Refusal to share to the fullest degree in the close amity of the leisure-time sweatshop is—for Mr. Riesman—a kind of ethical bohemianism. His autonomous consumer, sociable, trained, and in the know, is a critic of the distinctions between the Book-of-the-Month Club and the Reader's Subscription, Inc., marks the really good shows in his TV guide, buys educational comic books for his children, tastes the difference in fine after-dinner coffee, knows that the novel is a dead form and why. Bumper to bumper in the traffic home from work, or jammed into the commuter train, he has plenty of time to think. And he does think (thinking means worrying) while the radio blares "The House with the Stained Glass Window" or "The Magic of Believing," a little rock-and-roll philosophical number.

Does he have a moral problem, let's say, about leaving a changing neighborhood "for the sake of the children"? He is a liberal, of course, but after all, the Negroes who are moving in come from a different world, and he should not inflict his principles on his children. Still, there is a certain discomfort. He discusses it with his analyst. *Why* does he suffer from this moral qualm? Does it have some link with the ever-ambiguous relationship with parents? *What* moral problem? They are all psychological. Anxiety can be consumed like any product. And from his new, split-level, sapling-planted housing development he speeds into the city now ten miles further out.

We are a disappointed generation. We are a discontented people. Our manner of life says it aloud even if discreetly our public faces smile. The age of happy problems has brought us confusion and anxiety amid the greatest material comfort the world has ever seen. Culture has become a consolation for the sense of individual powerlessness in politics, work, and love. With gigantic organizations determining our movements, manipulating the dominion over self which alone makes meaningful communion with others possible, we ask leisure, culture, and recreation to return to us a sense of ease and authority. But work, love, and culture need to be connected. Otherwise we carry our powerlessness with us onto the aluminum garden furniture in the back yard. Power lawn mowers we can buy, of course.

The solution in our age of happy problems is not to install (on time) a central air-conditioning system and a color TV this year because the room air conditioner and the black-and-white TV last year did not change our lives in any important respect. The solution is not in stylish religious conversions or a new political party. The   9 answer is not even that Panglossian fantasy about "the autonomous personality" which will naturally emerge out of the fatal meeting of the other-directed consumer with a subscription to the *Saturday Review*.

The ache of unfulfilled experience throbs within us. Our eyes hurt. Vicarious pleasures buzz in our heads. Isn't there something   10 more, something more?

There is still awareness; there is still effort. "It should be every man's ambition to be his own doctor." This doesn't mean that he should not see a dentist when his tooth hurts, perhaps a psychoanalyst when his psyche hurts; but he must hold in mind the ideal maximum of humanity—the exercise of intelligence and desire within a context of active health. The Stoic philosophers had a great, although impossible, idea for these crowding times: cultivate your own   11 garden. We cannot retreat from the world any more—we never really could—but we can look for our best gardens within the world's trouble. There we must give ourselves silence and space; we can see what the will wants; we can make decisions. Only then—having come to terms with our own particularities—can we give the world more than a graceless, prefabricated commodity.

Hope? Some sweet Barbara is hope. And a work we love. And the strength, O Lord, not to accept the easy pleasures (easy anxieties) which have pleased us (made us anxious) so far. And the strength, O Lord, you who reign undefined above the psychoanalysts and the   12 sociologists, the market researchers and the advertising agencies, the vice-presidents and the book clubs, to refuse the easy solutions which have becalmed us so far.

Then with good belly luck we will be able to digest strong, irregu-   13 lar, yeasty black bread.

QUESTIONS AND PROBLEMS

1. Comment on the diction of the author. Does it suit his subject matter? Is parody involved?
2. This essay might have been reprinted under the heading "To Determine Cause and Effect."
   a. Explain why that heading would perhaps have been as correct as the one used.
   b. Defend its placement under "To Compare and Contrast." How serious do you think the author is concerning his main thesis?
3. Comment on the reference (Sec. III, par. 3) to Clifton Fadiman and Gilbert Highet. Is Gold making a serious point here? Is he being fair?
4. Is satire involved in the next paragraph? If so, is it effective? Do the references to Elizabeth Bowen, Arnold Toynbee, Jacques Barzun, and Evelyn Waugh tell us something important about the age, or about Gold?
5. What does the author mean when he refers to "a wife who is frantic to be a woman and a non-woman at the same time" (Sec. III, par. 4)?
6. What is meant by "ethical bohemianism," "autonomous consumer," "Panglossian fantasy"?
7. The author tells us, near the end of the essay, what the solution to our "happy problems" is *not*.
   a. What solutions does he suggest?
   b. Are they actual solutions?
   c. How does one go about accomplishing them?
8. Does the author view our culture in perspective? What reasons can you give to support or disprove the contention that he does? Is there evidence that he himself is untouched by the debilitating influences he cites?

SUGGESTIONS FOR WRITING

1. Write a familiar or humorous essay on television advertisements.
2. Write a serious essay in which you suggest solutions for the anxieties which plague the American today.
3. Compare and contrast your way of life as a college student with your life at home before you entered college.
4. Compare and contrast the day-to-day problems of the urban and the rural dweller. Develop a specific thesis.
5. Write a counterpart to Gold's essay in which you treat the three most serious problems which face man today.
6. Write a researched essay on the efforts of the government to secure truth in advertising.
7. Defend the "popular culture" which Gold attacks in his essay.
8. Read and review a how-to-live-a-fuller-life book. Assay both its value and its shortcomings.

SUGGESTIONS FOR FURTHER READING

Hannah Arendt, *The Human Condition* (Univ. of Chicago)
John B. Biesanz and Mavis Biesanz, *Modern Society*, 3rd ed. (Prentice-Hall)
C.E. Elias and others, eds., *Metropolis: Values in Conflict* (Wadsworth)
Eric Larrabee and Rolf Meyersohn, eds., *Mass Leisure* (Free Press)
Martin Mayer, *Madison Avenue, U.S.A.* (Harper; Pocket Books)
Vance Packard, *The Hidden Persuaders* (David McKay; Pocket Books)

ENGLISH AND AMERICAN EDUCATION
Sir Geoffrey Crowther

For the past three years I have been engaged, with my colleagues of the Central Advisory Council on Education in England, in a comprehensive study of the English educational system. I had some of my own education in the United States, and I have been a frequent visitor to America ever since. This double experience has bred in me   1
a growing sense of astonishment that two countries which share the same language, so many of the same cultural traditions and ways of life, whose political, religious, and social aspirations are so largely identical, should have educational systems so utterly different as to provide almost no basis for a comparison between them.

That is a strong statement, and my present purpose is to try to justify it. Let me first say, however, that I have no intention whatever of trying to show that one national system is, on balance, better   2
than the other; only that they are much more different than is usually realized.

The American and the English educational systems are different in purpose, structure, and method. Let us start with purpose. The two systems grew up in response to very different pressures and needs. In America, you have always been very conscious of the need to build up a new society. You have wanted to construct something bigger, richer, better than you have. This is said to arise from something in the American national character, but that seems to me to turn the logic upside down; it is the American national character that has arisen from the circumstances in which the American people have   3
found themselves. From the start it was necessary to create a supply of ministers of religion, of lawyers, and of skilled artisans—I place them in the order of importance in which they were regarded at the time. Later on there came the obvious necessity of incorporating the great waves of immigrants into your society. Still later came the great task, in which you are still engaged, of knitting your varied economic, social, and racial groups into the harmonious and balanced society in which the principles of democratic government can work properly.

Consciously or unconcsiously, American education has at all times been designed to serve these social purposes. It has been regarded as an instrument by which society can build its own future. From its nature, it has inescapably been concerned with the rank and   4
file of the people. Its chief concern for many generations has been to

do something to the masses—and I think the word is *to,* not *for*—in the interests of the American dream.

All this, of course, is platitude in America. What may not be quite so familiar is the contrast in the historical situation in England. We have never been very conscious of the necessity to build a new society. At all relevant times we have had a fully developed society already in being. And at all relevant times we have also, I am sorry to say, been on the whole pretty satisfied with the society we have. For most of the last two hundred years, American education has been designed to do a job of construction; English education has been designed primarily for maintenance, with improvement coming second. In the very latest period, perhaps, those attitudes have started to change. As with so many aspects of education, there seem to be the first signs of a tendency to change sides. Your education is becoming socially more conservative just when ours is becoming more consciously radical.

But that is a speculation for the future, on which I will not enlarge. I am talking of the influences of the past, which have shaped the structures of today. American education has always had to concern itself with the common man in his multitudes. The concern of English education has until very recently been with the maintenance of society, in the words of the old prayer which you will often hear in school and college chapels, "that there may never be wanting a succession of persons duly qualified to serve God in church and state." This is a conception which does not necessarily embrace the education of the great mass. There is a fine, rich, broad educational tradition in England. But it is not a tradition of education, above the minimum level, for the multitude. Post-primary education has always been thought of as a privilege in England; it was not until 1944 that the principle of secondary education for all was established, and it is hardly yet fully effective.

Let me pursue this contrast a little further. Let me give you two of the consequences, of which I would guess that one will shock you, while the other may perhaps surprise you more favorably.

I will start with the shocker. The consequence of our different attitude is that the sheer size, the volume or quantity, of English education is very much smaller than American. The age at which the legal compulsion to attend school expires is still only fifteen. Moreover, that is an effective leaving age, and more than four children out of five in fact leave school before they are sixteen. Of the sixteen-year-old age group—those between their sixteenth and seventeenth birthdays—only 22 per cent are still in full-time education. In the seventeen-year-olds, the figure falls to 13 per cent of the boys and 11 per cent of the girls. Among eighteen-year-olds, it is 8 per cent of the boys and 5.5 per cent of the girls.

What strikes Americans, I find, as even odder than these figures is the fact that we are not, as a nation, greatly disturbed by them, although many of us think they ought to be larger. But we cannot assume that public opinion is on our side. I am very doubtful whether there would be any support in public opinion for a policy of keeping the majority of children in school after sixteen, and I am certain that you would find hardly anyone in England who believes,   9 as you do, in keeping all children at school until eighteen. Our college students represent about 3 per cent of each age group, and there is an expansion program in hand that will raise it to about 5 per cent. Anybody who suggested that we needed any more than that would meet with the strongest resistance, and not least from the universities themselves.

This attitude does not arise from any lack of love for our children. It is not because we think we can't afford it. The proportion of our national income that we spend on general welfare services—social security, health, and the like—is about the highest in the world. It is not from lack of generosity or lack of means that we confine education after the middle teens to a minority. It is because we sincerely believe that it is the right thing to do, in the interests of the children themselves. After all, there can be no absolute rules about education. Nobody believes that any child should be allowed to leave school at twelve. I do not suppose a time will ever come when, even in America, it will become legal or compulsory for everyone to stay in full-time education until twenty-five. Where you fix the age between those limits is surely a matter of judgment. And why should it be the same age for all children? Our belief in England is that, balancing what can be got out of school against what can be got out of life, the average boy or girl has probably had the optimum dose after eleven years of schooling—and do not forget that we begin, by legal compulsion, at the age of five. Eleven years, after all, is one year out of every six or seven of the average lifetime.

Now let me give you the other side of the medal. Because education after fifteen or sixteen is confined to a minority, that minority gets every assistance that the state can provide. It is nowadays, to an overwhelming extent, a minority chosen for intelligence and attainment. There are, of course, still the independent schools, where very substantial fees have to be paid. But the pressure of numbers upon them is such that a stupid boy or girl will have great difficulty getting in. And in the state schools, selection is by merit only. But once selected, a boy finds himself with his foot not so much on a ladder as an escalator. He will have the best resources of the best schools concentrated on him. If he can secure a place in a university, and that also is a matter of selection by merit, the state will pay his tuition fees and his living expenses, not only during the session but during the vacation as well. There is no such thing as working your way through college in England. We do not need a National Merit Scholarship scheme because we have one already. Nor is this a recent thing. It has been expanded in recent years, but it has always existed.

Let me move on to structure. The outstanding difference here lies in the fact that we have a very much smaller degree of local control than you do. There are about 50,000 school boards in the United States, each of them, I suppose, more or less free to run the schools as it thinks best. That gives a total population in the average school board area of about 3500 persons. In England there are about 130 local education authorities, which gives an average population per area of about 300,000. Moreover, there are two other differences, apart from this sharp difference in size. Your school boards consist, I believe, in most states, of persons specially elected for the purpose, with no other duties. In England the schools are run by the county council, or the borough council, which is the general purpose government of the area.

Second, your school boards raise their own money by direct taxes, or at least the greater part of it. In England about 70 per cent of the expenditure of the local education authorities is met out of grants from the central government in London. There are advantages and disadvantages in this. It means that we do not have the enormous range in standards between rich areas and poor areas that you do. It means a much greater degree of standardization of conditions of employment among the teachers, and therefore of interchangeability between school and school and between area and area. But it also inevitably means a greater degree of uniformity imposed from the center. We think our system is decentralized, because it allows much more local freedom and variety than exist in the school systems of most Continental European countries. But there is no doubt that it is much more highly centralized than the American system.

The other great difference under the heading of structure is the principle of selection upon which our system is based. All children, except the minority in fee-paying schools, go to undifferentiated schools from the age of five to the age of eleven. At eleven or thereabouts, a proportion of them, varying from area to area but

11

12

13

14

averaging between 20 and 25 per cent, is selected for what we call grammar schools, which include children to the age of eighteen, though not all the pupils stay that long. The remainder go to what are called secondary modern schools, which include children to age fifteen and increasingly to sixteen, but no older.

You will see from this description that the crucial time for an English child is at the age of eleven or a little more. The selection test then applied—the famous or infamous eleven-plus examination—is supposed to be a classification purely by ability and aptitude, without any suspicion of being derogatory to those who are not selected. But, of course, everybody wants to be selected, and with the growing pressure of numbers as a result of the post-war bulge of population, the selection has been getting steadily more competitive. As the result of agitation, the Labor Party has adopted the policy of abolishing the eleven-plus examination by sending all children at that age to the same schools, the so-called comprehensive secondary schools. The Labor Party has moved toward this system in several of the areas where it controls the local council, and even in Conservative areas there is a distinct movement to experiment with systems that do not involve sending children to different schools at the age of eleven.

I have several times seen this movement quoted in America as evidence that English education is turning away from selection. I think this is a grave misunderstanding. The public objection to selection at eleven is social and political, not educational. It is an objection on the part of parents to having their children sent to different schools, not to their having different educations. And the remedies that are being applied are wholly in terms of institutions, not in terms of the education they provide. I know, for example, one large new comprehensive school built by a Labor council. Every child entering that school is tested and placed in one of fifteen "streams," differentiated by the children's intelligence and aptitude. This selection is done by the teachers; the parents have nothing to do with it; and the children are not even supposed to know which stream is which in intelligence grading. A child placed in one of the top streams will have an almost wholly different education from a child placed even in one of the middle streams. If this is not selection, I do not know the meaning of the term. But this is what we mean by a comprehensive school. Many people in England will tell you that the comprehensive school has been copied from the American comprehensive high school, some meaning it as a compliment, some as the reverse. I have often told them that they could hardly be more mistaken.

15

16

Nonselection—if that is the opposite of selection—as it is practiced in America is totally unknown in England. By nonselection I mean the principle of treating all children alike, allowing them to sort themselves out by their choice of courses, by what they find easy and difficult, or by their varying ambitions—with counseling   17
assistance, no doubt, but without any compulsory segregations. I am sure that your system seems as odd to us as ours does to you. There is no retreat from selection in England; the only change is that a growing number of people—but still a minority—think that the selection should be within a common school, not between schools.

The differences between the two countries in educational method make an enormous subject, and I must restrict myself to   18
four points out of many that it would be possible to make.

The first of these differences in method lies in the position of the teacher, in the relative positions of the teacher and the textbook. One of the things about American education that most strikes the English visitor is the importance you attach to textbooks. We have no parallel to that. To begin with, I do not think there are more than two or three, at most, of the local education authorities in England   19
that tell their schools what textbooks to use. That is left to the teacher, occasionally the principal, or the head of department in a large school. And in the higher grades, more often than not, there is not a textbook at all. A teacher will often recommend a book as covering the subject pretty well and as being useful for reference but will not make any attempt to go through it chapter by chapter.

This system places a much greater responsibility on the individual teacher, and I have often been asked in America whether we do not have a lot of trouble with it. So far as the political and social responsibility of the teacher is concerned, I cannot recall having heard of a single case arising through a teacher's being accused of using a book which seems offensive or objectionable to somebody in authority.   20
That is partly, perhaps mainly, because our system of large authorities and rather remote and indirect public control puts the individual teacher largely out of the reach of vigilance committees, whether of parents or of the local chamber of commerce. There is also a strong tradition against anything that smacks of political interference with the schools.

Educational responsibility, however, is another matter. Quite clearly, a system like ours, which places so much responsibility on the individual teacher, cannot work well unless the average standard of intelligence, knowledge, and teaching competence is high. Up to the present, we have been able to maintain that standard. It is partly, of course, a matter of numbers. In the whole of England last year there were only some 260,000 schoolteachers. We were a little short, but 300,000 would have given us all we need. And this is in a country about one quarter the size of the United States. I do not know how many schoolteachers there are in the United States, but I am very sure it is many more than four times 300,000. I do not see how you could possibly have coped with the enormous increase in the 21 American school population in the past forty years without being willing to take thousands of young men and women who needed close support from a textbook before they could teach. Indeed, under the pressure of rising numbers in the schools, I fear we shall find before long that we shall have to give the teacher more assistance, and that implies more external control on his teaching. This particular contrast is not, however, entirely a matter of numbers. It is partly also the result of a different tradition of teacher training, which, in England, has always laid a much greater emphasis on the content of what is to be taught than in America and much less on questions of pedagogic method.

The second difference in method is the absence in England of the course system which is so universal in your schools and colleges. Indeed, the word "course" has a wholly different meaning in the two countries. If you asked an English school child what courses he was taking, he wouldn't know what you meant. If you asked him what subjects he was taking, he would answer English, Latin, mathematics, history, and so forth. But that would not mean, as it would in America, that those were the subjects he had chosen to take. They 22 would be the subjects that his form, or class, was taking, and therefore that he was taking with the rest of the class. Until the boy is about fifteen or sixteen, it is unlikely that he or his parents have had any say in the choice of form in which he is placed. And at no age does he have any say in deciding the curriculum of that form. At the higher ages, there is a choice between three or four different curriculums, but each curriculum has to be taken, within narrow limits, as it stands.

Here, indeed, is a contrast with the American system. Perhaps it is not quite so sharp a contrast in practice as it is in principle, as I observe that, more and more, those American boys and girls who have ambition to gain admittance to a good college find their choice of courses in high school made for them by the college entrance requirements. But there is one important consequence for teaching that is worth bringing out. In an English school, in any year but one (and that one is what we call the fifth form year, about the age of fourteen or fifteen), you can assume that the pupils who are taking a subject in one year will be taking the same subject next year. The study of a subject can therefore be planned as a continuous process over a period of years. That is what we mean when we use the word "course." We mean a whole balanced curriculum of six or seven or   23 eight subjects, planned to continue over three or four or five years. Once a boy or girl enters on such a course, he or she will normally pursue it to the end. And all the boys and girls in a course will take substantially the same subjects, with perhaps slight options, as between a second classical or a second modern language. You will therefore understand how bewildered we are when we contemplate one of your neat, packaged, self-contained, nine-month courses, such as high school physics. It is no good asking an English schoolboy when he enters college how many years of French he has had at school. Two boys might both truthfully answer nine years. But they might mean totally different things, and neither one would mean what you thought he meant.

How, then, do we measure what a student has accomplished, if we cannot count up the number of courses he has satisfactorily taken? The answer is that we rely, to an extent wholly unknown to you, on general examinations. Every year—sometimes every term— the pupil has to take a written examination in all the subjects of the curriculum, and his further progress depends, sometimes entirely, on his performance in that examination. Most of these examinations are set and assessed within the school itself, by his own teachers. But at three crucial points in his career the examination is set and assessed by an external body. The first of these is the eleven-plus examina-   24 tion, which determines to which sort of secondary school the child should go. The second comes at fifteen or sixteen and is called the Ordinary Level of the General Certificate of Education, set and assessed by one of nine examining boards closely associated with the universities. This examination can be taken in any number of subjects from one upwards, but the most usual practice is to take it in from five to nine subjects. Third, there is the Advanced Level of the General Certificate of Education, which is taken at eighteen or thereabouts and which plays a large part in university entrance.

I have been describing the practice of the grammar schools; that is, the schools for the brightest 20 to 25 per cent of the children. Examinations, especially written examinations, play a much smaller part in the life of the less intelligent children. Even in this case, however, they play a much larger part than they do in America; and there is a rising demand for public examinations, at lower standards   25 of intelligence than those of the General Certificate of Education, for these less gifted children. I cannot honestly say that the children themselves clamor for examinations, but employers do, and therefore so do the parents. All the questions that Americans ask and answer in terms of the number and variety of courses a student has taken we ask and answer in terms of the examinations he has passed.

I have left to the last what is the sharpest difference of all between our two systems. This is our system of specialization, in which England is, I think, unique in the world. A student will take the examination for the Ordinary Level of the General Certificate of Education at the age of fifteen or sixteen in a wide range of subjects drawn both from the humanities and from the natural sciences. But once he has passed that examination, he will specialize. That is to say, he will devote two thirds, or perhaps even more, of his time in school to a narrow range of subjects. In one boy's case, it may be 26 physics, chemistry, and mathematics; in another's it may be chemistry and biology, or it may be history or modern languages and literature, or classical languages and philosophy. But, whatever the choice, the greater part of the pupil's attention, in the classroom and in his private study time, is given to his specialty, and he will take the advanced level examination at eighteen in his special subjects only. When he gets to the university, the specialization is even more intense. The range of subjects does not usually get any narrower, but the student gives 100 per cent of his time to it.

I have found that to Americans, and indeed to educationalists from every country in the world except England, this seems a very strange system indeed. Perhaps you will have difficulty in believing that I really mean what I say. So let me cite my own case, though it is now more than thirty years old. I was a modern languages specialist. For my last three years at school, from the ages of fifteen to eighteen, I studied mostly French and German language and literature, perhaps three or four hours a week of history, and one hour of 27 Scripture on Sundays. For another two years at Cambridge, even the history and the Scripture were cut out, and I studied French and German exclusively. Five years of my life were given to those languages. My experience was perhaps a little extreme; I think the admixture of general and contrasting subjects would nowadays, in a good school, be a little bigger. But the difference would not be great. The English boy or girl is a specialist from the age of fifteen or sixteen.

The advisory council of which I am chairman was specifically requested by the Minister of Education to review this system of specialization. We examined it most carefully and discussed it at great length, both with witnesses and among ourselves. In the end we came to the conclusion that we wanted to see it continued. We found that it was being pushed too far, and we have made a number of suggestions for removing what we think are abuses. But we have   28 reported in favor of this system of specialization. And that is a unanimous conclusion reached by a council made up of educators of all kinds. Perhaps you will find that fact as extraordinary as the system itself, and I must try to give you some of our reasons for thinking that, in this matter, we in England are in step and the whole of the rest of the world is out of step.

Let me begin by telling you of one argument that we reject. That is the argument that every intelligent citizen, or every educated man, ought to know something about each subject in a range so wide that it compels a balanced curriculum; that no one can afford to be ignorant of history, government, science, languages, and so forth. To this, we would give our answer in two parts. First, it is true that there are certain elementary skills and knowledges that everyone must   29 have—reading, writing, arithmetic, and several more. But these essential elements can be, and should be, provided by the age of sixteen. If you go on with them after that age, you will be wasting your time, because the knowledge you instill will be forgotten unless it can be attached to the main intellectual interest of a boy's or girl's life, which begins to emerge at about that age.

The second part of the answer is that it is only when you have got these essential elementary skills and knowledges out of the way that you can confront the real task of education. The acquisition of factual knowledge is by itself a poor test of any education and a lamentably poor test of the education of boys and girls of seventeen and eighteen. It has been said that the process of education is not to be compared to that of filling up an empty pot, but rather to that of lighting a fire. The proper test of an education is whether it teaches the pupil to think and whether it awakens his interest in applying his   30 brain to the various problems and opportunities that life presents. If these have once been done, then factual knowledge can easily be assimilated. If these have not been done, then no amount of nodding acquaintance with widely varying fields of human knowledge will equip a boy or girl with an educated mind. We in England argue the case for specialization not primarily on the score of the information it provides but because it awakens interest, teaches clear thinking, and induces self-discipline in study.

We believe that, if you can find which of the recognized intellectual disciplines most arouses a boy's interest—and we confine his choice to five or six recognized disciplines, chosen for their intellectual content, not for their vocational value—if you can let him spend his time on what interests him, but insist that he must work hard at it, go deep into it, follow it up in the library or the laboratory, get around behind the stage scenery that defines the formal academic subject, you will really be teaching him how to use the mind that God has given him. This sort of intensive study takes a great deal of time, and that is why it can only be applied, for any one student, to a restricted range of subjects. No doubt you will say that the boy must be very narrow as a result. That may be. Are you sure that being narrow is worse than being shallow? 31

I find that English education has a high reputation among Americans. I am often asked, for example, whether it is not true that the eighteen-year-old boy in England is a year or two ahead of his American contemporary. I always answer that question, or assertion, by asking some others. What boy? If an English boy is still at school at eighteen, he is necessarily in the upper quartile in intelligence. Are you comparing him with the average American high school graduate, 32 who is of average intelligence? And ahead in what? In the subjects to which he has been giving nearly all his time and attention for two years? It would be strange if he were not a long way ahead in those. Or over the whole range of a broad curriculum? He has been taught different things, by different methods, with a different purpose in view, in a different sort of school. There is no fair basis for a comparative judgment.

QUESTIONS AND PROBLEMS

1. What is the purpose of the opening paragraph of the essay?
2. After establishing that his purpose is to show contrast, Crowther classifies the areas in which he will develop that contrast. What is the classification? Does he further add subclasses? Note how tightly knit and well organized the essay is.
3. In par. 3 Crowther alludes to the early need of creating "a supply of ministers of religion, of lawyers, and of skilled artisans" and indicates that these are listed in order of importance.
   a. Why was this the order of importance in the early days of this country?
   b. What would you say are the needs to which American education must respond today?
4. Crowther refers to "the American dream" in par. 4.
   a. What is that dream?
   b. Is it adequately defined in the essay?
   c. Where do you find the definition?

5. Crowther finds (par. 5) signs of a shift from "construction" to "mainte-nance" in recent American education. Assuming that this shift has taken or is taking place, comment on the contemporary "student revolt" in this country in terms of that "maintenance."

6. Can you find arguments to support the idea that American higher education might well concentrate on 5 per cent of each college group (see English percentages, par. 9)? Assuming that by "higher education" one means educa-tion in the liberal arts, what changes would be necessary in the American system?

7. Discuss the English belief that "the average boy or girl has probably had the optimim dose [of formal education] after eleven years of schooling" (par. 10). Are there evidences that this may be true in our own country?

8. Roger Ascham, a leading English educator of the sixteenth century, main-tained that "Learning teacheth more in one year than experience in twenty; and learning teacheth safely, when experience maketh more miserable than wise" (*The Schoolmaster*, 1570). What shift in emphasis do you find in the present English system? Where does Crowther indicate this shift?

9. What are the social and political, as opposed to the educational, objections of the "eleven-plus" examination and its results (par. 15)? What are the educational pros and cons of selection and nonselection?

10. What are the arguments for and against system-wide adoption of textbooks? What of the teacher's right to assign texts which may be offensive to some members of the community—as Salinger's *The Catcher in the Rye* was to some people several years ago? Why does Crowther feel that *the* textbook has been necessary in America?

11. Discuss the English system of early specialization (par. 26) vs. the American system of later specialization. What are the advantages and the disadvantages of "general education" programs?

12. Crowther says (par. 30), "The proper test of an education is whether it teaches the pupil to think and whether it awakens his interest in applying his brain to the various problems and opportunities that life presents." Apply this test to your own public-school education. Apply it to the work you have had thus far in college.

SUGGESTIONS FOR WRITING

1. After research and conversation with older people, write an essay on "The Little Red School House." Develop by contrast.

2. Write an essay on the three major needs in American education today.

3. Compare (following research or from personal experience) public schools in a southern state with public schools in a northern state.

4. Refute the idea that "maintenance" (see par. 5) should be the order of the day in American education.

5. Write an essay on the subject, "Are We Overeducating?" Support one side or the other.

6. Using Roger Ascham's statement on learning vs. experience (see question No. 8, above) as a headnote, write an argumentative essay on the subject.

7. Contrast the kinds of needs which education filled in the early days of our republic and the kinds of needs it must fill today.

8. Write an essay on the meaning of academic freedom for either the teacher or for the student.

9. Argue the case for general vs. special specialized education, or vice versa.
10. Who should run the colleges? Draw up a plan for the equitable administration of all the affairs of a college or university.

SUGGESTIONS FOR FURTHER READING

Olive Banks, *Parity and Prestige in English Secondary Education* (Humanities)

Bernard Iddings Bell, *Crowd Culture* (Regnery)

Arthur A. Cohen, ed., *Humanistic Education and Western Civilization* (Holt, Rinehart & Winston)

Philip W. Cox and Blaine E. Mercer, *Education in Democracy: Social Foundations of Education* (McGraw-Hill)

David Daiches, "Education in Democratic Society," *Commentary*, April, 1960.

Harvard Committee, *General Education in a Free Society* (Harvard)

Robert M. Hutchins, *The University of Utopia* (Univ. of Chicago)

Brian Jackson and Dennis Marsden, *Education and the Working Class* (Monthly Review)

Thomas R. McConnell, *General Education* (Univ. of Chicago)

John Henry Newman, *The Idea of a University* (Doubleday; Holt, Rinehart & Winston)

Hyman G. Rickover, *American Education: A National Failure* (Dutton); *Education and Freedom* (Dutton)

Arthur E. Traxler, ed., *Positive Values in the American Educational System* (American Council on Education)

John Vaizey, *Control of Education* (Humanities)

Mark Van Doren, *Liberal Education* (Beacon)

IS THE WORLD SAFER FOR ANYTHING?

Henry Steele Commager

"The anniversary of Armistice Day should stir us to great exalta-
tion of spirit because of the proud recollection that it was our day, a
day above those early days of that never-to-be-forgotten November
which lifted the world to the high levels of vision and achievement   1
upon which the great war for democracy and right was fought and
won." So wrote the dying Woodrow Wilson on the fifth anniversary
of that day which had concluded the war to end war and to make the
world safe for democracy.

Surely the world had a right to exult when this greatest and most
terrible of wars dragged to its weary end. Militarism had been
crushed, aggression frustrated, tyranny ended, injustice rectified,
democracy vindicated, and peace assured; for now, after centuries of   2
yearning and striving, men of good will had set up a league to preserve peace. No more wars, no more tyranny—mankind had at last
sailed into the safe harbors of peace.

Rarely in history have such high hopes been dashed so low, and
Wilson added to his tribute the bitter lamentation that the glory of
Armistice Day was tarnished by the recollection that "we withdrew
into a sullen and selfish isolation which is deeply ignoble . . .
cowardly and dishonorable." So we did, but we were not alone in
selfishness or dishonor. Even before the guns fell silent over the
stricken battlefields of Europe, the great coalition that had won
victory had come apart. Russia, defeated and desperate, had plunged   3
into Communism; and the other partners, each with its own fears and
ambitions, glared at each other over the conference tables; while
Germany, embittered by defeat, plotted vengeance; and the most
ancient of empires fell apart. "Authority was dispersed," wrote Winston Churchill, "the world unshackled, the weak became the strong,
the sheltered became the aggressive, and a vast fatigue dominated
collective action."

Nineteen-eighteen did not usher in the millennium; it ushered in
a half century of conflict—turbulence, war, revolution, desolation,
and ruin on a scale never before seen or even imagined. It was a half
century that leveled more cities, ravaged more countries, subverted
more societies, obliterated more of the past, endangered more of the
future, cost more lives, and uncovered more savagery than any time
since the barbarians swarmed over Western Europe. Ancient nations
were overthrown, empires fragmented, principles of law subverted,   4
and traditional standards of morality repudiated. The era which was

to have seen the end of war ushered in instead the most terrible of wars, which rose to a climacteric in the most terrible of weapons; the era which was to have seen the triumph of democracy saw instead the triumph of tyranny; the era which was to have witnessed the triumph of science over inveterate ills heard instead the hoofbeats of the Four Horsemen of the Apocalypse.

Once again the blood-dimmed tide was loosed, and the world was sucked into war. Once again the "freedom-loving" nations triumphed; once again men of good will came together to set up a league that would preserve peace; once again major powers were excluded from the new organization—China, Japan, Germany—while those who controlled it used it as a stage on which to indulge their rivalries and voice their grievances. The great powers glared at each other with ceaseless animosity. Soon the hottest of wars was succeeded by the coldest, and we had Robert Frost to remind us that "for   5
destruction ice is also great and would suffice." During the whole quarter century after the fall of Italy, Germany, and Japan, war and violence were continuous: in India and Pakistan, in Israel and the Arab lands, in Greece and Turkey, in Algiers and Tunisia, Hungary and Berlin, Cuba and Haiti, Argentina and Bolivia, the Congo and Nigeria, Laos and Indonesia. If the great powers did not grapple with each other in global wars, they consoled themselves, as it were, with local wars in Korea and Vietnam, and with arming themselves for Armageddon.

How can we explain this long succession of blunders and tragedies almost without parallel in history? How could men whose resolution and courage had triumphed over mortal peril, whose skills and resourcefulness had enabled them to master nature, fail so greatly? They could control the great globe itself, but not themselves; solve infinite problems, but not finite; penetrate to the stars, but neglect the earth on which they stood. Noble in reason they doubtless were,   6
infinite in faculty, like a god in apprehension, but in action more like a dinosaur unable to adapt to an unfamiliar environment than like an angel. The contrast between intellectual talents and social accomplishments seemed to make a mockery of free will; the contrast between expectations and realities threw doubt on the theory of progress.

There were, no doubt, particular and immediate causes for the collapse of order after the first war. That war had bled victors and vanquished to exhaustion; it had killed off potential leaders of the new generation; it had left a heritage of confusion for victors and   7
bitterness for defeated; it had launched Communism in Russia and

revolution elsewhere; it had fatally weakened Britain's hold on her empire; it had left Americans baffled and disillusioned and prepared to embrace isolationism.

The Second World War had wasted even more human material and moral resources than the First, and had shattered, even more violently, the existing pattern of political life. But these are excuses rather than explanations. After all, Europe had been afflicted by previous wars, but had recovered and returned to her traditional position. And after all, the United States had been exempted from the wrath of both the great wars and had emerged from both with her resources unimpaired, yet she too suffered the malaise that afflicted the Old World. We must seek deeper causes for a change in the currents of history so great that it resembles rather a change in the tides of Nature herself. Nor are these hard to find.

First, and most fundamental, among the causes of our malaise is one that we stubbornly refuse to recognize: the emergence of the forgotten, the neglected, the disparaged, the impoverished, the exploited, and the desperate; one-half of the human race came out of the long dusk that hid it from our view and into the bright light of history. Here is not only the greatest revolution of our time but, by almost any test, the greatest revolution since the discovery of America and the shift in the center of gravity from the Mediterranean to the Atlantic and beyond. "The peoples of Europe," said Woodrow Wilson at the close of the first war, "are in a revolutionary state of mind. They do not believe in the things that have been practiced upon them in the past, and they mean to have new things practiced." That proved to be true of Russia—a truth even Wilson failed to recognize—and it proved even more true of the vast, heaving, turbulent peoples of Asia and Africa.

Stirred by the Wilsonian principle of self-determination after the First World War, and released by the breakup of the great empires and colonial systems after the Second, these peoples threw off their ancient bondage and struck for equality. Now they are determined to close, in a single generation, that gap of centuries which separated them from the peoples of the West—to close it peacefully if that is possible, otherwise through revolution and violence. They are determined to wipe out the century-long inferiority, the exploitation, the bondage which the West imposed upon them; to conquer poverty, ignorance, disease that afflict them disproportionately; and to take their equal place among the nations of the world. No wonder the whole globe is convulsed by this prodigious upheaval. The failure of the West, and particularly of the United States, to understand and

8

9

10

cooperate with this revolution is a greater blunder, by far, than the earlier failure of Europe to understand the significance of the American Revolution, or of the West, including the United States, to understand the significance of the Russian Revolution. It is a failure of global dimensions.

This was a revolution of two large continents—three if South America is included—against two smaller. No less ominous, it was a revolution of the colored races against the white. The exploitation, the inferiority, the bondage which the West had imposed upon Asia and Africa was racial as well as geographical. The subjugation of colored peoples by white had gone on for centuries until Europeans, in Old and New Worlds, came to assume that it was part of the cosmic order of things. White Europeans committed genocide against the native races of the Americas in the sixteenth and seventeenth centuries, destroying ancient civilizations, wiping out, by war and   11 disease, perhaps ten millions of Indians—one of the great holocausts of history. White Europeans filled the ranks of labor in the New World by enslaving millions of Africans—a business in which all the civilized nations of Europe engaged. White Europeans invaded Asia, imposed their will on old and proud peoples, and ruled over them with arrogance and violence. Nor was racial exploitation confined to Asia and Africa: It was carried to the New World and flourished for two centuries as slavery and for another as social and economic subjugation.

Here, then, is the second great cause of our current malaise: the racial revolution—a revolution which takes protean form in different countries and continents but has, almost everywhere, two common denominators: the refusal of all colored peoples to wear any longer   12 the badge of inferiority which whites have fastened on them, and the inability of most whites, in America and in Europe, to acknowledge their responsibility and their guilt or to realize that this long chapter of history is coming to an end.

One of the great paradoxes of history is that the revolt of the non-Western world against the West is being carried on with tools and principles fashioned by the West. The tools are science and technology; the principles are those of modern nationalism. Here is a third fundamental explanation of the crisis of our time: the ravages of   13 nationalism. For ours is, indubitably, the great age of nationalism: Within the past quarter century, some sixty nations have been "brought forth" while older nationalism has been given a new lease on life.

In its earlier manifestations—in the eighteenth and early nineteenth centuries—nationalism tended to consolidate, to centralize, to
mitigate particularism and parochialism, and to encourage administrative efficiency and cultural unity, especially in the United States,
Italy, and Germany. But almost from the beginning—in the Old
World and in Spanish America—nationalism stimulated fragmentation
along racial, linguistic, and religious lines; almost from the begin-   14
ning it exacerbated chauvinism, imperialism, and militarism. Whether
in the long run the advantages of political efficiency and cultural
self-consciousness will outweigh the disadvantages of national antipa-
thies and cultural chauvinism still remains to be decided. But it is
difficult to avoid the conclusion that the nationalism of our own
time is profoundly dangerous.

Alas, the new nations that have emerged from the disruption of
empires have imitated, or adopted, all the worst features of the old.
Small, they yearn to be large; weak, they pile up armaments; vulnerable, they seek alliances; insecure, they develop into police states;
without political traditions, they hover constantly on the brink of
civil war or anarchy; without viable economies, they are dependent
on richer neighbors; without cultural unity, they manufacture an
artifical culture and impose it by force; striving convulsively to be   15
independent, they become increasingly dependent and threaten the
peace of their neighbors and of the world. How many recent crises
have been precipitated by their ambitions and quarrels—quarrels exploited, all too often, by the great powers: the crisis of Berlin and
East Germany, the recurring crises of Arab-Israeli relations, the crises
of Cyprus, of the Congo, Algiers, Nigeria, Rhodesia, the crisis of
India and Pakistan, of North and South Korea, of Indonesia and Laos
and Vietnam.

These new countries, it will be said, are but following the bad
example of the older nations of the West. This is true enough, but
with two fateful differences: first, the new nations are committed to   16
ideologies that involve them with fellow believers everywhere and
engage them in larger quarrels; and, second, that they are operating
in a world shadowed by nuclear clouds.

For the triumph of malevolent over benevolent nationalism, the
great powers—and most of all the United States and Russia—bear a
heavy responsibility. Far from curbing competitive nationalism, they
have abetted it. To the new nations of Asia and Africa they provided
lavish military aid—the largest portion of American aid after the war,
for example, was military. They interfered high-handedly in the in-   17
ternal affairs of these new nations. They built up networks of alli-

ances designed to bring small nations into the orbit of large; they tried to divide the world into two armed camps with no room for neutralists. Nor did they for a moment curb their own chauvinism, their own commitment to military solutions of world problems, their own traditional nationalism and traditional sovereignty.

Closely related to the revolutionary upsurge of underprivileged peoples and the equally revolutionary impact of the new nationalism was the revolution precipitated by science and technology, and the rising expectations which it nourished. For the first time in history, science and technology seemed to bring the good life within the reach of men and women everywhere—the end of hunger, the wiping 18 out of contagious diseases, the prolongation of life, security from the elements, the preservation and development of natural resources, the pleasures of learning and of the arts. In the twentieth century, it was at least reasonable to hope that the burdens which had for so long afflicted mankind would be lifted.

Once again, expectations were to be disappointed. The gap between what men imagined and what they enjoyed had always been deep; now the gap between what men were taught to expect and what they actually received seemed intolerable. The machinery of life grew ever more elaborate, but the products of that machinery 19 became less and less gratifying. At the end of a generation of unparalleled advance in science and technology, mankind found hunger more widespread, violence more ruthless, and life more insecure than at any time in the century.

Nor was this disappointment confined to the backward peoples of the globe: Even in America, which boasted about limitless resources and the most advanced technology, poverty was familiar in millions of households, white as well as black; cities decayed, the 20 countryside despoiled, air and streams polluted; lawlessness, offical and private, was contagious; and war and the threat of war filled the minds of men with hatred and fear.

The symbol—more than the symbol—of this failure of science to bring expected rewards was the discovery and exploitation of nuclear energy. To release the energy of the atom was assuredly one of the greatest achievements in the history of science, and one that held out possibilities almost limitlessly benign. Instead, the United States and, after her, competing powers concentrated their scientific talents on harnessing atomic energy for war. As Churchill wrote prophetically in 1929: "Without having improved appreciably in virtue or enjoying wiser guidance, mankind has got into its hands for the first time the tools by which it can unfailingly accomplish its own extermination.

That is the point in human destinies to which all the glories and toils of men have at last led them." Nor was there any assurance that those who stood at the levers of control would refuse to use these 21 weapons of infinite destruction if they thought their own survival was at stake. After all, Americans had used them in 1945; after all, Americans, Russians, Chinese, and Frenchmen were carrying on continuous experiments to achieve even greater destructive power. And after all, prominent statesmen, not least those in the United States, did not hesitate to shake the raw head and bloody bones of nuclear destruction at intransigent opponents elsewhere on the globe. And if it could be said that only madmen would actually carry out such threats, the inevitable reply was that two madmen, Hitler and Stalin, had fought their way to power in the recent past, and that as yet the resourcefulness of mankind had not devised any way of preventing a repetition of this monstrous situation.

Finally, consider one of the great paradoxes of our day: at the time of the triumph of the experiemental method in science, we should abandon it in the realm of politics. Clearly, one of the causes—and one of the manifestations, too—of our malaise is the rejection of the practical, the relative, the organic view of society and politics, and the embrace of the doctrinaire, the absolute, and the static. The substitution of ideological for realistic policies is the hallmark of much of modern political philosophy, but it has not heretofore been characteristic of the American. In the name of doctrinaire notions of Aryan superiority, Hitler was prepared to bring down a Götterdämmerung upon his own country and the world; in the name 22 of doctrinaire Marxism, the Soviet was prepared to subvert all other governments; and in the name of "containment," the United States seems prepared to bustle about the globe putting down subversion and revolution. Our commitment, to be sure, has not been wholehearted; and the almost instinctive distaste of the American people for ideological principles has inspired widespread protest against the new departure. But even as the bankruptcy of the ideological approach to the great convulsive problems of the world becomes clearer, we seem to adopt the same approach to the issues of domestic politics.

There is nothing more implacable than ideological enmities or crusades—witness the religious wars of the sixteenth and seventeenth centuries—and one explanation of the peculiar ferocity of so many of our modern wars, even the American, is the ideological or quasireligious character. Ordinary rivalries and conflicts involve interests and issues that can be settled by negotiation and compromise. But ideo- 23 logical conflicts are moral, and honorable men find it difficult to compromise on principles or negotiate about morals. Woodrow Wilson had a more doctrinaire mind than Franklin Roosevelt, but Wilson could call for "peace without victory" while Roosevelt insisted on "unconditional surrender."

The three great powers that glare ceaselessly upon each other now, and whose conflicts shake the globe, are all committed to ideological positions which they find difficult to compromise. The leaders of all three nations know—as religious fanatics of the seventeenth century knew—that they are the pure of heart, that their cause is just, that they stand at Armageddon and battle for the Cause. Naturally, all three attempt to rally the smaller nations to their side, to enlist them in their crusades; and all are inclined to believe that those who are not with them are against them. None can tolerate deviation from the true faith. The Russians put down Hungarians and Czechs who transgress the scriptures; the Chinese punish dissenters even at the cost of civil war; the Americans will tolerate deviation in Guatemala or Santo Domingo and in Cuba only because they have succeeded in isolating it. 24

The ideological approach took over even in the American domestic arena—in politics, race relations, education, and elsewhere. It stigmatized the crusade of Joseph McCarthy against subversives, real or imagined; it sustains the ceaseless zeal of the House Un-American Activities Committee through the years in its search for Communists in government or in the universities; it provides moral fervor to George Wallace's arguments for white supremacy and logic to opponents of open-housing who proclaim that God is white. It characterizes, alike, students who think that the universities are all currupt and fit only to be burned because they do not instantly involve themselves in current affairs, a Vice Presidental candidate who thinks all demonstrations are pernicious, and Senators who are prepared to subvert the Constitution because Supreme Court judges do not automatically respond to obscenity with moral fervor. 25

The symptom of ideology is impatience, and its offspring is violence. Those who see the great turbulent issues of politics or law or society in simple terms of right and wrong are impatient with compromise or concession and even with reason. Impatience characterizes much of American life in the second half of the twentieth century: impatience of the young with the old, and of the old with the young; impatience with due process of law; impatience with old ideas rooted in tradition, and with new ideas that lack the authority of tradition; impatience with those who are neutral, and those who are 26 independent; impatience with the machinery of adjudication and arbitration; impatience with any solutions short of utopian.

And with impatience goes violence. This is natural enough: When men no longer believe in reason, when they no longer have confidence in the potentialities of history, they naturally turn to violence for the solution—or the liquidation—of their problems. Russia resorted to violence to get rid of the embarrassment of independence in Czechoslovakia; South Africa resorted to violence to dispose of   27 the awkward fact of a predominantly Negro population; the Arabs have no communications with the Israelis except by acts of violence; the United States elevates aimless violence against Vietnam to a philosophy. The connection between violence and ideology is not fortuitous but consequential.

In all of the great changes and developments that have characterized the last half century and condemned it to disorder, the United States has played a prominent part. It shared the failure to appreciate and support the great revolution of the underprivileged peoples; it shared—and indeed exemplified—the subordination of colored peoples to white; it stimulated and supported self-determination after the first war, and the breakup of ancient empires after the second; and did nothing to mitigate the ravages of chauvinistic nationalism. It   28 devoted a major part of its scientific energies to war and the preparation for war, and exalted the role and the power of the military. It embraced an ideological approach to the great problems of international politics and sought to imprison in ideological straitjacket the turbulent tides of history. In most of this, Americans departed from their own traditions and betrayed their own character. Is it too much to hope that we will return to our traditions and rediscover our true character?

QUESTIONS AND PROBLEMS

1. What is the effect on the reader of the quotation with which Commager begins his essay? What is the tone which it sets?
2. Commager writes (par. 4), "Nineteen-eighteen did not usher in the millennium; it ushered in a half century of conflict—turbulence, war, revolution, desolation, and ruin on a scale never before seen or even imagined." Outline in order of happening the major conflicts to which the author refers.
3. What were the immediate causes for the collapse of order after World War I?
4. What was the effect of Wilson's principle of self-determination?
5. List, in the order in which the author gives them, "the causes of our malaise," the causes for a change in the currents of history. Do you agree with Commager's order?
6. What is the meaning of the following: *cultural chauvinism, ideological policies, Götterdämmerung, containment.*

7. What symbolic meaning does the author give to the discovery and exploitation of nuclear energy?

8. Commager writes, "The symptom of ideology is impatience, and its offspring is violence" (par. 26). Comment in terms of student activism on college campuses.

9. In the final paragraph the author levels a number of charges against the United States. Do you find any which you can refute? If so, how would you do so?

10. The author ends with a question: "Is it too much to hope that we will return to our traditions and rediscover our true character?"
    a. To what traditions does he refer?
    b. What does he mean by "our true character"?
    c. Do you as a young person in the United States today agree with the need Commager refers to?

SUGGESTIONS FOR WRITING

1. Update Commager's essay by writing one on the period from the fiftieth anniversary of the World War I armistice to the present. Entitle it "1968—: Is the World Safer for Anything?"

2. Write a report on the involvement of the United Nations in a recent conflict. Draw conclusions as to the effectiveness of that involvement.

3. Interview veterans of two wars separated by some time. Compare and contrast their views of the effectiveness of warfare.

4. Write a satire on war as a solution for political questions.

5. Compare the organization and effectiveness of the League of Nations and the United Nations.

6. Compare and contrast the element of patriotism in two American wars.

7. Compare a specific social conflict in the United States with an actual war fought outside our shores.

8. Write an essay on "The Causes of Our Present Malaise."

SUGGESTIONS FOR FURTHER READING

Winston S. Churchill, *Blood, Sweat, and Tears* (Rolton)
Henry Steele Commager, *The Search for a Usable Past, and Other Essays in Historiography* (Knopf)
Foster R. Dulles, *America's Rise to World Power: 1898-1954* (Harper)
Dwight D. Eisenhower, *Peace with Justice* (Columbia)
Rodney Gilbert, *Competitive Coexistence* (Bookmailer)
Robert L. Heilbroner, *The Future as History* (Harper; Grove)
Henry A. Kissinger, *Nuclear Weapons and Foreign Policy* (Harper; Doubleday)
Walter Langsam, *The World Since 1919*, 7th ed. (Macmillan)
Walter Mills, *End to Arms* (Antheneum)
Franklin D. Roosevelt, *Selected Speeches, Messages, Press Conferences, and Letters*, ed. B. Rauch (Holt, Rinehart & Winston)

Walt W. Rostow, *The United States in the World Arena* (Harper)
John G. Stoessinger and Alan F. Westin, eds., *Power and Order* (Harcourt, Brace
    & World)
U. Thant, *Toward World Peace*, ed. Jacob Baal-Teshuva (Thomas Yoseloff)

TO DETERMINE
CAUSE AND EFFECT

When we ask *why?* we are frequently asking for causes, whether the result we are concerned about is an occurrence in our daily lives, an event in history, a matter of scientific or technological investigation, or any of our multitudinous concerns as human beings. Every day we note the effects of changes, and we become concerned with the causes which brought about those changes. Again, we constantly see changes occurring, and we wonder about the effects of these changes. And sometimes we wish to inquire into causes or probable causes and effects or probable effects even before either cause or result has touched us directly, as in matters of scientific investigation.

We search for causes in order to establish the principles of any science. In the search we become involved with both inductive and deductive methods of inference. We must apply tests. We must know if the causes we have determined upon are true causes, and we must know if they are inclusive, if they involve all factors which produce the effect. We must also ask if the causes we have determined upon are sufficient to produce the effect we have seen. We know that an event may follow another without any causal relationship: Lisbon was not destroyed by the great earthquake of 1755 because it was a city of sin; Robinson Crusoe was not marooned on a desert island because he had disobeyed his parents. The scientific investigator, having determined upon possible causes for a certain effect, isolates true causes by eliminating those which change the effect and those which, by their presence or absence, make no noticeable change in the effect. Finally, the investigator of causes of given results does not limit himself to the determination of inciting events. William Shakespeare may have poached a deer in Sir Thomas Lucy's park, but this possible occurrence did not make him a playwright. A raise in tuition does not in itself cause the burning of a college building. All causes, true and essential (not irrelevant) causes, and tested causes are required when determing the antecedents of a given result.

In studying the following essays, ask yourself if the causes found in certain effects are complete, true, and essential causes, and if the author has adequately tested those causes. In your own writing of essays employing this method of development, make a careful preliminary outline of your material, then check and recheck it, adding and eliminating as necessary until you are satisfied that you have omitted nothing essential, added nothing irrelevant, to explain the indicated result.

IN SEARCH OF A FUTURE
Notes and Comment from The New Yorker

On Tuesday, March 4th, in the Kresge Auditorium at the Massachusetts Institute of Technology, a group of scientists assembled, with students and others, to discuss the uses of scientific knowledge. There is nothing we might print in these columns that could be more urgent than the extemporaneous speech, made before that gathering by George Wald, professor of biology at Harvard and Nobel Prize winner, under the title "A Generation in Search of a Future." We therefore quote from it here at length: 1

"All of you know that in the last couple of years there has been student unrest; breaking at times into violence, in many parts of the world: in England, Germany, Italy, Spain, Mexico, Japan, and, needless to say, many parts of this country. There has been a great deal of discussion as to what it all means. Perfectly clearly, it means something different in Mexico from what it does in France, and something different in France from what it does in Tokyo, and something different in Tokyo from what it does in this country. Yet, unless we are to assume that students have gone crazy all over the world, or that they have just decided that it's the thing to do, it must have some common meaning. 2

"I don't need to go so far afield to look for that meaning. I am a teacher, and at Harvard I have a class of about three hundred and fifty students—men and women—most of them freshmen and sophomores. Over these past few years, I have felt increasingly that something is terribly wrong—and this year ever so much more than last. Something has gone sour, in teaching and in learning. It's almost as though there were a widespread feeling that education has become irrelevant. 3

"A lecture is much more of a dialogue than many of you probably realize. As you lecture, you keep watching the faces, and information keeps coming back to you all the time. I began to feel, particularly this year, that I was missing much of what was coming back. I tried asking the students, but they didn't or couldn't help me very much. 4

"But I think I know what's the matter. I think that this whole generation of students is beset with a profound uneasiness, and I don't think that they have yet quite defined its source. I think I understand the reasons for their uneasiness even better than they do. What is more, I share their uneasiness. 5

"What's bothering those students? Some of them tell you it's the Vietnam war. I think the Vietnam war is the most shameful episode in the whole of American history. The concept of war crimes is an American invention. We've committed many war crimes in Vietnam—but I'll tell you something interesting about that. We were committing war crimes in World War II, before the Nuremberg trials were held and the principle of war crimes was stated. The saturation   6 bombing of German cities was a war crime. Dropping those atomic bombs on Hiroshima and Nagasaki was a war crime. If we had lost the war, it might have been *our* leaders who had to answer for such actions. I've gone through all that history lately, and I find that there's a gimmick in it. It isn't written out, but I think we established it by precedent. That gimmick is that if one can allege that one is repelling or retaliating for an aggression, after that everything goes.

"And, you see, we are living in a world in which all wars are wars of defense. All War Departments are now Defense Departments. This is all part of the doubletalk of our time. The aggressor is always on the other side. I suppose this is why our ex-Secretary of State Dean Rusk went to such pains to insist, as he still insists, that in Vietnam   7 we are repelling an aggression. And if that's what we are doing—so runs the doctrine—everything goes. If the concept of war crimes is ever to mean anything, they will have to be defined as categories of *acts*, regardless of alleged provocation. But that isn't so now.

"I think we've lost that war, as a lot of other people think, too. The Vietnamese have a secret weapon. It's their willingness to die beyond our willingness to kill. In effect, they've been saying, You   8 can kill us, but you'll have to kill a lot of us; you may have to kill all of us. And, thank heaven, we are not yet ready to do that.

"Yet we have come a long way toward it—far enough to sicken many Americans, far enough to sicken even our fighting men. Far enough so that our national symbols have gone sour. How many of you can sing about 'the rockets' red glare, the bombs bursting in air' without thinking, Those are *our* bombs and *our* rockets, bursting   9 over South Vietnamese villages? When those words were written, we were a people struggling for freedom against oppression. Now we are supporting open or thinly disguised military dictatorships all over the world, helping them to control and repress peoples struggling for their freedom.

"But that Vietnam war, shameful and terrible as it is, seems to me only an immediate incident in a much larger and more stubborn   10 situation.

"Part of my trouble with students is that almost all the students I teach were born after World War II. Just after World War II, a series of new and abnormal procedures came into American life. We regarded them at the time as temporary aberrations. We thought we would get back to normal American life someday. 11

"But those procedures have stayed with us now for more than twenty years, and those students of mine have never known anything else. They think those things are normal. They think that we've always had a Pentagon, that we have always had a big Army, and that we have always had a draft. But those are all new things in American life, and I think that they are incompatible with what America meant before. 12

"How many of you realize that just before World War II the entire American Army, including the Air Corps, numbered a hundred and thirty-nine thousand men? Then World War II started, but we weren't yet in it, and, seeing that there was great trouble in the world, we doubled this Army to two hundred and sixty-eight thousand men. Then, in World War II, it got to be eight million. And then World War II came to an end and we prepared to go back to a peacetime Army, somewhat as the American Army had always been before. And, indeed, in 1950—you think about 1950, our international commitments, the Cold War, the Truman Doctrine, and all the rest of it—in 1950, we got down to six hundred thousand men. 13

"Now we have three and a half million men under arms: about six hundred thousand in Vietnam, about three hundred thousand more in 'support areas' elsewhere in the Pacific, about two hundred and fifty thousand in Germany. And there are a lot at home. Some months ago, we were told that three hundred thousand National Guardsmen and two hundred thousand reservists—so half a million men—had been specially trained for riot duty in the cities. 14

"I say the Vietnam war is just an immediate incident because as long as we keep that big an Army, it will always find things to do. If the Vietnam war stopped tomorrow, the chances are that with that big a military establishment we would be in another such adventure, abroad or at home, before you knew it. 15

"The thing to do about the draft is not to reform it but to get rid of it. 16

"A peacetime draft is the most un-American thing I know. All the time I was growing up, I was told about oppressive Central European countries and Russia, where young men were forced into the Army, and I was told what they did about it. They chopped off a 17 finger, or shot off a couple of toes, or, better still, if they could manage it, they came to this country. And we understood that, and sympathized, and were glad to welcome them.

"Now, by present estimates, from four to six thousand Americans of draft age have left this country for Canada, two or three thousand more have gone to Europe, and it looks as though many more were preparing to emigrate.   18

"A bill to stop the draft was recently introduced in the Senate (S. 503), sponsored by a group of senators that runs the gamut from McGovern and Hatfield to Barry Goldwater. I hope it goes through.   19 But I think that when we get rid of the draft we must also drastically cut back the size of the armed forces.

"Yet there is something ever so much bigger and more important than the draft. That bigger thing, of course, is the militarization of our country. Ex-President Eisenhower, in his farewell address, warned us of what he called the military-industrial complex. I am sad to say that we must begin to think of it now as the military-industri-   20 al-labor-union complex. What happened under the plea of the Cold War was not alone that we built up the first big peacetime Army in our history but that we institutionalized it. We built, I suppose, the biggest government building in our history to run it, and we institutionalized it.

"I don't think we can live with the present military establishment, and its eighty-billion-dollar-a-year budget, and keep America anything like the America we have known in the past. It is corrupting   21 the life of the whole country. It is buying up everything in sight: industries, banks, investors, scientists—and lately it seems also to have bought up the labor unions.

"The Defense Department is always broke, but some of the things it does with that eighty billion dollars a year would make Buck Rogers envious. For example, the Rocky Mountain Arsenal, on the outskirts of Denver, was manufacturing a deadly nerve poison on such a scale that there was a problem of waste disposal. Nothing daunted, the people there dug a tunnel two miles deep under Denver,   22 into which they have injected so much poisoned water that, beginning a couple of years ago, Denver has experienced a series of earth tremors of increasing severity. Now there is grave fear of a major earthquake. An interesting debate is in progress as to whether Denver will be safer if that lake of poisoned water is removed or is left in place.

"Perhaps you have read also of those six thousand sheep that suddenly died in Skull Valley, Utah, killed by another nerve poi-   23 son—a strange and, I believe, still unexplained accident, since the nearest testing seems to have been thirty miles away.

"As for Vietnam, the expenditure of firepower there has been frightening. Some of you may still remember Khe Sanh, a hamlet just south of the Demilitarized Zone, where a force of United States Marines was beleaguered for a time. During that period, we dropped on the perimeter of Khe Sanh more explosives than fell on Japan throughout World War II, and more than fell on the whole of Europe during the years 1942 and 1943. 24

"One of the officers there was quoted as having said afterward, 'It looks like the world caught smallpox and died.' 25

"The only point of government is to safeguard and foster life. Our government has become preoccupied with death, with the business of killing and being killed. So-called defense now absorbs sixty per cent of the national budget, and about twelve per cent of the Gross National Product. 26

"A lively debate is beginning again on whether or not we should deploy antiballistic missles, the ABM. I don't have to talk about them—everyone else here is doing that. But I should like to mention a curious circumstance. In September, 1967, or about a year and a half ago, we had a meeting of M.I.T. and Harvard people, including experts on these matters, to talk about whether anything could be done to block the Sentinel system—the deployment of ABMs. Everyone present thought them undesirable, but a few of the most knowledgeable persons took what seemed to be the practical view: 'Why fight about a dead issue? It has been decided, the funds have been appropriated. Let's go on from there.' 27

"Well, fortunately, it's not a dead issue. 28

"An ABM is a nuclear weapon. It takes a nuclear weapon to stop a nuclear weapon. And our concern must be with the whole issue of nuclear weapons. 29

"There is an entire semantics ready to deal with the sort of thing I am about to say. It involves such phrases as 'Those are the facts of life.' No—these are the facts of death. I don't accept them, and I advise you not to accept them. We are under repeated pressure to accept things that are presented to us as settled—decisions that have been made. Always there is the thought: Let's go on from there. But this time we don't see how to go on. We will have to stick with these issues. 30

"We are told that the United States and Russia, between them, by now have stockpiled nuclear weapons of approximately the explosive power of fifteen tons of TNT for every man, woman, and child

on earth. And now it is suggested that we must make more. All very   31
regrettable, of course, but 'those are the facts of life.' We really
would like to disarm, but our new Secretary of Defense has made the
ingenious proposal that now is the time to greatly increase our nuclear armaments, so that we can disarm from a position of strength.

"I think all of you know there is no adequate defense against
massive nuclear attack. It is both easier and cheaper to circumvent
any known nuclear-defense system than to provide it. It's all pretty   32
crazy. At the very moment we talk of deploying ABMs, we are also
building the MIRV, the weapon to circumvent ABMs.

"As far as I know, the most conservative estimates of the number
of Americans who would be killed in a major nuclear attack, with
everything working as well as can be hoped and all foreseeable pre-
cautions taken, run to about fifty million. We have become callous to   33
gruesome statistics, and this seems at first to be only another gruesome statistic. You think, Bang!—and next morning, if you're still
there, you read in the newspapers that fifty million people were
killed.

"But that isn't the way it happens. When we killed close to two
hundred thousand people with those first, little, old-fashioned urani-
um bombs that we dropped on Hiroshima and Nagasaki, about the   34
same number of persons were maimed, blinded, burned, poisoned,
and otherwise doomed. A lot of them took a long time to die.

"That's the way it would be. Not a bang and a certain number of
corpses to bury but a nation filled with millions of helpless, maimed,
tortured, and doomed persons, and the survivors huddled with their   35
families in shelters, with guns ready to fight off their neighbors trying to get some uncontaminated food and water.

"A few months ago, Senator Richard Russell, of Georgia, ended a
speech in the Senate with the words 'If we have to start over again
with another Adam and Eve, I want them to be Americans; and I   36
want them on this continent and not in Europe.' That was a United
States senator making a patriotic speech. Well, here is a Nobel laure-
ate who thinks that those words are criminally insane.

"How real is the threat of full-scale nuclear war? I have my own
very inexpert idea, but, realizing how little I know, and fearful that I
may be a little paranoid on this subject, I take every opportunity to
ask reputed experts. I asked that question of a distinguished professor of government at Harvard about a month ago. I asked him what
sort of odds he would lay on the possibility of full-scale nuclear war
within the foreseeable future. 'Oh,' he said comfortably, 'I think I   37
can give you a pretty good answer to that question. I estimate the

probability of full-scale nuclear war, provided that the situation remains about as it is now, at two per cent per year.' Anybody can do the simple calculation that shows that two per cent per year means that the chance of having that full-scale nuclear war by 1990 is about one in three, and by 2000 it is about fifty-fifty.

"I think I know what is bothering the students. I think that what we are up against is a generation that is by no means sure that it has a 38 future.

"I am growing old, and my future, so to speak, is already behind me. But there are those students of mine, who are in my mind always; and there are my children, the youngest of them now seven 39 and nine, whose future is infinitely more precious to me than my own. So it isn't just their generation; it's mine, too. We're all in it together.

"Are we to have a chance to live? We don't ask for prosperity, or security. Only for a reasonable chance to live, to work out our des- 40 tiny in peace and decency. Not to go down in history as the apocalyptic generation.

"And it isn't only nuclear war. Another overwhelming threat is in the population explosion. That has not yet even begun to come under control. There is every indication that the world population will double before the year 2000, and there is a widespread expectation of famine on an unprecedented scale in many parts of the world. 41 The experts tend to differ only in their estimates of when those famines will begin. Some think by 1980; others think they can be staved off until 1990; very few expect that they will not occur by the year 2000.

"That is the problem. Unless we can be surer than we now are that this generation has a future, nothing else matters. It's not good enough to give it tender, loving care, to supply it with breakfast 42 foods, to buy it expensive educations. Those things don't mean anything unless this generation has a future. And we're not sure that it does.

"I don't think that there are problems of youth, or student prob- 43 lems. All the real problems I know about are grown-up problems.

"Perhaps you will think me altogether absurd, or 'academic,' or hopelessly innocent—that is, until you think of the alternatives—if I say, as I do to you now: We have to get rid of those nuclear weapons. There is nothing worth having that can be obtained by nuclear war— nothing material or ideological—no tradition that it can defend. It is 44 utterly self-defeating. Those atomic bombs represent an unusable weapon. The only use for an atomic bomb is to keep somebody else from using one. It can give us no protection—only the doubtful satisfaction of retaliation. Nuclear weapons offer us nothing but a balance of terror, and a balance of terror is still terror.

"We have to get rid of those atomic weapons, here and every-   45
where. We cannot live with them.

"I think we've reached a point of great decision, not just for our nation, not only for all humanity, but for life upon the earth. I tell my students, with a feeling of pride that I hope they will share, that the carbon, nitrogen, and oxygen that make up ninety-nine per cent of our living substance were cooked in the deep interiors of earlier   46
generations of dying stars. Gathered up from the ends of the universe, over billions of years, eventually they came to form, in part, the substance of our sun, its planets, and ourselves. Three billion years ago, life arose upon the earth. It is the only life in the solar system.

"About two million years ago, man appeared. He has become the dominant species on the earth. All other living things, animal and   47
plant, live by his sufferance. He is the custodian of life on earth, and in the solar system. It's a big responsibility.

"The thought that we're in competition with Russians or with Chinese is all a mistake, and trivial. We are one species, with a world   48
to win. There's life all over this universe, but the only life in the solar system is on earth, and in the whole universe we are the only men.

"Our business is with life, not death. Our challenge is to give what account we can of what becomes of life in the solar system, this corner of the universe that is our home; and, most of all, what   49
becomes of men—all men, of all nations, colors, and creeds. This has become one world, a world for all men. It is only such a world that can now offer us life, and the chance to go on."

QUESTIONS AND PROBLEMS

1. In establishing cause and effect relationships the writer may either search for causes or attempt to determine effects. Which method does George Wald employ?
2. Is a lecture a dialogue (par. 4)? If it is, what is the expected contribution of the audience? Can a lecturer be rated as to effectiveness according to how much he makes his lecture a dialogue?
3. Analyze par. 6 beginning, "What's bothering those students?" (Remember that this is an "extemporaneous speech," as stated in par. 1.) Is the topic sentence developed?
4. In newspapers or news magazines, look up some of the statements on the Vietnam war by ex-Secretary of State Dean Rusk. Compare his position with Wald's. Are the positions of both men sound?

5. How many discoveries, how many major accomplishments of man date after your own date of birth? How many of them date after the birth of your father's generation? Your grandfather's?
6. Wald calls the Vietnam war "an immediate incident." Why? Is he justified in using this phrase?
7. Discuss pros and cons of the military draft. What is the most equitable system of drafting? What are the alternatives to drafting?
8. What does Wald mean when he says that we have "institutionalized" the army (par. 20)? Does the term in itself suggest a danger? What strengths and what weaknesses are suggested by the term?
9. Wald states (par. 21) his belief that we cannot "live with the present military establishment, and its eighty-billion-dollar-a-year budget, and keep America anything like the America we have known in the past." What are the arguments for keeping America as it was in the past? Are there valid arguments for not keeping America as it was?
10. Outline in the order of presentation Wald's reasons for student unrest. Then rearrange them, if necessary, in their order of importance for you personally. Are there differences between the two arrangements? Why?
11. This essay is reprinted under the heading "To Determine Cause and Effect." It is also an analysis of reasons for student unrest. Checking against Part I of the table of contents of this book, which other methods of development does Wald use in presenting his argument? Are there others he might have used to good effect?
12. Wald ends his essay with commitment to the "One World" idea. Name men of the past who have been so committed. Are recent events in Europe a step in the One World direction?

SUGGESTIONS FOR WRITING

1. Write an essay entitled "Where I Stand" in which you develop by the method of cause and effect your present position on one of the following: war, integration of the races, pacifism, universal higher education.
2. Bronislaw Malinowski, anthropologist and analyzer of warfare, once wrote: "At present, an international war, like World Wars I and II, is a civil war of mankind divided against itself." Using this quotation as a reference point, speculate on the possibilities of the achievement of One World.
3. Read the Charter of the United Nations and develop an essay on the possibilities and the probabilities of effective police powers within the framework of the U.N.
4. Study several newspaper reports on a recent outbreak of civil violence. Analyze the effect of police action during and after the outbreak.
5. Study one or more instances of student unrest or protest on your own campus. Develop an essay in which you either analyze the causes of the unrest or, if the issue has been resolved, evaluate the effects of the unrest or protest.
6. The author of this essay quotes a Harvard professor as estimating the possibility of full-scale nuclear war as about one to three in 1990, about fifty-fifty by the year 2000. Write an imaginative piece about the aftermath of such an attack on our own country.

7. Write a researched article on the estimated number of nuclear weapons ready for use today and the meaning of these figures in terms of "balance of power."
8. Defend "student power" as a healthy trend in higher education today.

SUGGESTIONS FOR FURTHER READING

Saul Aronow and others, eds., *Fallen Sky: Medical Consequences of Thermonuclear War* (Hill and Wang)

Waldo Beach, *Conscience on Campus* (Association Press)

F. Macfarlane Burnet, *2000 A.D.: A Biologist's Thoughts on the Next Forty Years* (Cambridge)

M. Stanton Evans, *Revolt on the Campus* (Regnery)

Richard M. Fagley, *Population Explosion and Christian Responsibility* (Oxford)

R.A. Falk, *Law, Morality, and War in the Contemporary World* (Praeger)

John Hersey, *Hiroshima* (Knopf; Bantam; Modern Library)

J.O. Hertzler, *Crisis in World Population: A Sociological Examination with Special Reference to the Underdeveloped Areas* (Univ. of Nebraska)

Everett L. Hunt, *Revolt of the College Intellectual* (Aldine)

Donald Keys, ed., *God and the H-bomb* (Random House)

Jesse Kornbluth, ed., *Notes from the New Underground* (Viking)

Thomas Mann, *The Coming Victory of Democracy* (Knopf)

National Association of Women Deans and Counselors, *Ethical Values and Student Behavior* (National Education Association)

Paul Ramsey, *War and the Christian Conscience* (Duke)

Kurt Vonnegut, Jr., *Slaughterhouse Five* (Delacourt)

THE RESTLESS SPIRIT OF THE AMERICANS
Alexis de Tocqueville

In certain remote corners of the Old World you may still sometimes stumble upon a small district which seems to have been forgotten amid the general tumult, and to have remained stationary while everything around it was in motion. The inhabitants are for the most part extremely ignorant and poor; they take no part in the business of the country, and they are frequently oppressed by the government; yet their countenances are generally placid, and their spirits light. 1

In America I saw the freest and most enlightened men, placed in the happiest circumstances which the world affords: it seemed to me as if a cloud habitually hung upon their brow, and I thought them serious and almost sad even in their pleasures. 2

The chief reason of this contrast is that the former do not think of the ills they endure—the latter are for ever brooding over advantages they do not possess. It is strange to see with what feverish ardour the Americans pursue their own welfare; and to watch the vague dread that constantly torments them lest they should not have chosen the shortest path which may lead to it. 3

A native of the United States clings to this world's goods as if he were certain never to die; and he is so hasty in grasping at all within his reach, that one would suppose he was constantly afraid of not living long enough to enjoy them. He clutches everything, he holds nothing fast, but soon loosens his grasp to pursue fresh gratifications. 4

In the United States a man builds a house to spend his latter years in it, and he sells it before the roof is on: he plants a garden, and lets it just as the trees are coming into bearing: he brings a field into tillage, and leaves other men to gather the crops: he embraces a profession, and gives it up: he settles in a place, which he soon afterward leaves, to carry his changeable longings elsewhere. If his private affairs leave him any leisure, he instantly plunges into the vortex of politics; and if at the end of a year of unremitting labor he finds he has a few days' vacation, his eager curiosity whirls him over the vast extent of the United States, and he will travel fifteen hundred miles in a few days, to shake off his happiness. Death at length overtakes him, but it is before he is weary of his bootless chase of that complete felicity which is for ever on the wing. 5

At first sight there is something surprising in this strange unrest of so many happy men, restless in the midst of abundance. The 6 spectacle itself is however as old as the world; the novelty is to see a whole people furnish an exemplification of it.

Their taste for physical gratifications must be regarded as the original source of that secret inquietude which the actions of the Americans betray, and of the inconstancy of which they afford fresh examples every day. He who has set his heart exclusively upon the pursuit of worldly welfare is always in a hurry, for he has but a limited time at his disposal to reach it, to grasp it, and to enjoy. The   7 recollection of the brevity of life is a constant spur to him. Besides the good things which he possesses, he every instant fancies a thousand others which death will prevent him from trying if he does not try them soon. This thought fills him with anxiety, fear, and regret, and keeps his mind in ceaseless trepidation, which leads him perpetually to change his plans and his abode.

If in addition to the taste for physical well-being a social condition be superadded, in which the laws and customs make no condition permanent, here is a great additional stimulant to this restless-   8 ness of temper. Men will then be seen continually to change their track, for fear of missing the shortest cut to happiness.

It may readily be conceived, that if men, passionately bent upon physical gratifications, desire eagerly, they are also easily discouraged: as their ultimate object is to enjoy, the means to reach that object must be prompt and easy, or the trouble of acquiring the   9 gratification would be greater than the gratification itself. Their prevailing frame of mind then is at once ardent and relaxed, violent and enervated. Death is often less dreaded than perseverance in continuous efforts to one end.

The equality of conditions leads by a still straighter road to several of the effects which I have here described. When all the privileges of birth and fortune are abolished, when all professions are accessible to all, and a man's own energies may place him at the top of any one of them, an easy and unbounded career seems open to his ambition, and he will readily persuade himself that he is born to no vulgar destinies. But this is an erroneous notion, which is corrected by daily experience. The same equality which allows every citizen to conceive these lofty hopes, renders all the citizens less able to realize them: it circumscribes their powers on every side, while it gives freer scope to their desires. Not only are they themselves powerless, but   10 they are met at every step by immense obstacles, which they did not at first perceive. They have swept away the privileges of some of their fellow-creatures which stood in their way; but they have opened the door to universal competition: the barrier has changed its shape rather than its position. When men are nearly alike, and all follow the same track, it is very difficult for any one individual to walk quick and cleave a way through the dense throng which surrounds and presses him. This constant strife between the propensities springing from the equality of conditions and the means it supplies to satisfy them, harasses and wearies the mind.

It is possible to conceive men arrived at a degree of freedom which should completely content them; they would then enjoy their independence without anxiety and without impatience. But men will never establish any equality with which they can be contented. Whatever efforts a people may make, they will never succeed in reducing all the conditions of society to a perfect level; and even if they unhappily attained that absolute and complete depression, the inequality of minds would still remain, which, coming directly from the hand of God, will for ever escape the laws of man. However democratic then the social state and the political constitution of a people may be, it is certain that every member of the community will always find out several points about him which command his own position; and we may foresee that his looks will be doggedly fixed in that direction. When inequality of conditions is the common law of society, the most marked inequalities do not strike the eye; when everything is nearly on the same level, the slightest are marked enough to hurt it. Hence the desire of equality always becomes more insatiable in proportion as equality is more complete.

Among democratic nations men easily attain a certain equality of conditions: they can never attain the equality they desire. It perpetually retires from before them, yet without hiding itself from their sight, and in retiring draws them on. At every moment they think they are about to grasp it; it escapes at every moment from their hold. They are near enough to see its charms, but too far off to enjoy them; and before they have fully tasted its delights, they die.

To these causes must be attributed that strange melancholy which oftentimes will haunt the inhabitants of democratic countries in the midst of their abundance, and that disgust at life which sometimes seizes upon them in the midst of calm and easy circumstances. Complaints are made in France that the number of suicides increases; in America suicide is rare, but insanity is said to be more common than anywhere else. These are all different symptoms of the same disease. The Americans do not put an end to their lives, however disquieted they may be, because their religion forbids it; and among them materialism may be said hardly to exist, notwithstanding the general passion for physical gratification. The will resists—reason frequently gives way.

In democratic ages enjoyments are more intense than in the ages of aristocracy, and especially the number of those who partake in them is larger: but, on the other hand, it must be admitted that man's hopes and his desires are oftener blasted, the soul is more stricken and perturbed, and care itself more keen.

QUESTIONS AND PROBLEMS

1. de Tocqueville visited the United States in 1831-32 and published his well-known *Democracy in America* in France in 1835. How many of the causes of the "restless spirit" of Americans still apply today?
2. In par. 2 de Tocqueville speaks of Americans as being "serious and almost sad even in their pleasures." Compare or contrast with present-day college students. What are the causes of what you find?
3. Apply the statements in par. 5 to present-day Americans. Consider housing, employment, politics, and travel.
4. Does the beginning of par. 10 describe America, or does it apply, rather, to the American Dream? Wherein would you find fault with de Tocqueville's point of view?
5. Compare de Tocqueville's impressions of Americans with those of a foreign student on your campus. What similarities do you find?
6. Compare this writer's observations with those of Arthur M. Schlesinger in "Our Ten Contributions to Civilization," pp. 170-178.

SUGGESTIONS FOR WRITING

1. Write a paper entitled "Americans are Optimists" in which you determine the chief causes of optimism on the part of the people of the United States.
2. Write a similar paper on "The Pessimism of Americans."
3. Determine the causes of the restless spirit of American college students. Write an essay in the manner of de Tocqueville.
4. Why is the United States government generous to peoples of foreign lands? Make this the subject of an essay developed by cause.
5. Write an essay on the effects of American generosity abroad. Limit your paper to one country or to only a few examples.

SUGGESTIONS FOR FURTHER READING

British Broadcasting Corporation, *Americans: Ways of Life and Thought* (Dufour)

J.G. Carney, *Americans Don't Always Do What the Romans Did* (Carlton)

Alexis de Tocqueville, *Democracy in America* (various publishers)

Charles Dickens, *American Notes* (Peter Smith; Oxford)

F.R. Dulles, *Americans Abroad* (Univ. of Michigan)

William J. Lederer and Eugene Burdick, *The Ugly American* (Norton; Fawcett)

Edward A. McCreary, *The Americanization of Europe* (Doubleday)

Harriett Martineau, *Society in America* (AMS [3 vols.] ; Peter Smith [abridged])

Mrs. Frances Trollope, *Domestic Manners of the Americans* (Whittaker, Treacher; Peter Smith)

WE ASK THE WRONG QUESTIONS ABOUT CRIME
William M. McCord

America is by far the most criminal nation in the world. On a per capita basis, Americans commit about twice as many assaults as Frenchmen, triple the number of rapes as Italians, and five times as many murders as Englishmen. From the price manipulations of Westinghouse-General Electric and the mass violence of Los Angeles down to the subway muggings and the petty thievery of juvenile gangs, it is apparent, in James Truslow Adams's words, that "lawlessness has been and is one of the most distinctive American traits." 1

Yet we are at the same time one of the most puritanical of peoples, forever searching for some means to cure, suppress or punish wicked tendencies. This urge to reform has produced that recurring phenomenon in American life, the investigating commission, of which the latest example is the National Crime Commission appointed by President Johnson. Unfortunately, however, he has asked this newest blue-ribbon panel to answer the wrong questions and it may well end its investigations without adding much to what we already know. 2

Why is drug addiction increasing among young people? This is probably the most sensitive of the five questions the Commission will consider. In posing it, the President's advisers—perhaps responding to the public's appetite for sensation—have misled the commission. Any reasonable discussion of juvenile drug addiction (which, in America, means primarily addiction to heroin) should start by clearing up several prevalent misconceptions. 3

Drug addiction is *not* increasing; in all probability it has declined since the turn of the century. In 1915 (the year after the Harrison Act declared opiate addiction illegal), responsible scientists estimated that 215,000 Americans were addicts; by 1922, the number dropped to 110,000 (undoubtedly, most of those who gave up the habit were not true addicts); by 1960, the Federal Bureau of Narcotics reported only 45,391 known addicts in America—a figure that, however open to criticism, is the best available and shows a declining rate of addiction. The average age of drug addicts has not changed. 4

Secondly, drug addiction does *not* cause crime; it may in fact decrease it. 5

Many juvenile addicts are, of course, criminal. The "junkie" is likely to rob or shoplift or burglarize. But the best study of the subject (Isidor Chein's "The Road to H") shows that drug addiction tends to redirect the potential delinquent from more serious crimes

toward those that will bring him the money to buy drugs. In all   6
probability, drug addicts are less prone to commit really violent
crimes like rape, assault or murder. The "flattening" effect of heroin
often causes sexual desire to disappear and also reduces aggressive-
ness. In some recorded cases, addiction has actually eliminated vi-
cious criminal tendencies.

Thirdly, drug addiction per se does not seriously injure mind or
body, as do barbiturates, alcohol or tobacco. Even after 50 years of
addiction in some cases, no discernible physical or mental harm has
been traced to the use of narcotics. Further, the habit can be cured.
Although hospital treatment has been discouraging (about 90 per   7
cent failure among adult addicts), Synanon, a group similar to Alco-
holics Anonymous, has reported a high degree of success and Chein's
research shows that 26 per cent of teen-age addicts spontaneously
cure themselves. Cured or not, however, many addicts continue to
work—indeed, some deteriorate only when taken off the drug.

The average juvenile drug addict is admittedly an unhappy person, plagued by a sense of futility and aimlessness. Typically, he
comes from a deprived ethnic group (97 per cent of youthful addicts
come from families affectd by divorce, desertion or open hostitity
between their members). He tries narcotics at an early age, usually by   8
15. Normally, he takes his first dose at the encouragement of a friend
rather than as a result of a "pusher's" influence. For such young
people—passive, dependent, loveless—the drug serves to reduce intolerable anxiety.

Should we deny them this satisfaction? For most addicts, drugs
are an indispensable psychological crutch, as important to them as
insulin is for the diabetic. To declare narcotics illegal may change the   9
ways in which disordered people control their anxiety but it does
nothing to cure the underlying condition; the *form* of misbehavior
changes, but the causes stay the same.

In fact, the evidence suggests that juvenile drug addiction should
not be considered a major social problem at all. The most civilized
approach for the President's commission would be to examine ways
of legalizing the dispensation of drugs under medical advice and prescription. England has long ago removed the problem from police
jurisdiction. As a result, some authorities claim, the nation has only   10
700 known addicts. Others take issue with this figure and a few
believe that drug addiction is on the rise. But Britain has apparently
eliminated illegal traffic in drugs and, what is most important,
stopped much of the criminal behavior which, in America, is inevitably associated with addiction.

A balanced appraisal of the English solution, rather than the study of even more intensive attempts to curb the supposed terrors of addiction, would thus seem to be the most fruitful avenue of investigation for the commission. The legalization of drug-taking (under medical supervision) might result in a slight increase in addic- 11 tion but I do not find this possibility frightening since: (1) addiction in itself does not appear physically harmful; (2) crimes prompted by the present necessity for purchasing drugs illegally would possibly decrease.

The second crucial question the commission has been asked to 12 consider is, Why does organized crime continue to expand?

Whether the ranks of organized crime *have* actually expanded remains a subject of debate. Certain facts are apparent: mobs of strike-breakers no longer find lucrative employment; gangland kill- ings, like the St. Valentine's Day massacre, have become a rarity. 13 And contemporary racketeers can seldom boast, like Al Capone, that "the biggest bankers and businessmen and politicans and professional men are looking to me to keep the system going."

Certainly, organized crime—labor racketeering, Mafia operations in gambling and vice, underworld penetration of sports and busi- ness—is still an important part of American life. Admittedly, the "invisible government" of the Mafia is highly institutionalized and its power affects police and politicians in many American cities. And clearly, as the Kefauver investigation hinted, gangsters have also, from time to time, found a receptive attitude in such respectable 14 organizations as Western Union, major telephone companies and Wall Street brokerage firms. But while recognizing, as a Fund for the Republic report concluded, that "the underworld is an independent power, vying with other great classes and movements in America for wealth and influence in our culture," it is salutary to view the prob- lem in its historical and sociological perspective.

New York's "Bowery Boys" and the "Dead Rabbits" of the eighteen-sixties, the gangs of the Far West in the eighteen-seventies and Chicago's "Mike McDonald Democrats" of the eighteen-eighties testify that organized crime has been an enduring, even a glamorized, element in American culture for 100 years. Racketeers flourish in catering to desires which Americans periodically declare illegal: 15 drink, sex, gambling or security from economic competition. No government can outlaw these human appetites; to the degree that it tries to do so, the organized underworld will continue to find ready customers. In our refusal to tolerate human weakness, we have pro- duced a legion of Lucky Lucianos and Frank Costellos.

Yet recent trends in America have led to a relative decline in the influence of such men. Once-illicit activities, like drinking, have returned to the domain of legitimate business. The economy is no longer as competitive as in the past. Labor unions have, by and large, won acceptance and there is little need for terrorism as a means of protecting workers in an era of surplus labor. All of these changes signal the passing of big-city, organized crime—at least in the form in which we have known it.

The means are also at hand to curb the racketeers even further, if the public conscience really demanded it. Robert Kennedy, as Attorney General, increased Justice Department prosecutions of organized crime from 17 in 1960 to 262 in 1963. The Los Angeles police, by internal house-cleaning and external vigilance, has almost eliminated the Mafia, reducing gang killings to an average of one a year. Even Chicago, under Chief O.W. Wilson, has tightened its laws, refurbished its police and begun to clean out the more poisonous elements. The answer to organized crime, therefore, lies in the effective pursuit of justice—and just possibly in the repeal of laws that take too little cognizance of mankind's foibles.

The third question the President put to the commission is, Why do one-third of parolees revert to crime?

According to the most authoritative research in this field (the recent studies of Prof. Daniel Glaser, who traced the histories of more than 1,000 men in the Illinois penal system), approximately one-third of parolees *do* return to a life of crime. But this rate of failure should not invite condemnation of present trends in penal reform. On the contrary, the evidence suggests that the spread of an enlightened approach to rehabilitation has markedly enhanced the effectiveness of the American prison.

In the nineteen-thirties, Sheldon and Eleanor Glueck of Harvard followed up hundreds of men who had been imprisoned in Massachusetts. They found that over 80 per cent reverted to crime, and the longer a man spent in prison, the greater were the chances of recidivism. Reform schools in the nineteen-thirties and nineteen-forties seemed equally ineffective. An evaluation of typical Eastern reformatories revealed that 85 per cent of inmates went on to commit crimes in adulthood.

Today, this rate of failure has been substantially reduced. Most states now practice "parole prediction," using statistical tables to forecast a man's performance on parole rather accurately. In Illinois, only 3 per cent of parolees with favorable predictions violated their trust, while 75 per cent of those regarded as bad risks reverted to crime. The State of Washington's parole predictions have so far proved 100 per cent accurate!

A second factor accounting for the decline in parole violations has been the modernization and humanization of the rehabilitation process. Federal prisons have introduced individual and group therapy; the relatively "open" prison system typified by Chino, California, has been widely adopted; new facilities for the criminally insane, like California's Vacaville, have been established; older prisons have tried such new techniques as San Quentin's group discussions for convicts and their families; and even conjugal visiting has been allowed in such an unlikely place as Mississippi.   22

Encouraged by the success of New Jersey's Highfields project and New York's Wiltwyck School, many of the nation's juvenile reformatories have also replaced the techniques of punishment with those of rehabilitation. This quiet, almost unreported revolution in the penal system demonstrates how the application of social science can benefit society.   23

Can the number of parole violations be even further reduced? Probably yes. Proven methods of treatment could be introduced in those states, particularly in the South, which have been almost untouched by prison reform. The parole program itself could be further improved by an expansion of staff, the establishment of more counseling centers, and particularly by easing the task of parolees seeking a legal way to make a living. (The Glaser research showed that 90 per cent of convicts seek legitimate employment for a month after leaving prison, but that their initial income amounts to only $80 a month and one-third of them are still unemployed after three months.)   24

A more radical solution might also deserve consideration by the National Crime Commission: the introduction of more "indeterminate sentences" with an attendant revision in legal concepts of punishment and responsibility. The accuracy of parole prediction indicates that certain types of intractable offenders cannot benefit from the present penal system. A man like Albert Fish, who murdered, cooked and ate a young girl, had repeatedly served time in prison, yet, by contemporary law, had not been considered insane and consequently had been released each time he had been suitably "punished."   25

Might it not be wiser to declare such men not responsible for their actions and make them liable to an indefinite, nonpunitive sentence? In varying degrees, Britain, Sweden and Denmark already   26 follow a policy of confining certain types of offenders to hospitals for an undetermined period.

Why does one man break the law and another living in the same circumstances does not? This was the fourth question, and one that the National Crime Commission will, I trust, dispose of expeditious-   27
ly. The circumstances which lead one man to crime and another to good citizenship are, in reality, always quite different.

I am personally acquainted with cases where a child has, it would seem, miraculously escaped the influence of a highly criminal environment. In one Boston family, for example, the eldest son became a   28
murderer and another boy committed violent sex crimes, but the youngest turned into a mild and harmless, if highly neurotic, book-
keeper.

Until recently, these variations were attributed to the mysterious workings of moral fiber or free will or chance but now criminology has   29
reached the point where nearly all the differences in "circumstances" can be weighed and calculated.

Research by the Gluecks has most dramatically demonstrated that distinctive factors that lead to crime can be identified early in life, even at the time when a child enters school. From the findings of their "Unraveling Juvenile Delinquency"—an analysis of the differing environments of delinquents and nondelinquents—the Gluecks constructed a prediction table based on such influences as parental   30
discipline, family cohesiveness and affection. Individual children can thus be graded on the risk of becoming delinquent. Even children in the same family can often receive a different score, since one child may be his mother's pet and the other treated as a black sheep, or one may have been born when his father was at home while another's arrival may have triggered the father's desertion.

The New York Youth Board used this scale to predict delinquen-
cy among boys starting school in one section of the city in 1952. Now they have reached adolescence, and preliminary reports indicate   31
that the board's predictions have turned out to be 89 per cent accu-
rate.

In a similar research project among boys who averaged 11 years of age in 1939, none of those raised in environments judged as the most "positive" had become criminal 25 years later while 91 per cent   32
of those who suffered the most negative influences had criminal records.

Clearly, when an adult's behavior can be predicted from a knowl-
edge of forces operating in childhood—influences which he could not conceivably control—society must begin to question the belief that a   33

person acts from willful intent, that he should be held personally responsible for his actions and that he deserves punishment for behaving in an evil fashion.

On the other hand, such new procedures raise the delicate question of how society should utilize them. What limits should be imposed? We may soon be faced with a momentous choice between intervening in a child's family, perhaps forcibly—in defiance of our conception of parents' rights to raise their own children—and not intervening even though we *know* they are injuring a child to the point where he may one day threaten society. 34

The President's commission would do well to examine these issues, for they will soon become a matter of wide debate. 35

Why does juvenile delinquency know no economic or educational boundaries? Focusing on this fifth question may again deflect the Crime Commission from more basic issues. Every type of American boy does, in fact, commit crimes, but persistent delinquents needing help seldom emerge from the privileged educated segments of American society. 36

Admittedly, one can find drug addiction in Darien, rich teen-age robbers in Phoenix, "sex orgies" at Stanford, and sophisticated burglars among Harvard's student body. These wealthy, educated youths do not normally appear on police blotters; their prominence and connections insure that they will not be labeled as delinquents. (As a teen-ager, I myself committed a flagrant and dangerous traffic violation which, properly, resulted in arrest. My best friend's father, however, judged the case, and I was released with friendly admonitions.) This double standard is a disgrace that the commission, as other groups have done, should expose and condemn. 37

Yet, while recognizing the universality of delinquency and class distortions in the statistics, every social scientist knows that the most brutal crimes are confined to that segment of society which has been thoroughly dehumanized, that professional stealing is most prevalent where the American Dream has been least fulfilled, and that gang warfare breaks out where American ideals of courage, brotherhood and manliness are taken seriously but with the fewest rewards. 38

Despite the bias in criminal reporting, one can be reasonably certain that young Negroes commit 30 per cent more larcenies, 60 per cent more murders and 70 per cent more assaults than whites. But on the other hand, white urban slum delinquents commit twice as many assaults, three times as many larcenies and four times as many rapes as their fellow Caucasians in rural areas. 39

Discrepancies like these have been noted in America since 1800 and they cannot be explained in terms of the nature of Negroes or Puerto Ricans or working-class whites, or whoever else, at the moment, happens to have reputation for delinquency. Urban Jews, Irish, Italians and Frenchmen have all previously been America's juvenile champions of crime—until they, in turn, found more useful and rewarding outlets in American life.   40

Boys who have to struggle up from the lowest social strata have traditionally been prone to delinquency. Our society, in psychologist Kenneth Kenniston's words, offers working-class boys "few prospects as dignified, exciting and challenging as truancy, gang warfare, vandalism and theft." The middle-class boy, in contrast, soon outgrows his indiscretions as he finds more opportunities open to him for a happier or more productive or more profitable existence.   41

Until the preconditions of crime—ethnic discrimination, family disintegration and the rest of the characteristic malaise of industrial civilizations—are eliminated, we cannot uproot the cancer of delinquency at the center of American life.   42

To eradicate crime in America will take a revolution. The National Crime Commission cannot turn America back into a poor, rural, village-based society where the crime rate was so much lower. Nor can the commission change the American tradition that honors the violent cowboy-gangster here. And clearly, a Presidential group cannot fundamentally change an entire social structure—one that forces Negroes in Watts or Puerto Ricans in Harlem or K.K.K. murderers in Alabama to pursue their ways of tragic, brutal, purposeless violence.   43

But the commission can accomplish two tasks. It can sweep away false questions about a new wave in drug addiction and a supposed growth in organized crime, and myths about "the good boy gone wrong" that continue to confuse the public. And it can propose solutions to new questions that the public, let alone its intellectual leaders, has hardly examined: 44

> What would be the impact of legalizing drug addiction?
> Should America legalize gambling and prostitution (thus depriving organized crime of these particular sources of income)?
> Should American lawyers abandon their concepts of "responsibility," "willful intent" and, in fact, the whole set of easily accepted but barely defensible assumptions about human nature that underlie contemporary law?
> Should judges revise their sentencing procedures, so that men would be treated in terms of their nature rather than their illegal acts?
> Should the state consider intervening in families that, with seeming inevitability, will produce criminals?

I have no pat answers to these questions and I am deeply worried about how they will affect our tradition of privacy, our belief in man's rationality and our conviction that some men (at least) have 45 the power to choose freely. But I am sure that by confronting these complex, essentially philosophical problems, the National Crime Commission can best fulfill its duty.

QUESTIONS AND PROBLEMS

1. How does McCord substantiate the charge he makes in the opening sentence? Is it possible to refute this statement? How?
2. In the opening paragraphs of his essay McCord makes three assertions to clear up "several prevalent misconceptions" regarding the relationship between drug addition and crime. Is the evidence he gives for each assertion sufficient for you to accept his claim?
3. What has been the English solution to the drug problem (par. 10)? Would this method of meeting the problem work in the United States?
4. What is the author's method of approaching the second question asked of the National Crime Commission (pars. 10 and following)? What is his method of argument throughout?
5. Explain or identify *ethnic group*, St. Valentine's Day massacre, Mafia, Kefauver investigation, Lucky Luciano.
6. Does the double standard in regard to misdemeanors and crimes by teenagers and young adults (par. 37) exist in your area? Explain.
7. Discuss the relationship between social and economic deprivation and crime which the author cites in par. 41. What is the future of crime in America after present-day "urban slum delinquents" find more useful and rewarding outlets?
8. "To eradicate crime in America," says McCord, "will take a revolution" (par. 43). To what extent is this revolution now going on?
9. Comment on each of the "new questions" which the author raises at the end of the essay. Which ones suggest practical solutions?

SUGGESTIONS FOR WRITING

1. Write an essay on the effect of legalized open use of drugs.
2. Investigate use of drugs by students. Write an essay in which you concentrate on the effects of such use.
3. Arrange an interview with an inmate of a local jail. Report your discussion with him on crime, stressing cause and effect.
4. Research a paper on the Mafia.
5. Assuming the correctness of the opening sentence of this essay, write an essay on the causes for America's being "by far the most criminal nation in the world."
6. Write a paper on "Student Crimes" in which you classify and analyze such "crimes."
7. Write an essay in definition of "The Juvenile Delinquent."
8. Compare and contrast your idea of *delinquency* with that of your parents.

SUGGESTIONS FOR FURTHER READING

Edward J. Allen, *Merchants of Menace: The Mafia* (Charles C. Thomas)

K.R. Eissler, ed., *Searchlights on Delinquency* (International University)

Morris L. Ernst and Alan U. Schwartz, *Privacy: The Right to Be Let Alone* (Macmillan)

Viktor E. Frankl, *Man's Search for Meaning* (Beacon; Washington Square)

Elmer H. Johnson, *Crime, Correction, and Society* (Dorsey)

Paul Talalay, ed., *Drugs in Our Society* (Johns Hopkins)

Paul W. Tappan, *Crime, Justice, and Correction* (McGraw-Hill)

TO DEFINE

To explain a word, an object, or an abstract idea we define (from the Latin *de + finire,* "to set the limits about"). Sometimes we define by using well-known synonyms, but when there are no available synonyms we must employ what is called *logical* definition. A logical definition is made up of two parts, a *genus,* or general class, in which the term to be defined belongs, and a *differentia,* one or more limiting expressions which distinguishes the term from all other members of that class. We may define a noun as a *name,* simply using a synonym which explains the original term. Or we may expand the definition to a logical one, as a dictionary would do, by stating that a noun is "a word that is the name of a subject of discourse (as a person, animal, plant, place, thing, substance, quality, idea, action, or state) and that in languages with grammatical number, case, and gender is inflected for number and case but has inherent gender."[1] Here we have set logical limits about the term to be defined. Likewise we might define "man" as "a human being," relying upon a synonym; or more specifically we may give the genus and differentia of a logical definition: "a bipedal primate mammal (*Homo sapiens*) that is anatomically related to the great apes but distinguished esp. by notable development of the brain with a resultant capacity for articulate speech and abstract reasoning, is usu. held to form a veritable number of freely interbreeding races, and is the sole recent representative of a natural family (*Hominidae*); *broadly:* any living or extinct member of this family."[1]

But a synonym, as was pointed out above, is not always available, and then a logical definition is demanded. There is no synonym for the term *paragraph,* but a logical definition gives it both a genus, or class (a paragraph is a unit of *discourse* . . .), and a differentia (. . . that *develops a single idea*). Likewise there is no synonym for the geometric term *triangle;* so a logical definition must be employed: "a polygon [genus] having three sides [differentia] ."[2] It is impor-

---

1.*Webster's Seventh New Collegiate Dictionary* (Springfield, Mass.: G. & C. Merriam Co., 1963.)
2.*Ibid.*

tant in all definitions that the genus not be omitted, that it be exact—neither too large nor too small—that it be adequately differentiated from other members of the genus, and that the term itself not be repeated in the definition. To say "A stadium is where athletic contests are held" is to omit altogether the genus, "a playing field." To define a magazine as "a monthly publication containing articles, stories, and poetry" is to make the genus too small, for not all magazines are published monthly. To define a pen as "something to write with" is to make the genus far too large. To say that a cow is "an animal that eats hay" is to give no adequate differentiation. If one says that a circle is a "circular figure" he is repeating the term to be defined, as Dr. Samuel Johnson, in his eighteenth-century dictionary, repeated both the words in "hatchet-faced" by defining this as "an ugly face; such, I suppose as might be hewn out of a block by a hatchet."

The requirements of logical definition, as well as the faults which creep into such definitions, are well kept in mind when definition is to be used as a method of presenting an idea in an essay, for logical definition is often the pattern followed in such essays. Yet any exposition developed by definition will do more than merely state a logical definition. It will employ what is called *extended* definition, or the development in detail of the meaning, or a suggested meaning, of a term. The extended definition is particularly important when one defines an abstract term or when one needs to explain the meaning of a highly technical term in ways which will be understandable to the ordinary reader. Sometimes this essay-definition will develop the meaning of a term by using repetition—saying the same thing over but in different words. Sometimes it will explain the term by giving its background. Sometimes it will use the device of comparison and contrast. Again, a negative approach may be employed: defining a term by telling what it is not. Usually illustration and example play an important part in development by definition, and frequently analogy is used. In fact, virtually all of the modes of essay development included in this book are available to the writer of the essay which defines. Watch for the various devices the writers of the following essays have employed in defining their central terms.

EXPRESSIVE LANGUAGE
LeRoi Jones

Speech is the effective form of a culture. Any shape or cluster of human history still apparent in the conscious and unconscious habit of groups of people is what I mean by culture. All culture is necessarily profound. The very fact of its longevity, of its being what it is, *culture,* the epic memory of practical tradition, means that it is profound. But the inherent profundity of culture does not necessarily mean that its *uses* (and they are as various as the human condition) will be profound. German culture is profound. Generically. Its uses, however, are specific, as are all uses . . . of ideas, inventions, products of nature. And specificity, as a right and passion of human life, breeds what it breeds as a result of its context.

Context, in this instance, is most dramatically social. And the social, though it must be rooted, as are all evidences of existence, in culture, depends for its impetus for the most part on a multiplicity of influences. Other cultures, for instance. Perhaps, and this is a common occurrence, the reaction or interreaction of one culture on another can produce a social context that will extend or influence any culture in many strange directions.

Social also means *economic,* as any reader of nineteenth-century European philosophy will understand. The economic is part of the social—and in our time much more so than what we have known as the spiritual or metaphysical, because the most valuable canons of power have either been reduced or traduced into stricter economic terms. That is, there has been a shift in the actual meaning of the world since Dante lived. As if Brooks Adams were right. Money does not mean the same thing to me it must mean to a rich man. I cannot, right now, think of one meaning to name. This is not so simple to understand. Even as a simple term of the English language, *money* does not possess the same meanings for the rich man as it does for me, a lower-middle-class American, albeit of laughably "aristocratic" pretensions. What possibly can "money" mean to a poor man? And I am not talking now about those courageous products of our permissive society who walk knowledgeably into "poverty" as they would into a public toilet. I mean, The Poor.

I look in my pocket; I have seventy cents. Possibly I can buy a beer. A quart of ale, specifically. Then I will have twenty cents with which to annoy and seduce my fingers when they wearily search for gainful employment. I have no idea at this moment what that seventy cents will mean to my neighbor around the corner, a poor

Puerto Rican man I have seen hopefully watching my plastic garbage   4
can. But I am certain it cannot mean the same thing. Say to David
Rockefeller, "I have money," and he will think you mean something
entirely different. That is, if you also dress the part. He would not
for a moment think, "Seventy cents." But then neither would many
New York painters.

Speech, the way one describes the natural proposition of being
alive, is much more crucial than even most artists realize. Semantic
philosophers are certainly correct in their emphasis on the final dicta-
tion of words over their users. But they often neglect to point out
that, after all, it is the actual importance, *power,* of the words that
remains so finally crucial. Words have users, but as well, users have
words. And it is the users that establish the world's realities. Realities
being those fantasies that control your immediate span of life. Usually they are not your own fantasies, *i.e.,* they belong to governments, traditions, etc., which, it must be clear by now, can make for   5
conflict with the singular human life all ways. The fantasy of America might hurt you, but it is what should be meant when one talks of
"reality." Not only the things you can touch or see, but the things
that make such touching or seeing "normal." Then words, like their
users, have a hegemony. Socially—which is final, right now. If you
are some kind of artist, you naturally might think this is not so.
There is the future. But *immortality* is a kind of drug, I think—one
that leads to happiness at the thought of death. Myself, I would
rather live forever . . . just to make sure.

The social hegemony, one's position in society, enforces more
specifically one's terms (even the vulgar have "pull"). Even to the
mode of speech. But also it makes these terms an available explanation of any social hierachy, so that the words themselves become,   6
even informally, laws. And of course they are usually very quickly
stitched together to make formal statutes only fools or the faithfully
intrepid would dare to question beyond immediate necessity.

The culture of the powerful is very infectious for the sophisticated, and strongly addictive. To be any kind of "success" one must
be fluent in this culture. Know the words of the users, the semantic 7
rituals of power. This is a way into wherever it is you are not now,
but wish, very desperately, to get into.

Even speech then signals a fluency in this culture. A knowledge
at least. "He's an educated man," is the barest acknowledgment of   8
such fluency . . . in any time. "He's hip," my friends might say. They
connote a similar entrance.

And it is certainly the meanings of words that are most important, even if they are no longer consciously acknowledged, but merely, by their use, trip a familiar lever of social accord. To recreate instantly the understood hierarchy of social, and by doing that, cultural, importance. And cultures are thought by most people in the world to do their business merely by being hierarchies. Certainly this 9 is true in the West, in as simple a manifestation as Xenophobia, the naive bridegroom of anti-human feeling, or in economic terms, Colonialism. For instance, when the first Africans were brought into the New World, it was thought that it was all right for them to be slaves because "they were heathens." It is a perfectly logical assumption.

And it follows, of course, that slavery would have been an even stranger phenomenon had the Africans spoken English when they first got here. It would have complicated things. Very soon after the 10 first generations of Afro-Americans mastered this language, they invented white people called Abolitionists.

Words' meanings, but also the rhythm and syntax that frame and propel their concatenation, seek their culture as the final reference for what they are describing of the world. An A flat played twice on the same saxophone by two different men does not have to sound the same. If these men have different ideas of what they want this note to do, the note will not sound the same. Culture is the form, the overall structure of organized thought (as well as emotion and spiritual pretension). There are many cultures. Many ways of organizing thought, or having thought organized. That is, the form of thought's passage through the world will take on as many diverse shapes as there are diverse groups of travelers. Environment is one organizer of 11 *groups,* at any level of its meaning. People who live in Newark, New Jersey, are organized, for whatever purpose, as Newarkers. It begins that simply. Another manifestation, at a slightly more complex level, can be the fact that blues singers from the Midwest sing through their noses. There is an explanation past the geographical, but that's the idea in tabloid. And singing through the nose does propose that the definition of singing be altered . . . even if ever so slightly. (At this point where someone's definitions must be changed, we are flitting around at the outskirts of the old city of Aesthetics. A solemn ghost town. Though some of the bones of reason can still be gathered there.)

But we still need definitions, even if there already are many. The dullest men are always satisfied that a dictionary lists everything in the world. They don't care that you may find out something *extra,* 12 which one day might even be valuable to them. Of course, by that time it might even be in the dictionary, or at least they'd hope so, if you asked them directly.

But for every item in the world, there are a multiplicity of definitions that fit. And every word we use *could* mean something else. And at the same time. The culture fixes the use, and usage. And in   13 "pluralistic" America, one should always listen very closely when he is being talked to. The speaker might mean something completely different from what we think we're hearing. "Where is your pot?"

I heard an old Negro street singer last week, Reverend Pearly Brown, singing, "God don't never change!" This is a precise thing he is singing. He does not mean "God does not ever change!" He means "God don't never change!" The difference, and I said it was crucial, is in the final human reference . . . the form of passage through the world. A man who is rich and famous who sings, "God don't never change," is confirming his hegemony and good fortune . . . or merely calling the bank. A blind hopeless black American is saying something very different. He is telling you about the extraordinary order   14 of the world. But he is not telling you about his "fate." Fate is a luxury available only to those fortunate citizens with alternatives. The view from the top of the hill is not the same as that from the bottom of the hill. Nor are most viewers at either end of the hill, even certain that, in fact, there is any other place from which to look. Looking down usually eliminates the possibility of understanding what it must be like to look up. Or try to imagine yourself as not existing. It is difficult, but poets and politicians try every other day.

Being told to "speak proper," meaning that you become fluent with the jargon of power, is also a part of not "speaking proper." That is, the culture which desperately understands that it does not "speak proper," or is not fluent with the terms of social strength, also understands somewhere that its desire to gain such fluency is done at a terrifying risk. The bourgeois Negro accepts such risk as profit. But does *close-ter* (in the context of "jes a close-ter, walk wi-thee") mean the thing as *closer*? Close-ter, in the term of its user, is, believe me, exact. It means a quality of existence, of actual physical disposition perhaps . . . in its manifestation as a *tone* and *rhythm*   15 by which people live, most often in response to common modes of thought best enforced by some factor of environmental emotion that is exact and specific. Even the picture it summons is different, and certainly the "Thee" that is used to connect the implied "Me" with, is different. The God of the damned cannot know the God of the damner, that is, cannot know he is God. As no Blues person can really believe emotionally in Pascal's God, or Wittgenstein's question, "Can the concept of God exist in a perfectly logical language?" Answer: "God don't never change."

Communication is only important because it is the broadest root of education. And all cultures communicate exactly what they have, a powerful motley of experience. 16

QUESTIONS AND PROBLEMS

1. What method does Jones use to define his "expressive language"? How is the essay developed?
2. Jones says, "The economic is part of the social—and in our time much more so than what we have known as the spiritual or metaphysical . . . " (par. 3). Why is this true? Discuss the *economic* as part of the *social* today.
3. How many terms are defined in this essay? Check some of them against their dictionary definitions. Which definition is more meaningful to you, Jones' or that in the dictionary?
4. In what sense does the author use the term *fantasy* in par. 5? What is "the fantasy of America"?
5. What does Jones mean when he says, "The dullest men are always satisfied that a dictionary lists everything in the world" (par. 12)? What is the "something *extra*" which one may find?
6. Explain the point Jones makes about the expression, "God don't never change" (par. 14). How does this example relate to the theme of the entire essay?
7. Discuss "speaking proper" (par. 15) in terms of your own background and education. What does Jones mean by "the terms of social strength"?
8. What is the "powerful motley of experience" (par. 16) which is communicated by the specialized terms of college students? Explain some of these terms by employing the kind of contrast Jones uses in explaining "God don't never change."

SUGGESTIONS FOR WRITING

1. Define the term *social justice* from the point of view of the bottom of the hill (see par. 14).
2. Draw up a lexicon of student jargon. Explain the terms carefully, using illustrations.
3. Define the term *culture* from the point of view of the contemporary student. How does your definition differ from that of Matthew Arnold in the nineteenth century: "Contact with the best that has been said and thought in the world"?
4. What is an educated man? Write an essay in which you expand upon and illustrate the meaning of the term today.
5. Write an essay on the specialized terms used by a social, economic, ethnic, or occupational group. Explain why the specialized terms are useful within the group.

SUGGESTIONS FOR FURTHER READING

Lester V. Berrey and Melvin Van Den Bark, *American Thesaurus of Slang* (Crowell)

Joseph Bram, *Language and Society* (Random House)

Lewis Herman and Marguerite Herman, *American Dialects* (Theatre Arts)

Dell Hymes, ed., *Language in Culture and Society* (Harper)

George A. Miller, *Language and Communication* (McGraw-Hill)

Vance Randolph and George P. Wilson, *Down in the Holler: A Gallery of Ozark Folk Speech* (Univ. of Oklahoma)

Edward Sapir, *Culture, Language, and Personality*, ed. David G. Mandelbaum (Univ. of California)

Robert A. Stewart, *Goldin Stairs* (Dietz)

W.T. Witham, *Americans as They Speak and Live* (Ungar)

THE HEART OF RADICALISM

Harvey Goldberg and
William Appleman Williams

What is it to be a radical, to take a position at once denounced as corrosive and welcomed as life-giving? In its most general meaning, the one that unifies otherwise disparate programs and ideas, it is to be of a certain temperament, to have a spirit of steadfastness which sustains man's adherence to principle over any opposition, except new truth. Henry Demarest Lloyd lost friends, Heywood Broun his employment, LaFollette a political party, Veblen all academic respectability, and John Brown life itself. But at the crucial moment of pressure, recantation seemed a far greater price than loss of constancy.   1

In this sense, "radical" defines a nature different in quality from the temporizing "liberal" spirit, so expert in weighing principle against expediency. Broun made the point with characteristic directness: "In the final court of reckoning I believe the angels will indulge in few long cheers for any liberal. With minor exceptions he's a trimmer. 'There is much to be said on both sides' is one of his favorite sayings, or 'The truth lies somewhere between the two.' Thus split, he conciliates. It is hard enough to draw the mote from any eye, and if a man must drop that every now and then to take a yank at some beam in the opposite camp, he will accomplish little in the space allowed us."   2

The substantive meaning of liberalism as a creed is not at stake here, for one may have a radical devotion to some of its cardinal principles. The main tenets of liberalism were recently summed up by Charles Frankel as faith in reason, devotion to civil liberties, subordination of clerical influence, government economic interference for the benefit of the many, and optimism about future progress. But if the advocate of any of these puts his words to rest at the doorstep of action, if, after sifting evidence through a maze of gray, he fights shy of supporting white over black, then he has bartered radical responsibility for liberal respectability. Joseph Conrad understood the process far better than some contemporary "liberal" intellectuals, who appear to find the current retreat from protest justified by "the large measure of common ground occupied by liberals and conservatives alike." In *Nostromo,* his great novel of 1904 about a South American republic in social ferment, he expressed a "feeling of pity for those men [the liberals], putting their trust in words of some sort, while murder and rapine stalked over the land. . . ." If   3 men can fall into the formalism of words in the face of frontal acts like "murder and rapine," then the plunge is far easier when the symptoms of life and injustice are more subtle.

Morris Cohen once set up as opposites the reckless, impetuous radical and the searching, critical liberal. Yet the radical proves to be sober who refuses to yield up his deeply conceived principles; and the liberal is reckless when he gambles with his beliefs. It is yet to be proved that the hairsplitter emerges from life with a much better harvest than a fistful of hair.   4

To be radical, then, is to be steadfast, but steadfast for what? The equation must be filled out in order to differentiate radicals from other varieties of extremists—nags and cranks espousing such assorted causes as perpetual motion and reincarnation, or rip-roaring reactionaries utterly devoted to the cause of feudalism (economic or social). Already the adjective "radical" has come into sociological literature to modify the noun "Right." In a perceptive study of right-wing political extremism in the United States, Seymour Lipset justified this use of the term. "This group is characterized as radical because it seeks to eliminate from American political life those persons and institutions which threaten either its values or its economic interests." So defined, "radical" fails of precision, requiring another term, like Right or Left, to give it substance.   5

But radicalism points to the unattained future, not the once-attained past. If radicals stand fast and want change, they desire also a society of greater liberty and equality. Perhaps the view of Comte, who divided the world into a party of order and a party of progress, was too extreme. But the general drift seems perfectly clear; and the radicals belong to the side of progress. In all its complex parts their creed had been summed up by Russell Fraser into this organic whole: "Radicalism is here affirmed to be, neither a handy surrogate for those disgruntled persons not fed at the breast of their mother, nor pleased in their choice of a father, nor yet an ardent interlude through which young romantics must travel on their way to the 'real world' beyond, but rather a way of life humanitarian in the best sense, because it entails the most entire, the most reckless in point of self-interest, indeed the most fanatic, consecration to the common weal."   6

The United States has had its radicals, a fair number, at times acting alone and at times in concert, men who devoted themselves exceedingly well to the common weal. But the truth must be faced, however disillusioning, that the richest tradition of American radicalism belongs to a small minority of courageous men and women; that   7 their achievements, while outweighing their numbers, included neither a lasting mass movement nor a profound shift of power; that a greater number of radicals than these have failed to measure up to the standards of profundity and constancy required of them.

What are the chief difficulties that have blocked the way of a genuine radical success? And what is the challenge that is now posed? The obstacles have been ideological and institutional, the difficulty of overcoming that popular American elixir of the frontier on the one hand and the problem of confronting hostile power on the other. But why bother at all to study the barriers or those who scaled them? The radical legacy is, in fact, the foundation upon which a   8 more humane America can be built. This convolution in which the seeming dead end of yesterday becomes the highroad of tomorrow appears to be the path upon which moves the continuity of history. And it is only through understanding and accepting this irony of history that contemporary radicals can grasp the meaning of the history of American radicalism, diagnose its present condition, and plan its future.

QUESTIONS AND PROBLEMS

1. In par. 1 the authors name five men each of whom lost something of value because of his radicalism.
   a. Does the mere mention of the five names make the point of the authors clear?
   b. Would it be helpful to know who these men were?
   c. Identify the ones you know something about and explain why they were radicals.
   d. Where would you go to find out something about the men whose names meant nothing to you on first reading?
   e. Why, according to the authors, did these men accept their losses rather than change their activities to avoid the losses?
2. Henry Demarest Lloyd once referred to himself as a "socialist-anarchist-communist-individualist-collectivist-cooperative-aristocratic-democrat."
   a. Define each of these terms, looking up the ones you are unsure of.
   b. He also referred to himself as a socialist and a democrat. Do these two terms embrace the meaning of the longer identification given above?
   c. He insisted that *socialist* and *democrat* are synonymous terms. Discuss in the light of present-day politics.
3. In par. 2 Heywood Broun refers to the liberal as a *trimmer*. Does the statement which follows this one make an adequate definition of the term?
4. What distinction do the authors make in par. 3 between "radical responsibility" and "liberal respectability"? What is the meaning of the last sentence of this paragraph?
5. Find the fingure of speech in par. 4. Is it a telling one, or is it too light for the serious subject of the essay? What is the value of such figures in an argumentative essay?

6. Russell Fraser, whose definition of radicalism is quoted in par. 6, has asked the question, "Why is one man damned for breaking with his past and another eulogized for it?" Comment on this question in terms of political radicals you know about. Comment on it in terms of student radicalism on college campuses.

7. Arthur Koestler, in his novel *The Gladiators*, states, "Blessed are those who take the sword in their hand to end the power of the Beasts; those who build towers of stone to gain the clouds, who climb the ladder to fight with the angel; for they are the true sons of man." Could this statement be used to support the position of either the conservative or the radical? Comment on the importance of point of view when defining such terms as *conservative* and *radical*.

8. What is the "irony of history" the authors refer to in the last paragraph? If one can accept this irony, does it support the need for radicalism in social and political life, or does it merely explain it?

SUGGESTIONS FOR WRITING

1. In Shelley's verse drama *Prometheus Unbound* the title character, who incurred punishment for bringing fire to Man after the Flood, affirms "Neither to change, nor falter, nor repent." Use this quotation as the title of an essay on ideal radicalism, reinforcing your definition by reference to contemporary radical reformers you have read about in the press.

2. Write two one-paragraph definitions of the radical, in one of which you take the point of view on the liberal and in the other the point of view of the conservative or the reactionary.

3. Write an analysis of student unrest on your campus, taking as nearly an objective point of view as you can. Write it as if it were a report you are making for the dean of your college.

4. Write an investigative paper on the subject of John Brown of Civil War fame, using as your thesis the unsoundness of the idea that he was a crazed, embittered misfit.

5. Compare and contrast your own present position on political and social matters with that of your father or with that of someone you know well in your father's generation. Again, analyze both positions as objectively as you can.

6. Charles Beard, the American historian, maintained that of the various motives which impel men to action, the most important throughout history has been the struggle for food, clothing, and shelter. In an essay, defend this statement.

7. Write one-paragraph definitions of the terms *justice, individualism, faith, equality*, and *brotherhood*.

8. Incorporating your one-paragraph definition (from No. 7) in it, write an extended essay on one of the above terms. Illustrate your definition by reference to specific persons and events.

SUGGESTIONS FOR FURTHER READING

Stephen Vincent Benét, *John Brown's Body* (Holt, Rinehart & Winston)
Heywood Broun, *It Seems to Me* (Harcourt, Brace & World)

Morris R. Cohen, *The Faith of a Liberal* (Holt, Rinehart & Winston)
Mark Holloway, *Heavens on Earth: Utopian Communities in America 1680-1880*
    (Peter Smith; Dover)
F.O. Matthiessen, *Theodore Dreiser* (Dell)
William Styron, *The Confessions of Nat Turner* (Random House)

PATRIOTISM

George Santayana

Patriotism is a form of piety. It is right to prefer our own country to all others because we are children and citizens before we can be travellers or philosophers. Specific character is a necessary point of origin for universal relations: a pure nothing can have no radiation and no scope. It is no accident for the soul to be embodied: her very essence is to express and bring to fruition the functions and resources of the body. Its instincts sustain her ideals and its relations her world. A native country is a sort of second body, another enveloping organism to give the will definition. A specific inheritance strengthens the soul. Cosmopolitanism has doubtless its place, because a man may well cultivate in himself, and represent in his nation, affinities to other peoples, and such assimilation to them as is compatible with personal integrity and clearness of purpose. Plasticity to things foreign need not be inconsistent with happiness and   1
utility at home. But happiness and utility are possible nowhere to a man who represents nothing and who looks out on the world without a plot of his own to stand on, either on earth or in heaven. He wanders from place to place, a voluntary exile, always querulous, always uneasy, always alone. His very criticisms express no ideal. His experience is without sweetness, without cumulative fruits, and his children, if he has them, are without morality. For reason and happiness are like other flowers—they wither when plucked. On the other hand, to be always harping on nationality is to convert what should be a recognition of natural conditions into a ridiculous pride in one's own oddities. Nature has hidden the roots of things, and though botany must now and then dig them up for the sake of comprehension, their place is still under ground. A man's feet must be planted in his country, but his eyes should survey the world.

Where parties and governments are bad, as they are in most ages and countries, it makes practically no difference to a community, apart from local ravages, whether its own army or the enemy's is victorious in war, nor does it really affect any man's welfare whether the party he happens to belong to is in office or not. These issues concern, in such cases, only the army itself, whose lives and fortunes are at stake, or the official classes, who lose their places when their leaders fall from power. The private citizen in any event continues in   2
such countries to pay a maximum of taxes and to suffer, in all his private interests, a maximum of vexation and neglect. Nevertheless,

because he has some son at the front, some cousin in the government, or some historical sentiment for the flag and the nominal
essence of his country, the oppressed subject will glow like the rest
with patriotic ardour, and will decry as dead to duty and honour
anyone who points out how perverse is this helpless allegiance to a
government representing no public interest.

In proportion as governments become good and begin to operate
for the general welfare, patriotism itself becomes representative and
an expression of reason; but just in the same measure does hostility
to that government on the part of foreigners become groundless and
perverse. A competitive patriotism involves ill-will toward all other
states and a secret and constant desire to see them thrashed and
subordinated. It follows that a good government, while it justifies   3
this governmental patriotism in its subjects, disallows it in all other
men. For a good government is an international benefit, and the
prosperity and true greatness of any country is a boon sooner or later
to the whole world; it may eclipse alien governments and draw away
local populations or industries, but it necessarily benefits alien individuals in so far as it is allowed to affect them at all.

Animosity against a well-governed country is therefore madness.
A rational patriotism would rather take the form of imitating and
supporting that so-called foreign country, and even, if practicable, of
fusing with it. The invidious and aggressive form of patriotism,
though inspired generally only by local conceit, would nevertheless
be really justified if such conceit happened to be well grounded. A
dream of universal predominance visiting a truly virtuous and intelligent people would be an aspiration toward universal beneficence. For   4
every man who is governed at all must be governed by others; the
point is, that the others, in ruling him, shall help him to be himself
and give scope to his congenial activities. When coerced in that direction he obeys a force which, in the best sense of the word, *represents*
him, and consequently he is truly free; nor could he be ruled by a
more native and rightful authority than by one that divines and
satisfies his true necessities.

A man's nature is not, however, a quantity or quality fixed unal-
terably and *a priori*. As breeding and selection improve a race, so
every experience modifies that individual and offers a changed basis
for future experience. The language, religion, education, and prejudices acquired in youth bias character and predetermine the direc-   5
tions in which development may go on. A child might possibly
change his country; a man can only wish that he might change it.

Therefore, among the true interests which a government should represent, nationality itself must be included.

Mechanical forces, we must not weary of repeating, do not come
merely to vitiate the ideal; they come to create it. The historical
background of life is a part of its substance, and the ideal can never
grow independently of its spreading roots. A sanctity hangs about
the sources of our being, whether physical, social, or imaginary. The
ancients who kissed the earth on returning to their native country
expressed nobly and passionately what every man feels for those
regions and those traditions whence the sap of his own life has been
sucked in. There is a profound friendliness in whatever revives primordial habits, however they may have been overlaid with later so-   6
phistications. For this reason the homelier words of a mother tongue,
the more familiar assurances of an ancestral religion, and the very
savour of childhood's dishes, remain always a potent means to
awaken emotion. Such ingrained influences, in their vague totality,
make a man's true nationality. A government, in order to represent the
general interests of its subjects, must move in sympathy with their
habits and memories; it must respect their idiosyncrasy for the same
reason that it protects their lives. If parting from a single object of
love be, as it is, true dying, how much more would a shifting of all
the affections be death to the soul.

Man is certainly an animal that, when he lives at all, lives for
ideals. Something must be found to occupy his imagination, to raise
pleasure and pain into love and hatred, and change the prosaic alternative between comfort and discomfort into the tragic one between
happiness and sorrow. Now that the hue of daily adventure is so dull,
when religion for the most part is so vague and accommodating,
when even war is a vast impersonal business, nationality seems to
have slipped into the place of honour. It has become the one eloquent, public, intrepid illusion. Illusion, I mean, when it is taken for
an ultimate good or a mystical essence, for of course nationality is a
fact. People speak some particular language and are very uncomforta-
ble where another is spoken or where their own is spoken differently.
They have habits, judgments, assumptions to which they are wedded,   7
and a society where all this is unheard of shocks them and puts them
at a galling disadvantage. To ignorant people the foreigner as such is
ridiculous, unless he is superior to them in numbers or prestige, when
he becomes hateful. It is natural for a man to like to live at home,
and to live long elsewhere without a sense of exile is not good for his
moral integrity. It is right to feel a greater kinship and affection for
what lies nearest to oneself. But this necessary fact and even duty of

nationality is accidental; like age or sex it is a physical fatality which can be made the basis of specific and comely virtues; but it is not an end to pursue, or a flag to flaunt, or a privilege not balanced by a thousand incapacities. Yet of this distinction our contemporaries tend to make an idol, perhaps because it is the only distinction they feel they have left.

QUESTIONS AND PROBLEMS

1. Look up the word *patriotism* in an unabridged dictionary. In what particular areas does Santayana extend the definition?
2. Define *cosmopolitanism, plasticity, a priori, primordial, intrepid.*
3. Restate in your own words Santayana's reasons why a man without a country has an unsatisfactory position in the world (par. 1).
    a. Are the reasons sound ones?
    b. Why are such a man's children "without morality"?
    c. Discuss the question in terms of the dream of "One World" by men of good will.
4. Discuss patriotism and the ordinary citizen, with particular reference to Santayana's point of view in par. 2.
5. "Animosity against a well-governed country is therefore madness" (par. 4).
    a. Discuss in terms of recents wars.
    b. Discuss in terms of minority-group struggles within our own country.
6. Relate to present-day communism the following statement (par. 4):

    "For every man who is governed at all must be governed by others; the point is that the others, in ruling him, shall help him to be himself and give scope to his congenial activities."

7. Transfer Santayana's concept of patriotism to a student's loyalty to his school. What points from Santayana's essay would be acceptable to you in making the latter definition?
8. What does Santayana mean when he says (par. 7), "Something must be found . . . to raise pleasure and pain into love and hatred. . . . "? Apply to civil rights problems in the United States.

SUGGESTIONS FOR WRITING

1. Write your own extended definition of patriotism.
2. Write an essay on "Patriotism in One World." Make it a comparison and contrast between national and international patriotism.
3. Select a country which the United States government and many of its people view with distrust. Examine the causes and the effects of that distrust.
4. Write an essay supporting the view that there should be one government for all the Americas, or argue that there should be two American governments, one North and one South, with some such border as the Panama Canal to separate the two.
5. Write a definition of loyalty, either on a national or on a personal basis.
6. Write an essay on the place of loyalty in a student-school situation.

7. Write an essay on the influence of the military establishment on national loyalty.
8. Consider the question of national loyalty and the economically disadvantaged. Form a thesis which you can argue.

SUGGESTIONS FOR FURTHER READING

Alan Barth, *Loyalty of Free Men* (Shoe String)

Leonard W. Doob, *Patriotism and Nationalism: Their Psychological Foundations* (Yale)

Harold M. Hyman, *To Try Men's Souls: Loyalty Oaths in American History* (Univ. of California)

James H. Jauncey, *I Believe in the American Way* (Zondervan)

J.P. Morray, *Pride of State* (Monthly Review)

John H. Schaar, *Loyalty in America* (Univ. of California)

John C. Wahlke, ed., *Loyalty in a Democratic State* (Heath)

WHAT'S BUGGING THE STUDENTS?
Irving Kristol

No one, except perhaps a few college administrators, mourns the passing of "the silent generation." But it must be said in its favor that at least one knew what the American university students of the 1950s were silent about, and why. They were conformist for plain, indeed, obvious and traditional, conformist reasons. We may have been distressed and vexed by this conformism; we were not mystified by it; whereas we are very much mystified by the nonconformism of the students of the sixties.

Many of the same middle-aged critics who so fervently and eloquently condemned the silent generation are now considerably upset and puzzled at the way students are "misbehaving" these days. One wanted the young to be idealistic, perhaps even somewhat radical, possibly even a bit militant—but not like this! It used to be said that the revolution devours its children. It now appears that these children have devoured this revolution.

What is it all about? One thing is fairly clear: the teach-ins, the sit-ins, the lay-downs, the mass picketing, and all the rest are not *merely* about Vietnam, or civil rights, or the size of classes at Berkeley, or the recognition of Red China. They are about these issues surely, and most sincerely. But there is, transparently, a passion behind the protests that refuses to be satisfied by the various topics which incite it. This passion reaches far beyond politics, as we ordinarily understand that term. Anyone who believes the turbulence will subside once we reach a settlement in Vietnam is in for a rude surprise. Similarly, anyone who thinks of present-day campus radicalism as a kind of overzealous political liberalism, whose extremism derives from nothing more than youthful high spirits, is deceiving himself. What we are witnessing is an event *in* American politics, but not *of* it.

Indeed, one of the most striking features of the new radicalism on the campus is that it is, in one sense, so apolitical. It is a strange experience to see a radical mood in search of a radical program; it is usually very much the other way around. These young American radicals are in the historically unique position of not being able to demand *a single piece of legislation* from their government—their "platform" is literally without one legislative plank. Their passion for "freedom now" coexists with a remarkable indifference to everything the United States government is doing, or might do, in this direction.

If one read every campus leaflet published these past two years and attended every campus or off-campus demonstration, and knew only what one learned from these sources, one would hardly be aware that the Johnson Administration had enacted in the area of civil rights the most far-reaching reforms in a century of legislative history. There has been no campus meeting to celebrate the passage   5 of the Civil Rights Act or the Voting Rights Acts. There has not even been any meeting criticizing these laws for "not going far enough." It's as if nothing had happened—or, to put it more precisely, as if whatever happens in Washington has nothing to do with the world the students live and act in.

The same sort of thing is to be seen with regard to the war on poverty, a topic upon which students will declaim passionately and with unquestionable sincerity. But it seems that their passion is so pure, their sensibility so fine, that these would be violated by a consideration of anything so vulgar as how to get more money into poor people's pockets. The recent increase in social security and the   6 medicare bill made their way through Congress without the benefit of so much as a benevolent nod from the campuses. Whenever I have mentioned the legislation in conversation, I have received an icy stare of incomprehension and disdain, as if I were some kind of political idiot who actually believed what he read in the New York *Times*.

Even in the single area where one would most expect specific and tangible proposals of reform, the organization of the multiversity, these have not made their appearance. For an entire year the students of the University of California at Berkeley have given dramatic evidence of dissatisfaction with their university experience—and does anyone know specifically what they would like, by way of improvement? The university officials certainly don't know, nor do the regents, nor do the faculty. Some outsiders *think* they know. Berkeley   7 is too large, they say, too anonymous; there is no possibility of a face-to-face community of scholars, young and old. This is true enough. But the Riverside branch of this same university is a small liberal arts college, with great intimacy and comfort, and for the past decade it has had much difficulty in attracting enough students. They all want to go to Berkeley, and the reason, they will explain, is: "That is where the action is."

The denunciations of the multiversity suspiciously resemble the way New Yorkers excoriate "megalopolis"—having come there in the first place, and determinedly remaining there, for no other reason than that New York *is* a megalopolis. All Americans will always insist that they adore small towns and detest great cities, but the move-   8 ment of population from towns to cities remains strangely unaffected. And Berkeley, even today, has far more student applications than it can handle; one might even say, *especially* today, for I understand that the number of applications has, in fact, slightly increased.

No, the upsurge of left-wing sentiment and left-wing opinion on the American campus today is not the sort of thing progressive parents and educators had in mind ten years ago when they benevolently urged students to become "socially committed" and "more idealistic." They naively wished them to have intelligent discussions of Vietnam, not to hurl insults and epithets at Averell Harriman (as happened at Cornell), or tear up their draft cards, or laud the Viet Cong. They wished them to be urbane and tolerant about sex, not to carry placards with dirty words, or demand the sale of contraceptives   9
in the college bookstore. They wished them to be concerned for civic and social equality for the Negro, not to denounce "white America" as a pious fraud, whose "integration" did not differ essentially from South Africa's apartheid, or express sympathy with a mindless (if occasionally eloquent) black nationalism. They wished—they wished, in short, that their children be just like them, only a wee bit bolder and more enlightened. Instead, these children are making it very clear that being just like their parents, progressive or not, is the fate they wish most desperately to avoid.

And this, I think, is the crux of the matter. The new student radicalism is so fundamentally at odds with our conventional political categories because it is, above all, an *existentialist* revolt. The term is unfortunately chic, and ambiguous, too. But in this context it   10
has a fairly definite meaning: the students are in rebellion, not so much because things are bad for them, or for others, but because things are what they are for them and for others.

Clues to the meaning of this rebellion may be found in two phrases that now appear ever more commonly in the left-wing cam-   11
pus vocabulary. The first is "organized America." The second is "participatory democracy."

"Organized America" is, quite simply, America, and not, as one might think, some transient bureaucratic excrescence on the body of America. As a matter of fact, today's students are immensely skillful in coping with bureaucracies and their paper work. They fill out forms and applications with a briskness and competence that startle the middle-aged observer. (I would guess that no one over the age of forty could properly fill out a college application form unless he received guidance from some kindly youngster.) What bugs the students is not these trivia but the society they emanate from—the affluent society, welfare state and all. The liberalism (and the radicalism, too) of the 1930s and 1940s has borne its fruit, and it tastes bitter to the children, setting their teeth on edge. That is why American students, amidst reasonably general prosperity and under a liberal Administration that is expanding the welfare state more aggressively and successfully than anyone had thought possible, feel more "alienated" than ever before. So many college students "go left" for the same reason that so many high school students "go delinquent." *They are bored.* They see their lives laid out neatly before them; they see themselves moving ahead sedately and more or less inexorably in their professional careers; they know that with a college degree even "failure" in their careers will represent no harsh punishment; they know "it's all laid on"—and they react against this bourgeois utopia their parents so ardently strove for.

One of the unforeseen consequences of the welfare state is that it leaves so little room for personal idealism; another is that it mutes the challenge to self-definition. All this is but another way of saying that it satisfies the anxieties of the middle-aged while stifling the creative energies of the young. Practically every college student these days understands what is meant by an "identity crisis": it is one of the cliches of the sixties. It is not, perhaps, too much to say that mass picketing on the campus is one of the last, convulsive twitches of a slowly expiring American individualism.

American youth, however, has had one grand idealistic experience: the civil rights movement. This has been the formative experience for the activists of the 1960s; it is this movement that gave them a sense of personal power and personal purpose; and it is the civil rights movement which instructed them in the tactics of civil disobedience that are now resorted to at the drop of a hat. Unfortunately, the civil rights movement has had one great drawback: so far from being a proper "dissenting" movement, it has behind it the President, Congress, the courts, the laws of the land, and a majority of public opinion. This fact helps explain why the younger militants have constantly pushed the movement toward "extremes"—for example, demanding utter, complete, and immediate *equality of condition* for the Negro, as against mere equality of opportunity.

Such equality of condition is what "freedom now" has come to mean. And since this demand cannot be fulfilled without repealing three centuries of history, and since even Lyndon Johnson hasn't figured out a way to do this, there is some satisfaction in such a maneuver. The trouble is that the students do not know how to fulfill this demand either, and are even running out of extremist slogans; which is why so many of them are receptive to the idea of switching their attention to Vietnam, where they can be more splendidly, less ambiguously, in "the opposition."

A second theme of student radicalism today, and a polar twin to the concept of "organized America," is the idea of "participatory democracy." This is a vague notion, but a dynamic one. It expresses a profound hostility toward, and proposes an alternative to, everything that is impersonal, manipulative, "organized" in the American political process. Indeed, many of these students simply dismiss American democracy as a sham, a game played by the "power structure" for its own amusement and in its own interests. *True* democracy, they insist, can only mean direct democracy, where the people's will is expressed and legislated by the people themselves rather than by elected representatives, most of whom achieve office by deceit and retain office through the substantial support offered them by the vested interests. 16

One is reminded by this of nothing so much as the Russian Narodniki ("populists," our textbooks call them) of the end of the nineteenth century. They, too, were largely middle-class students who selflessly turned their backs on the careers the Czarist bureaucracy offered them. They, too, "returned to the people," leaving the fleshpots of Petrograd for the villages of the interior, much as our students leave their comfortable homes in New York or Chicago for Southern ghettos and slums. And they, too, were hostile to the nascent liberal institutions of their day, seeing political salvation only in a transformed and redeemed people rather than in improvements in any kind of system of representative government. It is also interesting to recall that, though they were as individuals the gentlest and most humane of their time, they nevertheless believed in the justice and efficacy of terrorism against the status quo and assassination against its spokesmen. 17

The analogy is, of course, very superficial: the United States today is not Czarist Russia of yesterday. But it is nevertheless illuminating, because it helps reveal the inner logic of the idea of "participatory democracy," a logic which proceeds from the most exemplary democratic premises to the most illiberal conclusions. Though few students these days learn it in their social studies course, the Founding Fathers of the American republic were exceedingly familiar with the idea of "participatory democracy"; as a matter of fact, this was what the word "democracy" usually meant prior to 1789. They rejected "participatory democracy" (they called it "direct democracy") in favor of "representative government" for two 18 reaons. First, they didn't see how it could work in so large and complex a nation, as against a small city-state. Second, and more important, they thought it inconsistent with the idea of free government—that is, a government that respected the liberties of the individual. For participatory democracy requires that all people be fit to govern; and this in turn requires that all people *be made* fit to govern, by rigid and uniform educational training, constant public indoctrination, close supervision of private morals and beliefs, and so forth. No legislator can be as free as a private citizen, and to make all the people legislators is willy-nilly to abolish the category of private citizen altogether.

This, of course, is exactly what the Communists do, after their own fashion. They claim to exemplify a truer, more "direct," more "participatory," more "popular" democracy than is to be found in the representative institutions of the bourgeois West. The claim has a certain plausibility, in that regimes established by mass movements and mass revolutions certainly "involve the people" more than does   19
any merely elected government. The semblance of "involvement" is perpetuated, as we know, through the mass organizations of the Communist state, and the fact that it is done under compulsion, and becomes more of a farce with every passing Communist year, is one of the inner contradictions both of the Communist system and of the myth of direct democracy itself.

These contradictions our left-wing students are not entirely unaware of. Though many of them are, to one degree of another, either pro-Communist or belligerently "neutralist," theirs is a very qualified and unconventional version of this attitude; which is why conventional anti-Communist propaganda tends to pass them by. They are,   20
for instance, extraordinarily uninterested in the Soviet Union, and they become ever less interested to the degree that the Soviet Union liberalizes its regime—that is to say, to the extent that the Soviet Union becomes merely another "organized" system of rule.

What they seek is a pure and self-perpetuating popular revolution, not a "planned economy" or anything like that. And this is why they are so attracted to Castro's Cuba and Mao's China, countries where the popular revolution has not yet become "bourgeoisified." As for mass terror in Cuba and China—well, this actually may be taken as a kind of testimony to the ardor and authenticity of the   21
regime's revolutionary fervor. Our radical students, like other radical students before them, find it possible to be genuinely heartsick at the injustices and brutalities of American society, while blandly approving of injustice and brutality committed elsewhere in the name of "the revolution."

Like other radical student generations before them, they are going to discover one day that their revolution, too, has been betrayed, that "organized society" is what revolutions establish as well as destroy. One hopes they will not be made too miserable by their disillusionment. One also hopes, it must be added, that they won't make *us* too miserable before that day arrives. 22

QUESTIONS AND PROBLEMS

1. This essay might have been placed under the heading "To Compare and Contrast." If it is an essay in definition, what exactly is being defined?
2. Does the author leave you with the impression that he got his information from students or that what he wrote depended upon assumptions—or even prejudice? Cite proof from the essay.
3. Is the purpose of Kirstol's essay clear? Exactly what is the purpose?
4. Explain the meaning of *existential, populist, left-wing, apartheid, identify crisis.*
5. What is the difference between "participatory democracy" and the present democratic structure in the United States?
6. Why is Kristol's analogy between the Russian populists of Czarist days and student radicalism today a superficial one? Explain.
7. Although Kristol's essay was written only a few years ago, motivating factors of the student revolt may have changed. Does the author's point in par. 4 still apply? If not, cite instances.
8. What does the author mean when he says (par. 10), "the students are in rebellion, not so much because things are bad for them, or for others, but because things are what they are for them and for others"? Do you agree with him?
9. How does Kristol explain, in part, what's bugging the students by showing what is not bugging the students?
10. Outline the steps Kristol takes to explain the "new radicalism": first, telling what it is not concerned with, second . . . , etc. Is the method of comparison and contrast carried through the essay?

SUGGESTIONS FOR WRITING

1. What basic changes have taken place in the college curriculum over the past generation? Through an interview with a college professor or through checking old catalogues of your college, compare today's curriculum with that of some definite time in the past.
2. Make the same comparison of college social life and social regulations.
3. It is frequently asserted, particularly by the tub-thumping fraternity, that we must maintain "our American way of life." Write an essay on definition of this term.
4. Contrast "our American way of life" today with that of the post-World War I or World War II era.
5. Explain and analyze either a major student demand on your campus or a recent student demonstration.
6. Find out something about the philosophy of existentialism. Write a definition of it in your own terms.

7. Explain, from the student point of view, what is wrong with "organized America." Define the term.
8. Make a study of student activism in one of the countries of South America. Use specific illustrations.
9. Define the term *revolt* as it applies to student activism.
10. Write an essay in definition of *leadership* as it applies to the members of your own generation.

SUGGESTIONS FOR FURTHER READING

Albert T. Anderson and Bernice P. Biggs, *Focus on Rebellion* (Chandler)
Waldo Beach, *Conscience on Campus* (Association Press)
Edward Cain, *They'd Rather Be Right* (Macmillan)
M. Stanton Evans, *Revolt on the Campus* (Regnery)
Rose K. Goldsen and others, *What College Students Think* (Van Nostrand)
Everett L. Hunt, *The Revolt of the College Intellectual* (Aldine)
Harry H. Lunn, *The Student's Role in College Policy-Making* (American Council on Education)
National Association of Women Deans and Counselors, *Ethical Values and Student Behavior* (National Education Association)
Elizabeth Sutherland, ed., *Letters from Mississippi* (McGraw-Hill)
Howard Zinn, *SNCC* (Beacon)

THE WHITE POWER STRUCTURE

Allan Morrison

Since the Negro revolt ignited the fire that had been smoldering for generations and shook America out of its complacency about the racial problem, a key phrase, uttered by many of its leaders as well as rank and file shock troops, has echoed around the land: the White Power Structure. Seldom defined, the term has become a vital part of the lexicon of the civil rights movement, and a convenient synonym for the vast complex of governmental authority, economic power and military leadership which runs our society and maintains the status quo against which the Negro is rebelling. This complicated structure of authority is the target of the Negro protest movement's most vocal and militant spokesmen. The phrase is not heard from the lips of the more moderate Negro leaders like the NAACP's Roy Wilkins or the National Urban League's Whitney Young, but to the younger Negro militants, whose economic philosophy veers left of center, it has become both a watchword and a rallying cry.

The Negro freedom movement is understandably fragmented, and its leaders and component groups differ as to ideology, tactics, timing and priorities, but all agree that they face a common enemy, an impersonal hierarchy which possesses the power to keep Negroes in a pathological condition. But it is not always clear to those who are involved in the civil rights struggle who precisely are the people who make up the power structure which governs the country economically, politically and militarily. There is a general vagueness in "the movement" about the identities of the men who occupy the pivotal positions from which they can make major decisions affecting the destinies of millions.

To succeed, a revolution's leadership must understand the nature of its adversary and decide how best to deal with him. The Negro protest movement, emerging from its protest stage, is learning more about its opposition and how it operates. Like the labor upsurge of the 30s, the Negro movement has had to do its homework and discover who occupies the command posts of our economy and society. In its struggles with monopolies in the basic industries, the CIO hired trained economists to whom facts were weapons. Economic and scientific political research is no less essential to today's civil rights fighters.

Every important revolution in history has been conducted against an identifiable and visible enemy—a class or a nation—from which it sought either basic reforms, partial surrender of power, or total abdi-

cation. The French Revolution was an uprising against a feudal aristocracy blocking the way of a new dynamic bourgeoisie struggling   4
for power. England's industrial revolution broke the political power
of the landed aristocracy and made possible the growth of capitalism
in that country. The American Revolution crushed a colonial system.
The Russian Revolution wiped out czarism and a society ruled by a
feudal nobility.

The Negro revolt of the 60s is being fought for such recognizable
goals as equality, justice, full opportunity to develop and enjoy citizenship and an end to the humiliation of segregation which breeds
inferiority. This is a unique revolt which does not seek an end to the
existing society or the destruction of its rulers. The Negro's leaders   5
repeatedly declare that the revolt is not aimed at the 173 million
whites who make up the predominant group, but against a relatively
small but rarely identified power structure composed of people who
really run the country and from whom it seeks to wrest fundamental
concessions and reforms either through persuasion or direct action.

America's power structure, consisting of the highest influence-
wielding economic, political and military circles, probably numbers
no more than 5,000 persons. They are the same forces against whom
the nation's labor movement and liberals find themselves arrayed on
many policy questions. To Negroes, this powerful elite group has
another important dimension: color. For those who run the coun-   6
try's biggest corporations, control the machinery of state and direct
the military establishment are white. "There is a cultural and institutional tradition that white people exploit Negroes," said the eminent
Swedish economist Gunnar Myrdal in his classic study of the U.S.
race problem *An American Dilemma.* "Discrimination against Negroes is thus rooted in this tradition of economic exploitation."

Though the central enemy is recognized in a very loose sense as a
white elite occupying the seats of power, the Negro movement for
equality cannot present a unified national strategy against the men of
power, some of whom are invisible and faceless. "We know that the
white power structure exists," a CORE official stated, "but it is so   7
scattered, so huge and so powerful that it is often difficult to mount
an effective strategy against it." The civil rights movement makes its
demands on the power structure and backs these up with demonstrations on the national, regional and local levels.

The 1963 March on Washington asserted the Negro's mood to the
entire White Establishment including the Kennedy Administration.
But after the pageantry and the speeches ended, the ten top March
leaders conferred with the late President Kennedy, Chief Executive

of the nation. The confrontation there was with the No. 1 symbol of   8
government. The historic Selma-Montgomery march, though national
in its impact, was essentially for Negro voting rights on the local
level, and the marcher's chief antagonists were Sheriff James G. Clark
of Selma and Alabama's notorious Governor George C. Wallace.

Clark represented the power structure of his county, fighting
viciously to prevent Negroes there from participating in local government; while Wallace symbolized the state and Deep Southern regional power structures. From Washington to Bogalusa, La., the civil   9
rights movement has been probing for the sensitive pressure points at
which it must fight its battles against bigotry. But it must first know
where the seats of real power are and who occupies them.

What, first of all, is power? Bertrand Russell once defined power
as "the production of intended effects," giving power the quality of
a property which can be owned by an individual or a group.
"Power," wrote political scientist Harold D. Lasswell, "is participation in the making of decisions." The late English economist, Profes-   10
sor R.H. Tawney, a socialist by philosophy, said: "Power may be
defined as the capacity of an individual or group of individuals, to
modify the conduct of other individuals or groups in the manner
which he desires."

The structure of power in America is centered in three major
institutions, which by their centralized influence and the great consequences of the decisions which they make, shape great events and
determine developments. These are the economy, the political system, and the military establishment. In all of these areas executive
and administrative powers have increased in recent years to an awesome degree. The most powerful persons in the nation, therefore, are   11
those who control these institutions. If this premise is accepted, then
we must conclude that real power in the U.S. is concentrated in the
hands of a few thousand individuals, headed by a power elite of
political leaders and government officials, five-star generals and ad-
mirals, and the main owners and chief executives of the biggest industrial corporations.

Those who are members of the power structure blandly deny
that they are powerful, while, outside it, numerous economists, political scientists and self-styled radical intellectuals reject the notion
that such a group exists. But the U.S. power system is now clearly
discernible. What used to be called "the invisible government" is now   12
largely visible. A growing centralization of power in a narrowing
circle of politicans, industrialists and military leaders has endowed

the big decisions which they make with a greater significance than at any time in the history of man.

The core of America's power system is the highly concentrated group of men who own and manage big property. These are the corporate rich who include the chief executives of the top corporations. Who are the industrial overlords of the United States today? In the 1950s a comprehensive survey was made of the 900 top executives in U.S. industry culled from the nation's 250 largest industrial companies, 25 biggest railroads and 25 biggest utilities. Total yearly sales **13** for the 300 top companies examined were $122 billion. Officers included in the study were either chairmen, presidents, executive vice presidents or plain vice presidents. The characteristics of this powerful group of industry executives are the same today: white, college-trained, hired in their 20s, served their corporations for 30 years, age between 50 and 60, and annual salaries in the $70,000–$80,000 range.

In the East, where economic and political power in the U.S. is concentrated, a white-Anglo-Saxon-Protestant establishment holds **14** sway but its power and authority are diminishing and it is feeling the pressure to open its ranks to formerly excluded groups like the Jews.

Racial and religious prejudices are weakening the power of certain circles of the financial and industrial power structure and threatening their continued control over the public. In a remarkable book, *The Protestant Establishment: Aristocracy and Caste in America,* E. Digby Baltzell writes: " . . . in order for an upper class to maintain a continuity of power and authority, especially in an opportunitiarian and mobile society such as ours, its membership must, in the long **15** run, be representative of the composition of society as a whole." The present power structure of the U.S. is clearly not representative of the population. There are no non-whites on either the national cabinet,* the U.S. Joint Chiefs of Staff, or the executive bodies of the National Association of Manufacturers, the U.S. Chamber of Commerce, the American Bankers Association or the National Industrial Conference Board.

Indications are that if American society is going to survive on its present bases, its leadership structure will have to be reorganized by the admission of groups traditionally excluded from it. Its future, if **16** it has one, will rest on whether it can establish one valid principle of

---

*Robert C. Weaver was appointed Secretary to the recently created Department of Housing and Urban Development in January, 1966, the first Negro to hold a cabinet post.

discrimination: on the basis of accomplishment and qualification rather than on ethnic or racial considerations.

Until the election in 1960 of John Fitzgerald Kennedy to the presidency, the U.S. political leadership elite was confined to the white-Anglo-Saxon-Protestant caste. Kennedy's break-through symbolized an ethnic-religious reorientation of the establishment on the power level which has not yet taken in the Negro. Jews are still victims of the cast line in the establishment as Negroes are of the color line. Jews constitute an important and influential part of the leadership of American science, education, arts and business, but are generally excluded from the top circles of the power structure. An example: one in every seven graduates of the Harvard Business School is Jewish, but of the carefully selected trainees from business who return to Harvard for the Advanced Management Program only one in 200 is Jewish. [17]

At the top of the pyramid of the U.S. economy about 150 people earn a million dollars or more a year, another 400 or so receive between $500,000 and a million. Some 1,500 persons earn from $250,000 to $500,000. These are the propertied since the income of two-thirds of the people in the $100,000–$1,000,000 bracket is derived from dividends, capital gains, estates or trusts. The thrust of the civil rights movement to desegregate the national housing market has very grave implications for most of these upper-income Americans. [18]

High finance undergirds the power structure. A number of powerful oligarchies like the Rockefellers, Ford, General Motors, and the J.P. Morgan and DuPont interests have commanding positions. Ten years ago the Rockefeller family holdings were reported as $3,515 million, but the total assets of Rockefeller-controlled interests exceeded $61 billion. The DuPont family fortune in 1956 was estimated at $4,660 million in corporate assets, while the Mellon family interests totalled $3,769 million. All of the great American family fortunes, for better or worse, belong in the power structure picture. A handful of multimillionaire families, like the Rockefellers and Rosenwalds, have consistently given generous assistance to Negro education. [19]

Certain sections of big business have made substantial contributions to Negro advance through the United Negro College Fund. Contributions from industry to Negro education have reached unprecedented levels since the civil rights drive began. "I attribute it to the growing recognition by the leaders of government and industry that the Negro people in the United States must now be brought to the [20]

level of full and effective citizenship," explains Dr. Frederick D.
Patterson, president of the United Negro College Fund, which has
raised $90 million since its founding in 1944, more than 75 per cent
of which has come from business, industry and foundations.

Dispensing benefactions to the Negro is a tradition with a few
wealthy white families which pre-dates the Civil War. The Rockefellers are a notable example. During slavery one Rockefeller aided
fugitive slaves to escape via the legendary Underground Railroad.
Today, New York's Governor Nelson Rockefeller entertains Martin
Luther King Jr. as a private dinner guest at the State Mansion in
Albany, N.Y.; John D. Rockefeller III is the earnest chairman of the
national council of the United Negro College Fund; Rodman C.   21
Rockefeller, son of Nelson, is co-chairman of the Interracial Council
for Business Opportunity which seeks to encourage the growth of
small Negro businesses; Winthrop Rockefeller has long been an active
supporter of the National Urban League. But these are isolated examples of philanthropy and concerrn for human rights by individual
members of one of the most powerful dynasties in American life and
are by no means typical of their class.

"Many of the leaders of American business and industry now
recognize that the Negro has to receive the same education as other
American youth and has to have the same opportunities for employment and expression as other Americans, and that the failure to
provide this is a drag on the national economy and a source of
embarrassment to American leadership among the free peoples of the
world," concludes Dr. Patterson. A capital development fund drive
for $50 million launched by the United Negro College Fund in 1963
received large contributions from some of the leading units of the   22
corporate power structure. The Ford Foundation gave $18 million,
the Carnegie Corporation $2½ million, the Ford Motor Company
$500,000, the Kresge Foundation $500,000 and Standard Oil of N.J.
$500,000. Such efforts by corporate wealth to raise Negroes' educa-
tional level are small but represent a kind of trend toward undoing
the grievous damage done to the Negro by racial discrimination over
many generations. Nowadays when big business helps the Negro it is
not motivated necessarily by idealism but by self-interest.

The leaders of the National Urban League, the one Negro leadership organization which maintains steady contact with substantial
elements of the white power structure, have no illusions about why
U.S. businessmen and industrialists are slowly opening the doors of
economic opportunity to Negores. "The power structure," says
Whitney Young Jr., executive director of the League, "is no longer a   23

monolithic body of a few people who make the big decisions. Power is located in centers of influence. Power is in the labor movement as well as the civil rights movement. The major corporations of the country have belatedly but quite soundly decided that they must intervene in the civil rights struggle."

Within the last few years a small number of American corporations in the top bracket have authorized participation in the National Urban League's Commerce and Industry Council of 45 company executives, many of whom are included in the top 1,000 U.S. corporation officials belonging to the national economic power structure. "The leaders of industry are becoming more liberal and sensitive   24 about the racial crisis mainly out of enlightened self-interest," remarks Whitney Young Jr. "They know that they can't sell the U.S. free enterprise system to foreign dark-skinned peoples when black people in America don't get their fair share of the rewards of the system."

The men who control the power and wealth of the higher corporate world have realized that business cannot function effectively and profitably on racial tension, conflict and violence. Such conditions   25 are unhealthy for business. Racial boycotts of industrial concerns have greatly perturbed captains of industry.

The power structure in recent years has shown increasing anxiety that the wealthy state it operates might be threatened and damaged by such internal disorders as strikes, riots and racial outbreaks and protests. Beyond the fear of the destruction of its power, profits and   26 interests by domestic convulsions, the power system is now obsessed by a fear that their entire society might be swept away in a nuclear war.

As in the economy, a small but wilful band of powerful men, numbering no more than 75, occupies the command posts of the executive branch of the federal government where high policy is made and executive decisions settled. This top circle of the country's governing apparatus consists of the president, vice-president, the cabinet, and the heads of the main government agencies, departments and commissions. Except for three Negroes—Robert C. Weaver, direc-   27 tor of the Housing and Home Finance Agency, Carl Rowan, U.S.I.A. director, and Hobart Taylor, who is a special counsel with the President's executive staff—this hierarchy of government is a white club.* Few are professional politicans or have been trained in party politics.

---

*Robert C. Weaver appointed Secretary, Department of Housing and Urban Development, January, 1966; Carl Rowan, resigned U.S.I.A. directorship, 1965; Hobart Taylor appointed director, Import Export Bank, 1965.

The White House staff and the cabinet represent the pinnacle of political power in America, but there is within Congress a special power structure of key decision makers.

All of the members of Congress, both the House of Representatives and the Senate, must be considered in the national political power system to a degree because they contribute to the making of legislative decisions which have national and international consequences, but only two of the six Negro members of the House of Representatives, Congressmen Adam Clayton Powell and William   28
Dawson, possess meaningful power by virtue of being the chairmen of strategic congressional committees. Powell and Dawson, it should be noted, owe their membership in the power structure, not to the dominant white majority but to big-city constituencies which are practically all-Negro.

Since the 1880's the U.S. Senate has been an all-white body. No Negro has ever served in a federal cabinet, but if President Johnson decides to make Robert Weaver the first head of the proposed department of housing and urban development this lily-white tradition will have been broken. The cabinet is nominally the president's council of advisers, but its authority has declined in recent years. A powerful body, the seven member National Security Council now   29
wields much of the power formerly held by the cabinet. A strategic planning agency located at the very apex of the governmental structure, the NSC is really the country's top board of directors for the nation's security. The Council's authority and scope are vast, and embrace military strategy, nuclear policy, economic aid and some domestic questions. The President relies on its membership for advice on crucial issues.

Enormous power to advise, plan and manage the nation's defenses and its offensive capabilities reside in the U.S. Joint Chiefs of Staff, a five-man council of military advisers to the President, the   30
National Security Council and the secretary of defense. The Joint Chiefs of Staff do not make national policy but plan for war.

Labor is a definite factor in the American structure because it controls the organization of most of the national labor market, because its union treasuries contain hundreds of millions of dollars and because the Negro revolution has been forced to confront it squarely as a major institution responsible for the exclusion of black workers from skilled trades. Before the rise of the CIO in the 30s, U.S. labor presented the Negro with an agonizing dilemma: whether to oppose it along with the rest of the power structure, or join forces with it and work for racial reforms from inside. "There are really two power   31 structures, one corporate and the other labor," observes A. Philip Randolph, sole Negro member of the A.F.L.-C.I.O. executive council and now the elder statesman of the Negro rights movement. "The Negro has to decide which of these forces he wants to ally himself with. The labor power structure offers the greatest opportunity for economic advancement. First, labor is not free, and the Negro is not free. There is, therefore, a natural alliance between labor and the Negro. Neither labor nor the Negro has yet recognized this natural affinity."

Randolph notes that corporate power in the U.S. is white and will probably remain so. "I don't see any change coming soon in the racial composition of the power structure," he says pessimistically. "A few Negroes have been admitted to lower managerial positions in   32 the structure, but real power is held by the whites. The power structure is all white because Negroes have never possessed investment capital in any quantity to enter it."

The Negro revolt moves into its next phase armed with the weapons of the strongest, most sweeping civil rights laws ever passed in history. A decisive period of implementation of this legislation has now opened up. To achieve their constitutional and human rights, Negroes will have to employ many tools and techniques. To complete the unfinished revolution, Negores will make the transition from protest to planning for freedom, from propaganda to prepara-   33 tion to use widening opportunities. In the mid-1960s, the Negro revolt has learned a great deal about what the power structure is and who comprise it. The inclusion of seven Negroes in the top 5,000 of the higher circles is no measure of a pattern of integration but merely underlines the grim reality that the nation's power structure is 99.998 per cent white.

QUESTIONS AND PROBLEMS

1. The author defines "power structure" by first giving a definition of *power* and then the meaning of *structure* (pars. 10-11).
    a. What differences do you find in the two definitions?
    b. What are the three major institutions within the structure?
    c. Is any important institution omitted? Defend your answer.
2. What is the tone of the essay? When is that tone first established?
3. In par. 4 the author writes, "Every important revolution in history has been conducted against an identifiable and visible enemy—a class or a nation—from which it sought either basic reforms, partial surrender of power, or total abdication." Cite examples of some of these revolutions and explain.
4. What points of similarity and dissimilarity can you find between the American Revolution (the War of Independence) and the Negro protest movement?

5. This essay was written in 1965. Outline the progress of the Negro protest movement from that date to the present.
6. The author makes a distinction (par. 1) between the position of "the more moderate Negro leaders" and "the younger Negro militants." Does the author belong to one or the other group? Defend your answer.
7. Discuss the relationship of other minority groups to the white power structure—the Jews, for example, or the American Indians. Would any of Morrison's arguments apply to such groups?
8. Comment on the fact that Morrison cites so many monetary figures in his essay.
9. What relationship does the author establish between the men in high finance and the wealthy who dispense benefactions to the Negro?
10. In his conclusion, Morrison spells out the "next phase" of the Negro revolt. What steps does he say must be taken? Which have already been taken or started?

SUGGESTIONS FOR WRITING

1. Write an essay on the progress of the Negro revolt from 1965 to the present day.
2. Write an argument supporting the need of "revolution" on the part of some other minority group, as for example the American Indian, or some economically disadvantaged group, as the migratory workers.
3. Defend or oppose the need of radical revolution in a changing society.
4. Write an essay in definition entitled "The True Liberal."
5. Write an argumentative essay on the power of the military establishment in the United States.
6. Write a research paper on one of the great American educational and/or charitable foundations.
7. Write an essay in which you attempt to assess the position of the Negro in American society fifty years from now.
8. Write an essay in definition of one of the following:
    a. The Un-Christian Christian
    b. The Philosophy of "If"
    c. The Typical Suburban Family
    d. The College Student.

SUGGESTIONS FOR FURTHER READING

See list under "Blood Lust," pp. 183-184.

TO CLASSIFY
AND ANALYZE

Classification enables us to organize the various bits of knowledge we acquire throughout life, to relate the pieces to one another in meaningful ways. To make such relationships we must have a basis of classification, either one or several characteristics common to all the members of a given group. To determine the common denominator or denominators we use the devices of comparison and contrast and of analysis, for only after we have examined thoroughly the objects, events, or ideas to be classified can we determine the members of any one group. Chaos results if we do not use careful examination as the basis of classification. To classify adequately is to analyze with care.

The most readily available example of classification is that used by the scientist. And it is the most exact. The botanist, for example, examines in minute detail the likenesses and differences of plants, noting such qualities as root system, stem formation, leaf shape, and characteristics of the reproductive system. The similarities so found become the basis for the classes into which the plants are put. After large classes have been established, the scientist forms the various subclasses, ever narrowing the classifications. Without such exactness the plant world would be for us a meaningless jumble.

More often than not the nonscientist makes use of a less exacting kind of classification, one which is sometimes called loose or literary classification. On the basis of an examination we may classify students as superior, satisfactory, or failures. We may classify man's political leanings as left-wing, right-wing, or dead center. We classify the various subjects offered in college by departments and sometimes add subclasses—English: English Literature, English Composition; Philosophy and Religion: Philosophy, Religion. Imagine the chaos if all the courses offered in a college were merely listed at random in the college catalogue—or even if they were listed alphabetically by title. Classification, it is clear, brings order out of chaos.

For all classification there must be a governing principle. That principle may be determined by shape, by size, by color, by time, by place, by degree of education, by political persuasion, by moral standards, by any of a countless number of characteristics. In the kind of loose classification most of us use in our daily lives there need be no attempt at all-inclusiveness. One writer may classify the various kinds of students as four types; another writer may have determined upon six, or only three. This determination is a reflection of his analysis of the subject. It is also affected by the degree of persuasion he brings to the subject. In other words, the writer's point of view determines the classification. But one basic rule holds for all classification: the classes must be mutually exclusive; they must not overlap. If a classification were made of roots, stems, leaves, buds, flowers, and roses, we have inexact classification, as two of the categories overlap. If a classification is made up of Republican, conservative, radical, Democrat, and Sociolist, we find the same fault of overlapping categories. But college students may be classified as freshmen, sophomores, juniors, and seniors; technical and exact limits are set by the schools for each of these classes. On the other hand, freshmen, sophomores, juniors, seniors, men, and women would not be an acceptable classification, as the last two items in the classification result from a different controlling principle than the first four. The writer who uses the device of classification must be sure of his controlling principle, must adhere to it, and must have mutually exclusive elements in that classification. This is why teachers of writing often insist that the student begin with an outline, for an outline quickly reveals faults in classification.

Analysis implies the separation of a subject or of a unit of meaning into its component parts. A writer's preliminary outline of an essay is both a classification and a schematic presentation of his analysis of his subject. The table of contents of a book may likewise be an analysis—but only a partial one—of its subject, a list of the component parts of the whole. And yet neither is a full analysis until the author's controlling purpose is made clear. He must have a valid principle or basis of division, and the divisions must be consistent with this basis. The author's purpose governs the kind of analysis he makes.

The writer who classifies and analyzes must, then, make sure that the divisions of his subject are mutually exclusive, that they do not overlap, and that their total equals the original subject. He may classify and analyze novels according to the principle of subject matter. He may classify and analyze men according to background, education, and profession. He may analyze matter according to solids, liquids, and gases. But he may not logically analyze novels according to romantic subjects, women writers, stories of violence, novels of social consciousness, and the well-paid writer. He would be inconsistent if he classified and analyzed the types of men as Caucasian, Mongolian, anthropologists, and college graduates, for he would be shifting from one principle of analysis to another. Nor would the chemist analyze matter as solids, liquids, gases, and compounds.

One writer's analysis will not necessarily agree with that of another. Think of an analysis of the conditions which create a high incidence of crime in thickly populated urban centers. An analysis by a resident of such an area, a man born and raised in a ghetto, is likely to be quite different from that of an economically advantaged man who merely passes through the ghetto on his way to his office. And of the hundreds of books which have been written to teach students how to be better writers there is wide variance in method of meeting the problem. Analysis frequently becomes, then, a matter of argument; a writer's purpose is often to persuade the reader that his is the best analysis.

In reading the following essays, ask yourself if the principle of division is clear and if the divisions themselves are mutually exclusive. Also determine if the total of the divisions is the same as the professed topic. Finally, ask yourself if the method of division is a valid one, if it clarifies the subject. For the latter is, after all, the reason for a writer's using classification and analysis as his method of presenting his subject.

OUR TEN CONTRIBUTIONS TO CIVILIZATION
Arthur M. Schlesinger

Since the United States has now become the leader of the free
world, our allies are asking, and we ourselves should be asking, what
this portends for the future of civilization. The key to the answer, I   1
suggest, lies in what I venture to call America's seminal contributions
of the past. In my view there have been at least ten.

The Right of Revolution

First and foremost stands the concept of the inherent and universal right of revolution proclaimed in the Declaration of Independence: the doctrine that "all men are created equal" possessing "unalienable rights" to "life, liberty, and the pursuit of happiness," with
the corollary that governments derive "their just powers from the
consent of the governed" and that therefore the people have the
right to supplant a government "destructive of these ends" with one   2
which they believe "most likely to effect their safety and happiness."
True, the history of England provided precedents for the men of
1776, and the Age of Enlightenment supplied intellectual support;
but the flaming pronouncement, followed by its vindication on the
battlefield, made the doctrine ever afterward an irrepressible agency
in "the course of human events."

Europe was the first to respond. In 1789 occurred the great
French Revolution, the forerunner of two later ones of the French
people during the nineteenth century; and neighboring countries
were not slow to follow. A series of revolts, centering in 1830 and   3
1848, drove the Turks from Greece, overturned or strove to overturn
illiberal governments through most of the rest of the Continent, and
hastened political reforms in other lands to forestall popular upheavals.

These convulsions all had their internal causes, but in every instance the leaders derived inspiration from America's achievement of
popular rule as well as from its freely expressed interest in their
similar aspirations. Presidents, Congresses, and civic gatherings ap-
plauded the uprisings, and American volunteers actually fought in
the Greek war of liberation. After Russia helped Austria to suppress
the Hungarian rebellion, a United States warship late in 1851
brought the Magyar patriot Kossuth to this country, where he received the honors of an American hero. The citizens of Springfield,
Illinois, for example, rallied to his cause in words which have a fresh   4

and poignant significance for us today. Affirming "the right of any people . . . to throw off . . . their existing form of government, and to establish such other in its stead as they may choose," they condemned the "interference of Russia in the Hungarian struggle" as "illegal and unwarrantable" and asserted that "to have resisted Russia . . . would have been no violation of our own cherished principles . . . but, on the contrary, would be ever meritorious, in us, or any independent nation." Abraham Lincoln, then in private life, was one of the authors of the resolutions.

The doctrine of revolution, however, had still broader implications. The European eruptions in most instances sought merely to replace domestic regimes; the American revolt, to cast off a distant yoke. It was the first of the great colonial insurrections, an example all the more potent because Washington's ill-trained soldiers defeated the mightiest nation in the world. The Spanish dependencies to the 5
south took heed and early in the nineteenth century won their freedom. Then, oddly enough, came a setback to the trend as a large part of Asia and Africa and many islands of the Pacific fell under the sway of Old World powers. And after a time even the United States, forgetful of its own once colonial status, followed suit.

But in the twentieth century the two world wars radically changed the situation, recalling the United States to its historic heritage, crippling the military strength of the European imperialist countries, and awakening subject peoples everywhere to their right of self-determination. America led the way by relinquishing its Carib- 6
bean protectorates and granting independence to the Philippines, and soon the Old World governments fell into line, some voluntarily to anticipate the inevitable, as in the case of England, and others because they were unable to quell native rebellions, as in the cases of France and Holland.

Although more than a century and a half has elapsed since America proclaimed the right of revolution, these events of our own day evidence its continuing vitality. Lest I be accused of claiming too much for a precedent so far in the past, consider the words of President Sukarno of Indonesia three and a half years ago in his address of 7
welcome to the Bandung Conference. This Asian-African gathering, the first of its kind in history, brought together delegates from twenty-nine nations, most of them newly free. "The battle against colonialism," Sukarno declared,

> has been a long one, and do you know that today is a famous anniversary in that battle? On the eighteenth day of April, one thousand seven hundred and seventy-five, just one hudnred and eighty years ago, Paul

Revere rode at midnight through the New England countryside, warning of the approach of British troops and of the opening of the American War of Independence, the first successful anticolonial war in history. About this midnight ride the poet Longfellow wrote:

> A cry of defiance and not of fear,
> A voice in the darkness, a knock at the door,
> And a word that shall echo for evermore. . . .

Yes [he concluded], it shall echo for evermore . . . until we can survey this our own world, and can say that colonialism is dead.

The Principle of Federalism

Because of the difficulties experienced under the Articles of Confederation, the Constitution of 1787 established a partnership of self-governing commonwealths with an overall elective government powerful enough to protect and promote their joint concerns and—what was not less important—with a provision for admitting later states on a plane of full equality. This was something new in history; Tocqueville called it "a great discovery in modern political science," for no other people had ever devised a federal structure over so large an area or with a central government chosen by popular vote or on such generous terms for future members. It offered mankind a key to the age-old problem of reconciling legitimate local interests with the general good.

Mexico, Argentina, and other Latin American countries adopted variants of the plan, and so did Germany and Austria-Hungary. Britain applied it to two of its largest colonies, Canada and Australia, and in the twentieth century recast most of its empire into a Commonwealth of Nations on the same basis. More dramatically, the principle caused men to conceive of some sort of federation of the world, first in the League of Nations and then in the United Nations, both sponsored by American Presidents; and in the not too distant future it promises to bring about a United States of Western Europe.

The Consent of the Governed

Neither the doctrine of revolution nor the principle of federalism necessarily ensured that the government so established would rest on the consent of the governed. This was an entirely different matter, as the history of Latin American dictatorships as well as that of other nations proves. But, as we have seen, it was a basic tenet of the founders of the United States and may well be regarded as America's third contribution to humanity.

The framers of the Constitution spurned European tradition by rejecting a monarchy, a nobility, or a hereditary legislative chamber, placing their trust in a government of the people, by the people, and for the people, one which should rule by counting heads instead of breaking them. Starting with a somewhat limited number of voters but in better proportion than in any other country, the suffrage was broadened generation by generation until it came to include all adults of both sexes; and at every point America set the pace for the Old World. The underlying philosophy was not that the common man is all-wise, but only that he can govern himself better than anyone else can do it for him.

11

The Status of Women

Women played a man's part as well as a woman's in taming the wilderness, and until very recently, moreover, they were fewer in number than the opposite sex and hence commanded a high scarcity value. From early times foreign observers marveled at the unusual educational opportunities open to them, their immunity from molestation when traveling alone, their freedom to go out of the home to agitate for temperance, antislavery, and other reforms. "From the captain of a western steamboat to the roughest miner in California," wrote one visitor, "from north, south, east, and west, we hear but one voice. Women are to be protected, respected, supported, and petted."

12

The organized feminist movement arose earlier in the United States than in any other nation not because American women enjoyed so few privileges but because they had so many that they demanded more—in short, all those exercised by their husbands and brothers, including that of suffrage. The famous women's rights convention at Seneca Falls, New York, in 1848, the first in the history of the world, turned the Declaration of Independence to account by proclaiming "all men and women are created equal" with the same unalienable rights to "life, liberty, and the pursuit of happiness." It took the women many years to achieve that goal, but in time they succeeded, and every victory spurred their sisters in other lands to similar endeavors.

13

The Melting Pot

A fifth contribution of the United States has been the fusing of many different nationalities in a single society. America has been in the best sense of the term a melting pot, every ingredient adding its

particular element of strength. The constant infusion of new blood
has enriched our cultural life, speeded our material growth, and pro-   14
duced some of our ablest statesmen. Over 17 million immigrants
arrived in the single period from the Civil War to World War I—more
than America's total population in 1840—and today English and
Scottish blood, the principal strain in colonial times, constitutes considerably less than half the whole.

Many other peoples, it is true, are also of mixed origin; but the
American achievement stands alone in the scale, thoroughness, and
rapidity of the process and, above all, in the fact that it has been the
outcome not of forcible incorporation but of peaceful absorption.
Significantly, the very nationalities which had habitually warred with   15
one another in the Old World have lived together in harmony in the
New. America has demonstrated for everyone with eyes to see that
those things which unite peoples are greater than those which divide
them, that war is not the inevitable fate of mankind.

Our most tragic failure has involved our Negro citizens, now a
tenth of our number. Taken forcibly from Africa, trammeled in slavery for two and a half centuries, denied their constitutional rights
after emancipation in the states where most of them lived, this ill-
used race has been a standing reproach to our professions of democracy and has enabled Communist spokesmen as well as other foreign
critics to impugn the very principle of human equality on which the   16
republic was founded. Nevertheless, even these injured people have
not been unwilling Americans, as the Irish before winning their freedom were unwilling Britons; they have only been unwilling to be
halfway Americans or second-class citizens. Hence they have unhesi-
tatingly rejected the blandishments of Soviet propaganda. Fortunately they can now at long last look forward to the final rectification of
the wrongs they have so patiently endured.

Freedom of Worship

The recognition that the relations between man and his Creator
are a private affair into which government must not intrude contra-
vened the age-long European practice of uniting church and state and
imposing harsh restrictions on dissenters. The Amercan system was a
legacy of colonial times, when the theological motive for settlement
was intesnse and the multiplicity of denominations suggested the
need for mutual forbearance. Rhode Island, Maryland, and Pennsyl-   17
vania in the persons of Roger Williams, Lord Baltimore, and William
Penn set the pattern to which the Bill of Rights of the federal Constitution gave nationwide sanction. Religion by choice was the natural

counterpart of government by consent, and, contrary to Old World belief, the separation of church and state did not in fact weaken either but strengthened both.

The Public School

The principle of government by consent made it imperative that the people be literate and well informed if they were to vote intelligently. To ensure this essential condition, statesmen agreed that society must at its own initiative and expense supply the means of 18 schooling. This, too, broke drastically with the Old World concept that education should be a privately financed undertaking for the upper classes, the rank and file supposedly having little need for any in what was deemed to be their permanently inferior station.

New England inaugurated the practice in colonial days; then, with the swift extension of the franchise during the first half of the nineteenth century, it was adopted throughout the North and later in the South. Free public education thus became the article of American faith it has continued to be ever since. From the United States 19 the plan spread in modified form around the world. Japan, for example, in 1872 made it the cornerstone of its program of modernization. Probably America has conferred no greater boon on mankind, for popular education is the seedbed of virtually all other human aspirations.

Voluntary Giving

Foreigners have always criticized the American for his pursuit of the almighty dollar, but have seldom gone on to note that he has in unparalleled degree returned the fruits of his labors to society. If he has been hardheaded about making money, he has, so to speak, been softhearted about spending it. This constitutes the American version 20 of the Old World concept of *noblesse oblige* carried to a point the Old World has never approached. Even long before Carnegie and Rockefeller amassed their colossal fortunes, men and women of modest means gave freely to schools, churches, foreign missions, colleges, hospitals, charities, and other projects for social betterment.

In the twentieth century this same concern has led men of wealth to set up some four thousand philanthropic foundations staffed with experts to administer the funds with maximum usefulness and for nearly every conceivable object of human benefit. Their programs, exceeding all earlier bounds, include the control of epidemic diseases 21 and far-reaching researches in the natural and social sciences. Even so, the lion's share of the more than 6.5 billion dollars devoted to altruistic purposes last year still derived from other than foundation sources.

And, increasingly, Americans have extended their beneficence to foreign peoples. Over a century ago popular subscriptions helped relieve Irish suffering during the terrible potato famines of the 1840s and later aided with equal generosity the victims of natural catastrophes in other lands. And, besides the work of the Red Cross in peace and war, the great foundations have in our own day improved health, educational, and agricultural conditions in many countries. In the same tradition the private organization known as CARE has, since   22 World War II, channeled gifts of food, clothing, medicine, and the like to the needy of Europe, Asia, Africa, and Latin America. Thanks to this ingrained trait of the national character, the government found it easy to mobilize our people behind the Marshall Plan, a costly tax-supported program for repairing the war-stricken economies of Western Europe. Though these official undertakings were in part designed to halt the spread of Communism, they arose from deeper springs of human compassion and have no parallel in history.

Technology

Mechanical ingenuity, or what today is called technological knowhow, contrary to common belief is by no means a late development. From the mid-eighteenth century on, the people, confronted with a chronic shortage of labor and the problems arising from formidable distances and poor communications, devised means to overcome these handicaps as well as to ameliorate other conditions of life. The record is truly remarkable. Before the end of the nineteenth   23 century Benjamin Franklin, Eli Whitney, and their successors produced such epochal inventions as the lightning rod, the cotton gin, the steamboat, the metal plow, the harvester, vulcanized rubber, the sewing machine, the telegraph, the telephone, and the electric light, among others. In still other instances they greatly improved on what had come to them from abroad.

The upshot was not only to transform American life but that of peoples everywhere. President Truman therefore was not occupying wholly new ground when in 1949 he proposed his Point Four Program to make "the benefits of our scientific advances and industrial progress available for the improvement and growth of underdeveloped areas" and thus "help them realize their aspirations for a better life." Under this program the United States has sent experts in indus-   24 try, engineering, and agriculture to many lands; built roads and bridges in Iran, irrigation works in India, and fertilizer plants in Korea; and endeavored in countless other ways to remove the obstacles that have barred less enterprising countries from the advantages of modern civilization. Just as the government has made our philanthropic impulse a vital instrument of foreign policy, so also it has done with our technological skill.

Evolutionary Progress

The United States is often considered a young nation, but in fact it is next to the oldest continuous government in the world. The reason is that the spirit of its people has always been empirical and pragmatic, dedicated to equalitarian ends but willing to realize them by flexible means. In the European sense of the term, America's 25 major political parties are not parties at all, because they do not divide over basic ideologies. Neither wishes to overturn or replace the existing political and economic order; they merely desire to alter it at slower or faster rates of speed.

One of our proudest achievements has been the creation of a system of controlled capitalism that yeilds the highest living standards on earth and has made possible a society as nearly classless as man has ever known. The profit system as it has developed in America is a multiprofit system, sharing its benefits with all segments of society: capital, labor, and the consuming masses. Yet even this was 26 not due to a preconceived blueprint; it too was the result of trial and error. Unprincipled businessmen had first to be brought to heel by government restraints and the growing power of organized labor before they came to learn that they must serve the general good in pursuing their selfish interests. Now labor is feeling the restraint.

Even our creed of democracy is no fixed and immutable dogma. Thus the statesmen of the early republic, though they were stalwart champions of private enterprise, chose to make the post office a government monopoly and to confide the schools to public ownership. Since then, by fits and starts, and most recently under the New Deal, the United States has taken on many of the characteristics of a 27 welfare state. This has occurred, however, not under the banner of socialism or of any other "ism," but simply because the Americans hold with Lincoln that "the legitimate object of government is to do for a community of people whatever they need to have done but cannot do at all, or cannot do so well for themselves, in their separate and individual capacities."

Viewed as a whole, the contributions of America to civilization will be seen to have been for the most part in the nature of methods or proccesses. They have aimed to release men from political and religious disabilities, from ignorance and poverty, from backbreaking toil. They have struck at the fetters which from time immemorial the Old World had fastened on human beings. They have opened the   28 doors of opportunity for the many while still assuring them to the few, in the belief that everyone should have an equal chance to be as unequal as he can without denying the same right to others. In brief, they have sought to substitute fluidity for rigid class distinctions as the vital principle of social well-being. And the consequence has been a general leveling of society upward instead of downward.

But what of the future? I recall what a thoughtful Hollander said to me a few years after World War II. Observing that Europe's age of greatness was now over and that Americans must henceforth take the lead in the advancement of civilization, he wondered whether they would be equal to the task. Plainly he had grave doubts, for like most foreigners he thought of us as having been only beneficiaries of the bounty of the Old World without making any creative returns in   29 kind. But for an American historian the answer is clear. The true measure of our past contributions lies in the very fact that they have become so woven into the life of mankind that my Dutch friend was unaware of them. If we can only preserve our free institutions and our faith in the untrammeled human spirit, we shall triumphantly meet the challenge now before us.

QUESTIONS AND PROBLEMS

1. Why does Schlesinger begin his list of ten contributions with "The Right of Revolution"?
2. Are the items in his list given according to historical sequence or order of importance? If you were to employ the latter classification, would the items be given in a different order? Explain.
3. Schlesinger says (par. 6) that the United States has been recalled to its historical heritage, which includes "awakening subject peoples everywhere to their right of self-determination." Why then can not our government—and thus presumably most of our citizens—support the change in government in Cuba, for example? Can this complex problem be explained by another of the "contributions"? Which one?
4. Carlyle once said that democracy means "despair of finding any Heroes to govern you, and contented putting up with the want of them." Ernst Jonson has said, "Democracy means that the opinions of a majority, no matter how arrived at, must of necessity be just and wise; that if enough people believe a thing to be true it must be true." Contrast these statements with Schlesinger's, in the section entitled "The Consent of the Governed," on the philosophy which underlies universal suffrage.

5. Do you agree with the reason Schlesinger gives for the fact that organized feminism arose earlier in the United States than in any other nation (par. 13)? Are there other possible reasons?
6. If, as is undoubtedly true, voluntary giving is one of our great contributions to civilization, how does one explain the "Yankee Go Home!" attitude, particularly in some South American and Asian countries, in light of our heavy contributions to the peoples and governments of those areas?
7. Schlesinger stresses the strengths of popular education (par. 19). Are there weaknesses which might be cited in popular education in the United States today? If so, what are they?
8. Discuss possible drawbacks to the technological revolution which America has fostered (pars. 23-24). Has progress in this area brought unalloyed good?
9. Not all nations have accepted "One of our proudest achievements . . . a system of controlled capitalism . . . " (par. 26). Why?
10. Check over the list of ten contributions. Would you add an eleventh, or even a twelfth? What would they be?

SUGGESTIONS FOR WRITING

1. Schlesinger says (pars. 16), "our Negro citizens . . . can now at long last look forward to the final rectification of the wrongs they have so patiently endured." This essay was written in 1959. Write a report on the positive steps which have been taken since that time.
2. Make a study of a leading American philanthropist and his contributions to civilization.
3. The tax-exempt status of charitable, educational, and religious foundations has often been questioned. Write an essay on the limits to which a foundation may go to maintain that status.
4. Determine the five major contributions of your own college or university to American life.
5. Write a paper on a revolution which the United States, which contributed "first and foremost" the right of revolution, has not supported. Analyze the reasons why support was not forthcoming.
6. Using the contribution of "The Consent of the Governed" as a basis, take either the positive or the negative point of view on the right of college students to govern themselves.
7. Should college students determine their own curriculum, select their own faculty? Discuss both the pros and the cons of this issue.
8. Some Americans consider all public ownership and all social legislation to be socialism; others hold with the view of Abraham Lincoln as quoted in par. 27. Defend one position or the other.
9. Write an essay on "Our Eleventh Contribution to Civilization."

SUGGESTIONS FOR FURTHER READING

Richard M. Abrams and L.W. Levine, *The Shaping of Twentieth Century America* (Little, Brown)
Jacques Barzun, *God's Country and Mine* (Vintage)
Charles A. Beard and Mary R. Beard, *Beards' New Basic History of the United States*, rev. ed. (Doubleday)
Bernard Iddings Bell, *Crowd Culture* (Regnery)

Theodore C. Blegen, ed., *Land of Their Choice: The Immigrants Write Home* (Univ. of Minnesota)

James Bryce, *Reflections on American Institutions* (Fawcett)

Edward McNall Burns, *The American Idea of Mission* (Rutgers)

Jules Davids, *America and the World of Our Time*, rev. ed. (Random House)

Henry M. Pachter, *Collision Course: The Cuban Missile Crisis and Coexistence* (Praeger)

Roger Shinn, ed., *Search for Identity: Essays on the American Character* (Harper)

Alexis de Tocqueville, *Democracy in America* (various publishers)

Arnold J. Toynbee, *America and the World Revolution* (Oxford)

THE BLOOD LUST

Eldridge Cleaver

The boxing ring is the ultimate focus of masculinity in America, the two-fisted testing ground of manhood, and the heavyweight champion, as a symbol, is the real Mr. America. In a culture that secretly subscribes to the piratical ethic of "every man for himself"—the social Darwinism of "survival of the fittest" being far from dead, manifesting itself in our ratrace political system of competing parties, in our dog-eat-dog economic system of profit and loss, and in our adversary system of justice wherein truth is secondary to the skill and connections of the advocate—the logical culmination of this ethic, on a person-to-person level, is that the weak are seen as the natural and just prey of the strong. But since this dark principle violates our democratic ideals and professions, we force it underground, out of a perverse national modesty that reveals us as a nation of peep freaks who prefer the bekini to the naked body, the white lie to the black truth, Hollywood smiles and canned laughter to a soulful Bronx cheer. The heretical mailed fist of American reality rises to the surface in the velvet glove of our every institutionalized endeavor, so that each year we, as a nation, grind through various cycles of attrition, symbolically quenching the insatiable appetite of the *de facto* jungle law underlying our culture, loudly and unabashedly proclaiming to the world that "competition" is the law of life, getting confused, embarrassed, and angry if someone retorts: "Competition is the Law of the Jungle and Cooperation is the Law of Civilization." 1

Our mass spectator sports are geared to disguise, while affording expression to, the acting out in elaborate pageantry of the myth of the fittest in the process of surviving. From the Little League to the major leagues, through the orgiastic climax of the World Series; from high school football teams, through the college teams, to the grand finale of the annual bowl washouts; interspersed with the subcycles of basketball, track, and field meets—all of our mass spectator sports give play to the basic cultural ethic, harnessed and sublimated into national-communal pagan rituals. 2

But there is an aspect of the crystal of our nature that eschews the harness, scorns sublimation, and demands to be seen in its raw nakedness, crying out to us for the sight and smell of blood. The vehemence with which we deny this obvious fact of our nature is matched only by our Victorian hysteria on the subject of sex. Yet, we deny it in vain. Whether we quench our thirst from the sight of a

bleeding Jesus on the Cross, from the ritualized sacrifice in the elevation of the Host and the consecration of the Blood of the Son, or
from bullfighting, cockfighting, dogfighting, wrestling, or boxing,   3
spiced with our Occidental memory and heritage of the gladiators of
Rome and the mass spectator sport of the time of feeding Christians
and other enemies of society in the lions in the Coliseum—whatever
the mask assumed by the impulse, the persistent beat of the drum
over the years intones the chant: Though Dracula and Vampira must
flee the scene with the rising of the sun and the coming of the light,
night has its fixed hour and darkness must fall. And all the lightbulbs
ever fashioned, and all the power plants generating electricity, have
absolutely no effect on the primeval spinning of the earth in its orbit.

In America, we give maximum expression to our blood lust in the
mass spectator sport of boxing. Some of us are Roman enough to
admit our love and need of the sport. Others pretend to look the
other way. But when a heavyweight championship fight rolls around,   4
the nation takes a moral holiday and we are all tuned in—some of us
peeping out of the corner of our eye at the square jungle and the
animal test of brute power unfolding there.

Every institution in America is tainted by the mystique of race,
and the question of masculinity is confused by the presence of both
a "white" man and a "black" man here. One was the master and the
other was the slave until a moment ago when they both were declared to be equal "men"; which leaves American men literally without a unitary, nationally viable self-image. Whatever dim vision of
masculinity they have is a rough-and-ready, savage mishmash of violence and sexuality, a dichotomized exercise and worship of physical
force/submission to and fear of physical force—which is only one
aspect of the broken-down relationship between men and women in   5
America. This is an era when the models of manhood and woman-
hood have been blasted to dust by social upheaval, as the most
alienated males and females at the bottom of society move out of
"their places" and bid for their right to be "man" and "woman" on
an equal basis with the former masters and mistresses. These, in turn,
are no longer seen by themselves and others as supermen and super-
women, but only as men and women like all other. And in this
period of social change and sexual confusion, boxing, and the heavyweight championship in particular, serves as the ultimate test of masculinity, based on the perfection of the body and its use.

QUESTIONS AND PROBLEMS

1. Explain the meaning of "social Darwinism" (par. 1).
2. Cleaver uses powerful adjectives to color the meaning of many of the terms he uses, as "*ratrace* political system" (par. 1).
   a. Find several other examples in the essay.
   b. What is the effect of these highly limiting or "definition" adjectives on you as a reader?
   c. Cleaver is a shrewd, not a careless, writer. Yet obviously many readers will not agree with his use of the adjectives he has selected. Then why does he use them?
3. Cleaver uses standard descriptive terms also, as "white lie" in par. 1. Others are calculated to shock the reader to awareness (just as Coleridge in *The Rime of the Ancient Mariner* shocks us by qualifying the word *white* by writing, "white as leprosy"). Which qualifying adjective in the opening paragraph produces this shock? What is its meaning?
4. Why are our mass spectator sports "geared to disguise . . . the acting out in elabroate pageantry of the myth of the fittest" (par. 2)? Does Cleaver prove this point?
5. What is meant by "our Victorian hysteria on the subject of sex" (par. 3)?
6. Why does a heavyweight championship fight occasion a national "moral holiday" (par. 4)?
7. How would you state the theme of this essay?
8. Cleaver does not here explain a process but an attitude. Does he do so effectively? Is a deeper purpose hidden in this explanation?

SUGGESTIONS FOR WRITING

1. Write an essay on the psychology of the spectator.
2. Make a study of the social conditions of one black American family in your community.
3. Write an explanation of why some Negro leaders favor separation of blacks and whites. If possible, use a local campus situation.
4. Interview five black American students on your campus. Explain their positions on leading campus issues.
5. Write an essay on "blood lust" in college football.

SUGGESTIONS FOR FURTHER READING

James Baldwin, *Nobody Knows My Name* (Dial); *The Fire Next Time* (Dial)
Francis L. Broderick and August Meier, *Negro Protest Thought in the Twentieth Century* (Bobbs-Merrill)
Claude Brown, *Manchild in the Promised Land* (Macmillan)
Eldridge Cleaver, *Soul on Ice* (McGraw-Hill)
W.E.B. DuBois, *Souls of Black Folk* (Fawcett)
The Editors of *Ebony*, *The White Problem in America* (Johnson Publishing Co.)
Nat Hentoff, *The New Equality* (Viking)
Charles S. Johnson and others, *Into the Main Stream* (Univ. of North Carolina)

James W. Johnson, *Autobiography of an Ex-Coloured Man* (Knopf)
LeRoi Jones, *Home: Social Essays* (William Morrow)
Martin Luther King, Jr., *Why We Can't Wait* (Harper)
Saunders Redding, *Lonesome Road: The Story of the Negro in America*
    (Doubleday)
Charles E. Silberman, *Crisis in Black and White* (Random House)
Whitney M. Young, *To Be Equal* (McGraw-Hill)

WHY MEN FALL IN LOVE
George Wiswell

Consider, for a moment, the plight of the man on the other side of the room. Until this moon-smitten moment he was, as far as the world could see, a free, stalwart male, capable of functioning rationally in his business and personal life, outwardly content and, perhaps, with a weather eye out for casual companionship, accustomed to accepting what windfalls blew his way. Or maybe he thought he was happily married.   1

Now, abruptly, he sees a girl. *The* girl. He may have seen her before. Not necessarily. In either case, the symptoms of humanity's oldest malady begin popping out over him like a pox. He dissolves into a stupor of manic ecstasy. In one moment he has symphonic dreams of the music he could make with this woman; in the next he is roweling himself with doubts as to whether or not she feels anything for him. He hangs around aching to have her look at him or say something that will make his day worthwhile, yet in terror that the glance or word might ruin it. In between draughty, sentimental sighs, he is wont to behold himself as the luckiest of men, not seeming to care or realize that in the throes of this euphoria, which may last a few hours, days, or possibly years, his judgment is reduced to jelly and his liberty to slavery.   2

There's nothing organically wrong. He's just in love, or, as Shaw put it, overestimating the difference between one woman and another.   3

How, then, did he get that way?   4

For answers we went to those who ought to know (women), those who might remember (men), those who think they know (authors), and those who are still trying to find out (psychiatrists and psychologists).   5

The women in general placed themselves in one of two convenient categories: those who wish they knew and those who are sure. The latter have an unquenchable suspicion that the quickest way to a man's heart is through his hormones, that beauty *in toto* or beauty in particular—breasts, legs, eyes, lips, hair, necks, scents, etc.—brought into action at the opportune time will cause even the most imperturbable clod to yield to sex appeal. Although this notion is disproved every day (beauty can catch a man's eye but not his heart), it persists and is perpetuated in the advertising pages of ladies' magazines and is perhaps one reason so many agency executives leave estates while so many women die spinsters.   6

The amateur female authorities are less dogmatic. Marlene Dietrich, who, on the word of Ernest Hemingway, knows more about love than "anybody in the world," is abundantly and durably endowed with sex appeal, yet she senses something subtler is involved   7
in bringing the man to gaff. Femininity, she says, is a woman's greatest asset, her magnetic field to which the man is drawn and which he wants to enter since the scissors cut the cord.

"It is in you [the woman] that he looks for his ideal," Miss Dietrich wrote to her sisters and advised them to "live up to the images he has of you [to] guide your way around the stones on   8
which you would stub your Cinderella toes, whatever happens. They are mysteriously the reason why you are loved."

Helen Lawrenson, who has contributed lively essays on various aspects of amour to this and other magazines, believes a man can fall in love with a girl without ever looking at her feet. He does it, Miss Lawrenson wrote us, to "fill a deep mental and physical need." The girl "corresponds to an image somewhere in his subconscious, perhaps of his mother, perhaps of a storybook princess, perhaps of a   9
childhood ideal or half-remembered fantasy. This is what happens when a man looks at a girl and suddenly, out of all the women he sees, she, and she alone, becomes illuminated in some special way which makes her stand out, desirable and unique, from all the others."

Men, on the average, take an agnostic view. They shrug and say, "Who knows? Who knows why you get enraptured over a few bars of a Beethoven symphony, or a scrap of poetry, or a patch of color and   10
form on a canvas? You come across the girl. At the time, you like or need her. You take her. That's that. From then on you get along as best you can."

Those who have been scalded by this even go along with Sam Levenson's story about the father listening to his schoolboy son describe a Moslem marriage and the rite of keeping the bride veiled until after the ceremony. The boy observes how strange it is that "in Arabia you don't know who your wife is until after the wedding."   11
The father nods and mutters: "In New York, too." Those who still have a few illusions and are guarding them carefully take refuge in Chekhov's conclusion: "There is but one incontrovertible truth about love—it is a great mystery."

Another angle, popularly held among males, puts the laurel (or thorns) on the head of the man. Its spokesman could be this successful young publicity man who explained it over a Martini before catching a commuters' express to Westport, wife and children:

"Sooner or later you get tired tomcatting around. It's not just that 12
the variety gets monotonous. After a while you get scared. Where are
you going to end up? That's when it happens. You make a peace
with your libido, concentrate on the best girl around, and settle
down."

Poets and peasants, playwrights and philosophers, the fellow
down the street who fell in love only last week and the girl who got
him—all have had a fling at describing what it's like (good), but when 13
they try to tell how it happened they usually founder in platitude,
confusion, hypocrisy or evasion.

Enter science. No fanfare of trumpets, just the sharp, insistent
cries of discovery from the psychiatrists against the drum roll of 14
statistics from the psychologists. It is a discordant concerto, but it
plays some new tunes.

The analysts now believe that a man does not fall in love. He
jumps in. Jumps because he is suffering from internal discontent,
feelings of guilt and anxiety of which he may not even be aware. 15
These derive from a complicated emotional struggle which, put simply if not precisely, goes something like this:

In matters of love, the inner man is made of three warring forces:
the ego-ideal (a subconscious image of the man you think you ought
to be), the daimonion, or unconscious conscience (roughly, a demon
or evil spirit dwelling within that keeps flailing you, again subconsciously, with intimations of your inadequacies and imperfections),
and the ego (your consciousness, the man you think you are). Ac- 16
cording to this theory, credited to Dr. Edmund Bergler, and similar
ones exposed by most practising psychiatrists, the demon is always
confronting the ego with reminders that it is failing to measure up to
the ego-ideal, and the difference between reality and expectation is
paid off with stirrings of guilt, depression, dissatisfaction.

These feelings may be vague or completely obscured. The man
may deny them and say he is just a bit moody or a trifle off the 17
beam.

Nevertheless they exist, say the psychiatrists, and when they become intolerably acute the man will seek and damn soon find the
first woman on whom he can project his ego-ideal, that is, see in her
symbolically all the great things he is supposed to be himself, and get
from her the constant reassurances (that the demon is always demanding) of what a fine and noble fellow he is. (Thus the familiar:
"Oh, Algernon, you have such a nice way of doing things.") This 18
projection, or transference, is accomplished in a blink, as swift and
silent as the flight of Cupid's arrow. Thereafter the man is wholly

and irrevocably in love, wildly out of control emotionally, but feeling buoyant and happy because he has relieved himself of his tensions and recriminations which were as painful psychically as Chinese water torture is physically.

To see the transference at work, reflect upon the case of Budd Schulberg, aurhor of *What Makes Sammy Run?* In Hollywood shortly after publication of the book, which is a devastating dissection of a ruthless and unscrupulous movie-town "operator," Schulberg   19 found himself being privately and publicly attacked by members of the film colony who apparently regarded the novel either as a pack of monstrous lies or as the betrayal of a family secret.

One night at a large party, Schulberg recalls, "I was bitterly and conclusively told off by a well-known actress I had always admired. I felt awful. A girl was there. I hadn't met her before. We got talking   20 and she sort of mentally held my hand the rest of the night. I was in love before the party was over." They were later wed and are still married.

Schulberg may not have known exactly what happened, but the   21 psychiatrists say they do.

Again—a prominent New York designer who had buried himself in his career and at thirty-eight had avoided any deep female attachments. He was in an auto accident in which another man was killed. Although completely exonerated, he could not forget the incident. It   22 weighed on him. He became morose and self-reproachful. He leaped suddenly into love with a woman who for years had been a casual acquaintance, for whom he had shown theretofore little more than apathy.

In both these instances the demon within was abetted by clearly discernible outside forces. Such aid is unnecessary in most cases, the   23 psychiatrists maintain, there being masochist enough in all of us to do the trick.

Psychiatry also detects unmistakable ingredients of narcissism in the mixture of love. The lover sees in his beloved his own ego-ideal. Her looks are secondary to the images of himself he finds in her. Thus conventional beauty has no effect on causing a man to love,   24 though it is seldom a deterrent. And behind the beloved, there disports the man's ego, "basking in the manic intoxication of being loved" (Bergler).

Although he died a century before this idea achieved the dignity of a scientific theory, Stendhal tagged it when he wrote in his *On Love:* " . . . people, with their paroxysms of love, in love on credit, if one may say so, throw themselves at the objects of their affection. . . . Before any of the sensation which is the consequence of the nature of an object has time to reach them, they endow the object, from a distance, and before even seeing it, with that imaginary charm of which they have an inexhaustible supply within themselves. On drawing closer to the object, they see it, not as it really is, but as they have created it, and they take a delight in themselves under the guise of the object which they have set on too high a pedestal."

Psychiatrically speaking, then, love is the inevitable result of guilt feelings. It is attained by the transference, which is consciously indiscriminate and which Bergler calls "an act of despair" in a mood of panic. It can save a man from melancholy and desperation, but it does not come equipped with any manufacturer's guarantees of quality or length of performance. A relapse of considerable and often fatal severity can usually be predicted. Unless a man can find his way out through some work he enjoys, advancement in his career, or some other sublimation, he is odds-on to get all his old dissatisfactions back again and wind up directing them against the woman. In short, hating her. As Friar Laurence warned Romeo: "These violent delights have violent ends."

And this would account, too, for that old banality, ricochet love. A psyche on the rebound is apt to be tightly knotted with discontent, distress and despondency.

Since this theory rhymes poorly with moon or June, it is unpopular with sentimentalists and song writers. If it vexes the reader as well, if it robs his idea of love of its wonder and romance, he may sip some consolation from Nietzche's observation that "not the smallest charm of a theory is that it can be refuted."

It is, however, mirrored often in literature. Shakespeare said that love is blind, that it "looks not with the eyes, but with the mind." Congreve called it a "frailty of the mind." And Hawthorne wrote solemnly that "the world owes all its onward impulses to men ill at ease." Also, presumably, most of its marriages.

It also finds support, if not concurrence, in the opinions of some of our finest modern writers. Here is what Henry Green, author of *Loving, Nothing,* and other novels, wrote us on the subject:

> A man falls in love because there is something wrong with him. It is not so much a matter of his health as it is of his mental climate; as, in winter, one longs for spring. He gets so he can't stand being alone. He may imagine he wants children, but he doesn't, at least not as women do. Because once married and with children of his own, he longs to be alone again.
>
> A man who falls in love is a sick man. . . . Before he's in love he's in a weak condition, for which the only prognosis, and he is only too

aware of this, is that he will go on living. And, in his invalidism, he doesn't feel he can go on living alone. . . .

I am, of course, assuming that love leads to marriage. Unrequited love is to be avoided at all costs. If a married man falls in love with a third party and hasn't the courage to leave his wife, he is like a man who takes off his belt, ties it round the branch of a tree, and hangs himself in the loop while his trousers fall around his ankles. If an unmarried man finds unrequited love then there is even more the matter with him.

30

The love one feels is not made for one but made by one. It comes from a lack in oneself . . . a deficiency. . . .

We are all animals, and therefore we are continually being attracted. That this attraction should extend to what is called love is a human misfortune cultivated by novelists. It is the horror we feel of ourselves, that is, of being alone with ourselves, which draws us to love, but this love should happen only once, and never be repeated, if we have, as we should, learnt our lesson, which is that we are, all and each one of us, always and always alone.

Selah!

A sunnier, but still somber, opinion is rendered by James A. Michener, author of the short stories, *Tales of the South Pacific,* to which Rodgers and Hammerstein added music and sugar to get the immensely popular *South Pacific.* (And if attendance figures to that production are a clue, a landslide majority of the population prefers to conceive of love as a paradisical confection of wooing and courtship compounded with shoes and rice. It stayed away in hordes from other plays like *The Immoralist,* a more sardonic, though psychologically accurate study of an unhappy marriage.) Mr. Michener, whose recent best-selling novel, *Sayonara,* dealt centrally with love, contributed the following paragrpah to our informal forum:

31

I suppose a man decides to fall in love because subconsciously he knows there's a better way to live than living alone. I doubt that sex is the motivating power. I doubt that mimicking his companions who settle down with one girl is the driving force. Certainly security can't be, for the most insecure men in the world are those who have to worry about the girls they've fallen in love with, or married. And economics certainly can't play a part, because any single man with a good income is plain nuts, financially speaking, to take on a mistress or a wife. So I conclude men fall in love because of their subconscious awareness that in spite of all the perils and dissatisfactions, living with a human being of the opposite sex is a spiritual completion that can be gained in no other way. It's a hell of a price to pay, but it's worth it.

Once more the subconscious, the "sickness" of Mr. Green's interpretation, the unconscious conscience and ego-ideal of the psychiatrists. If a man is driven to love by inner needs, conscious speculation on his part concerning the type of girl he wants is likely to be fruitless and idle. He may claim that when he goes for a girl, she will be blonde, lushly curved, and in other respects reminiscent of, say, Marilyn Monroe. When his time comes, he may easily pass Miss Monroe on the street without noticing her, so consumed is he in his 32 preoccupation with an angular brunette on the mold of Katharine Hepburn. Tenements and low-cost housing developments are full of husbands who, when single, swore they would marry for money, and psychiatrists' couches are hot from the backs of men who rejected and fled mother only to marry her in the form of another woman. When a man loves, he loves. There is little he can do to stop or control it.

Both the psychiatrists and psychologists agree that love and sex are fairly distinct emotions. Sex is a physical drive, a lust for momentary pleasure, a demanding desire for another body. Love is a psychic urge, a grab at ecstasy, an overwhelming interest in another life. 33 Theodor Reik, one of the world's foremost authorities (he was a psychoanalyst both in Europe and the United States), says: "Although they are different, love and sex, like whiskey and water, mix marvelously well."

Should a man be powerfully attracted to a woman, yet uncertain whether it was his mind or his membranes involved, he probably could arrive at a quick and conclusive answer a few hours after an experiment in the handiest bedroom-laboratory. But, as the analysts would hurriedly add, the well-adjusted man who already has a love in his life—work, sweetheart, wife, or family—would be extremely unlikely to allow himself to get into circumstances under which he 34 might like to run the test. The neurotic, on the other hand, tries it again and again by actively seeking out the situation and courting the temptation (which the analysts term "the allure of the forbidden"). He is dependent on this condition for his excitement, which is one reason his marriages go sour. Since sex is not "forbidden" in wedlock, it soon loses its appeal.

"There are periods in our lives," Andre Maurois wrote us, "when we feel predisposed to love. Adolescence is one, another begins toward fifty. At such moments our body is in quest of a possible 35 mistress. The first lovable woman then encountered will awaken strong feelings. In other words we fall in love with love and choose whoever happens to be there.

"Sometimes much depends on circumstances. If a man is shy, he may feel encouraged by a forced intimacy. Because he happens to be 36 alone with a woman . . . he suddenly becomes more daring. A durable love may ensue.

"But in many cases," adds the honored master of French letters, "a man falls in love because a woman wants him to. If she has any charm he seldom resists her first advances. If she knows the game and how to retreat after she has excited interest and desire, the male animal will follow. . . . " 37

While that concept has attractive Parisian overtones and would no doubt charm scenarists, it probably would not completely satisfy either the iatrists or ologists. The two branches of study agree on a few points but they disagree on many. They are like boxers who touch gloves in the center of the ring, then proceed to hammer each 38 other's brains out the rest of the round. In some analytic circles, Kinsey is an ugly word or possibly a disease; similarly, most psychologists would rather be caught lying with their statistics than conceding much validity to many psychiatric theories which apply, they feel, only to a small percentage of the population.

Psychologists, generally, believe that men fall in love because they think it will fill basic and ordinary needs—social and/or economic improvement, sexual gratification, the desire to be approved of. How and when a man is drawn to a woman is conditioned by childhood experiences. He will respond automatically in adulthood to the same type of woman from whom he received the best treatment as a youngster. The lad, for example, who underwent a lot of 39 scolding and restraint from a brown-eyed, brunette mother, yet got tender attention and a happy time from a blonde and blue-eyed nurse, will, as surely as the hounds of Pavlov salivated at the sound of the bell, make straight for the blondes when picking a wife or a sweetheart, even though—as is often the case—the childhood events may only be dimly or inaccurately remembered, or forgotten entirely.

The psychologists also claim that we are in continual conflict with our culture (ourselves, the psychiatrists would say) and that this has an effect on why we love and the way we do it. We are, they say, capable of loving several people at one time. The exclusivism thrust 40 upon us by convention is an ogre, constantly sniping at our mental well-being, for it causes us to squelch emotions that were better unleashed.

"Not in our present society, but ideally," one New York clinician and lay analyst told us, "a man would have a primary love object, a wife and family, let's say, then have affairs on the side—rarely, spo- 41 radically or steadily—all his life, as he wanted them, as he needed them. This would satisfy his basic needs of security and variety.

"I daresay there are some men, gifted with uncommon tact and discretion, who manage to live this way today. But most men rightly think they couldn't get away with it. The pressures against it are enormous.

"Biologically we are promiscuous. Yet our normal propensity for love takes a beating because our social attitudes hurt, frustrate and inhibit all except monogamous love. We are ashamed to admit that we fall in love over and over again. That's why you hear people calling their past loves infatuations and their present infatuation love. There's no difference. A man falls in love because it is biologically and psychologically normal. He should, of course, marry for love, but he'd be in a terrible spot if he married everybody he loved."

Max Lerner, a syndicated professional ponderer of love and sexual problems for the masses, believes this struggle (which psychologist Robert Lindner has defined as a clash between "the imperative of fidelity and the pressure of human biopsychic nature") a waning one. Increasingly more men, he notes, are adopting "operative codes" that acknowledge but do not obey "formal" ones. "Eventually the gap between them is narrowed ... Kinsey's material on the changing patterns of sexual behavior ... shows that there is a reaching for greater freedom of sexual choice [in] a society which ... is increasingly oriented toward claims to personal happiness rather than to traditional codes." The point here is that the psychologists apparently contend that there is more to mull in what makes a man *not* fall in love than in why he does.

Any psychiatrist in fighting trim would come up swinging at such reasoning. He would first throw a jab—love is not logical but unconscious—then follow up with a flurry by explaining the illogical and contradictory workings of the unconscious in terms of Freud's story about the man who returned his neighbor's pot in damaged condition and was reproached: "First," said the man, "I never borrowed the pot. Second, when you handed it to me it was already broken. Third, I gave it back to you undamaged." Finally, hoping the opponent is reeling, he would fling a haymaker claim that the "normal," well-integrated man *is* monogamous, falling in love only once or twice in a lifetime, and that any susceptibility to numerous affairs is evidence of neurosis.

The psychologist: Love is biologic, normal, healthy, vigorous.

The psychiatrist: Love is a powerful counterattack against masochistic feelings of guilt.

42

43

44

45

So goes the battle. Both contestants being strong newcomers to science (psychology has the edge in weight and experience, but psychiatry has speed and the vitality of youth), the match may go into late rounds. Somewhere along the way they may uncover the true reason why a man falls in love. Just as two of hydrogen and one   46
of oxygen = water, it may be precise, factual and dull. But recognizing it, knowing what causes it, we may be able to do something constructive about diminishing the boredom, misery and misunderstanding that are often the consequence of the act.

Whatever the outcome, it will be, inescapably, some extension of the answer struck by Alistair Cooke, facile emcee of TV's "Omnibus" and thoughtful commentator on American foibles, triumphs and mores for the British press and radio. When we asked him if he   47
knew what made a man fall in love, Mr. Cooke frowned uncomfortably, then beamed.

"Of course," he replied. "A woman."

QUESTIONS AND PROBLEMS

1. Wiswell analyzes the matter of falling in love by searching for reasons. He presents his search as an organized one.
   a.   To what three groups did he go in search for the reasons?
   b.   Was the scope of the search broad enough?
   c.   Do the groups he went to constitute a valid classification?
2. The author classifies the women he went to for answers into two categories. What are they? Is there a possible third category?
3. What answers do the men give to the question posed in this essay?
4. Having stated the three areas (or classes) of his search, Wiswell later brings in, or seems to bring in, a fourth. What is this group? Is it a logical part of his classification?
5. Can this essay be easily outlined? Try outlining it. Is the result a logical outline?
6. What, in matters of love, are the three warring forces in man? Explain them. Are the definitions Wiswell gives of these forces adequate for understanding them?
7. How is the use of specific example brought into the subject of the essay? Does the use of examples improve the analysis?
8. From Wiswell's observation of the psychiatrist's view of why men fall in love is it possible to argue that both marriage and divorce stem from the same inner need?
9. Love and sex are presented as rather distinct emotions. How is each term defined?
10. Why is it that people frequently call "their past loves infatuations and their present infatuation love" (par. 43)?

SUGGESTIONS FOR WRITING

1. Should college students marry? Write an essay defending marriage for young people while still in college.
2. Read Shakespeare's *Antony and Cleopatra*. Then write an essay explaining the methods Shakespeare used to remove the sordidness from the association of the two main characters and cause their love to be viewed as grand and ennobling.
3. Defend or refute the idea that guilt feelings cause men to fall in love.
4. Analyze the relationship between love and hate in the association of a man and a woman.
5. Analyze a view of love presented by Hemingway in "The Short Happy Life of Francis Macomber" or by Fitzgerald in *The Great Gatsby*.
6. What are the dangers of marriage? Classify them either from a man's or from a woman's point of view.
7. What is the basis of the "warfare" between men and women? Analyze this problem in a light essay.
8. Write an essay on the subject of divorce in which you analyze the various causes.

SUGGESTIONS FOR FURTHER READING

Derrick S. Bailey, *The Mystery of Love and Marriage* (Harper)

Denis de Rougemont, *Love Declared: Essays on the Myths of Love* (Pantheon Beacon)

Leslie A. Fiedler, *Love and Death in the American Novel* (Meridian)

Wallace Fowlie, *Love in Literature: Studies in Symbolic Expression* (Indiana)

Ignace Lepp, *The Psychology of Loving* (Taplinger; New American Library)

Karl A. Menninger and Jeanetta L. Menninger, *Love Against Hate* (Harcourt, Brace & World)

Douglas N. Morgan, *Love: Plato, the Bible and Freud* (Prentice-Hall)

THE DISCOVERY OF WHAT IT MEANS
TO BE AN AMERICAN
James Baldwin

"It is a complex fate to be an American," Henry James observed, and the principal discovery an American writer makes in
Europe is just how complex this fate is. America's history, her aspirations, her peculiar triumphs, her even more peculiar defeats, and her
position in the world—yesterday and today—are all so profoundly   1
and stubbornly unique that the very word "America" remains a new,
almost completely undefined and extremely controversial proper
noun. No one in the world seems to know exactly what it describes,
not even we motley millions who call ourselves Americans.

I left America because I doubted my ability to survive the fury of
the color problem here. (Sometimes I still do.) I wanted to prevent
myself from becoming *merely* a Negro; or, even, merely a Negro
writer. I wanted to find out in what way the *specialness* of my   2
experience could be made to connect me with other people instead
of dividing me from them. (I was as isolated from Negroes as I was
from whites, which is what happens when a Negro begins, at bottom,
to believe what white people say about him.)

In my necessity to find the terms on which my experience could
be related to that of others, Negroes and whites, writers and non-
writers, I proved, to my astonishment, to be as American as any
Texas G.I. And I found my experience was shared by every American   3
writer I knew in Paris. Like me, they had been divorced from their
origins, and it turned out to make little difference that the origins of
white Americans were European and mine were African—they were
no more at home in Europe than I was.

The fact that I was the son of a slave and they were the sons of
free men meant less, by the time we confronted each other on European soil, than the fact that we were both searching for our separate   4
identities. When we had found these, we seemed to be saying, why,
then, we would no longer need to cling to the shame and bitterness
which had divided us so long.

It became terribly clear in Europe, as it never had been here, that
we knew more about each other than any European ever could. And
it also became clear that, no matter where our fathers had been born,   5
or what they had endured, the fact of Europe had formed us both,
was part of our identity and part of our inheritance.

I had been in Paris a couple of years before any of this became
clear to me. When it did, I, like many a writer before me upon the

discovery that his props have all been knocked out from under him, suffered a species of breakdown and was carried off to the mountains   6 of Switzerland. There, in that absolutely alabaster landscape, armed with two Bessie Smith records and a typewriter, I began to try to re-create the life that I had first known as a child and from which I had spent so many years in flight.

It was Bessie Smith, through her tone and her cadence, who helped me to dig back to the way I myself must have spoken when I was a pickaninny, and to remember the things I had heard and seen and felt. I had buried them very deep. I had never listened to Bessie   7 Smith in America (in the same way that, for years, I would not touch watermelon), but in Europe she helped to reconcile me to being a "nigger."

I do not think that I could have made this reconciliation here. Once I was able to accept my role—as distinguished, I must say, from   8 my "place"—in the extraordinary drama which is America, I was released from the illusion that I hated America.

The story of what can happen to an American Negro writer in Europe simply illustrates, in some relief, what can happen to any American writer there. It is not meant, of course, to imply that it happens to them all, for Europe can be very crippling, too; and, anyway, a writer, when he has made his first breakthrough, has sim-   9 ply won a crucial skirmish in a dangerous, unending and unpredictable battle. Still, the breakthrough is important, and the point is that an American writer, in order to achieve it, very often has to leave this country.

The American writer, in Europe, is released, first of all, from the necessity of apologizing for himself. It is not until he *is* released from the habit of flexing his muscles and proving that he is just a "regular guy" that he realizes how crippling this habit has been. It is not necessary for him, there, to pretend to be something he is not, for   10 the artist does not encounter in Europe the same suspicion he encounters here. Whatever the Europeans may actually think of artists, they have killed enough of them off by now to know that they are as real—and as persistent—as rain, snow, taxes or businessmen.

Of course, the reason for Europe's comparative clarity concerning the different functions of men in society is that European society has always been divided into classes in a way that American society never has been. A European writer considers himself to be part of an   11 old and honorable tradition—of intellectual activity, of letters—and his choice of vocation does not cause him any uneasy wonder as to whether or not it will cost him all his friends. But this tradition does not exist in America.

On the contrary, we have a very deep-seated distrust of real intellectual effort (probably because we suspect that it will destroy, as I hope it does, that myth of America to which we cling so desperately). An American writer fights his way to one of the lowest rungs 12 on the American social ladder by means of pure bull-headedness and an indescribable series of odd jobs. He probably *has* been a "regular fellow" for much of his adult life, and it is not easy for him to step out of that lukewarm bath.

We must, however, consider a rather serious paradox: though American society is more mobile than Europe's, it is easier to cut across social and occupational lines there than it is here. This has something to do, I think, with the problem of status in American 13 life. Where everyone has status, it is also perfectly possible, after all, that no one has. It seems inevitable, in any case, that a man may become uneasy as to just what his status is.

But Europeans have lived with the idea of status for a long time. A man can be as proud of being a good waiter as of being a good actor, and in neither case feel threatened. And this means that the actor and the waiter can have a freer and more genuinely friendly 14 relationship in Europe than they are likely to have here. The waiter does not feel, with obscure resentment, that the actor has "made it," and the actor is not tormented by the fear that he may find himself, tomorrow, once again a waiter.

This lack of what may roughly be called social paranoia causes the American writer in Europe to feel—almost certainly for the first time in his life—that he can reach out to everyone, that he is accessi- 15 ble to everyone and open to everything. This is an extraordinary feeling. He feels, so to speak, his own weight, his own value.

It is as though he suddenly came out of a dark tunnel and found himself beneath the open sky. And, in fact, in Paris, I began to see the sky for what seemed to be the first time. It was borne in on me—and it did not make me feel melancholy—that this sky had been 16 there before I was born and would be there when I was dead. And it was up to me, therefore, to make of my brief opportunity the most that could be made.

I was born in New York, but have lived only in pockets of it. In Paris, I lived in all parts of the city—on the Right Bank and the Left, among the bourgeoisie and among *less miserables,* and knew all kinds of people, from pimps and prostitutes in Pigalle to Egyptian bankers 17 in Neuilly. This may sound extremely unprincipled or even obscurely immoral: I found it healthy. I love to talk to people, all kinds of people, and almost everyone, as I hope we still know, loves a man who loves to listen.

This perpetual dealing with people very different from myself caused a shattering in me of preconceptions I scarcely knew I held. The writer is meeting in Europe people who are not American, whose sense of reality is entirely different from his own. They may love or hate or admire or fear or envy this country—they see it, in any case, from another point of view, and this forces the writer to reconsider many things he had always taken for granted. This reassessment, which can be very painful, is also very valuable.

This freedom, like all freedom, has its dangers and its responsibilities. One day it begins to be borne in on the writer, and with great force, that he is living in Europe as an American. If he were living there as a European, he would be living on a different and far less attractive continent.

This crucial day may be the day on which an Algerian taxi-driver tells him how it feels to be an Algerian in Paris. It may be the day on which he passes a cafe terrace and catches a glimpse of the tense, intelligent and troubled face of Albert Camus. Or it may be the day on which someone asks him to explain Little Rock and he begins to feel that it would be simpler—and, corny as the words may sound, more honorable—to *go* to Little Rock than sit in Europe, on an American passport, trying to explain it.

This is a personal day, a terrible day, the day to which his entire sojourn has been tending. It is the day he realizes that there are no untroubled countries in this fearfully troubled world; that if he has been preparing himself for anything in Europe, he has been preparing himself—for America. In short, the freedom that the American writer finds in Europe brings him, full circle, back to himself, with the responsibility for his development where it always was: in his own hands.

Even the most incorrigible maverick has to be born somewhere. He may leave the group that produced him—he may be forced to—but nothing will efface his origins, the marks of which he carries with him everywhere. I think it is important to know this and even find it a matter for rejoicing, as the strongest people do, regardless of their station. On this acceptance, literally, the life of a writer depends.

The charge has often been made against American writers that they do not describe society, and have no interest in it. They only describe individuals in opposition to it, or isolated from it. Of course, what the American writer is describing is his own situation. But what is *Anna Karenina* describing if not the tragic fate of the isolated individual, at odds with her time and place?

The real difference is that Tolstoy was describing an old and dense society in which everything seemed—to the people in it, though not to Tolstoy—to be fixed forever. And the book is a mas-   24 terpiece because Tolstoy was able to fathom, and make us see, the hidden laws which really governed this society and made Anna's doom inevitable.

American writers do not have a fixed society to describe. The only society they know is one in which nothing is fixed and in which the individual must fight for his identity. This is a rich confusion,   25 indeed, and it creates for the American writer unprecedented opportunities.

That the tensions of American life, as well as the possibilities, are tremendous is certainly not even a question. But these are dealt with in contemporary literature mainly compulsively; that is, the book is more likely to be a symptom of our tension than an examination of   26 it. The time has come, God knows, for us to examine ourselves, but we can only do this if we are willing to free ourselves of the myth of America and try to find out what is really happening here.

Every society is really governed by hidden laws, by unspoken but profound assumptions on the part of the people, and ours is no exception. It is up to the American writer to find out what these   27 laws and assumptions are. In a society much given to smashing taboos without thereby managing to be liberated from them, it will be no easy matter.

It is no wonder, in the meantime, that the American writer keeps running off to Europe. He needs sustenance for his journey and the best models he can find. Europe has what we do not have yet, a sense   28 of the mysterious and inexorable limits of life, a sense, in a word, of tragedy. And we have what they sorely need: a new sense of life's possibilities.

In this endeavor to wed the vision of the Old World with that of the New, it is the writer, not the statesman, who is our strongest arm. Though we do not wholly believe it yet, the interior life is a real life,   29 and the intangible dreams of people have a tangible effect on the world.

QUESTIONS AND PROBLEMS

1. Why was it of value for Baldwin—as for other Americans—to go to Europe in order to find an answer to the question suggested by the title?
2. Outline the steps in Baldwin's discovery. Are they given in a logical order?

3. Is the author's analysis primarily intellectual or emotional, or a combination of both? Cite proof from the essay.

4. Explain what caused the "species of breakdown" which Baldwin refers to in par. 6. How did Bessie Smith help Baldwin?

5. What is the difference between "role" and "place" as Baldwin uses the terms in par. 8)?

6. Can the necessity of flexing one's muscles and proving that one is a "regular guy" (par. 10) have a "crippling" effect on a college student in the United States? Give examples.

7. Is Baldwin correct in saying that Americans "have a very deep-seated distrust of real intellectual effort" (par. 12)? Cite examples to prove or disprove.

8. In reference to Baldwin's comment on "status" in par. 13, what is the basis of status in American life? What are some positive and some negative effects of this basis?

9. Baldwin refers twice to the "myth of America" (pars. 12 and 26). What is this myth?

10. What does Baldwin mean when he says, in the last paragraph, that "the intangible dreams of people have a tangible effect on the world"? Illustrate the meaning from contemporary American history.

SUGGESTIONS FOR WRITING

1. If you have been abroad, analyze your feelings about being an American in a foreign land.

2. Write an essay on the place of the intellectual in American life.

3. Write a research paper on an American writer's experience in living abroad: Ben Franklin, James Fenimore Cooper, Hemingway, F. Scott Fitzgerald, Baldwin—anyone who interests you.

4. Contrast the typical American way of life of members of any economic class with its European counterpart.

5. Read F. Scott Fitzgerald's *The Great Gatsby*. Use it as the basis for an analysis of "The American Dream."

6. Write a paper on the subject, "The Discovery of What it Means to Be a Negro"—or a member of any other minority group in the United States.

7. Write an analysis of "The White Problem" from the point of view of a Negro.

8. "With Freedom and Justice for All"—discuss the reality today of this idealistic statement of American principle.

SUGGESTIONS FOR FURTHER READING

Stuart G. Brown, *Memo for Overseas Americans: The Many Meanings of American Civilization*, rev. ed. (Syracuse)

Harlan Cleveland and others, *Overseas Americans* (McGraw-Hill)

John A. Garraty and Walter Adams, *From Main Street to the Left Bank* (Michigan State Univ.)

Ernest Hemingway, *A Moveable Feast* (Scribner)

Gertrude Stein, *The Autobiography of Alice B. Toklas* (Vintage)

THE CULT OF THE PRESENT
Kenneth Keniston

Some outlooks make the past their psychological center and look back nostaligically to the pleasures of lost times. Others, like the traditional American ethos, look primarily to the future, considering both present and past mere preparations for what is to come. Still others consciously focus on the present, which is seen as the central aspect of time and history, the rationale of behavior and the raison   1 d'etre of life. Each of these temporal orientations accentuates its characteristic mode of experience: a focus on the past emphasizes memory, history, conservation, and nostalgia; one on the future stresses anticipation, planning, saving, and preparation; and concern with the present almost invariably involves a focus on experience, consumption, sentience, activity, and adventure in the here and now.

Of these three orientations, it is abundantly clear that the alienated focus consciously on the present. Their philosophies emphasize the irrelevance of the past and their pessimism about the future. They reject long-range idealism in favor of the personal and situational needs of the moment; they tell us of their lack of future plans; they experience time as decline or stagnation rather than progress or growth. So, too, in their daily lives they are addicted to passionate intellectual inquiry in the service of present needs rather than to efforts to acquire skills for the future. They are detached observers   2 of their worlds, searching for ways to intensify and heighten the present, not for the wisdom of the past or for lessons for the future. Though the present is often dull, boring, or depressing to them, they can seldom escape it by pleasant fantasies about what was or what is to come. The future is closed by their pessimism; and even their fantasies of past infantile bliss are unconscious and would be unacceptable to their conscious selves. Whatever conscious meaning their lives may have is given by immediacy, experience, the here and now.

The cult of the present can take many forms, ranging from the quest for Nirvana to drug addiction, from aesthetic appreciation to violent delinquency. But we can distinguish two possible directions in any effort to intensify the present. One is a search for adventure, active, outgoing, and vigorous, which emphasizes the role of the actor in *creating* experience, in making new and heightened experiences for himself. An adventurous approach to experience leads to an   3 equation of self and activity, in which the individual seeks to become what he does, in which emphasis is on the process rather than on the product, in which the actor tries to find and reveal himself through his activity. In our own time, such an emphasis can be seen in forms as different as action painting and juvenile delinquency; in both cases, meaning derives from action.

The more passive form of the cult of the presnt is the *search for sentience,* and it is this search that characterizes the alienated. Here the self is defined not by action, but by perception; and meaning is created by heightened receptivity and openness. Experience is defined as subtlety, sensitivity, and awareness: the purpose of existence is not to alter the world so as to create new experiences, but to alter the self so as to receive new perceptions from what is already there. Whereas the adventurous seeks to change the world so that it stimulates him in new ways, the sentient seeks to change himself so that he is more open to stimulation. The experiencer thus seeks above all to refine himself as perceiver, cultivating "awareness," "openness," and "sensitivity." Along with a search for heightened perceptiveness goes a desire for heightened responsiveness—"genuine" feeling, direct passion, pure impulse, and uncensored fantasy. Some seek sentience through aesthetic sensitivity, others through continual self-examination, others by vicarious experience of the lives of others. The essential quest is the effort to perceive and feel deeply, clearly, intensely, truly.

A major component of this quest is the *search for a breakthrough.* The alienated value most those moments when the barriers to perception crumble, when the walls between themselves and the world fall away and they are "in contact" with nature, other people, or themselves. These times of breakthrough are relatively rare, for much of their lives seem to them dull, depressed, and ordinary. But when such moments come, the alienated describe them in mystical terms, emphasizing the loss of distinction between self and object, the revelation of the meaning of Everything in an apparently insignificant detail, the ineffability of the experience, the inherent difficulty in describing a moment which transcends ordinary categories of language. At other times, a breakthrough may be achieved with a person in a "moment of truth," when the two understand each other in what seems a miraculously total way. Or a breakthrough may be to the inner self, involving a feeling of inner communication and psychic wholeness which—though ephemeral—can profoundly affect the individual later.

Implicit in the search for a breakthrough is the conviction of alienated subjects that they are *constricted by conventional categories,* imprisoned by the usual ways of seeing the world, of coping with their own feelings and fantasies, of dealing with other people, even of channeling inner impulse into activity. One subject described human relations in terms of people attempting to communicate through airtight space suits; others feel that they are bound and hampered in their search for experience by the conventional categories of our culture. Their laboriously acquired educations often seem to them to have built a dark screen between themselves and the   6 world, a distorting filter which blocks clear perception. Despite their occasional breakthroughs, alienated subjects feel that they are unduly constricted in expressing their feelings; that they have lost the capacity for spontaneous appreciation of the world which they once had in childhood; that they are unduly shut off from their own fantasies and feelings. Though most observers would question these self-appraisals, they are a major motive in the continual effort of the alienated to attain more immediate contact with objects, and a further expression of their inability to tolerate any restraint or self-limitation.

For many alienated youths, the search for sentience entails still another corollary, the *desire for self-expression.* This is rarely a desire to remedy wrongs or to reform society. Instead, it grows out of their conviction that they have, for brief moments, achieved some truer and more total perception of the world than have most of their fellows. For some, the desire to express this perception has led to an interest in writing, the theater, or painting. We usually see artistic efforts as attempts to communicate and, in this measure, assume they require an audience; but for the alienated, the external audience   7 is relatively unimportant. Their crucial audience is internal: they write or act or paint for themselves, to structure, order, and confirm their own experience, more as subjective catharsis, perceptual therapy, or self-justification than as an effort to reveal to an outer audience. The desire for self-expression thus becomes a facet of their effort to enhance experience, to structure and organize it in new ways that will not obscure its meaning, to order the chaos of sensation with personal form.

The meanings of the cult of the present for these young men are complex. In part, it is a response to a conscious desire to escape their pasts and avoid their futures, but it is more than this. The alienated feel hemmed in and constrained by their worlds (and, unconsciously, by their unruly fantasies and feelings); they reject the culture which shaped them; they chafe under even the ordinary categories through which most men filter experience and feeling. To some extent, they   8 are incapable of employing these categories, for their experience has disposed them to see the world differently; but in part, their ideology dictates that they should *choose* to reject these categories. They are extraordinarily aware of the blinders of selective awareness and inattention which many men use to hide the seamier sides of their lives from themselves; and though the alienated have, in fact, blinders of their own, they are at least different and unconventional blinders.

The notion of a breakthrough also has multiple meanings. A breakthrough means an ability to slough off the restrictive categories through which most men interpret their lives to themselves; it involves a kind of experience which is above all characteristic of early childhood, when perception was in fact less structured by adult categories and blindnesses, when wisdom comes from the mouths of babes because they have yet to learn what can be noticed and said without fear of adult reprisal. Even in their intense conscious orientation to the present, these youths therefore manifest an *un*conscious desire to recapture the qualities of experience that, they vaguely recall, characterized their early lives. Ultimately they seek to regain the relatively undifferentiated and uncategorized view of the world they had as small children, and to achieve the same total understanding and fusion with another that they had with their mothers.   9

The cult of the present is, however, not only a theme of alienation, but is found in other forms among many young people. Indeed, among the defining characteristics of American youth culture—the special world of American adolescents and young adults—are a concentration on the present, a focus on immediate experience, an effort to achieve "genuineness," "directness," "sincerity" in perception and human relations. We see this cult in both forms—as a search for external stimulation and for internal transformation—in many of the deviant behaviors of our society: in the search for adventure among   10 delinquent gangs, in the use of drugs to break through the gates of perception, in the "beat" quest for "kicks." And in less extreme form, a similar emphasis on the present exists in the increasing American stress on consumption rather than saving, on the "rich, full life" in the present rather than the deferred goals and future satisfactions of an earlier society. All of this suggests that the alienated are reacting to a problem which transcends the peculiarities of their individual lives, and that the cult of the present is a response to historical pressures which affect alienated and unalienated alike.

QUESTIONS AND PROBLEMS

1. Why do the alienated focus consciously on the present? Why is focus on the future not possible for them?
2. Why does the author refer to the *cult* of the present?

3. Define or explain *sentience*, Nirvana.
4. Explain the "cult of the present" in terms of recent "hippie" or "beat" movements among young people.
5. What is the basis of revolt against conventions—at any time, in any place? Why do conventions stifle many of the young?
6. Relate the "cult of the present" to present-day attitudes of students regarding education.
7. Relate the cult to some present-day experiments in art, as expressed, for example, in the essay on *Pop Art*, pp. 43, 44. Relate it to contemporary experimental drama.
8. In telling the reader what the alienated reject or avoid (as in par. 8), does Keniston also tell us why they do so? Give some of your reasons for the rejection.
9. Explain what young adults mean when they say they want to achieve "genuineness," "directness," "sincerity" (par. 10).
10. What is the relationship between the "cult of the present" and the use of drugs?

SUGGESTIONS FOR WRITING

1. After reading one of Jack Kerouac's books (*On the Road,* for example, or *The Subterraneans*), analyze the Kerouacian "hero."
2. Analyze the alienation of Benjamin Braddock in Charles Webb's novel, *The Graduate.* Or analyze the same character from the point of view of the movie version.
3. Write an analysis of the rebellion of the so-called beat generation.
4. Write an essay in analysis of Thoreau as an early-day beatnik.
5. Write an argumentative essay on the failure of social and political Darwinism.
6. Read one or two copies of an "underground" newspaper. Analyze its assumptions, its political attitudes, its basic motivations.
7. Write on the theme of adolescence, using an American novel—Twain's *The Adventures of Huckleberry Finn,* Crane's *The Red Badge of Courage,* Wolfe's *Look Homeward, Angel,* McCullers' *The Heart is a Lonely Hunter,* Salinger's *The Catcher in the Rye,* for example—as a basis.

SUGGESTIONS FOR FURTHER READING

Peter Blos, *On Adolescence* (Free Press)
Erik Erikson, *Youth: Change and Challenge* (Basic Books)
Paul Goodman, *Growing Up Absurd* (Random House)
Kenneth Keniston, *The Uncommitted: Alienated Youth in American Society* (Harcourt, Brace & World)
Karl A. Menninger, *Man Against Himself* (Harcourt, Brace & World)
Fritz Pappenheim, *Alienation of Modern Man* (Monthly Review)
Thomas F. Parkinson, ed., *Casebook on the Beat* (Crowell)
David Riesman, *The Lonely Crowd* (Yale)
Gerald Sykes, ed., *Alienation* 2 vols. (Braziller)

Allen Wheelis, *The Quest for Identity* (Norton)
Winston White, *Beyond Conformity* (Free Press)
Elias Wilentz and Fred McDurrah, *The Beat Scene* (Citadel)

TO ARGUE AND PERSUADE

You may write an argumentative exposition to explain or to persuade, but usually an element of persuasion exists in all argumentative writing. As any topic developed by argument and/or persuasion automatically suggests more than one point of view, it is requisite that the writer of such an essay comprehend the facts and the evidence related to his topic. It is not enough that he understand the topic from his point of view; in order to argue with conviction and to persuade with authority, he must know all sides of the question. Only in this way can he marshal the evidence he needs to argue persuasively his position on the matter.

Cause, effect, and proof are fundamental to any argumentative essay. Only after these factors are carefully evaluated can one begin to develop a subject by argument and persuasion. They are, furthermore, the bases on which you test any argument you read or listen to. Through careless reading and listening the unwary frequently accept points of view which are not tenable to those who take a reasoned approach to a subject.

The cause or causes must, as we have already seen (p. 105), be true causes, not merely tangential details, and they must be inclusive, omitting no essential factors. In addition, the causes must be sufficient to produce the effects attributed to them. Let us consider an example. A teacher is dismissed from his post in a university. A group of students protest, claiming that the dismissal was an arbitrary and authoritarian act of the administration. The student senate enters the fray, citing the dismissal as yet one more instance of students not being consulted on matters of vital concern to the student body. A call goes out for boycotting classes, the administration building is occupied by students, and a demand is made that the students be given equal voice with the faculty and the administration on all matters of university policy, course offerings, and hiring and retention of faculty. The question raised by this sequence of events is this: Was the firing of the faculty member the cause or merely the inciting incident?

Not only must the writer of argument be careful of causes, of the facts he is dealing with, but he must also be careful of his reasoning on these facts so as to offer acceptable proof for his argument. That reasoning may be by inductive or by deductive inference. And the reasoning may be further supported by appeal to authority. If he uses inductive reasoning he finds particular facts which will support a general conclusion. His problem is to be sure he has based his conclusions on a sufficient number of cases lest his readers object that he has been too selective. Nor may he omit instances in which his conclusions have been contradicted; he must, rather, explain the apparent contradictions. For he must not give the impression that he has distorted or overelaborated his evidence.

If the writer of the argument uses deductive reasoning to establish his point, he makes use of general principles rather than particulars. Given a general principle of wide acceptability, he may prove a particular point by the logical process of deductive reasoning. The old syllogism concerning the mortality of Socrates, with its acceptable major premise, its acceptable minor premise, and its assured conclusion, is an example:

> Major premise: All men are mortal.
> Minor premise: Socrates is a man.
> Conclusion: Therefore Socrates is mortal.

In using deductive reasoning the writer must be certain that both major and minor premises will be generally accepted as true. He must, in addition, be certain that he has used the same terms in the same way in both major and minor premises. In the example above, *men* and *man* have the same meaning and are used in the same way. But note what happens to the logic of the argument in the following syllogism:

> Major premise: No cat has nine tails.
> Minor premise: One cat has one more tail than no cats.
> Conclusion: Therefore one cat has ten tails.

The problem is compounded when one avoids the double negative:

> Major premise: It is either raining or it is not raining.
> Minor premise: It is not raining.
> Conclusion: Therefore it is raining.

In both syllogisms the major premise may be accepted as true. But the minor premise of the "cat" syllogism is irrelevant to the logical deduction, and the minor premise of the "raining" syllogism requires the double negative, "It is not *not* raining," to be acceptable. Because of the faulty minor premises, both syllogisms result in unacceptable conclusions.

Citing authority can also lead to questionable or unsound conclusions if the authorities are not chosen with great care. Shakespeare uses many military terms and gives accounts of battles, yet, in spite of the fact that his name is a household word, he cannot be cited as an authority on military affairs. Aristotle was once the authority on natural science, but scientific investigation of an inductive nature has revealed that he can hardly be considered so today. Mohammed is an authority for Mohammedans but not necessarily for Christians. The American Association of Manufacturers speaks with great authority for many of its members, yet what it maintains may carry little conviction for a Socialist. So training and experience, passage of time, changes in the body of knowledge, and prejudice are elements to be considered in appealing to authority.

Reading essays developed by argument and persuasion is one of the best possible methods of sharpening one's critical powers. And writing such essays will probably make you more aware than you have been of the fallacies which creep so easily into our reasoning process.

BLACK, WHITE, COLORED
Marston Bates

We have, in the United States, become burdened with a whole complex of attitudes and beliefs about race that forms a frighteningly explosive mixture. The problems are clearly social rather than biological, arising out of developments in the cultural history of Western civilization as a whole, and of the United States in particular. The solutions will also necessarily involve cultural change. Yet race—geographical variation within an animal species—is a biological phenomenon, which may give me some excuse for contributing to the mass of verbiage that has been generated in the discussion of racial problems. 1

Our vocabulary annoys me. I find "white" a particularly silly term for peoples of European and Near Eastern origin. Albinos, who may turn up almost anywhere, might be called white; but with that exception I can't see how the word would apply to any human skin. "Of the color of snow or milk" the dictionary says of white. My efforts to imagine a human complexion blending into a snowbank are unavailing. Ermine may be white, but not people. Europeans, when they stay out of the sun, tend to be lighter than most other people; but the best term for this would seem to be "paleface," allegedly used by the American Indians. 2

There are all sorts of troubles with connotations when we use "white" and "black." One of the subsidiary meanings of "white" is "morally or spiritually pure or stainless"; and the *Oxford English Dictionary* has another subsidiary meaning (7b): "free from malignity or evil intent; beneficent, innocent, harmless, esp. as opposed to something characterized as *black*." We have, for instance, the difference between white magic and black. We of European descent might like to think of ourselves as white in this sense of being innocent and beneficent; but such a belief is hardly held up by history. 3

The problem was already bothering me back in 1952 when I wrote the chapter on "The Varieties of Tropical Man" in *Where Winter Never Comes*. I suggested there that we might be better off if we used words based on Greek: "leucoderm" for white skin; "melanoderm" for black; "xanthoderm" for yellow; "erythroderm" for red. It would seem to me much more difficult to get upset about leucoderms versus melanoderms than about white versus black. 4

There isn't, of course, any chance of influencing change in vocabulary, but it is still fun to play with the idea. White superiority, in the Greek-based vocabulary, would become "leucodermosis," which has an appropriately diseased sound. Black Power might comparably become "melanodermosis." I know some Negroes who suffer from acute forms of melanodermosis. This is perfectly understandable, but hardly helpful in solving the problems of coexistence. It is a more reasonable disease than leucodermosis—one wonders why it has not affected everyone labeled "Negro"—but it still seems unhealthy. In its acute form it becomes "leucophobia," a hatred for all palefaces.

The Greek terms would give a new perspective on segregation. Restaurants and bars could put up signs saying "Only Leucoderms Will Be Served," which would look appropriately ridiculous. And it might be possible to work out a quarantine for real estate agents infected with malanophobia. At least such a label would seem appropriate for this particular kind of social disease.

One of the problems of racial names stems from the accident by which the aboriginal Americans came to be called Indians. This leaves us with the awkward necessity of always using an adjective to show whether American or Indian Indians are meant. One solution has been to call the Americans "Amerinds," but this sounds to me more like a label for a variety of fruit than for a variety of people. Erythroderm doesn't help much in this case, since the need is not so much for ridicule as for a workaday word.

I was surprised to read in the article by Sol Tax in the insert on warfare in the December, 1967, issue of *Natural History* that the Indian wars of our past had great popular support. On reflection, however, this is understandable. The Indians were generally considered inferior, and we wanted their lands—so we took them. But our hatred of the Indians has subsided since we have them out of the way nicely herded into reservations on land for which we have little use. The problems of leucoderm-erythroderm relations remain and have been dealt with in various articles in this magazine (for example, an article on the Cree in the May, 1967, issue and one in the Iroquois in the June-July, 1967, issue). We have, to a varying but large extent, undermined the values of the Indian cultures without replacing them with our own—creating a situation that looks unsatisfactory to almost everyone. Must the Indians be Westernized, absorbed into our society? Cultural diversity appeals to me as a "good thing" in itself; but not if it has to be maintained artificially on fenced reservations, dealing with vanishing cultures as we deal with vanishing wildlife.

The situation of the erythroderms in the United States is thus very different from that of the melanoderms. The Africans were torn out of their native cultures and thrust into ours. Over the generations they have acquired our values; they are Americans, which makes the caste discrimination all the more painful and senseless. James Baldwin has given a sensitive description of his personal discovery of his Americanism in *Notes of a Native Son,* and his experience is surely far from unique. Here, incidentally, we have the case of an extremely good writer who happens to have the wrong skin color. 9

Wrong? It is odd that a beautiful skin should be a handicap; and I, at least, find the darker human skins more attractive than the pale ones. This must be generally true if one can judge by the amount of time paleface people spend in trying to darken their skins. Suntan lotions, sunlamps, and beaches for sunbathing form a considerable industry. This leucoderm preoccupation with getting dark must look ridiculous to a melanoderm; it certainly makes melanophobia seem odd. 10

There is, of course, no such thing as a "race" in any objective sense. Some students recognize three or four races, others thirty or more, but in no case is it possible to draw sharp lines. Ashley Montagu and a few other anthropologists think it would be helpful if we abandoned the word "race" altogether and since human differences are undeniable, wrote about "ethnic groups." I can't see that this would help much. Anyway, they have about as much chance of changing vocabulary as I have of persuading people to use "leucoderm" instead of "white." The real need in many of these cases is not so much to substitute words as it is to desensitize the words we already have. 11

The differences among groups of people, which we classify as racial traits, are puzzling. They include skin color, hair form and distribution, facial features, and body build, as well as differences in blood chemistry and presumably in other aspects of internal anatomy and physiology. For most of these traits I cannot see any adaptive value, although many students of the subject would disagree with me. Dark skin color, for instance, at first appears to be an adaptation to warm climates. But in the infrared parts of the spectrum involved in heat transfer, all human skin acts as a "black body," absorbing and radiating heat with equal efficiency. All efforts to show racial differences in heat toleration have failed. (Relevant studies have been summarized in an article by H.F. Blum, entitled "Does the Melanin Pigment of Human Skin Have Adaptive Value?" *Quarterly Review of Biology,* January 1961.) Some of the proposed adaptive explanations seem to verge on the absurd: that the epicanthic fold of the Mongolian eye is a protection against the glare of snowfields; or that the same Mongolians have little facial hair because ice crystals forming in a beard would be inconvenient. 12

But it is difficult to explain many human features, whether they characterize particular races or the species as a whole. Desmond Morris, in a thought-provoking book, *The Naked Ape,* has looked at the possible evolutionary background of many human peculiarities; his ideas, whether valid or not, should at least stimulate discussion. He reviews, for instance, the various explanations of our lack of body $\quad$ 13 fur: that it makes it easier to catch lice and fleas; that primitive man was a messy feeder and could not keep fur clean; that the loss of fur was a consequence of the acquisition of fire; that the fur was lost during an aquatic stage in human evolution. He seems himself to favor the idea that the naked body would have a cooling advantage in the quick spurts of running by early hunters.

Leucoderms don't come out very well if we compare different races in biological terms. The trait of hairlessness, for instance: leucoderms have more body hair than any other human type, which would make them backward in comparison with the more hairless melanoderms and xanthoderms. The lips form another human peculiarity, the inside lining of the mouth coming outside (Morris thinks this $\quad$ 14 serves as a sexual signal). The melanoderms would win here too, with their thicker lips. In general, the melanoderms seem to be the most advanced of racial varieties—and Africa appears to be the center of human evolution—which gives no help to people suffering from leucodermosis.

But generalization of this sort is dangerous. I found a book by the distinguished biochemist Roger Williams, entitled *You Are Extraordinary,* particularly interesting in this respect. Williams is attacking the concept of the "normal" or "average" man, which could apply equally well to the average for any race. We all know that individuals look different and have distinctive fingerprints; if we stop $\quad$ 15 to think we realize that each has a different smell—as every bloodhound knows. Our insides differ greatly: stomachs come in all sorts of shapes and sizes; the heart is even more variable than the stomach; sense organs differ in acuity from person to person; and so on through all aspects of our anatomy and physiology.

We have to be careful then in generalizing about man or about different races. It isn't the race that counts, but the individual; and each individual is different. I particularly like an analogy made by Williams: "Social science built on the average man would be like United States geography built upon the concept of the 'average state': It has an area of 72,000 square miles and a population of over 3.5 million. It has about 1,200 square miles of fresh water lakes and 37 square miles of salt lake. Its highest mountains are about 6,000 $\quad$ 16 feet high. About 5,000 square miles of it lie in the Arctic regions, where the ground is frozen the year round (permafrost). It has a shoreline of about 150 miles. The average state produces yearly about ½ million barrels of oil; 300,000 tons of coal; 50,000 pounds of copper; 10 million bushels of wheat; 3 million pounds of tobacco; 1 million bales of cotton; about 150,000 tons of citrus fruit and 9,000 tons of pineapples."

No one fits the average. We are not black, white, or colored. We   17
are individuals, you and me.

QUESTIONS AND PROBLEMS

1. What is the purpose of the author when he suggests that only albinos are white (par. 2), that the dictionary definition of the word includes "beneficent, innocent, harmless" (par. 3)? What tone does he adopt here?
2. Is the tone continued in pars. 4, 5, and 6? What do you find wrong with using the terms the author suggests?
3. Bates once wrote, "I suspect that in the end, what with the promiscuity of the wandering Scandinavians and the low cultural resistance of the blackfellows, human races will disappear."* Beginning with this somewhat irreverent statement, argue for or against the notion that races as we have considered them in the past will not long survive.
4. Bates is not very happy with the coinage "Amerinds" for American Indians (par. 7). Are such terms as Nisei, Mexican-Americans, and Afro-Americans acceptable to you? What name would you suggest for the white Americans which Bates finds so inaptly termed?
5. Discuss the problem of the Negro in reference to the author's comment in par. 9. What is the feeling of Negro leaders today on this matter? What is the tone of the last sentence of the paragraph? Does the tone continue in par. 10?
6. Sharp inroads have been made on racial prejudice in recent years. Name some decisive events or actions which have helped to reduce such prejudice.
7. How is prejudice against the American Indian revealed? What steps might be taken to better the social position of the Indian?
8. Bates' method of developing this essay has depended heavily upon the use of specific examples, often absurd or near-absurd ones. Where does his main argument come? How does he make it graphic?

SUGGESTIONS FOR WRITING

1. Make a new classification to take the place of our conventional terms for races. Argue for its adoption.
2. Investigate the economic and social conditions of the American Indian today. Argue for specific improvements.
3. Write a review of Desmond Morris' *The Naked Ape*. (See introduction to "The Book Review" section, pp. 327-328.)
4. Write an essay on the meaning of race on the campus of your school.

---

* *Marston Bates*, Where Winter Never Comes (Charles Scribner's Sons, 1952).

5. Write a sketch of the "average student" at your school, following the pattern of Bates in par. 16.
6. Write an essay on paternalism as it applies to the American Indian.
7. Using two or three prominent examples, develop a paper on the contributions which individual Negroes have made in one field of endeavor—literature, art, business, the ministry, etc.
8. Write an argument against the separation of college students into freshman, sophomore, junior, and senior classes.

SUGGESTIONS FOR FURTHER READING

M.F. Ashley Montagu, *The Concept of Race* (Free Press); *The Idea of Race* (Univ. of Nebraska); *Man's Most Dangerous Myth: The Fallacy of Race* (World)

Marston Bates, *Where Winter Never Comes* (Scribner); *Man in Nature* (Prentice-Hall)

H.F. Blum, *Time's Arrow and Evolution* (Peter Smith)

Margaret Mead, *Anthropology, a Human Science* (Van Nostrand)

Desmond Morris *The Naked Ape* (McGraw-Hill)

Roger J. Williams, *Free and Unequal: The Biological Basis of Individual Liberty* (Univ. of Texas); *You Are Extraordinary* (Random House)

LIFE, LIBERTY, AND THE PURSUIT OF WELFARE
Joseph Wood Krutch

"Welfare" is one of the key words of our time. What too many men now seem to desire is not virtue or knowledge or justice, but welfare. To the majority the word sums up the principal object of government and, indeed, of all social institutions.　1

Had you asked a Greek philosopher what the purpose of government should be, he would have said something about the maintenance of justice. And had you pressed him to say in what justice consists, he would have replied—not very satisfactorily—"In assuring to every man that which is rightfully his."　2

A medieval theologian would have added something about the City of God and the extent to which a community of mortals might approximate it. On the other hand that brutal seventeenth-century realist, Thomas Hobbes, would have gone to the other extreme. To him the principal aim of government is simply the maintenance of order, the taming of that state of nature which is anarchy of war. And the state of anarchy, he would have added, is so terrible that any government is better than no government.　3

Finally, had you posed the same question to an eighteenth-century philosopher, he would have said something to the effect that the chief purpose of government is not simply the maintenance of order, but the assurance to each man of his inalienable rights. And if you had asked him what these inalienable rights are, he would have answered in some form not too different from that of the Declaration—"Life, liberty and the pursuit of happiness."　4

In any event, it is obvious that none of these formulas is entirely satisfactory to most people today. They do not explicitly reject life, liberty and the pursuit of happiness, but they obviously consider them something less than enough. The invention of the term "welfare state" to describe something more than the democratic state is an expression of this dissatisfaction. It is intended to define a new ideal, which its proponents would call an extension of the ideal of a merely democratic state.　5

If it be objected that the philosophers, theologians and social critics cited above did not actually speak for the masses and that the great majority of the people would always have preferred "welfare" to the less easily understood goods proposed to them, the answer is that even if this be granted, it is not crucial to the argument which follows. The fact remains that the power of the masses is now for the first time decisive and that the sociologists and political scientists　6

218 To Argue and Persuade

most influential today tend both to accept this fact and to concur in
regarding "welfare" as the chief legitimate aim of government.

In a broad, general way we all know what welfare so used implies, what specific laws and institutions are called welfare measures,
and what are the premises upon which they are advocated. No one
would object very much if I said that the welfare state assumes, not
only that men should be protected against those who would deprive
them of their right to life, liberty and the pursuit of happiness, but
that it should go beyond mere protection to something more positive. All men not only must be guaranteed their liberties but also, to   7
a very considerable extent, "looked after." Many of the arguments
both for and against the policy of looking after people are too familiar to need mentioning. But certain fundamental questions are seldom asked. What is the ultimate definition of welfare—in what does
it consist, and who decides what it is? Or, to put the question in a
simpler form: Does the promotion of welfare mean giving people
what they want or seem to want or think they want, or does it
consist in giving them what they ought to have?

The answer implied in various specific welfare proposals is sometimes the one and sometimes the other. But few have ever dared to
put the question boldly and to give a positive answer one way or
another. If welfare means that people get what they want, then   8
which wants of which people come first? If welfare means giving
them what they ought to have, then who decides what they ought to
have, and on the basis of what criteria is the decision made?

This last is a very tough question indeed for an age which has
rejected absolutes and enthusiastically embraced both cultural and
moral relativism. One of the few bold answers I have ever encountered was given by David Thompson, a lecturer in history at Cambridge
University. "The welfare state," said he, "exists to promote whatever   9
the community regards as beneficial and good. If the community
regards automobiles, TV sets and football pools as of greater value than
better schools, more generous care for old people, and a creative use
of leisure, then the democratic state will provide more automobiles,
TV sets and football pools."

In the course of the article Mr. Thompson gives the impression
that he has preferences of his own and that they are not what he
believes to be those of most people. But he does not appear to have
his tongue in his cheek when he yields to the only definition of
democracy and the only definition of welfare which his relativistic
philosophy will permit. Like most of our contemporaries, he is unwilling to consider the possibility that what the community regards   10

as valuable is not the only possible standard by which values may be judged. Nor, as a matter of fact, can anyone escape such a conviction unless he is willing to assume what most today refuse to assume, namely, that some basis for calling one thing intrinsically and absolutely better or righter or higher than another can be found somewhere: In nature, in reason or in the law of God—all of which are independent of either custom or majority opinion.

Refuse, as most sociologists, psychologists and anthropologists do refuse, to make such an assumption, and you are driven to the conclusion which Mr. Thompson accepts: That nothing is better or more desirable than anything else except insofar as more people want it. Thus he comes to defend democracy not because of any conviction that its decisions are wiser by some independent standards than those arrived at by other forms of government, but simply because any decision which has majority sanction is wise and right by the only possible definition of those terms. 11

If, as most people seem to assume, the normal is merely the average, if the good life is whatever the majority thinks or has been persuaded to think it is, if what men should do is whatever they do do, then it must follow that the desirable is whatever is most widely desired, and that democracy means that what the majority admires is necessarily to be called excellent. Mr. Thompson himself may prefer what he calls "the creative use of leisure" to TV sets and football pools, but he is too broad-minded—as we now call it—to suppose that such a preference is anything more than just another one of those tastes about which there is no disputing. 12

Laissez faire is generally supposed to describe the social theory diametrically opposed to that of the welfare state, but here one sort of *laissez faire* is exchanged for another. Though the economy is to be planned, society is to be allowed to drift intellectually and culturally with whatever economic, technological or other currents may vary in this direction or that. 13

Under democracy of the older sort the most fundamental right of the citizen was assumed to be the pursuit of happiness. The welfare state substitutes welfare—usually defined in material terms—for happiness. But by way of compensation it assures the citizen that his right is not merely to pursue happiness but to attain welfare; and under this arrangement we lose something as well as, perhaps, gain something. Though we may pursue whatever kind of happiness seems to us most worth pursuing, the welfare which is going to be assured us must be mass-produced, whether it is defined, under a dictator- 14 ship, as what the dictator thinks we ought to have, or, as in our society, by what the majority wants or has been persuaded to want.

If I object that to define welfare as whatever most people seem to want tends to mean more things and fewer ideas and, in general, tends toward the vulgarest possible conception of what constitutes the good life, I will be told that the answer is education—that, given   15
enough schools, and schools that are good enough, the community will want what is truly most desirable; and that, if properly educated, it will provide for itself and ultimately reach a truly acceptable definition of welfare.

But despite all the schooling which Americans get, many of them do not seem to be very effectively learning any ideals or cultivating any interests other than those which seem to prevail among the   16
uneducated. High-school graduates and college graduates also very frequently prefer television and shinier automobiles to any of the more intellectual and less material forms of welfare.

This fact brings us again up against the unanswered question and it suggests that education is failing to help people to achieve an acceptable definition of welfare for the same reason that the ideal of   17
welfare itself is failing—because, in other words, we are unable to give any definition of education except the same kind of definition we give of welfare.

If students do not want classical literature, philosophy or science, if they do want sports, courses in movie appreciation and in the accepted social conventions, then, just as the other things constitute welfare, so these things must constitute education. Once the school, like the church, tended to embody a protest, or at least a countervailing influence, against what the other forces in society tended to   18
make of that society and of man himself. The church held that man undisciplined by religion was wicked. The school held that unless he was educated, he would be ignorant and crass. But both the church and the school seem now to have fallen in love with the world as it is. They talk more and more about adjustment—and by that to mean "adjustment to things as they are."

The church halfheartedly, the school with real enthusiasm, gives up the attempt to direct society and is content to follow it, like the political leader who watches where the mob is going, puts himself at the head of it and says, "Follow me." Educators so-called have said, "Don't teach literary English; teach acceptable English." If, as a New York commission recently has proposed, children are not interested   19
in the classics, don't waste time trying to arouse their interests; give them something they are interested in—teach them how to drive

automobiles, how lipstick is best applied or, and this is part of one actual course in a Midwestern institution of learning, how to order groceries over the telephone.

These are the things many of the students will be doing; this is what their lives will be made up of. And if the business of education is to prepare for life, then these are the things that they ought to be taught. But the statement so commonly made, that education should be a preparation for life, is meaningless unless the kind of life it is supposed to prepare for is specified. If education is properly defined as hardly more than what anthropologists call "acculturation," then it is worth taking account of the fact that most children get much more of their education in this sense from advertisements, moving pictures, television, popular songs and so on, than they do from school. Preparation for life as the schools are tending to define it is much better accomplished by those institutions outside the school system than by those within it.

It would, of course, be inaccurate as well as unfair to leave the impression that there is no protest against the ideals and practices of the schools as typified by the examples just given. During the past few years such protests have grown from a whisper to an outcry. Various organizations, notably the Council for Basic Education, have been formed to combat the prevailing tendencies. The latter especially has conducted a vigorous campaign of propaganda, buttressed by news bulletins, which report both outrageous examples of denatured education and reforms in the directions of which it approves.

Such protests have had their effect. In California, for instance, the recent report of a state-appointed commission puts itself squarely on record as finding the prevailing aims and methods of the school system to be in many instances radically undesirable.

Even more important perhaps is the fact that many parents have expressed their dissatisfaction and called for reform. The National Education Association, a very powerful and well entrenched group, has bitterly resented most such criticism, but if the tide has not actually turned, it looks as though it might be on the point of turning.

Nevertheless, it is not enough merely to ridicule current extravagances, to call for a return to the three R's and to insist that education does not consist in miscellaneous instruction in such varied specific subjects as safety rules for automobilists, the use of consumer credit and the current conventions governing "dating." Neither is it enough to say only that schools should be concerned primarily with the intellect and that those who talk about "educating the whole

child" seem to forget that his head is part of him. Any rational   24
theory must be based upon some conviction that the man of whom
the child is the father ought to be in mind, in taste and in convictions
something more that what he will be if he is allowed to follow only
his simplest inclinations and whatever happens to be the current
conventions of his group. In other words, what is necessary is a
standard of values. Education is simply not changing people as much
as it should.

Many critics of our society have said that we lack standards. This
has been said so often by preachers and by the makers of commencement addresses that we have almost stopped asking what, if anything,
it means to say that our society "lacks standards." But that we do
lack standards for welfare and standards for education is obvious.   25
Welfare turns into vulgar materialism because we have no standard by
which to measure it. Education fails because it also refuses to face
the responsibility of saying in what education consists. Both tend to
become merely what people seem to want.

To any such complaint most sociologists, psychologists and educators will shrug and say, "Perhaps. But where can you find standards other than those which are set by society itself? Who is arrogant   26
enough to set them up? Where can the authority for such standards
be found?"

Most periods of human history have believed that they could be
found somewhere outside mere custom. They have usually been
sought in one or all of three places: (1) In the revealed will of God;   27
(2) in the operation of right reason, supposedly capable of defining
good and evil; (3) in something permanent in human nature itself.

If I say this to the modern relativist, he replies that none of these
things will any longer do. (1) God no longer exists. (2) Though man
is capable of thinking instrumentally—that is to say, capable of
scheming to get what he wants—there is no such thing as pure reason
capable of reaching an absolute; and whenever men have thought
they were doing so, they were, in fact only rationalizing their desires
or the customs of their particular country. (3) What we call "human   28
nature" is merely the result of the conditioning of the individual,
either by the society in which he lives or by the peculiar experiences
which have happened to be his. Since neither God nor pure reason
exists, and since human nature in infinitely variable, it is evident that
morals are merely mores, or custom; that right reason is merely a
rationalization of the prejudices of the individual or his society; and
that human nature is merely what social circumstances have made it.

If all these characteristic modern convictions—or lack of convictions—are sound, then we must agree that whatever most people want is welfare, and that whatever pupils think they would least dislike doing in school is education. It is then useless to ask whether society is going in the right direction or whether men today are leading a good life. Nothing is absolutely better than anything else; things are what they are and will be what they will be, and we cannot control or direct. We must follow where events may lead us. 29

Before accepting this counsel of despair once and for all, it would be worth while to ask again if it really is certain that all three of the conceivable bases upon which some standard might be founded really are merely illusory. Each of them might be taken up in turn. One might ask again does God exist; one might ask again is right reason a mere figment of the imagination? Does human nature exist? 30

I here raise only what is perhaps the least difficult of all these questions—the last one. Granted that man may be conditioned in various ways, is it nevertheless true that there are limits to the extent to which he can be conditioned? Is it true that human nature tends to return to some norm, that it is not limitlessly conditionable? And is it possible that to some extent one thing is better or higher or more valuable than another because human nature tends persistently to think that it is? Or, to put the question in its most general form, is there a good life which might be loosely defined as "that which is in accord with the most fundamental and persistent wants, desires and needs of human nature"? 31

If ours is the richest and most powerful civilization that has ever existed, but if it is also the most anxious and ill at ease, is that in part because human nature needs something more than the wealth and power it has acquired? Is it possibly because human nature needs to believe just what modern thought has forbidden it to believe—that is, that morals are more than mores and that value judgments are more than merely rationalized prejudices? Once you insist that human nature as such does not exist, all the relativisms of our time—cultural, moral and social—inevitably follow. So, almost in desperation, let us ask again, "How good is the evidence that there is no such thing as human nature, that it is nothing but what experience or culture has made it?" 32

We must begin by remembering that the theory that human nature is nothing in itself is not actually new. In that enormously influential seventeenth-century book, *Leviathan* by Thomas Hobbes, the theory is already implicit. Hobbes attempts to account for all the

phenomena of human life by assuming that there is nothing innate in
man except the ability to receive stimuli, the ability to react to them
and the desire to experience pleasure. There is, accordingly, nothing   33
in the mind which has not been first in the senses. There are no such
things as innate ideas or desires other than the simple desire to experience pleasure or to exercise power, which latter is said to be the
same thing. Hence man becomes whatever experience makes him
and, to use the phrase which became popular later, he is born with a
blank slate upon which anything may be written.

We have enormously complicated this theory. We have drawn
from it many deductions. But we have added little if anything essentially new. The whole of modern relativism seems to follow logically
from Hobbes. If the human mind begins as a blank slate upon which
anything may be written, then morals are only mores, our ideas of
what is good or evil, just or unjust, beautiful or ugly, seemly or   34
unseemly, are simply learned from the society in which we grow up.
Nothing is eternally or inherently better than anything else—cultures
vary from time to time and from place to place, but there is no
external standard by which one may be judged as better than another. Incidentally, this complete abandonment of the right to judge
we now commonly call "getting rid of our prejudices."

Contemporary anthropologists are fond of pointing out that
what was considered right and desirable in one society was not so
considered in another. Already by the end of the nineteenth century
the historian Lecky could assert in his *History of European Morals*
that there is no act which has not at one time or place been commanded as a duty and at another time or place forbidden as a sin—
which is to say again that morals are only mores. Or, as a contempor- 35
ary college textbook on psychology, written by a professor at the
University of Southern California, puts it in a very short chapter on
morals, "We call a man moral when he acts in accord with the laws
and customs of his society"—by which definition, no doubt, a Nazi
who took part in the persecution of the Jews would be a moral man,
and one who did not would be an immoral one.

In a world which has no definitely rejected transcendental sanc-
tions for either codes of morals or standards of value, the question
whether human nature itself might supply them becomes enormously
important. Is the usual negative answer really justifiable? Shall we   36
one day swing again in a different direction and discover evidence
now neglected that human nature is something in itself and does
provide certain absolutes, valid at least within the human realm?

Have the anthropologists, for instance, been so preoccupied with
the collection of materials to demonstrate the enormous differences

between cultures that they have overlooked some things which are 37 common to all? Have the experimental psychologists been so busy conditioning both men and animals that they have paid little attention to the resistance to conditioning which both can put up?

One little breeze in psychological doctrine might seem to point in this direction. Some skeptical psychologists have begun to wonder whether instinct on the one hand and the conditioned reflex on the 38 other really can account for all of the behavior of living organisms. Certain sufficiently obvious facts have recently been re-emphasized.

Consider three of them which seem ludicrously simple. (1) Birds know by instinct how to fly and do not have to be taught, though mother birds sometimes seem to be teaching them. This is an example of instinct. (2) Seals do not instinctively know how to swim, but they learn very easily how to swim when they are taught by their parents. (3) You would have a very hard time indeed teaching most 39 songbirds to swim. In other words, there are not just two classes of animal behavior—that which is inborn and that which is learned. There is also a third and possibly an enormously important one— namely, that behavior which is not inborn, though the ability to learn it easily is.

Considering such facts, some have begun to wonder whether the same might be true not only of skills but throughout the whole psychic realm of beliefs, tastes, motives, desires and needs. The thesis of the moral relativist is—to take an extreme case—that since no one is born with an innate idea that dishonesty and treachery are evil, then the conviction that they are evil can be nothing but the result of social education, and the opposite could just as easily have been 40 taught, since value judgments are merely the rationalized prejudices of a given culture. May it not be true on the contrary that certain ideas are much more easily learned than others, and that what the eighteenth century called natural law, natural taste and the rest, is real—consisting in those beliefs and tastes which are most readily learned and most productive of health and happiness?

Perhaps you can condition an individual or a society to think and behave unnaturally just as you might possibly teach a robin to swim, but men who have been conditioned to think or behave unnaturally are unhappy—as unhappy and as inefficient as swimming robins. Perhaps Hobbes was right to the extent that no ideas are innate; but if the capacity to entertain readily some ideas and not others is innate, 41 then it comes down to much the same thing. As Alexander Pope wrote nearly two and a half centuries ago, "Nature affords at least a glimmering light; the lines, though touched but faintly, are drawn

right"—which is to say that the faint lines on the not quite blank
slate constitute the reality behind the idea of a normal human being.

What Pope thought of as a metaphor may be an accurate biological statement. On the not quite blank slate the lines are touched too
faintly to constitute an automatic instinct—they may even be destroyed by resolute conditioning and education—but they are rather
like a latent image on a photographic plate, imperceptible until   42
developed, though development will reveal only what already exists.
If this is true, then there is no such thing as human nature. What we
are born with is not a blank slate, but a film bearing already a latent
image.

No doubt, as Pope himself said elsewhere, as experimental
psychologists prove in the laboratory and as dictators as well as
educators have too often demonstrated, the lines may be overlaid,
and the unnatural may cease to seem a creature of hideous mien. But
the conditioners have to work hard. Men, I suspect, believe must   43
more readily in the reality of good and evil than they accept cultural
relativism. Perhaps that means that belief in the reality of good and
evil is according to nature and the modern tendency to dismiss them
as mere prejudices of culture is fundamentally unnatural.

Such as assumption is at least one which no valid science forbids,
and if we make even such a minimum assumption, we can be saved
from the nihilism of the present-day social, cultural and moral relativism. We have again some point of reference now lacking in every
inquiry which sets out to determine what kind of society or educa-   44
tion or culture would be best for us. One thing is no longer as good
as another provided only it can be shown or made to exist. We would
no longer need to talk only about what can be done to men or what
we might possibly be able to make them into, for we would be able
to talk again about what men are in themselves.

We would have the beginning of a basis for a definition of welfare
and a definition of education such as we now totally lack. We could
say, for example, that welfare is not merely what people at a given   45
moment believe they want, but that which experience has proved to
be conducive to health and happiness.

We could say that education is not whatever a pupil thinks he
wants in school, but that it is that which experience has shown will
lead to a true understanding of his own nature, his own needs and his 46
own wants. We could say the ideal of education is not conformity,
not acculturation, but the full development of human nature's potentialities.

We could say that the normal is not the same thing as the average, but rather that the normal is normative—that is to say, that by which a thing is to be judged. And we could add that the normal 47 human being is not the average human being, but the thing to which human nature aspires.

To attempt to determine what is part of permanent human nature is to undertake no easy task. To distinguish between what is truly natural and what is merely conditioned is extremely difficult. But to conclude that the question is actually a meaningful one is already to have concluded something vastly important. We talk much today about the extent to which we can control nature and our destiny, of how we have taken the future of the human race into our hands. But control implies some idea of the direction in which you 48 want to go. We have the power, perhaps, but what good is the power unless we know what we want to do with it? "Give me a fulcrum for my lever, and I will move the world," said Archimedes. But a fulcrum for a lever is exactly what we lack. It implies a point of support which is necessary if you are going to move the world. We are trying to lever society without having any fulcrum on which to rest the lever and, in the absence of any other, we might possibly find it in some understanding of fundamental human nature.

However much there may be still to learn about human nature, certain of its characteristics seem to me obvious enough to suggest 49 some of the ways in which our society has been going wrong.

The first of these permanent characteristics seems to me to be that man is inveterately a maker of value judgments. His idea of what constitutes right and wrong conduct, of what is just or unjust, has been—perhaps will continue to be—extremely diverse. But he has nearly always believed that good and evil, justice and injustice, are 50 realities which it is of the first importance to define and to cherish, while moral and cultural relativism—the idea that morals are nothing but mores and that one society is not absolutely better than another is so profoundly unnatural a conviction that it has seldom been entertained for long and is destructive of human welfare when it is.

Closely related to the value judgment is the idea of justice. Men have varied enormously, irreconcilably, over the question of what constitutes justice. But they have nearly always believed that there is some such thing and that they should adhere to it. Part of that feeling is, I believe, the conviction that acts should have consequences, and that the way you are treated should be in some degree 51 affected by the way in which you behave. A spoiled child, one who never pays any penalty for his follies or misdeeds, one who is given what some of the modern educators call "uncritical love," is usually an unhappy child because something fundamental in his human nature tells him that acts should have consequences and makes him profoundly uneasy in a world where they do not.

Similarly I believe that a society is unhappy if it holds—as so many sociologists now profess to hold—that no man should be held responsible for his imprudences or his crimes. He may be glad to escape those consequences, but he is finding himself in a world with-   52
out justice, in a world where the way in which you act has no effect upon the way in which you are treated. And I believe that, like the spoiled child, he is profoundly uneasy in that unnatural situation.

I believe that it is also in accord with fundamental human nature to want some goods other than the material, that a society which defines the good life as merely a high standard of living and then defines the high standard of living in terms of material things alone is one which, in that respect, is denying expression to a fundamental characteristic of man. Few societies, whether primitive or not, have ever accepted the belief that welfare thus narrowly defined is the one and only supreme good. Men have sought all sorts of other things—   53
they have sought God, they have sought beauty, they have sought truth or they have sought glory, militarily or otherwise. They have sought adventure; they have even—so anthropologists tell us—sometimes believed that a large collection of dried human heads was the thing in all the world most worth having. But seldom if ever, so it seems to me, have the confessedly sought only what is now called "welfare."

This is a mere beginning. You may dispute, if you like, even the few general statements I have made about permanent human nature. But if you admit that some things are and some things are not in   54
accord with human nature, then you have grasped an instrument capable of doing something which few men today seem able to do, namely, attempt a rational criticism of things as they are.

QUESTIONS AND PROBLEMS

1. What does Krutch mean by "welfare"? How does he use contrast to make his meaning clear by the time the reader comes to pars. 5, 6, and 7?
2. Krutch says (par. 7) that many of the arguments for and against welfare are too familiar to need mentioning. However, give some of these arguments.
3. How do the questions Krutch asks in pars. 7 and 8 contribute to a definition of welfare?
4. Discuss present-day social work among the economically disadvantaged in urban areas from the point of view of Krutch's question, "Does the promo-

tion of welfare mean giving people what they want or seem to want or think they want . . . ?" (par. 7).

5. What basic problems are involved in giving people "what they ought to have"?
6. What does Krutch mean by "cultural and moral relativism" (par. 9)?
7. Discuss David Thompson's statement (par. 9) from the point of view of practical democracy.
8. In par. 12 Krutch states the assumption, "the good life is whatever the majority thinks or has been persuaded to think it is."
   a. Are there weaknesses in this definition? What are they?
   b. Who are the persuaders? How effective are they?
9. Discuss "pursuit of happiness" in terms of the United States Government today. Are there conflicts in the definition of "happiness" which a vast number of people would hold and that which the government holds? Explain.
10. Discuss the demands of college students for new kinds of courses—in movie making or movie appreciation, for example—in light of the proposition that education will cause people to want fewer things and more ideas and will give them a conception of what the good life is. Do college students want "adjustment to things as they are" (par. 18)?
11. Consider the proposition that "whatever pupils think they would least dislike doing in school is education" (par. 29). Examine the statement in view of the courses you and your friends are taking or plan to take in college.
12. Discuss the three bases for making absolute judgments which Krutch names in pars. 10 and 27.
13. How does Krutch arrive at the definitions of welfare and education which he gives in pars. 45 and 46? Has he built the essay to these conclusions logically?
14. Several groups—student demonstrators, leaders of riots—have maintained that they should not be held legally responsible for certain activities for which the law normally holds a man responsible. Do you agree or disagree with Krutch's view as expressed in par. 52? Defend your point of view.

SUGGESTIONS FOR WRITING

1. Write an essay on "Education in Utopia," giving the student's view of the ideal educational system.
2. Develop your own definition of welfare. Take issue, if you wish, with Krutch's ideas.
3. In an essay, prophesy the nature of the welfare state in the year 2001.
4. Write a satire on the decision-makers who decide "what the people ought to have."
5. Make a study of contemporary advertising from the point of view of the statement, "the good life is whatever the majority . . . has been persuaded to think it is."
6. Analyze the curriculum of your school from the point of view of Krutch's proposition that education "is that which experience has shown will lead to a true understanding of [the pupil's] own nature, his own needs and his own wants" (par. 46).
7. Argue for or against traditional vs. experimental courses in the college curriculum.

8. Write an essay on the social responsibility of the American, or on the social responsibility of the college student.

SUGGESTIONS FOR FURTHER READING

K. Arrow, *Social Choice and Individual Values*, 2nd ed. (Wiley)

Ralph J.D. Braibanti and Joseph J. Spengler, eds., *Tradition, Values, and Socioeconomic Development* (Duke)

Valdeman Carlson, *Economic Security in the United States* (McGraw-Hill)

Peter Gay, *The Dilemma of Democratic Socialism* (Collier)

Joseph Wood Krutch, *The Measure of Man: On Freedom, Human Values, Survival and the Modern Temper* (Bobbs-Merrill)

Frank C. Laubach, *The World Is Learning Compassion* (Revell)

R.W. Livingstone, *Education and the Spirit of the Age* (Oxford)

Walter G. Muelder, *Foundations of the Responsible Society* (Abingdon)

New York University, *The Obligation of Universities to the Social Order* (New York Univ.)

Wilhelm Ropke, *Welfare, Freedom and Inflation* (Univ. of Alabama)

William T. Tucker, *The Social Context of Economic Behavior* (Holt, Rinehart & Winston)

CLASSROOM WITHOUT WALLS
Marshall McLuhan

It's natural today to speak of "audio-visual aids" to teaching, for we still think of the book as norm, of other media as incidental. We also think of the new media (press, radio, TV) as *mass media* and think of the book as an individualistic form—individualistic because it isolated the reader in silence and helped create the Western "I." Yet it was the first product of mass production. 1

With it everybody could have the same books. It was impossible in medieval times for different students, different institutions, to have copies of the same book. Manuscripts, commentaries, were dictated. Students memorized. Instruction was almost entirely oral, done in groups. Solitary study was reserved for the advanced scholar. The first printed books were "visual aids" to oral instruction. 2

Before the printing press, the young learned by listening, watching, doing. So, until recently, our own rural children learned the language and skills of their elders. Learning took place outside the classroom. Only those aiming at professional careers went to school at all. Today in our cities, most learning occurs outside the classroom. The sheer quantity of information conveyed by press-magazines-film-TV-radio far exceeds the quantity of information conveyed by school instruction and texts. This challenge has destroyed the monopoly of the book as a teaching aid and cracked the very walls of the classroom so suddenly that we're confused, baffled. 3

In this violently upsetting social situation, many teachers naturally view the offerings of the new media as entertainment, rather than education. But this carries no conviction to the student. Find a classic that wasn't first regarded as light entertainment. Nearly all vernacular works were so regarded until the 19th century. 4

Many movies are obviously handled with a degree of insight and maturity at least equal to the level permitted in today's textbooks. Olivier's *Henry V* and *Richard III* assemble a wealth of scholarly and artistic skill, which reveals Shakespeare at a very high level, yet in a way easy for the young to enjoy. 5

The movie is to dramatic representation what the book was to the manuscript. It makes available to many and at many times and places what otherwise would be restricted to a few at few times and places. The movie, like the book, is a ditto device. TV shows to 50,000,000 simultaneously. Some feel that the value of experiencing a book is diminished by being extended to many minds. This notion is always implicit in the phrases "mass media," "mass entertain- 6 ment"—useless phrases obscuring the fact that English itself is a mass medium.

Today we're beginning to realize that the new media aren't just mechanical gimmicks for creating worlds of illusion, but new languages with new and unique powers of expression. Historically, the resources of English have been shaped and expressed in constantly new and changing ways. The printing press changed not only the quantity of writing but also the character of language and the relations between author and public. Radio, film, TV pushed written   7 English toward the spontaneous shifts and freedom of the spoken idiom. They aided us in the recovery of intense awareness of facial language and bodily gesture. If these "mass media" should serve only to weaken or corrupt previously achieved levels of verbal and pictorial culture, it won't be because there's anything inherently wrong with them. It will be because we've failed to master them as new languages in time to assimilate them to our total cultural heritage.

These new developments, under quiet analytic survey, point to a basic strategy of culture for the classroom. When the printed book first appeared, it threatened the oral procedures of teaching and created the classroom as we now know it. Instead of making his own text, his own dictionary, his own grammar, the student started out with these tools. He could study not one but several languages. To-   8 day these new media threaten, instead of merely reinforce, the procedures of this traditional classroom. It's customary to answer this threat with denunciations of the unfortunate character and effect of movies and TV, just as the comic book was feared and scorned and rejected from the classroom. Its good and bad features in form and content, when carefully set beside other kinds of art and narrative, could have become a major asset to the teacher.

Where student interest is already focused is the natural point at which to be in the elucidation of other problems and interests. The educational task is not only to provide basic tools of perception but   9 also to develop judgment and discrimination with ordinary social experience.

Few students ever acquire skill in analysis of newspapers. Fewer have any ability to discuss a movie intelligently. To be articulate and discriminating about ordinary affairs and information is the mark of an educated man. It's misleading to suppose there's any basic difference between education and entertainment. This distinction merely   10 relieves people of the responsibility of looking into the matter. It's like setting up a distinction between didactic and lyric poetry on the ground that one teaches, the other pleases. However, it's always been true that whatever pleases teaches more effectively.

QUESTIONS AND PROBLEMS

1. McLuhan writes, "Today we're beginning to realize that the new media aren't just mechanical gimmicks for creating worlds of illusion, but new languages with new and unique powers of expression" (par. 7). How does this essay bear out that statement?
2. José y Ortega y Gasset once defined culture as that which a man has in his possession when he has forgotten everything he has read. Does McLuhan's essay reinforce this definition?
3. Discuss McLuhan's contention that "Today in our cities, most learning occurs outside the classroom" (par. 3). What is the quality of the word *monopoly* two sentences further on?
4. Why does the author object to the term "mass media" (par. 6)? Do you agree with the implication he finds in the use of the term?
5. McLuhan defines the educational task as "not only to provide basic tools of perception, but also to develop judgment and discrimination with ordinary social experience" (par. 9). How does he suggest the new media can be of aid in this task?
6. McLuhan has speculated whether rebellion in the classroom and rebellion against the book are the result of our electronic age. Comment on this possibility.
7. The author says that it is "misleading to suppose there's any basic difference between education and entertainment" (par. 10). Discuss the relationship between the two in terms of your own experience as a student.
8. Reply to McLuhan's statement, "Find a classic which wasn't first regarded as light entertainment" (par. 4) by naming several.

SUGGESTIONS FOR WRITING

1. Write an argument in opposition to McLuhan's position. Entitle it "But There Will Always Be the Book."
2. Write a research paper on the invention of printing by movable type in the Western world.
3. McLuhan refers to the time—actually not very long ago—when students were required to memorize—great swatches of poetry, for example. Write a defense of memorizing as a form of pedagogy; or write an argument against memorizing in education.
4. Write your own "Classroom Without Walls" on contemporary education outside the school.
5. Write a review of a recent movie or a television "special," stressing the educational quality of the production.
6. Defend "the book" as central to education.
7. What influences have radio, television, and movies had on language? Develop by use of example.
8. Investigate the present use of electronic aids in primary school classrooms. Compare with those in use when you were in the primary grades.
9. Write an essay on "Education as Entertainment."
10. Read McLuhan's *The Medium Is the Massage*. Write a paper explaining the author's basic points.

SUGGESTIONS FOR FURTHER READING

Jack Behar and Ben Lieberman, "Paradise Regained, or McLuhanacy?" *Teacher's College Record*, April, 1966.

William D. Boutwell, ed., *Using Mass Media in the Schools* (Appleton-Century-Crofts)

Edgar Dale, *Mass Media and Education* (Univ. of Chicago)

Benjamin DeMott, "Against McLuhan." *Esquire*, August, 1966.

Lewis A. Dexter and David M. White, eds., *People, Society, and Mass Communications* (Free Press)

Norman Jacobs, ed., *Culture for the Millions?* (Beacon)

Marshall McLuhan, *Explorations in Communications* (with E.S. Carpenter) (Beacon); *The Gutenberg Galaxy: The Making of Typographic Man* (Univ. of Toronto); *Understanding Media: The Extensions of Man* (McGraw-Hill); *The Medium Is the Massage* (with Quentin Fiore) (Random House)

Gerald E. Stearn, ed., *McLuhan, Hot & Cool* (Dial)

ADDRESS AT GETTYSBURG
Abraham Lincoln

Four score and seven years ago our fathers brought forth on this continent a new nation, conceived in Liberty and dedicated to the proposition that all men are created equal. 1

Now we are engaged in a great civil war, testing whether that nation, or any nation so conceived and so dedicated, can long endure. We are met on a great battle-field of that war. We have come to dedicate a portion of that field as a final resting place for those who here gave their lives that that nation might live. It is altogether fitting and proper that we should do this. 2

But, in a larger sense, we can not dedicate—we can not consecrate—we can not hallow this ground. The brave men, living and dead, who struggled here have consecrated it far above our poor power to add or detract. The world will little note nor long remember what we say here, but it can never forget what they did here. It is for us the living, rather, to be dedicated here to the unfinished work which they who fought here have thus far so nobly advanced. It is rather for us to be here dedicated to the great task remaining before us—that from these honored dead we take increased devotion to that cause for which they gave the last full measure of devotion—that we here highly resolve that these dead shall not have died in vain—that this nation, under God, shall have a new birth of freedom—and that government of the people, by the people, for the people shall not perish from the earth. 3

November 19, 1863

QUESTIONS AND PROBLEMS

1. Outline Lincoln's address to show the relationship among the various parts he develops.
2. We are told that Lincoln's address was given scant attention in the press of the day. Do you consider it a persuasive statement? Why?
3. Compare Lincoln's statement with the typical political address. What qualities does it have which have made it endure as a classic? What does it tell you about Lincoln the man?
4. Can the address be easily paraphrased? Can a précis be made of it? Try.
5. Comment on the words Lincoln uses. Is the diction highly allusive? Are the words generally more denotative or connotative? What is the total effect?

SUGGESTIONS FOR WRITING

1. Write an address in dedication of a memorial—one already existing or one which may come in the future—on your campus. Limit it to the length of two typewritten pages.

2. Write an essay on the *spirit* of the Address at Gettysburg. What does it tell us about the people whom Lincoln represents?
3. Write a "Gettysburg revisited" type of paper in which you assess the accomplishments of the past century and more of which Lincoln would have been proud.
4. Is the spirit of Gettysburg dead today? Assess the nature of American commitment to ideals.
5. Write a "Vietnam Address"—as quiet and controlled as Lincoln's, and as true for today as Lincoln's address was for his day.

BRINGING SCIENCE UNDER LAW
Harvey Wheeler

In referring to science and technology here, I am invoking the distinction Linus Pauling once made between "developmental" science and what is ususally called "pure" science. By developmental science Pauling did not mean merely technology nor did he mean only bureaucratized science, i.e. the mass cooperative endeavor that takes place in great institutes and business corporations. Rather, he had in mind the day-to-day work of the brilliant men who are exploring the implications of the breakthroughs made by first-magnitude geniuses.

One distinctive feature of developmental science is its rapid technological transformation. In fact, the pace of technological application is such that developmental science these days is almost immediately converted into technology. In speaking of science in this article, I have this in mind. I am not, in a word, concerned with the basement-and-garret science of the lonely pioneering genius.

H.W.

A shock reverberated through the intellectual establishment of the West in the mid-twentieth century when it became apparent that science was not necessarily incompatible with totalitarianism. The West had previously "proved" on paper that science required the so-called free market in ideas, a John Stuart Mill type of liberal democracy, in order to flourish. This, it now became clear, was simply not true.   1

There had been an even more disturbing revelation earlier. Nazi Germany had shown that even the most "ethical" of the professions, medicine, was capable of turning its humanitarian code into a license to perform gruesome experiments on living people. While this was chilling, it also seemed at the time to be too perverse to be a threat   2
elsewhere. Now, however, with authoritarianism increasing throughout the West, and with organ transplants becoming commonplace, we are beginning to have vague fears that something similar to the Nazi corruption of medical science might be looming for all of us.

A third shock occurred after World War II when we learned that our own American scientists had eagerly produced history's most awesome weapons, hardly stopping to consider that moral issues   3
might be involved in their decision to do so. Science, these eminent men insisted, was ethically neutral.

Recently, a technological development renewed our concern. Dramatic developments in mathematical logic, cybernation, systems analysis, and the planning-programming-budgeting approach to ad-

ministrative control have been giving us reason of late to believe that
a science-spawned managerial revolution may yet be in the offing.   4
During the past twenty years or so, it has begun to appear that
management may gain access to techniques and tools that could be
used to achieve their managerial ends without concern for the public
good.

The appearance of a new technology, of course, need not necessarily be a matter of concern unless another factor is present; that is,
the new technology and its practitioners must be engaged in doing
something that intimately affects the public interest. When this happens there are grave potentials for harming, as well as benefiting,   5
society. The question, then, arises as to whether or not we can or
should act collectively to inhibit the harmful effects that may result
from the bad uses of sciences and technology. This is our present
problem.

Currently many solutions are being offered. One is to find some
way of revivifying the classical idea of the profession. Another is to
create some sort of government agency charged with coördinating   6
science policy. Both solutions strike me as seriously deficient. Nothing less than an entirely new look at science will suffice. This requires
discussion of what has come to be known as the scientific revolution.

The process by which the A-bomb was created pointed up the
inner political logic of that revolution. It also laid bare the corrosive
impact developmental science is having on our traditional liberal
democratic dogmas and practices. The birth of the bomb demonstrated once and for all that neither the people, their elected repre-   7
sentatives, nor even bureaucratic experts are competent any longer to
"legislate" about scientific problems. The traditional deliberative
processes of Western democracy, it is clear, were undermined when it
became apparent that they could not cope with the implications of
contemporary science for public policy.

But there was also a positive side. The implications of the new
science ranged far beyond the interests and activities of the scientific
establishment itself; fundamental scientific innovations, such as those
relating to atomic energy and solid-state physics, furnished the
foundations on which the very shape of society would be built in the
future. Important scientific discoveries had always brought about
profound social changes, of course. But as long as these discoveries   8
occurred infrequently and without conscious anticipation, much less
design, one could not say that they were called forth politically.
However, with the maturity of the sciences, Francis Bacon's *New
Atlantis* became a prescription for the present rather than a fanciful

vision of the future. The time, then, had arrived when science made it possible to "legislate" the shape of the future.

This shifted politics to a new plane. Those who had produced the atom bomb were actually the first to see that they had wrought not only a scientific but a political revolution—legislatures might continue to operate in their accustomed fashion, politicians might continue to campaign for office as of old, but those who were really determining the outlines of the future belonged to the scientific, rather than the political, establishment. As a consequence of these developments, the significance of today's scientific revolution can be summarized simply: The revolution has brought about social transformations; relationships between theory and practice that seemingly had been firmly established by the Industrial Revolution were reversed. This change means, among other things, that in the world created by the scientific revolution the critical force in society will no longer be the flow of capital but scientific and technological innovation. The most fateful struggles in that society will be fought over the efforts to direct and control these innovations. This is where constitutionalization comes in.

Our notion of legislation and/or constitutionalization has long been built on two assumptions, neither of which is now acceptable. The first was that men of common prudence and wisdom are capable of understanding every political problem that needs to be understood. The second was that such men could make laws to deal with these problems. The scientific revolution is undermining the first of these assumptions by posing problems too technical for laymen to fathom. It is undermining the second by making it impossible for legislatures to lay the foundation for the future. The result is already evident; we either have to invent new procedures for handling science policy or be ruled by technology.

How do we deal with the problem? At first blush, it might seem enough merely to strengthen our governing institutions with more scientific advisers. But this is not enough; it won't do. The reason is that the scientific expert has to be such a narrow specialist he cannot acquire the general knowledge necessary to grasp the social and philosophical implications of even those technical matters on which he is an acknowledged expert. The same thing applies in reverse. The generalist's knowledge of any one specialty is not thorough enough for him to master the complex problems now associated with science and technology.

There is a philosophical issue here. It turns on a very old argument about science—one as old as the temptation of Adam and Eve,

the curiosity of Pandora, or Prometheus' defiance of the gods. Per-   12
haps of all such myths, the Doctor Faustus story is the most pertin-
ent.

That myth embodied the essential ethic of medieval science—
something the men of the Middle Ages took very seriously. Remember they did not look upon science as ineffectual. On the contrary,
everyone believed in its power—black magic it was called—just as   13
everyone believed in white magic, the power of miracles. But one
magic was satanic and the other godly. One defied God and incurred
His wrathful retribution; the other entailed His bountiful intervention.

The war between the two varieties of magic was carried over into
attacks on magicians who practiced the black arts of alchemy and
astrology and employed spells, secret words, cabalistic designs,
talismanic charms, and amulets to gain power over the spirits who—it
was widely believed—were in control of human events. As the various
departments of magic matured into the post-medieval sciences, the
pioneers were anxious to purge science of this reliance on supernatur-   14
al forces. At the same time they were eager to proclaim their own
religious orthodoxy. Such, at least, was the aim of Copernicus,
Galileo, Brahe, and Vesalius. It was also the later concern of Descartes, Bacon, Newton, and Leibnitz. But, though science was changing the face of the earth, the theologians still looked at the world in
the old manner. As a result, the old war between black and white
magic turned into a new war between science and religion.

The leading early apologist for the new view of science was
Francis Bacon. Bacon claimed that science had no theological significance; like heaven and earth, theology and science were simply different realms of truth. To make his case, Bacon and his followers
invoked the Biblical text that distinguished between the things owing
to Casesar and those owing to God. They argued from it that a man   15
could be faithful to one and yet serve the other. Beyond this, Bacon
held that there was something intrinsically humanistic about science.
It advanced human knowledge, which in turn contributed to human
progress. The only thing necessary, then, was to keep science free of
dogma and authority.

Bacon's position in time became the professional ideology of
science, to such an extent that it seemed to be a self-evident truth.
All seemed to be going well—the ideology went largely unchalleng-   16
ed—until the contemporary scientific revolution reopened certain
ethical issues that had remained closed since the seventeenth century.
We are, in a sense, then, back to Doctor Faustus.

Recall that the Faustian legend was informed with a view that had science dependent on the special intervention of supernatural forces. Medieval science had sought for ultimate power and knowledge—omnipotence and omniscience, the attributes of God. The scientists of that period, in a word, had pursued the most fundamental quests. They tried to plumb directly to the secrets of the creation of life. They sought the magical elixir that would bring everlasting youth, searched for the philosopher's stone that would convert the baser metals into the finer, puzzled over the secret "signatures" of events that would unlock the mysteries of past and future and produce control over the paths of the planets and the vagaries of the weather. They propitiated spirits who could empower them to move mountains, change men into different shapes, and permit moving 17 about through space and time at will. With such goals, the prospects for science were more revolutionary, and the risks incurred by its practitioners far more dangerous, than what was to come later. Medieval science, then, faced up to the questions about men who would play God. The advent of the early-modern sciences required a new informal "contract" in place of the older one Faustus had negotiated with Satan. According to the new pact, scientists would abandon all the quests that were disturbing to theologians in return for freedom to work without interference. As scientists they would stay out of God's province, concerning themselves only with the problems of this world. Theologians and philosophers for their part would stop pillorying science. Francis Bacon drafted this "contract" for the Anglo-Saxon world; it was also described by Descartes and Leibnitz.

Although modern science abandoned an over-all ethic, it did adopt a kind of internal code. The scientist was supposed to maintain his methodological and intellectual honesty, but that was all. Hence, from a deeper standpoint, early-modern science was ethically barren, and proud of it. This, however, will no longer do. Science today is once more delving into something like the quests pursued by medieval magic. For example, the deliberate synthesis of miracle fabrics, exotic metals, and precious stones has become an everyday occurrence. The genetic code through which the rudimentary substances 18 of life are ordered into their distinctive shapes and functions has been deciphered. The French physicist Pierre Auger has even suggested that molecular biologists may succeed in recalling previously extinct animal forms from the burial grounds of history. The contemporary scientist must, then, face the ethical problem Doctor Faustus confronted. Unfettered freedom for developmental science is no longer tolerable. Scientists themselves recognize it, as was evident in the bad consciences of some of those who built the atom bomb.

The distinguished physicist Max Born has pointed to a source for the ethical corrosion in modern science. For men to be ethical they must perceive the moral implications of the alternative actions open to them. This is not necessarily a pragmatic or utilitarian view of ethics, for even if one holds that such things as murder are evil the hard question comes when we have to decide in a given case exactly what constitutes "murder" and whether or not there are circumstances that might justify it. Ordinarily, ethical judgments of this kind are not too difficult. If a military commander orders a subordinate to commit a crime against humanity, the soldier may decide he has no alternative but to obey. However, he cannot claim ignorance of the ethical issue. The case of the scientist, though, is somewhat   19
different. When a scientist sets out to produce atomic bombs or death rays, the preliminary research may be on such an abstract level that the connection between pure science and the purpose for the research effectively disappears. The scientists working on such projects can dispel any ethical qualms they might have by intoning the traditional ideology: any augmentation of knowledge must be good. In short, ethical judgments require making a connection between actions and effects, and it is this connection that science dissolves. Moreover, the full implications of a scientific discovery may not become completely apparent for many years. A scientist may work in full innocence only to learn years later that he helped produce a horror.

It has always been true, of course, that an action in the present may have unforeseeable harmful effects in the distant future. The invention of the automobile is an all too familiar illustration. A similar separation—not in time but in function—accompanies bureaucratization. Bureaucracy transforms people into impersonal functionaries. This was one reason Nazi concentration-camp executives could go about their duties seemingly detached from the atrocities they administered. A similar effect occurs when science becomes bureaucratized—the individual scientist deals with so minute a seg-   20
ment of the over-all project that he becomes almost as detached from the implications of his work as Adolf Eichmann alleged he was. Now contemporary science is raising this separation between actions and their effects to a new level. The more profound a scientific innovation, the more universal its potential applications—and the more difficult it becomes to foresee its extended effects. Professor Born's mournful conclusion was that the contemporary scientific revolution

has destroyed ethics, ushering mankind into a new world that is not only post-industrial but post-ethical.

Ethics is philosophical but practical; science is logical and mathematical in form. The result is that scientific knowledge accumulates from generation to generation like the compound interest on savings deposits. Each new scientist stands on the shoulders of those who have gone before, leaving behind him a hundred more who will do the same in turn. Each fledgling scientist begins his career by mastering the distilled essences of the work of his predecessors; his lifetime is devoted to adding elements to the accumulated scientific edifice. **21** He need not, indeed, start out by retracing all the laborious steps that have brought science from its earliest beginnings to its present elevated state. If that were necessary, the progress of science would be limited to how much of it could be assimilated anew by each successive neophyte: science could not develop beyond the limits of scientific powers one man could bring to bear in the course of a single lifetime.

This latter condition, however, was roughly the case before the advent of modern science. Prior to that, the quest for both scientific and ethical knowledge proceeded in much the same way. Both were **22** subject to similar limitations and neither could systematically develop and accumulate its findings. Bacon, realizing this, was right in seizing upon augmentation as the trademark of early-modern science.

When, in the seventeenth century, science acquired this power of augmentation, the growth of scientific knowledge shot up at an exponential rate, while ethical knowledge remained, and remains to this day, much as before. The social effect of such knowledge—that is, its capacity for good—is limited by the amount of wisdom individual men can acquire during their lifetime, for one does not assimilate the truth of an ethical precept the way one grasps the truth of a mathematical solution. On the contrary, one must first become a philoso- **23** pher to perceive the validity of the teachings of the wise men who have gone before. Coue was wrong, with his doctrine that every day in every way we are getting better and better. His error, and that of the doctrine of progress, was in assuming that the augmentation observable in the sciences was applicable to moral philosophy. On the contrary, moral philosophy has progressed but little during its entire twenty-five hundred years of history.

Each man must learn and apply ethical truths for himself. This is an additional basis for the contemporary separation between science and ethics. As science progresses cumulatively the problems it poses become progressively more numerous and complex. The gap between science and ethics widens with each passing hour. Some relief might develop were science able to extend human longevity, permitting us to devote more time to the quest for wisdom. Short of this, however, the only solution would appear to lie in a concerted effort to consti- 24 tutionalize science, so that its progress and development can be subjected to planning and control. A new ethic of science must be developed. We face a genuine culture crisis. This would be true even if, improbably, science were to grind to a halt and technological developments based on it were to cease. If today's life scientists are correct, the present crisis will shortly take an even more ominous turn.

The life sciences—biology, genetics, and so forth—are on the brink of a revolutionary development that will usurp the primacy that the physical sciences have enjoyed for over three hundred years. But note one difference: tampering with life processes demands ethical norms. Sciences that deal with life processes cannot avoid questions concerned with the goals, ends, and purposes of life. The tragedy, however, is that such questions do not interest most scientists, while philosophers by and large are not interested in what science is doing. Nonetheless, anything connected with the life processes involves ethics. It is *there,* unavoidable, lying at the heart of the life sciences. Yet, the biological sciences matured under the hegemony of the physical sciences—and, more's the pity, their recent spectacular advances have come from molecular biology, whose operating as- 25 sumption is that life processes can be reduced to the principles of physics. The life sciences, then, have reached maturity with the amoral pursuit of "objectivity" that long characterized the physical sciences. Inasmuch as life is intrinsically normative, the contemporary ethical poverty of biology must be due to some more fundamental development that made this distortion seem plausible. I suggest it was the ancient maneuver whereby all nature, life as well as inert matter, was made profane. The maneuver predated modern science by nearly sixteen hundred years. It can be traced back to that point in the Western tradition when both nature and society were secularized. The striking fact is that not science but Christianity turns out to be the culprit.

Prior to the advent of Christianity there had been no secular society and there had been no secular view of nature in Western tradition. On the contrary, as with practically every other known culture, society and nature were regarded as intrinsically sacral. This, of course, was the point at issue between the early Christians and the ancient Romans. The Christians' way of stating this was that the one true God forbade their participation in the rituals of any other god. Viewed in the light of today's enlarged perspective, this commandment was preposterous. Worse, it smacked of the colossal effrontery 26 of the unlettered. The urbane Romans, ironically destined to be known as pagans (peasants), pointed out that what Christians over-dramatically objected to as Emperor worship was but the ritual celebration of the social order. That occurred in almost every society. Similar Roman rituals also celebrated the natural order. But the early Christians—today's Jehovah's Witnesses make much the same point— narrowly restricted the sacral to the attributes of their own remote triune God.

The issue was brought to a head four centuries later in the dramatic showdown between Saint Augustine and Bishop Faustus. Bishop Faustus represented the West's last chance to reject the hard-shell eschatology of the Christian extremists. But Augustine won that momentous battle and proceeded to establish the dualistic doctrine of the divine heavenly city and the corrupt city of this world as the 27 official world view of the Western tradition. What Augustine wrought was, in effect, the birth of an ideology that ultimately permitted Western science to take an amoral approach to nature. In the light of the scientific revolution of our times, the Augustine-Faustus debate must be revived, overturned, and an ethical view of man, society, and nature reëstablished.

How would the control of developmental science, what I call constitutionalization, work? Perhaps the A.E.C., Telstar, and the T.V.A. can serve as examples. A public corporation for developmental science can be chartered and given its constitution. Civilian control can be installed and charged with the responsibility for several functions that are now not being performed at all. Most obvious is the need for an ombudsman to process public complaints as well as 28 complaints from scientists inside the Establishment. The ombudsman should have positive, as well as negative, or corrective, functions. That is, in addition to investigating alleged evils he should also see that the scientific enterprise achieves its publicly approved goals. This would require a special court system of adjudication, complete with appeal procedures.

To approach science in this way requires a new conception of constitutional theory—an architectonic approach to the politics of science. In such a framework, intellectual endeavors would be thought of in broad political terms, rather than merely in terms of the narrow desires of those who wish to pursue knowledge for its own, or their own, sake. It would also require fresh thought about

problems such as representation, which we thought the eighteenth century had put to rest for all times. If there is to be a new kind of public corporation for science, if it is to be under civilian control, and if the public will is to make its voice heard, then there must be some way for that will to find expression. This raises the "legislative"   29
question of how to furnish science with responsible policy-forming and goal-establishing functions. We know that the scandalous scientific boondoggling of the recent past must be prevented. Scientists themselves have publicized certain unsavory aspects of "big science"—the space program and the Mohole project are examples. In addition to the fact that science may harm us, scientists sometimes make incredibly bad judgments about the conduct of their own affairs. Hence, science must be provided with a specially designed legislature, and, for civilian control to work, there must be participation by citizens as well as by professional scientists.

It may be that the envisioned public corporation should have a bicameral legislature, one house composed of scientists and the other of public members. One way to conceive of this would be to follow our traditional Constitutional wisdom and put financial controls and ratification powers in the public chamber and reserve the responsibility for initiating projects for the scientific chamber, with special provision for joint sessions. The proposal for a bicameral approach to   30
science planning and policy formation immediately raises the question of a separation of powers, a checks-and-balances feature. Each house would exercise restraint on the other; concerted action would require the coöperation of both. Obviously, this new constitutionalized scientific order should not slavishly follow the established American Constitutional separation-of-powers mechanism, but certain analogues do seem promising.

This raises the question of federalism. The general Constitutional idea of federalism is "subsidiarity." It means a preference for the local over the centralized solution to problems. There may be a need in the scientific order for a special version of this principle. This should be considered in the context of a proposed bill of rights for science. Subsidiarity dictates that every possible scientific issue be   31
dealt with at decentralized levels, rather than being disposed of in centralized institutions. One of the chief sources of the evils we now observe in "big science" derives primarily from its centralization. Perhaps something like an anti-trust approach to science ought to be provided for. This might be the best way to protect local autonomy for our centers of scientific research.

This brings us to the necessity of educating the general public about leading scientific issues. Each sector could serve this need in its own characteristic manner. Representatives from the public sector would have to qualify for office in some way and the best way would be for them to stand for election on the basis of general programs for the development of science. Scientists, in qualifying themselves for selection by their peers, would be required to address themselves to   32 more technical issues. Their educational role would be to uncover the extended social implications of the scientific matters at issue. A useful example was the Pauling-Teller debates a few years ago. These debates brought about a widespread public discussion of complex scientific issues. What I have proposed would regularize such public debates about the basic issues of science policy, conducted regularly by leading scientists.

There is a danger that in democratizing science we may submit it to the whims of public opinion. Many feel this would be better than leaving it to the scientists, but, of course, neither is ideal. Science is not the private property of scientists any more than the economy is the private property of businessmen, or the government the private property of politicans. Corruption occurs when scientists forget this. Actually, a scientist is much like a real-estate investor who has   33 bought property in the path of an expanding city. When the value of his possession rises he begins to talk and act as if *he* were responsible for it. However, the individual scientist is merely the one who happens to be "in possession" at the time that knowledge is provided by massive institutional, economic, and political forces of his day. Perhaps we need a new Henry George to point out that if anybody "owns" science, it is the people themselves.

In setting our own house in order, we must face the serious problem that concerns our universities and the relationships between developmental science and the proper approach to higher education. Revelations about Project Camelot and defense-oriented university research programs have made it obvious that developmental science has already distorted our educational processes and corrupted the idea of the university. The constitutional approach allows us to correct this by separating the big developmental scientific institutes and   34 laboratories from the universities, placing them instead under public corporations. Indeed, *all* our present professional and technical schools should properly be transferred to some such public corporation, freeing the university to safeguard the philosophic needs, the theoretical integrity, and the educational properties of the pursuit of knowledge without the contamination that political, financial, and practical needs now impose.

Two things that have corrupted the sciences and professions, of course, are money and power. Whenever an endeavor becomes extremely powerful or highly profitable, its moral integrity is threatened. This would make it appear that the only people capable of maintaining an ethic for a profession are the young, before they have used it to become rich and influential. We might recall a proposition once put forward by Harold Laski. He claimed that the effective regulators of the American judiciary were the law journals, which are run   35 by the young before they have made any money practicing law. Perhaps we can somehow institutionalize the critical and ethical talents of youth and focus them on the conduct of the sciences, as is now done for the judiciary by the law journals. Perhaps what we need, among other things, is a number of science review journals devoted primarily to the social, political, and ethical implications of developmental science.

There must be some way of protecting the integrity of the scientific enterprise from corruption by either scientist or non-scientist. Traditionally such aims have been achieved through bills of rights. We are concerned here with matters such as academic freedom, the rights of students and teachers, the needs of the new Linus Paulings, the Oppenheimers, the Thorstein Veblens, and all who aspire to similar status. We are reminded once again that intellectuals are not necessarily those best qualified to understand the true needs of their own enterprise—just as businessmen are not necessarily those best qualified to understand the true needs of the economic order. Yet today's bureaucratic scientist continues to echo the nineteenth-century businessman's individualist ideology. A hundred years ago the laissez-faire ideology may have been adequate for the needs of both scientists and society. Today, however, the arguments for unhampered science are as irrelevant as the arguments for free private   36 enterprise by mammoth corporations, or the arguments for an unregulated press by the mass-media monopolies. Three-quarters of research and development grants are for directed research. A monopoly already exists in science, and scientific freedom is largely a myth. Already, grave issues concerning intellectual freedom have arisen. Are there any projects the scientist has a right to refuse to work on? Lewis Branscom has made it clear that even if present trends continue unhampered some kind of bill of rights for science and letters will have to be instituted. The archaic ideology of science and the overweening hubris of the scientist must somehow be brought down to size. The most obvious way to do this is to provide for the constitutionalization of science in a special polity combining principles of both democracy and the rule of law. Within this context the liberties appropriate to intellectual endeavors can find proper expression and preservation.

A bill of rights reënforces the aforementioned need for a special court system. It would be necessary to provide for a prosecutor, subpoena power, and trial-like hearings. It is not possible for the common law side of our judicial system to assimilate easily these novel problems of adjudication. We will need a new jurisprudence of science, comparable to that we have developed for administrative law. 37

Policy formation for science means planning. It may well be that the essential nature of planning in the future will become subsumed under science policy—any other outcome would be almost inconceivable. No matter what problem we come up against—planning for the city of the future, demographic planning, resource conservation and development planning, or transportation planning—each begins from a scientific foundation and all have to be integrated into an over-all developmental program for the scientific enterprise. This requires Constitutional provision for science planning—a need that underscores the failure of our present Constitution to provide for planning of any kind. Even if science as such were to present no Constitutional issue, the need for planning should. A number of additional problems would remain even if all the innovations proposed above were to work perfectly. One of these is the relationship between the scientific and the military establishments. Three supplementary control devices may be required. One is a post-audit. This should be thought of in two ways: first, as a simple technical and financial post-audit to find out how appropriations were spent and whether irregularities occurred. But there must also be a *substantive* post-audit to inspect what actually was done in carrying out stated policies. This can be thought of as a retrospective application of planning-programming-budgeting techniques. We need to know whether space-program research and development was diverted into electronics R & D with commercial marketing potentials; whether funds for molecular biology were diverted into pharmacological research; and on down the line. Institutionalized post-audit devices are not sufficient because, as with the Army Inspector General and the federal regulatory agencies, the inspector tends to become a part of the system he inspects. Something similar to the British Commission of Inquiry is needed as well, and its quadrennial reports could coin- 38

cide with the planning process and electoral campaings. Such a commission, if staffed by men of eminence and independence, would
guarantee a quality to its reports so often produced by Presidential
commissions.

Another issue of major importance is the larger ecological aspect
of the scientific order. What *is* this scientific order? What are its
boundaries? Taken most broadly, its boundaries are those of the
universe itself. This means no nation by itself can constitutionalize
its own science. Suppose America had decided to develop solid-state
physics and transistor applications to maximize their usefulness to
the public good and avoid the dislocations too rapid exploitation
brings. Similar questions concerning the computer are actually before
us. It may be that intensive research on the cultural implications of
the computer should be carried out before we start using it to make
everything from shoes to teaching machines, flooding the consumer
market with hastily conceived gadgetry. In Russia, there was insuffi-
cient hardware for immediate application when the computer first
appeared. As a result, the Russians were forced, as they had been   39
earlier in the field of rocketry, to address themselves first to the
theoretical implications of the computer while they waited for the
hardware to become more widely available. It may be that this simple technological lag permitted them to take a wiser view of the role
of the computer than we had in this country, where it seeped
through the technological order as a result of the extension of ballis-
tics-control devices to industrial and administrative processes. But
the Russian example also makes clear that no one country, not even
a dictatorship, can really plan in the realm of developmental science.
The history of the transistor shows that Japan, or some other country, may come along and flood the world market. Ultimately what is
needed, then, is a concerted effort on a world level. It makes little
difference what one nation decides to do about the transistor if any
other is able to do the contrary.

So it is apparent that there is an international, or transnational,
aspect to the problem of constitutionalizing science. We already have
transnational industrial corporations. Perhaps the scientific order in
its constitutional mode must follow the example of the transnational
industrial combine. Perhaps both in unison will provide us with ave-   40
nues leading toward world order. In any case, the problem of world
order is here, built into contemporary developmental science. There
is no way to avoid it, and we must recognize that efforts to control
science must be integrated throughout the world.

QUESTIONS AND PROBLEMS

1. Wheeler argues that the days when scientists could be left free to do anything they wanted are finished—or should be. Why?
2. How does he tie our contemporary medical capability in transplanting human organs to the threat of developmental science?
3. He indicates, "American scientists had eagerly produced history's most awesome weapons, hardly stopping to consider that moral issues might be involved in their decision to do so" (par. 3).
   a. What are some of these moral issues?
   b. What was the defense of the scientists?
   c. What would be the effect of the sentence if the word *eagerly* were omitted?
4. One solution offered to the problem presented by developmental science is, Wheeler notes, the creation of "some sort of government agency charged with coordinating science policy." What are some of the scientific discoveries of the past which would have been hampered, if not entirely suppressed, if governments had had that power?
5. Why is it possible that scientists working on such projects as atomic bombs or death rays may hardly be concerned with the moral implications of their work? Why, according to Wheeler, may there be no clear connection between actions and effects?
6. Compare the first reactions to the invention of the automobile with the reaction when mass-production of vehicles was instituted and with problems raised by the concentration of automobiles today.
7. What comparison does Wheeler make to illustrate the accumulation of scientific knowledge from generation to generation?
8. Identify or explain: Linus Pauling, Coue, Bacon's *New Atlantis*, Dr. Faustus, Adolph Eichmann, the A.E.C., ombudsman, Thorstein Veblen, Robert Oppenheimer.
9. Outline Wheeler's plan for "constitutionalization" or control of developmental science. Why must science be provided with a specially designed legislature?
10. Wheeler maintains that certain revelations "have made it obvious that developmental science has already distorted our educational processes and corrupted the idea of the university" (par. 34).
    a. Discuss this assertion in terms of student protests on some major university campuses.
    b. What is the involvement of your own school in such programs? If the school is involved, what are the reasons for this involvement? If not involved, why not?
11. Why, according to Wheeler, can no single nation constitutionalize its own science? What universal factors are involved in effective control of developmental science?

SUGGESTIONS FOR WRITING

1. Write a paper on "Science and World Order" in which you develop the argument that world order can prevail only after there is adequate control of world science.

2. Investigate the scientific research being undertaken on your campus for out-side agencies and corporations. Develop an argument in favor of or against what you find.
3. Many college and university science teachers are calling for more required courses in science. Develop the pros and cons of an increased requirement in science at your school.
4. In many states, to be certified for secondary school teaching in any subject students are required to have taken from fourteen to sixteen semester hours of work in life and physical science, including physical geography and mathematics. Justify or argue against this requirement.
5. Write a satire directed against the use of the computer in so many areas of modern life.
6. Investigate and report upon computer science as a career.
7. Write a paper in which you distinguish between the terms *pure science* and *developmental science*.
8. Write a paper on the validity of Christopher Marlowe's play *Dr. Faustus* as a message for scientists today.
9. Compare medieval and modern warfare.
10. Investigate the role of the United Nations in bringing the fruits of modern scientific technology to developing nations.

SUGGESTIONS FOR FURTHER READING

Francis Bacon, *The New Atlantis* (various publishers)
Gustav Bergmann, *The Philosophy of Science* (Univ. of Wisconsin)
Max Born, *Physics and Politics* (Basic Books)
Jacob Bronowski, *Science and Human Values*, rev. ed. (Harper)
Eugene Burdick and Harvey Wheeler, *Fail Safe* (McGraw-Hill; Dell)
Arthur H. Compton, *The Human Meaning of Science* (Univ. North Carolina)
Christopher Marlowe, *Dr. Faustus* (various publishers)
Norman Moss, *Men Who Play God* (Harper & Row)
J. Robert Oppenheimer, *Science and the Common Understanding* (Simon and Schuster)
Linus C. Pauling, *No More War!*, enlarged ed. (Apollo)

TO DESCRIBE

The use of description as a method of developing a thesis or topic is as old as the essay itself. Two types of descriptive writing are used: one, which may be called "practical description," is employed, as we have already seen, in the method of development by explanation or process; the other, which may be called, for want of a better term, "pure description," is used when the writer determines to make his point by way of the senses, the emotions, the pictorial imagination. It is with this latter type of development that we are dealing here.

Whereas the former type of description may be said to make its appeal directly to the intellect, the method of pure description enlists additional appeals. Grace Brown, in an earlier essay, gave us a practical and interesting description of the process of making a cake. But we were not making the cake with her. The essayist who employs the kind of description with which we deal here "takes us along," so to speak. Description becomes the vehicle for the thought. Thoreau, in "Walden," wants to tell us some important things about man and nature. To do so he takes us to Walden Pond; we build the cabin with him, live there with him. E.B. White takes us back to Walden Pond ninety-four years later; we ride with him in his automobile, see the sights with him, and get the point of his essay. Dylan Thomas tells us something important about childhood and about memories of childhood in an essay of almost pure description which is rich in image and which appeals to our five senses; his essay is not expository in method and yet makes his particular point far better, I think we can agree, than a purely expository essay on the subject would have done.

Most essays are not so heavily descriptive as that of Dylan Thomas. But the careful writer enlists the aid of description whenever it serves to bring his point home to the reader in an interest-catching way. As a reader of the essays in this book you will note again and again instances in which description has been used to advantage by careful and accomplished writers. As a writer of essays you should bear in mind the value of appealing to the pictorial imagination of your readers, of having them join you, so to speak, inside the essay rather than merely standing on the margin of the page.

A writer appeals to the pictorial imagination through the use of what is frequently called *imagery*. Imagery refers to the "images" presented by the writer—not visual reproduction of a scene nor direct appeal to senses of smell, hearing, taste, touch (a writer cannot make us *smell* a word) but appeal to the senses of the mind. A dictionary describes *image* as "a mental representation of anything not actually present to the senses." The term *image,* then, refers to words which affect the senses of the mind. When William Holder wrote that a girl's voice "was as the night breeze on a parched land" he gave us a mental impression of a sound. When Dylan Thomas, in an essay which follows, describes a holiday as "a tune on an ice-cream cornet" he gives us not a sound but a mental impression of holiday joy in a child. William Beebe calls up associations—mental impressions of smells—when he describes the odor of the jungle as "acrid, sweet, spicy, and suffocating."

Imagery, as can be seen from the above examples, has, therefore, reference both to literal words and to words used figuratively. Dyland Thomas' holiday is a tune played on an ice-cream cone. Thomas Hardy, in *The Woodlanders,* describes the western sky as being "aglow like some vast foundry wherein new worlds were being cast." In the example given above, William Holder says that the girl's voice is like the night breeze. Milton has a line in which "brooding Darkness spreads his jealous wings." Robert Herrick admonishes girls, "Gather ye rosebuds while ye may." All of these figures (metaphor, simile, personification are illustrated) imply imagery, the writer's appeal to the mental senses. The essayist makes the same appeals when he uses description as the vehicle for carrying his ideas. Notice these few additional examples from the essays which follow:

Before I had done I was more the friend than the foe of the pine tree. (Thoreau)

Better paint your house your own complexion; let it turn pale or blush for you. (Thoreau)

It was June and everywhere June was publishing her immemorial stanza.... (White)

Automobiles, skirting a village green, are like flies that have gained the inner ear.... (White)

... foolish, mulish, religious donkeys on the unwilling trot. (Thomas)

I remember most the children playing, boys and girls tumbling, moving jewels, who might never be happy again. (Thomas)

Haight-Ashbury had survived the Summer of Love, but it seemed mortally wounded. (McNeill)

Even after the hordes, he [the shopkeeper] was holding his hill. (McNeill)

Imagery, the calling up the senses of the mind—whether of sight, sound, smell, taste, touch, or motion—serves the essayist as well as the poet and the writer of fiction.

FROM WALDEN

Henry David Thoreau

Near the end of March, 1845, I borrowed an axe and went down to the woods by Walden Pond, nearest to where I intended to build my house, and began to cut down some tall, arrowy white pines, still in their youth, for timber. It is difficult to begin without borrowing, but perhaps it is the most generous course thus to permit your fellow-men to have an interest in your enterprise. The owner of the axe, as he released his hold on it, said that it was the apple of his eye; but I returned it sharper than I received it. It was a pleasant hillside where I worked, covered with pine woods, through which I looked out on the pond, and a small open field in the woods where pines and hickories were springing up. The ice in the pond was not yet dissolved, though there were some open spaces, and it was all dark-colored and saturated with water. There were some slight flurries of snow during the days that I worked there; but for the most part when I came out on to the railroad, on my way home, its yellow sand-heap stretched away gleaming in the hazy atmosphere, and the rails shone in the spring sun, and I heard the lark and pewee and other birds already come to commence another year with us. They were pleasant spring days, in which the winter of man's discontent was thawing as well as the earth, and the life that had lain torpid began to stretch itself. One day, when my axe had come off and I had cut a green hickory for a wedge, driving it with a stone, and had placed the whole to soak in a pond-hole in order to swell the wood, I saw a striped snake run into the water, and he lay on the bottom, apparently without inconvenience, as long as I stayed there, or more than a quarter of an hour; perhaps because he had not yet fairly come out of the torpid state. It appeared to me that for a like reason men remain in their present low and primitive condition; but if they should feel the influence of the spring of springs arousing them, they would of necessity rise to a higher and more etheral life. I had previously seen the snakes in frosty mornings in my path with portions of their bodies still numb and inflexible, waiting for the sun to thaw them. On the 1st of April it rained and melted the ice, and in the early part of the day, which was very foggy, I heard a stray goose groping about over the pond and cackling as if lost, or like the spirit of the fog.

So I went on for some days cutting and hewing timber, and also studs and rafters, all with my narrow axe, not having many communicable or scholar-like thoughts, singing to myself,—

1

Men say they know many things;
But lo! they have taken wings,—
The arts and sciences,
And a thousand appliances:
The wind that blows
Is all that anybody knows.

I hewed the main timbers six inches square, most of the studs on two
sides only, and the rafters and floor timbers on one side, leaving the
rest of the bark on, so that they were just as straight and much   2
stronger than sawed ones. Each stick was carefully mortised or
tenoned by its stump, for I had borrowed other tools by this time.
My days in the woods were not very long ones; yet I usually carried
my dinner of bread and butter, and read the newspaper in which it
was wrapped, at noon, sitting amid the green pine boughs which I
had cut off, and to my bread was imparted some of their fragrance,
for my hands were covered with a thick coat of pitch. Before I had
done I was more the friend than the foe of the pine tree, though I
had cut down some of them, having become better acquainted with
it. Sometimes a rambler in the wood was attracted by the sound of
my axe, and we chatted pleasantly over the chips which I had made.
     By the middle of April, for I made no haste in my work, but
rather made the most of it, my house was framed and ready for the
raising. I had already bought the shanty of James Collins, an Irishman who worked on the Fitchburg Railroad, for boards. James Collins' shanty was considered an uncommonly fine one. When I called
to see it he was not at home. I walked about the outside, at first
unobserved from within, the window was so deep and high. It was of
small dimensions, with a peaked cottage roof, and not much else to
be seen, the dirt being raised five feet all around as if it were a
compost heap. The roof was the soundest part, though a good deal
warped and made brittle by the sun. Doorsill there was none, but a
perennial passage for the hens under the doorboard. Mrs. C. came to
the door and asked me to view it from the inside. The hens were
driven in by my approach. It was dark, and had a dirt floor for the
most part, dank, clammy, and aguish, only here a board and there a
board which would not bear removal. She lighted a lamp to show me
the inside of the roof and the walls, and also that the board floor
extended under the bed, warning me not to step into the cellar, a   3
sort of dust hole two feet deep. In her own words, they were "good
boards overhead, good boards all around, and a good window,"—of
two whole squares originally, only the cat had passed out that way
lately. There was a stove, a bed, and a place to sit, an infant in the

house where it was born, a silk parasol, gilt-framed looking-glass, and a patent new coffee-mill nailed to an oak sapling, all told. The bargain was soon concluded, for James had in the meanwhile returned. I to pay four dollars and twenty-five cents to-night, he to vacate at five to-morrow morning, selling to nobody else meanwhile: I to take possession at six. It were well, he said, to be there early, and anticipate certain indistinct but wholly unjust claims on the score of ground rent and fuel. This he assured me was the only encumbrance. At six I passed him and his family on the road. One large bundle held their all,—bed, coffee-mill, looking-glass, hens,—all but the cat; she took to the woods and became a wild cat, and, as I learned afterward, trod in a trap set for woodchucks, and so became a dead cat at last.

I took down this dwelling the same morning, drawing the nails, and removed it to the pond-side by small cartloads, spreading the boards on the grass there to bleach and warp back again in the sun. One early thrush gave me a note or two as I drove along the woodland path. I was informed treacherously by a young Patrick that neighbor Seeley, an Irishman, in the intervals of the carting, transferred the still tolerable, straight, and drivable nails, staples, and spikes to his pocket, and then stood when I came back to pass the time of day, and look freshly up, unconcerned, with spring thoughts, at the devastation; their being a dearth of work, as he said. He was there to represent spectatordom, and help make this seemingly insignificant event one with the removal of the gods of Troy.   4

I dug my cellar in the side of a hill sloping to the south, where a woodchuck had formerly dug his burrow, down through sumach and blackberry roots, and the lowest stain of vegetation, six feet square by seven deep, to a fine sand where potatoes would not freeze in any winter. The sides were left shelving, and not stoned; but the sun having never shone on them, the sand still keeps its place. It was but two hours' work. I took particular pleasure in this breaking of   5 ground, for in almost all latitudes men dig into the earth for an equable temperature. Under the most splendid house in the city is still to be found the cellar where they store their roots as of old, and long after the superstructure has disappeared posterity remark its dent in the earth. The house is still but a sort of porch at the entrance of a burrow.

At length, in the beginning of May, with the help of some of my acquaintances, rather to improve so good an occasion for neighborliness than from any necessity, I set up the frame of my house. No man was ever more honored in the character of his raisers than I.

They are destined, I trust, to assist at the raising of loftier structures
one day. I began to occupy my house on the 4th of July, as soon as
it was boarded and roofed, for the boards were carefully feather-
edged and lapped, so that it was perfectly impervious to rain, but
before boarding I laid the foundation of a chimney at one end,
bringing two cartloads of stones up the hill from the pond in my
arms. I built the chimney after my hoeing in the fall, before a fire   6
became necessary for warmth, doing my cooking in the meanwhile
out of doors on the ground, early in the morning: which mode I still
think is in some respects more convenient and agreeable than the
usual one. When it stormed before my bread was baked, I fixed a few
boards over the fire, and sat under them to watch my loaf, and
passed some pleasant hours in that way. In those days, when my
hands were much employed, I read but little, but the least scraps of
paper which lay on the ground, my holder, or tablecloth, afforded
me as much entertainment, in fact answered the same purpose as the
Iliad.

It would be worth the while to build still more deliberately than
I did, considering, for instance, what foundation a door, a window, a
cellar, a garret, have in the nature of man, and perchance never
raising any superstructure until we found a better reason for it than
our temporal necessities even. There is some of the same fitness in a
man's building his own house that there is in a bird's building its own
nest. Who knows but if men constructed their dwellings with their
own hands, and provided food for themselves and families simply
and honestly enough, the poetic faculty would be universally developed, as birds universally sing when they are so engaged? But alas!
we do like cowbirds and cuckoos, which lay their eggs in nests which   7
other birds have built, and cheer no traveller with their chattering
and unmusical notes. Shall we forever resign the pleasure of construction to the carpenter? What does architecture amount to in the experience of the mass of men? I never in all my walks came across a
man engaged in so simple and natural an occupation as building his
house. We belong to the community. It is not the tailor alone who is
the ninth part of a man; it is as much the preacher, and the merchant, and the farmer. Where is this division of labor to end? and
what object does it finally serve? No doubt another *may* also think
for me; but it is not therefore desirable that he should do so to the
exclusion of my thinking for myself.

True, there are architects so called in this country, and I have
heard of one at least possessed with the idea of making architectural
ornaments have a core of truth, a necessity, and hence a beauty, as if

it were a revelation to him. All very well perhaps from his point of view, but only a little better than the common dilettantism. A sentimental reformer in architecture, he began at the cornice, not at the foundation. It was only how to put a core of truth within the ornaments, that every sugarplum, in fact, might have an almond or caraway seed in it,—though I hold that almonds are most wholesome without the sugar,—and not how the inhabitant, the indweller, might build truly within and without, and let the ornaments take care of themselves. What reasonable man ever supposed that ornaments were something outward and in the skin merely,—that the tortoise got his spotted shell, or the shell-fish its mother-o'-pearl tints, by such a contract as the inhabitants of Broadway their Trinity Church? But a man has no more to do with the style of architecture of his house than a tortoise with that of its shell: nor need the soldier be so idle as to try to paint the precise *color* of his virtue on his standard. The enemy will find it out. He may turn pale when the trial comes. This man seemed to me to lean over the cornice, and timidly whisper his half truth to the rude occupants who really knew it better than he. What of architectural beauty I now see, I know has gradually grown from within outward, out of the necessities and character of the indweller, who is the only builder,—out of some unconscious truthfulness, and nobleness, without ever a thought for the appearance and whatever additional beauty of this kind is destined to be produced will be preceded by a like unconscious beauty of life. The most interesting dwellings in this country, as the painter knows, are the most unpretending, humble log huts and cottages of the poor commonly; it is the life of the inhabitants whose shells they are, and not any peculiarity in their surfaces merely, which makes them *picturesque;* and equally interesting will be the citizen's suburban box, when his life shall be as simple and as agreeable to the imagination, and there is as little straining after effect in the style of his dwelling. A great proportion of architectural ornaments are literally hollow, and a September gale would strip them off, like borrowed plumes, without injury to the substantials. They can do without *architecture* who have no olives nor wines in the cellar. What if an equal ado were made about the ornaments of style in literature, and the architects of our Bibles spent as much time about their cornices as the architects of our churches do? So are made the *belles-lettres* and the *beaux-arts* and their professors. Much it concerns a man, forsooth, how a few sticks are slanted over him or under him, and what colors are daubed upon his box. It would signify somewhat, if, in any earnest sense, *he* slanted them and daubed it; but the spirit having departed out of the

8

tenant, it is of a piece with constructing his own coffin,—the architecture of the grave,—and "carpenter" is but another name for "coffin-maker." One man says, in his despair or indifference to life, take up a handful of the earth at your feet, and paint your house that color. Is he thinking of his last and narrow house? Toss up a copper for it as well. What an abundance of leisure he must have! Why do you take up a handful of dirt? Better paint your house your own complexion; let it turn pale or blush for you. An enterprise to improve the style of cottage architecture! When you have got my ornaments ready, I will wear them.

Before winter I built a chimney, and shingled the sides of my house, which were already impervious to rain, with imperfect and   9
sappy shingles made of the first slice of the log, whose edges I was obliged to straighten with a plane.

I have thus a tight shingled and plastered house, ten feet wide by fifteen long, and eight-feet posts, with a garret and a closet, a large window on each side, two trap-doors, one door at the end, and a brick fireplace opposite. The exact cost of my house, paying the usual price for such materials as I used, but not counting the work, all of which was done by myself, was as follows; and I give the details because very few are able to tell exactly what their houses cost, and fewer still, if any, the separate cost of the various materials which compose them:—   10

Boards	$ 8.03½,	mostly shanty boards.
Refuse shingles for roof and sides	4.00	
Laths	1.25	
Two second-hand windows with glass	2.43	
One thousand old brick	4.00	
Two casks of lime	2.40	That was high.
Hair	0.31	More than I needed.
Mantle-tree iron	0.15	
Nails	3.90	
Hinges and screws	0.14	
Latch	0.10	
Chalk	0.01	
Transportation	1.40	I carried a good part on my back.
In all	$28.12½	

These are all the materials, excepting the timber, stones, and sand, which I claimed by squatter's right. I have also a small wood-   11
shed adjoining, made chiefly of the stuff which was left after building the house.

QUESTIONS AND PROBLEMS

1. Thoreau's essay is an account of his building a hut, an object to be made. But the hut becomes something more than a mere object; it is a symbol. Explain the symbolism.
2. In the opening sentence Thoreau says, "I borrowed an axe."
   a. What tone is set at the very outset of the essay?
   b. How does this expression fit the theme of the essay?
   c. Relate the opening sentence to the last sentence of the essay. What device of exposition is used?
3. Study the descriptive detail of the essay. Cite passages which are particularly effective.
4. Thoreau's exposition deals with building a house. What is the value of the passages on the birds, snakes, etc., he finds at Walden Pond?
5. Does Thoreau use an impressionistic manner or does he rely more on concrete details? What is the value of his method for this kind of essay?
6. Thoreau writes (par. 2), "... I usually carried my dinner of bread and butter, and read the newspaper in which it was wrapped. ... " What is the contribution of this passage to the meaning of the essay?
7. Comment on the statement (par. 3), "... I made no haste in my work, but rather made the most of it. ... "
   a. What philosophy of life is revealed in this statement?
   b. Relate the statement to education, to study.
8. How does Thoreau, in spite of the fact that there is a great deal of factual information in the essay, manage to keep the emphasis on human values? Cite examples.
9. Relate Thoreau's comments (par. 7) on simplicity, honesty, and the development of the poetic faculty with Wordsworth's theories of poetry and the common man.
10. Discuss Thoreau's theory of architecture.
    a. Make a concise statement of his theory.
    b. Relate the theory to contemporary architecture.
    c. Do your newest campus buildings fit the theory?
    d. What is the meaning of the statement, "They can do without *architecture* who have no olives or wines in the cellar" (par. 8)?

SUGGESTIONS FOR WRITING

1. Write an essay on something you have built, a camp you have set up, or some other activity of this kind. Follow Thoreau's method of giving factual information and yet stressing human values.
2. Write an essay on the values external nature has for you, stressing descriptive detail.
3. Describe a structure you have seen—a house, a church, a public building— which has some fame because of its architecture or because it was designed by a famous architect.
4. Describe and comment upon the most unusual house or building in your home town.
5. Write an impressionistic piece on a great cathedral or a famous castle you have visited. Concentrate on meanings more than on detail.

6. Write an essay on the essential harmony between one of your campus buildings and the activities which go on inside it.
7. Make a plan for the ideal college campus—the University of Utopia.
8. Investigate the functional value of a particular kind of architecture, illustrating your essay with one important example.

SUGGESTIONS FOR FURTHER READING

Henry Adams, *Mont Saint-Michel and Chartres* (various publishers)
E.R. De Zurko, *Origins of Functionalist Theory* (Columbia)
Joseph Hudnut, *Architecture and the Spirit of Man* (Harvard)
Frank Lloyd Wright, *Architecture: Man in Possession of His Earth* (Doubleday)
Harry Ransom, ed., *People's Architects* (Univ. of Chicago)

WALDEN—JUNE 1939

E.B. White

Miss Nims, take a letter to Henry David Thoreau. Dear Henry: I thought of you the other afternoon as I was approaching Concord doing fifty on Route 62. That is a high speed at which to hold a philosopher in one's mind, but in this century we are a nimble bunch.

On one of the lawns in the outskirts of the village a woman was cutting the grass with a motorized lawn mower. What made me think of you was that the machine had rather got away from her, although she was game enough, and in the brief glimpse I had of the scene it appeared to me that the lawn was mowing the lady. She kept a tight grip on the handles, which throbbed violently with every explosion of the one-cylinder motor, and as she sheered around bushes and lurched along at a reluctant trot behind her impetuous servant, she looked like a puppy who had grabbed something that was too much for him. Concord hasn't changed much, Henry; the farm implements and the animals still have the upper hand.

I may as well admit that I was journeying to Concord with the deliberate intention of visiting your woods; for although I have never knelt at the grave of a philosopher nor placed wreaths on moldy poets, and have often gone a mile out of my way to avoid some place of historical interest, I have always wanted to see Walden Pond. The account which you left of your sojourn there is, you will be amused to learn, a document of increasing pertinence; each year it seems to gain a little headway, as the world loses ground. We may all be transcendental yet, whether we like it or not. As our common complexities increase, any tale of individual simplicity (and yours is the best written and the cockiest) acquires a new fascination; as our goods accumulate, but not our well-being, your report of an existence without material adornment takes on a certain awkward credibility.

My purpose in going to Walden Pond, like yours, was not to live cheaply or to live dearly there, but to transact some private business with the fewest obstacles. Approaching Concord, doing forty, doing forty-five, doing fifty, the steering wheel held snug in my palms, the highway held grimly in my vision, the crown of the road now serving me (on the righthand curves), now defeating me (on the lefthand curves), I began to rouse myself from the stupefaction which a day's motor journey induces. It was a delicious evening, Henry, when the whole body is one sense, and imbibes delight through every pore, if I

1

2

3

4

may coin a phrase. Fields were richly brown where the harrow, drawn by the stripped Ford, had lately sunk its teeth; pastures were green; and overhead the sky had that same everlasting great look which you will find on Page 144 of the Oxford Pocket Edition. I could feel the road entering me, through tire, wheel, spring, and cushion; shall I have intelligence with earth too? Am I not partly leaves and vegetable mold myself?—a man of infinite horsepower, yet partly leaves.

Stay with me on 62 and it will take you into Concord. As I say, it was a delicious evening. The snake had come forth to die in a bloody S on the highway, the wheel upon its head, its bowels flat now and exposed. The turtle had come up too to cross the road and die in the attempt, its hard shell smashed under the rubber blow, its intestinal yearning (for the other side of the road) forever squashed. 5 There was a sign by the wayside which announced that the road had a "cotton surface." You wouldn't know what that is, but neither, for that matter, did I. There is a cryptic ingredient in many of our modern improvements—we are awed and pleased without knowing quite what we are enjoying. It is something to be traveling on a road with a cotton surface.

The civilization round Concord to-day is an odd distillation of city, village, farm, and manor. The houses, yards, fields look not quite suburban, not quite rural. Under the bronze beech and the blue spruce of the departed baron grazes the milch goat of the heirs. 6 Under the porte-cochere stands the reconditioned station wagon; under the grape arbor sit the puppies for sale. (But why do men degenerate ever? What makes families run out?)

It was June and everywhere June was publishing her immemorial stanza: in the lilacs, in the syringa, in the freshly edged paths and the sweetness of moist beloved gardens, and the little wire wickets that preserve the tulips' front. Farmers were already moving the fruits of their toil into their yards, arranging the rhubarb, the asparagus, the strictly fresh eggs on the painted stands under the little shed roofs with the patent shingles. And though it was almost a hundred years 7 since you had taken your ax and started cutting out your home on Walden Pond, I was interested to observe that the philosophical spirit was still alive in Massachusetts: in the center of a vacant lot some boys were assembling the framework of a rude shelter, their whole mind and skill concentrated in the rather inauspicious helter-skeleton of studs and rafters. They too were escaping from town, to live naturally, in a rich blend of savagery and philosophy.

That evening, after supper at the inn, I strolled out into the twilight to dream my shapeless transcendental dreams and see that the car was locked up for the night (first open the right front door, then reach over, straining, and pull up the handles of the left rear and the left front till you hear the click, then the handle of the right rear, then shut the right front but open it again, remembering that the key is still in the ignition switch, remove the key, shut the right front again with a bang, push the tiny keyhole cover to one side, insert 8 key, turn, and withdraw). It is what we all do, Henry. It is called locking the car. It is said to confuse thieves and keep them from making off with the laprobe. Four doors to lock behind one robe. The driver himself never uses a laprobe, the free movement of his legs being vital to the operation of the vehicle; so that when he locks the car it is a pure and unselfish act. I have in my life gained very little essential heat from laprobes, yet I have ever been at pains to lock them up.

The evening was full of sounds, some of which would have stirred your memory. The robins still love the elms of New England villages at sundown. There is enough of the thrush in them to make song inevitable at the end of the day, and enough of the tramp to make 9 them hang round the dwellings of men. A robin, like many another American, dearly loves a white house with green blinds. Concord is still full of them.

Your fellow-townsmen were stirring abroad—not many afoot, most of them in their cars; and the sound which they made in Concord at evening was a rustling and a whispering. The sound lacks steadfastness and is wholly unlike that of a train. A train, as you know who lived so near the Fitchburg line, whistles once or twice 10 sadly and is gone, trailing a memory in smoke, soothing to ear and mind. Automobiles, skirting a village green, are like flies that have gained the inner ear—they buzz, cease, pause, start, shift, stop, halt, brake, and the whole effect is a nervous polytone curiously disturbing.

As I wandered along, the *toc toc* of ping pong balls drifted from an attic window. In front of the Reuben Brown house a Buick was drawn up. At the wheel, motionless, his hat upon his head, a man sat, listening to Amos and Andy on the radio (it is a drama of many scenes and without an end). The deep voice of Andrew Brown, emerging from the car, although it orginated more than two hundred 11 miles away, was unstrained by distance. When you used to sit on the shore of your pond on Sunday morning, listening to the church bells of Acton and Concord, you were aware of the excellent filter of the intervening atmosphere. Science has attended to that, and sound now maintains its intensity without regard for distance. Properly sponsored, it goes on forever.

A fire engine, out for a trial spin, roared past Emerson's house, hot with readiness for public duty. Over the barn roofs the martins dipped and chittered. A swarthy daughter of an asparagus grower, in culottes, shirt, and bandanna, pedalled past on her bicycle. It was   12 indeed a delicious evening, and I returned to the inn (I believe it was your house once) to rock with the old ladies on the concrete veranda.

Next morning early I started afoot for Walden, out Main Street and down Thoreau, past the depot and the Minuteman Chevrolet Company. The morning was fresh, and in a bean field along the way I flushed an agriculturalist, quietly studying his beans. Thoreau Street soon joined Number 126, an artery of the State. We number our   13 highways nowadays, our speed being so great we can remember little of their quality or character and are lucky to remember their number. (Men have an indistinct notion that if they keep up this activity long enough all will at length ride somewhere, in next to no time.) Your pond is on 126.

I knew I must be nearing your woodland retreat when the Golden Pheasant lunchroom came into view—Sealtest ice cream, toasted sandwiches, hot frankfurters, waffles, tonics, and lunches. Were I the proprietor, I should add rice, Indian meal, and molasses— just for old time's sake. The Pheasant, incidentally, is for sale: a chance for some nature lover who wishes to set himself up beside a pond in the Concord atmosphere and live deliberately, fronting only the essential facts of life on Number 126. Beyond the Pheasant was a place called Walden Breezes, an oasis whose porch pillars were made of old green shutters sawed into lengths. On the porch was a distorting mirror, to give the traveler a comical image of himself, who had miraculously learned to gaze in an ordinary glass without smiling. Behind the Breezes, in a sun-parched clearing, dwelt your philosophi-   14 cal descendants in their trailers, each trailer the size of your hut, but all grouped together for the sake of congeniality. Trailer people leave the city, as you did, to discover solitude and in any weather, at any hour of the day or night, to improve the nick of time; but they soon collect in villages and get bogged deeper in the mud than ever. The camp behind Walden Breezes was just rousing itself to the morning. The ground was packed hard under the heel, and the sun came through the clearing to bake the soil and enlarge the wry smell of cramped housekeeping. Cushman's bakery truck had stopped to deliver an early basket of rolls. A camp dog, seeing me in the road, barked petulantly. A man emerged from one of the trailers and set forth with a bucket to draw water from some forest tap.

Leaving the highway I turned off into the woods toward the pond, which was apparent through the foliage. The floor of the forest was strewn with dried old oak leaves and *Transcripts*. From beneath the flattened popcorn wrapper *(granum explosum)* peeped the frail violet. I followed a footpath and descended to the water's edge. The pond lay clear and blue in the morning light, as you have seen it so many times. In the shallows a man's waterlogged shirt undulated gently. A few flies came out to greet me and convoy me to your cove, past the No Bathing signs on which the fellows and the girls had scrawled their names. I felt strangely excited suddenly to be snooping around your premises, tiptoeing along watchfully, as though not to tread by mistake upon the intervening century. Before I got to the cove I heard something which seemed to me quite wonderful: I heard your frog, a full, clear *troonk*, guiding me, still hoarse and solemn, bridging the years as the robins had bridged them in the sweetness of the village evening. But he soon quit, and I came on a couple of young boys throwing stones at him. 15

Your front yard is marked by a bronze tablet set in a stone. Four small granite posts, a few feet away, show where the house was. On top of the tablet was a pair of faded blue bathing trunks with a white stripe. Back of it is a pile of stones, a heap of stones, Henry. In fact the hillside itself seems faded, browbeaten; a few tall skinny pines, bare of lower limbs, a smattering of young maples in suitable green, some birches and oaks, and a number of trees felled by the last big wind. It was from the bole of one of these fallen pines, torn up by the roots, that I extracted the stone which I added to the cairn—a sentimental act in which I was interrupted by a small terrier from a nearby picnic group, who confronted me and wanted to know about the stone. 16

I sat down for a while on one of the posts of your house to listen to the blue-bottles and the dragonflies. The invaded glade sprawled shabby and mean at my feet, but the flies were tuned to the old vibration. There were the remains of a fire in your ruins, but I doubt that it was yours; also two beer bottles trodden into the soil and become part of earth. A young oak had taken root in your house, and two or three ferns, unrolling like the ticklers at a banquet. The only other furnishings were a DuBarry pattern sheet, a page torn from a picture magazine, and some crusts in wax paper. 17

Before I quit I walked clear round the pond and found the place where you used to sit on the northeast side to get the sun in the fall, and the beach where you got sand for scrubbing your floor. On the eastern side of the pond, where the highway borders it, the State has built dressing rooms for swimmers, a float with diving towers, drinking fountains of porcelain, and rowboats for hire. The pond is in fact a State Preserve, and carries a twenty-dollar fine for picking wild flowers, a decree signed in all solemnity by your fellow-citizens Walter C. Wardell, Erson B. Barlow, and Nathaniel I. Bowditch.   18 There was a smell of creosote where they had been building a wide wooden stairway to the road and the parking area. Swimmers and boaters were arriving; bodies splashed vigorously into the water and emerged wet and beautiful in the bright air. As I left, a boat-load of town boys were splashing about in mid-pond, kidding and fooling, the young fellows singing at the tops of their lungs in a wild chorus:

> Amer-ica, Amer-i-ca, God shed his grace on thee,
> And crown thy good with brotherhood
> From sea to shi-ning sea!

I walked back to town along the railroad, following your custom. The rails were expanding noisily in the hot sun, and on the slope of   19 the roadbed the wild grape and the blackberry sent up their creepers to the track.

The expense of my brief sojourn in Concord was:

Canvas shoes	$1.95 ⎫	gifts to take	
Baseball bat	.25 ⎬	back to a boy	20
Left-handed fielder's glove	1.25 ⎭		
Hotel and meals	4.25		
In all	$7.70		

As you see, this amount was almost what you spent for food for eight months. I cannot defend the shoes or the expenditure for shelter and food: they reveal a meanness and grossness in my nature which you would find contemptible. The baseball equipment, how-   21 ever, is the sort of impediment with which you were never on even terms. You must remember that the house where you practiced the sort of economy which I respect was haunted only by mice and squirrels. You never had to cope with a shortstop.

QUESTIONS AND PROBLEMS

1. Writing nearly a century after Thoreau, E.B. White considers what progress has been in the intervening years.

a. What value does he find in the new developments?

b. How does he use description to present what he finds?

2. What is the chief difference between a "scientific" description and the kind of description White employs?

3. Cite examples of the use of irony in putting across White's point of view.

4. Like Thoreau, White sets a tone at the very outset of his essay.

   a. What is that tone?

   b. Is it appropriate to his essay? Why or why not?

   c. How does it differ from the tone of Thoreau's original essay?

   d. Is there a relationship between the opening and the closing paragraphs of White's essay?

5. How does White use image throughout the essay to establish the contrast he is pointing out?

6. Comment on the "century of progress" theme as revealed by White's essay. Considering both essays, which way of life is the more appealing to you? Why?

7. How does White use descriptions of external nature to deepen the contrast he is presenting?

8. Contrast the activity at Walden Pond in Thoreau's day and in White's. Is White's essay nostalgic? Can you defend the present situation at Walden?

SUGGESTIONS FOR WRITING

1. Contrast your home, or your home town, as it is at the present time with your early recollections of it.

2. Take a bike or an auto trip along a country road near your campus. Describe what you find in such a way as to present a point of view.

3. Study maps and pictures of your campus as it was in its early days. Compare and contrast with the present-day campus. What conclusions can you draw?

4. Write a letter to an American writer of the past (other than Thoreau) in which you describe the present-day conditions of a place he described in one of his works.

5. Visit an old house or other building which is falling into decay. Make an imaginative contrast with what it once was.

SUGGESTIONS FOR FURTHER READING

Seymour M. Farber and Roger H.L. Wilson, ed., *The Air We Breathe: A Study of Man and His Environment* (Charles C. Thomas)

Owen Garrigan, *Man's Intervention in Nature* (Hawthorn)

Hans Huth, *Nature and the American: Three Centuries of Changing Attitudes* (Univ. of California)

Joseph Wood Krutch, *Twelve Seasons* (Apollo)

Norman Lacey, *Wordsworth's View of Nature* (Shoe String)

HOLIDAY MEMORY

Dylan Thomas

August Bank Holiday*—a tune on an ice-cream cornet. A slap of
sea and a tickle of sand. A fanfare of sunshades opening. A wince and
whinny of bathers dancing into deceptive water. A tuck of dresses. A   1
rolling of trousers. A compromise of paddlers. A sunburn of girls and
a lark of boys. A silent hullabaloo of balloons.

I remember the sea telling lies in a shell held to my ear for a
whole harmonious, hollow minute by a small, wet girl in an enor-   2
mous bathing suit marked Corporation Property.

I remember sharing the last of my moist buns with a boy and a
lion. Tawny and savage, with cruel nails and capacious mouth, the
little boy tore and devoured. Wild as seedcake, ferocious as a hearth-   3
rug, the depressed and verminous lion nibbled like a mouse at his half
a bun and hiccupped in the sad dusk of his cage.

I remember a man like an alderman or a bailiff, bowlered and
collarless, with a bag of monkeynuts in his hand, crying "Ride 'em,
cowboy!" time and again as he whirled in his chairaplane giddily   4
above the upturned laughing faces of the town girls bold as brass and
the boys with padded shoulders and shoes sharp as knives; and the
monkeynuts flew through the air like salty hail.

Children all day capered or squealed by the glazed or bashing sea,
and the steam-organ wheezed its waltzes in the threadbare play-   5
ground and the waste lot, where the dodgems dodged, behind the
pickle factory.

And mothers loudly warned their proud pink daughters or sons
to put that jellyfish down; and fathers spread newspapers over their   6
faces; and sandfleas hopped on the picnic lettuce; and someone had
forgotten the salt.

In those always radiant, rainless, lazily rowdy and skyblue summers departed, I remember August Monday from the rising of the
sun over the stained and royal town to the husky hushing of the   7
roundabout music and the dowsing of the naphtha jets in the seaside
fair: from bubble-and-squeak to the last of the sandy sandwiches.

There was no need, that holiday morning, for the sluggardly boys
to be shouted down to breakfast; out of their jumbled beds they
tumbled, and scrambled into their rumpled clothes; quickly at the
bathroom basin they catlicked their hands and faces, but never forgot to run the water loud and long as though they washed like   8

---

*A legal holiday in Great Britain on which the banks are closed.

colliers; in front of the cracked looking-glass, bordered with cigarette cards, in their treasure-trove bedrooms, they whisked a gap-tooth comb through their surly hair; and with shining cheeks and noses and tidemarked necks, they took the stairs three at a time.

But for all their scramble and scamper, clamour on the landing, catlick and toothbrush flick, hairwhisk and stair-jump, their sisters were always there before them. Up with the lady lark, they had prinked and frizzed and hot-ironed; and smug in their blossoming dresses, ribboned for the sun, in gymshoes white as the blanco'd 9 snow, neat and silly with doilies and tomatoes they helped in the higgledy kitchen. They were calm; they were virtuous; they had washed their necks; they did not romp, or fidget; and only the smallest sister put out her tongue at the noisy boys.

And the woman who lived next door came into the kitchen and said that her mother, an ancient uncertain body who wore a hat with cherries, was having one of her days and had insisted, that very 10 holiday morning, in carrying, all the way to the tramstop, a photograph album and the cutglass fruitbowl from the front room.

This was the morning when father, mending one hole in the thermos-flask, made three; when the sun declared war on the butter, and the butter ran; when dogs, with all the sweet-binned backyards 11 to wag and sniff and bicker in, chased their tails in the jostling kitchen, worried sandshoes, snapped at flies, writhed between legs, scratched among towels, sat smiling on hampers.

And if you could have listened at some of the open doors of some of the houses in the street you might have heard:—

"Uncle Owen says he can't find the bottle-opener—"
   "Has he looked under the hallstand?"
"Willy's cut his finger—"
   "Got your spade?"
"If somebody doesn't kill that dog—"
"Uncle Owen says why should the bottle-opener be under the
   hallstand?"   12
   "Never again, never again—"
"I know I put the pepper somewhere—"
   "Willy's bleeding—"
"Look, there's a bootlace in my bucket—"
   "Oh come *on,* come *on*—"
"Let's have a look at the bootlace in your bucket—"
   "If I lay my hands on that dog—"
"Uncle Owen's found the bottle-opener—"
   "Willy's bleeding over the cheese—"

And the trams that hissed like ganders took us all to the beautiful beach.

There was cricket on the sand, and sand in the spongecake, sand-flies in the watercress, and foolish, mulish, religious donkeys on the unwilling trot. Girls undressed in slipping tents of propriety; under invisible umbrellas, stout ladies dressed for the male and immoral sea. Little naked navvies dug canals; children with spades and no ambition built fleeting castles; wispy young men, outside the bathing-huts, whistled at substantial young women and dogs who desired   13
thrown stones more than the bones of elephants. Recalcitrant uncles huddled, over luke ale, in the tiger-striped marquees. Mothers in black, like wobbling mountains, gasped under the discarded dresses of daughers who shrilly braved the gobbling waves. And fathers, in the once-a-year sun, took fifty winks. Oh, think of all the fifty winks along the paper-bagged sand.

Liquorice allsorts, and Welsh hearts, were melting. And the sticks   14
of rock, that we all sucked, were like barbers' poles made of rhubarb.

In the distance, surrounded by disappointed theoreticians and an ironmonger with a drum, a cross man on an orange-box shouted that   15
holidays were wrong. And the waves rolled in, with rubber ducks and clerks upon them.

I remember the patient, laborious, and enamouring hobby, or   16
profession, of burying relatives in sand.

I remember the princely pastime of pouring sand, from cupped hands or bucket, down collars of tops of dresses; the shriek, the   17
shake, the slap.

I can remember the boy by himself, the beachcombing lone-wolf, hungrily waiting at the edge of family cricket; the friendless fielder,   18
the boy uninvited to bat or to tea.

I remember the smell of sea and seaweed, wet flesh, wet hair, wet bathing-dresses, the warm smell as of a rabbity field after rain, the smell of pop and splashed sunshades and toffee, the stable-and-straw smell of hot, tossed, tumbled, dug and trodden sand, the swill-and-gaslamp smell of Saturday night, though the sun shone strong, from the bellying beer-tents, the smell of the vinegar on shelled cockles, winkle-smell, shrimp-smell, the dripping-oily back-street winter-smell   19
of chips in newspapers, the smell of ships from the sundazed docks round the corner of the sandhills, the smell of the known and pad-dled-in sea moving, full of the drowned and herrings, out and away and beyond and further still towards the antipodes that hung their koala-bears and Maoris, kangaroos and boomerangs, upside down over the backs of the stars.

And the noise of pummelling Punch and Judy falling, and a clock tolling or telling no time in the tenantless town; now and again a bell from a lost tower or a train on the lines behind us clearing its throat, and always the hopeless, ravenous swearing and pleading of the gulls, donkey-bray and hawker-cry, harmonicas and toy trumpets, shouting and laughing and singing, hooting of tugs and tramps, the clip of the chair-attendant's puncher, the motorboat coughing in the bay, and the same hymn and washing of the sea that was heard in the Bible.

"If it could only just, if it could only just," your lips said again and again as you scooped, in the hob-hot sand, dungeons, garages, torture-chambers, train tunnels, arsenals, hangars for zeppelins, witches' kitchens, vampires' parlours, smugglers' cellars, trolls' grog-shops, sewers, under the ponderous and cracking castle, "If it could only just be like this for ever and ever amen." August Monday all over the earth, from Mumbles where the aunties grew like ladies on a seaside tree to brown, bear-hugging Henty-land and the turtled Ballantyne Islands.

"Could donkeys go on the ice?"
"Only if they got snowshoes."

We snowshoed a meek, complaining donkey and galloped him off in the wake of the ten-foot-tall and Atlas-muscled Mounties, rifled and pemmicanned, who always, in the white Gold Rush wastes, got their black-oathed-and-bearded Man.

"Are there donkeys on desert islands?"
    "Only sort-of-donkeys."
"What d'you mean, sort-of donkeys?"
    "Native donkeys. They hunt things on them!"
"Sort-of walruses and seals and things?"
    "Donkeys can't swim!"
"These donkeys can. They swim like whales, they swim like any-
        thing, they swim like—"
    "Liar."
"Liar yourself."

And two small boys fought fiercely and silently in the sand, rolling together in a ball of legs and bottoms. Then they went and saw the pierrots, or bought vanilla ices.

Lolling or larriking that unsoiled, boiling beauty of a common day, great gods with their braces over their vests sang, spat pips, puffed smoke at wasps, gulped and ogled, forgot the rent, embraced, posed for the dicky-bird, were coarse, had rainbow-coloured armpits,

winked, belched, blamed the radishes, looked at Ilfracombe, played
hymns on paper and comb, peeled bananas, scratched, found sea-   24
weed in their panamas, blew up paper-bags and banged them, wished
for nothing. But over all the beautiful beach I remember most the
children playing, boys and girls tumbling, moving jewels, who might
never be happy again. And "happy as a sandboy" is true as the heat
of the sun.

Dusk came down; or grew up out of the sands and the sea; or
curled around us from the calling docks and the bloodily smoking
sun. The day was done, the sands brushed and ruffled suddenly with
a sea-broom of cold wind. And we gathered together all the spades   25
and buckets and towels, empty hampers and bottles, unbrellas and
fishfrails, bats and balls and knitting, and went—oh, listen, Dad!—to
the Fair in the dusk on the bald seaside field.

Fairs were no good in the day; then they were shoddy and tired;
the voices of hoopla girls were crimped as elocutionists; no cannon-
ball could shake the roosting coconuts; the gondolas mechanically   26
repeated their sober lurch; the Wall of Death was safe as a governess-
cart; the wooden animals were waiting for the night.

But in the night, the hoopla girls, like operatic crows, croaked at
the coming moon; whizz, whirl, and ten for a tanner, the coconuts
rained from their sawdust like grouse from the Highland sky; tipsy
the griffon-prowed gondolas weaved on dizzy rails, and the Wall of   27
Death was a spinning rim of ruin, and the neighing wooden horses
took, to a haunting hunting tune, a thousand Beecher's Brooks as
easily and breezily as hooved swallows.

Approaching, at dusk, the Fair-field from the beach, we scorched
and gritty boys heard above the belabouring of the batherless sea the   28
siren voices of the raucous, horsy barkers.

"Roll up, roll up!"

In her tent and her rolls of flesh the Fattest Woman in the World
sat sewing her winter frock, another tent, and fixed her little eyes,
blackcurrants in blancmange, on the skeletons who filed and snig-   29
gered by.

"Roll up, roll up, roll up to see the Largest Rat on the Earth, the
Rover or Bonzo of vermin."

Here scampered the smallest pony, like a Shetland shrew. And
here the Most Intelligent Fleas, trained, reined, bridled, and bitted,   30
minutely cavorted in their glass corral.

Round galleries and shies and stalls, pennies were burning holes
in a hundred pockets. Pale young men with larded hair and Valen-
tino-black sidewhiskers, fags stuck to their lower lips, squinted along

their swivel-sighted rifles and aimed at ping-pong balls dancing on fountains. In knife-creased, silver-grey, skirt-like Oxford bags, and a sleeveless, scarlet, zip-fastened shirt with yellow horizontal stripes, a collier at the strength-machine spat on his hands, raised the hammer, and brought it Thor-ing down. The bell rang for Blaina.

Outside his booth stood a bitten-eared and barn-door-chested pug with a nose like a twisted swede and hair that startled from his eyebrows and three teeth yellow as a camel's, inviting any sportsman to a sudden and sickening basting in the sandy ring or a quid if he lasted a round; and wiry, cocky, bow-legged, coal-scarred, boozed sportsmen by the dozen strutted in and reeled out; and still those three teeth remained, chipped and camel-yellow in the bored, teak face.

Draggled and stout-wanting mothers, with haphazard hats, hostile hatpins, buns awry, bursting bags, and children at their skirts like pop-filled and jam-smeared limpets, screamed, before distorting mirrors, at their suddenly tapering or tubular bodies and huge ballooning heads, and the children gaily bellowed at their own reflected bogies withering and bulging in the glass.

Old men, smelling of Milford Haven in the rain, shuffled, badgering and cadging, round the edges of the swaggering crowd, their only wares a handful of damp confetti. A daring dash of schoolboys, safely, shoulder to shoulder, with their fathers' trilbies cocked at a desperate angle over one eye, winked at and whistled after the procession past the swings of two girls arm-in-arm: always one pert and pretty, and always one with glasses. Girls in skulled and cross-boned tunnels shrieked, and were comforted. Young men, heroic after pints, stood up on the flying chairaplanes, tousled, crimson, and against the rules. Jaunty girls gave sailors sauce.

All the Fun of the Fair in the hot, bubbling night. The Man in the sand-yellow Moon over the hurdy of gurdies. The swingboats swimming to and fro like slices of the moon. Dragons and hippogriffs at the prows of the gondolas breathing fire and Sousa. Midnight roundabout riders tantivying under the fairy-lights, huntsmen on billygoats and zebras hallooing under a circle of glow-worms.

And as we climbed home, up the gas-lit hill, to the still house over the mumbling bay, we heard the music die and the voices drift like sand. And we saw the lights of the Fair fade. And, at the far end of seaside field, they lit their lamps, one by one, in the caravans.

QUESTIONS AND PROBLEMS

1. Description is generally based on the use of more than one—or all—of the sense impressions. How many of the five senses does Thomas appeal to in this descriptive essay?
2. How is the child's prayer, "If it could only just be like this for ever and ever amen" (par. 21) linked to adult nostalgia? What is the nostalgia?
3. Analyze Thomas' prose style. How do the poet and the prose writer come together in this essay? Cite examples, not overlooking Thomas' use of alliteration.
4. Explain the terms "ice-cream cornet," "deceptive water," "A rolling of trousers," "A compromise of paddlers," "a lark of boys," "A silent hullabaloo of balloons" (par. 1). What do these images contribute to the mood of the essay?
5. Define and cite examples from the essay: *image, alliteration, internal rhyme, rhythm.*
6. Read the essay aloud. Is the prose Thomas uses particularly adapted to hearing? Why?
7. Choose four or five descriptive passages which particularly arrested your attention. Why did they do so?
8. Explain the statement (par. 12), "Willy's bleeding over the cheese—" Why is it an effective climactic statement in this exchange of comment?
9. Explain the use of Thomas' short paragraphs. What does this style of paragraphing contribute to the essay?
10. What is the indirect meaning of the essay, as opposed to the direct description of the August bank holiday?

SUGGESTIONS FOR WRITING

1. Write a descriptive essay which embodies a Romantic view of childhood.
2. Write a realistic description of childhood without Romantic overtones.
3. Write a critical essay in comparison of Oliver Goldsmith's poem "The Deserted Village" with George Crabbe's poem "The Village."
4. Write an analysis of Thomas' descriptive essay as an example of prose-poetry.
5. Analyze Katherine Mansfield's understanding of children as expressed in her short story "The Doll's House."
6. Write a descriptive account of a holiday you had as a child. Center it on a single incident, as Thomas does, rather than on an extended vacation. Concentrate on bringing in the sense impressions.
7. Read Kenneth Grahame's essays based on reminiscence of childhood in his volumes *Dream Days* and *The Golden Age.* Write an essay on Grahame's understanding of the essential nature of childhood.
8. Write an essay on your own interpretation of "The Golden Age." What was "The Golden Age" in your life? Through use of description, try to make that time vivid for your reader.

SUGGESTIONS FOR FURTHER READING

Charles S. Brooks, *Prologue* (Harcourt, Brace)
Samuel L. Clemens, *The Adventures of Huckleberry Finn* (various publishers);
   Autobiography (Harper & Row)

Peter Coveney: *Poor Monkey: The Child in Literature from Rousseau's Emile to the Freudian Novelists* (Dufour)

Kenneth Grahame, *The Golden Age, and Dream Days* (Dufour; New American Library)

AUTUMN IN THE HAIGHT: WHERE HAS LOVE GONE?
Don McNeill

The season changed, and the moon thrusts of the Autumn Equinox preoccupied the many people in Haight-Ashbury who chart by planetary movement. Others participated in the Equinox celebration, a pleasant event which has become a tradition here in the past few seasons. This celebration was of special note, because two traditional American Indian medicine men decided at the last minute to attend. The medicine men, Rolling Thunder and Shaymu, came to the Straight Theatre on Haight Street and helpers hurried to the street with handbills reading "QUICK INDIANS WANT TO SEE YOU." The natives came, and, in front of the Straight, Rolling Thunder met Shaymu, and Shaymu said, "Let us adopt these people, who are called hippies, as our children. They have been disowned." Rolling Thunder agreed, and the Indians and many of their new children went to the country to dance all night around a fire on a beach.   1

The vast majority of the younger residents of Haight-Ashbury just hung around the street, aware of neither the Equinox nor of their new family. Most were unaware because they didn't care. They had more pressing problems: to find some bread to get home, to find a place to crash for the night, or to find some speed so they could forget about the night. Haight Street was lined with people with problems.   2

Most of the tourists were gone, and with them their funny money, which really didn't matter because they only clogged the streets and not much of the money filtered back into the community anyway. But the community was certainly short of bread. The Haight-Ashbury Medical Clinic, which had given free medical treatment to 13,000 people since June without any financial or moral support from government or foundation sources, finally closed its doors, defeated and depleted, on September 22. The Digger Free Store was in debt and the proprietor threatened to split to New York unless the $750 in back rent materialized. The Switchboard, which maintained a volunteer legal staff of thirty lawyers and had found crash pads for up to 300 pilgrims a night, was doing fine until it received some contributions. They spent the money before the checks bounced, and needed $1000 to survive. Most of the communes in the country still depended on outside support, and even the free food in the Panhandle, which began to resemble a bread line, threatened to fold without more funds.   3

Haight-Ashbury had survived the Summer of Love, but it seemed 4
mortally wounded.

It could have been worse. Estimates in the spring had doubled
the estimated 50,000 saints and freeloaders who came to the Haight
seeking the love and free life that the papers had promised. The
subdivided flats in the bay-windowed houses—the rule to Haight-
Ashbury as tenement apartments are to the East Side—stretched to 5
accommodate guests. There were no hunger riots, and the now de-
funct free medical clinic kept the threatened plague and pestilence in
check. The pilgrims were fed and housed—with occasional free music
and drugs thrown in—and the panhandlers on Haight Street were still
asking for quarters in October.

As I arrived, there were kids on many corners with packs on their
backs and thumbs stuck out trying to leave. The people I met, many
of whom had been here before the Human Be-In and the Summer of
Love (some of whom had coined the words), were exhausted and
dejected, rather like a bartender counting unbroken glasses after an 6
all-night brawl. Yet they were counting broken spirits and their few
veteran friends who had not yet split for the sanctum of an unpubli-
cized commune in the country. They were the hosts of the Summer
of Love and now, after the Autumn Equinox, it was time to clean
up.

There's not much reason now to go to Haight Street unless it's to
cop. The street itself has a layer of grease and dirt which is common
on busy sidewalks in New York but rare in San Francisco, a film that
comes from bits of lunch, garbage, and spilled coke ground into the
cement by the heels of Haight Street strollers. It is not a pleasant
place to sit, yet hundreds do, huddled in doorways or stretched out 7
on the sidewalk, in torn blankets and bare feet, bored voices begging
for spare change, selling two-bit psychedelic newspapers that were
current in the spring, and dealing, dealing, dealing. The dealing is my
strongest impression of Haight Street. The housewives with their
brownie cameras miss the best part of the show.

It's not hard to cop in the Haight. If you look remotely hip and
walk down the street, a dozen anxious peddlers should approach you
to offer their goods. It is something that may happen once a day on
St. Mark's Place. Here I am asked several times on each block
whether I want to buy, or occasionally sell, grass, acid, meth, kilos,
lids, matchboxes or, in the case of one ambitious (and, I think, mad) 8
merchant, "Owsley tabs, mescaline, psilocybin coated grass, or anything, anything you want." The merchant was young, fat, owlish-
looking, perspiring and unshaven. He had an entourage of several

pre-adolescent kids swathed in Army blankets. "I know the stuff is good," he said. "I try it all myself."

The pace of dealing picks up at night, when the dark provides some protection. Walking down Haight Street at night, the offers are whispers in the shadows or in the crowds. Mostly it's acid. But street acid is usually a combination of a taste of acid fortified with any-thing from methedrine to strychnine. There have been a lot of bad trips here lately, because there has been a lot of bad acid.   9

Even in October some new stores are opening, latecomers for the left-overs of the poster and bead market, but it should be a rough winter for the bead game, with no assurances that next summer the circus will come to town again. Enlightened natives have spread out all over town from Haight-Ashbury. Anyone curious about hippies can pick up a hitchhiker or find some on his own block. Unlike Greenwich Village, the shops are not an attraction in themselves. The same goods are sold in more attractive shops all over town.   10

I did find one merchant who wanted nothing to do with the psychedelic market. I needed some matches so I went into a liquor store on Haight Street off Clayton and, rather than hassle the thin, white-haired man at the counter, I bought a pack of cigarettes, which he gave me with a pack of matches. Then I asked for an extra pack of matches.   11

He eyed me severely.

"You got matches, right here," he said, tapping the pack of matches with the nail of his index finger.

"I'd like an extra pack," I said. "I'll pay you for them."

He shook his head. "No," he said, "you got matches right here. One pack is all you need. One pack of cigarettes. One pack of matches. What do you need more for?"

I pulled out my other pack of cigarettes. "For these," I said. "That's what I came here for."   12

"What happened to the matches you got with those?" he shouted triumphant with the evidence, finding me guilty of all the dope-fiend-marijuana-puffing sins that the mind of a liquor-store keeper could imagine. Even after the hordes, he was holding his hill. He was doing his bit.

The street is the heart of the Haight. It is where everyone first realized that they had company on their trip. It is reality—a hard fact to stomach when you're fifteen and strung out on meth and it's midnight and you've got no place to crash except a doorway. With-out the coffee houses and bars of the beats, the street is the scene, a hell of a scene, with tourists and runaways and dealers and burners   13 and the holy Angels with their bikes and the gaudy stores as a backdrop.

A schism exists between the street and the elite in Haight-Ashbury. The same is true in New York. The elite of the Haight-Ashbury scene are even more aware of it, and they have occasionally tried to bridge the gap, without much success. Chester Anderson began the Communication Company over a year ago, hoping to keep the street in touch and control with an "instant newspaper" of enticing handbills. The handbills fascinated the fringes but bored the masses. Anderson was finally purged and split several months ago for 14 Florida. The Diggers tried harder, attacking the needs of the neighborhood with free food and free stores and free theatre and free thought. They convinced Jay and Ron Thelin, pioneer proprietors of the Psychedelic Shop, to forsake free enterprise and just be free. The shop became a lounge for the street and finally died October 6 with the proprietors in debt, in love, and enlightened. On that day, the elders decided to put an end to it all.

The idea was kindled at a meeting earlier in the week at Happening House, a beautiful Victorian mansion just off the Panhandle on Clayton Street, which opened at the end of the summer to serve as a community center. The idea was to have a three-day funeral for the death of hip—of the death of the Haight—and most of the meeting was spent trying to determine just what had died. But all agreed that 15 a funeral was a good idea. "The idea of a few people going down Haight Street," sighed *Oracle* editor Allen Cohen. "The idea, the symbols, go through walls, through windows, through air, through mountains. Through the media, it will hit millions of people." The media giveth and the media taketh away. . . .

The next day was a day of preparation and press conferences. I walked into the Psychedelic Shop in the late afternoon to find CBS News waiting in line behind a local television station to interview 16 Ron Thelin in his tiny office at the back of the shop. A tiny enameled American flag hung from Thelin's freshly pierced ear.

The funeral notices had been printed. They were small, stiff cards, bordered in black, reading "HIPPIE. In the Haight-Ashbury district of this city, Hippie, devoted son of Mass Media. Friends are invited to attend services beginning at sunrise, October 6, 1967, at Buena Vista Park."

Saturday morning the little windows in the parking meters up and down Haight Street were all painted white, and the faithful gathered before dawn at the top of the hill in Buena Vista Park to 17 greet the sun. The sun rose on time, and they rang bells and breathed

deeply and exhaled OM, the first sound in the Universe. Then the
pallbearers lifted the fifteen-foot coffin, to be filled with the artifacts   18
of hip, and bore it down the long hill to the street. They paused to
kneel at the crossroads of Haight and Ashbury and brought the coffin to rest for the moment in front of the Psychedelic Shop, which
had a huge sign reading "BE FREE" in place of its famous mandala.
Then the elated mourners swept the street, in preparation for the
procession at noon.

At noon a huge banner was stretched across the street. It read
"DEATH OF HIPPIE, FREEBIE, BIRTH OF THE FREE MAN."
The coffin was carried to the Panhandle, where more newspapers,
beads, fruit, cookies, posters, flowers, and buttons were added to the   19
remains. A banner was held up reading "The Brotherhood of Free
Men is Born." And, as the procession began, the crowd sang Hare
Krishna, but slowly, as a dirge.

The procession moved slowly down the Panhandle towards
Golden Gate Park. First came a legion of photographers, walking
backwards, and then the coffin, over ten struggling pallbearers, and
then a hippie laid out on a stretcher, holding a flower to his chest,
and then about 200 mourners, some in elaborate costume, some
shaking tambourines, some carrying babies, some dodging cameras.
When it reached the park the procession turned left, now with a
police escort, whose job seemed to be to keep the procession jammed
onto the sidewalk. Six blocks later they turned left again, hauling the   20
coffin up the steep hill on Frederick Street, and at the top of the hill
they turned again on Masonic Street, which goes steeply downhill, to
complete the circle of the Haight. The coffin picked up speed as it
moved downhill, the photographers jumped to get out of the way,
and the dead hippie squirmed to stay on the stretcher. And then,
halfway down the steep Masonic Street sidewalk, their path was
blocked.

A Cadillac had been left parked in a driveway.

The funeral procession came to a crushing halt, and the police
escort—a lone cop—sauntered over and began to write out a parking   21
ticket.

"Move the car," someone yelled. The owner walked out of the
house and began to argue with the cop.   22

"Hassle him later," they yelled. "Move the car!"

The cop gave the man a ticket, and the owner returned to his
house. The Cadillac remained in the driveway and the pallbearers   23
were groaning.

At which point the cop consented to let the procession by-pass 24
the car in the street.

The procession ended where it began, in the Panhandle. The
hippie on the stretcher rose from the dead, looking punchy, and the
banners were used to kindle a fire under the huge coffin. The flames
took to it quickly and rose ten feet in the air as the crowd cheered. 25
They danced in a circle around the burning coffin and the camera-
men and, as the charred coffin crumbled and the fire died down, free
men began to leap over the flames. Then the crowd gasped with
horror as they saw the fire engines approach.

"The remains!" someone yelled. "Don't let them put it out!"
The crowd blocked the firemen and spokesmen argued with the chief
as his men readied their hoses. When the hoses were ready, the crowd
parted, and the coffin disappeared in a monster cloud of spray and 26
black smoke. The fire was out in seconds, and the firemen moved in
with shovels to break apart the smouldering remains. A few diehards
were still arguing with the chief, but the mourners had already begun
to wander off.

Saturday, the *Chronicle* reverently reported that the Hippie was
dead, but by Monday they were back in business again, with their
daily quota of copy from the Haight. The banner remained strung
across Haight Street for a week, as a reminder, and the Psychedelic
Shop was closed and boarded up, and the parking meters were 27
cleaned of the white paint. But the kids still panhandled and sold
newspapers and lounged in the doorways, and the occasional tourist
still gawked from behind the locked doors of his car. Nothing had
changed. It all was the same.

But an exorcism is a subtle thing, and some of the dejection that
plagues the Haight in the wake of the Summer of Love did appear to
be gone. When a phalanx of fourteen cops swept down Haight Street
Tuesday in a daylight raid to net runaways, the community re- 28
sponded with vigor and outrage and, despite threats by Police Chief
Cahill, the raids were not repeated. The heat was on and the Haight
kept cool.

Within a few weeks, the Switchboard was out of debt and danger,
and a series of well-attended benefits brought a generous reserve of
funds into the coffers of the clinic, which reopened in late October.
The Straight Theatre, which was denied a dance permit by an ever- 29
harassing city, held huge "Dance Classes" (for which permits are not
needed) to the accompaniment of the Grateful Dead. And the Dig-

gers were delivering free meat to communes and distributing 5000 copies of a twenty-page free magazine called *Free City*.

The elders now harbor hopes that San Francisco will indeed become a "free city." If any city can, it can, but it must be born, not made. The hippie was made but the community called Haight-Ashbury was born, and it was a virgin birth—an evolutionary experiment and experience. It was beautiful, I am told, in the golden age before the Human Be-In which awoke the media to the precious copy lying untapped on the south side of Golden Gate Park. "Were you here a year ago?" people ask. If you were, then you know.   30

But then the seekers came en masse, enticed by the media. "They came to the Haight," a handbill relates, "with a great need and a great hunger for a loving community. Many, wanting to belong, identified with the superficial aspects of what 'hippie' was. They didn't drop out but rather changed roles.   31

"As a result the tone of Haight-Ashbury changed. With many people coming in expecting to be fed and housed, the older community tried to fulfill their needs. Rather than asking them to do their thing, the community tried to give them what they came for. The community tried to be something it wasn't.   32

"The early members tried to save the community and as a result it began to die. It began to die because in the effort to save it the individuals lost themselves. Without individual selves the community started to become a shell with little within; to maintain the community feeling, meetings replaced relationships and organization replaced community.   33

"By the end of the summer we were forming organizations to save something that no longer existed. Community is a creative thing and saving is only a holding action. By desperate clinging, we lost."   34

They lost, but they learned.   35

QUESTIONS AND PROBLEMS

1. What part does description play in this essay? What other devices does the author employ?
2. Is this indeed an essay? Defend it as belonging in that category.
3. Define or explain within the context of the essay "funny money," "short of bread" (par. 3), "to cop" (par. 7), "no place to crash" (par. 13).
4. Why was the "funeral" a failure? What did it set out to accomplish which was not accomplished?
5. Where does the author lay the blame for this failure? Discuss generally the effect of various media on such movements as that called "hippie."

SUGGESTIONS FOR WRITING

1. Write an essay in definition of "Hippie Culture."
2. Write an explanation of what "grass" (or "acid," "meth," etc.) is and what its effects on the user are reputed to be.
3. Describe an impromptu event on your own campus, developing as you write a thesis or point.
4. The author says, at the end of the essay, "Community is a creative thing. . . . " Describe and explain the community of students as a creative force.
5. Use description as the main method of developing an essay on the success or failure of your high school or college in achieving a reasonable goal.

TO NARRATE

Narration has to do with relating happenings. The happenings themselves may be actual events or they may be fictitious. In most forms of imaginative writing the narration is of prime importance, but in the essay the narration is subordinate to the main purpose, the presentation of a thesis or idea.

The relating of facts or experiences by way of *story* is surely the oldest form of artistic—as opposed to practical—communication by means of language. When used by the essayist, the specific experience or chain of events being narrated will point out a general experience or prove a point. Francis Parkman, in his narratives of experiences on the California and Oregon trails, gives us insight into the character and the lives of the Indians, the traders, the men who peopled the West. George Orwell, in "Shooting an Elephant," condemns an entire political and economic system.

The narrative essay is frequently written in the first person, as in autobiographical episodes which have ideas to communicate or points to make. Orwell uses this method in his essay illustrating the meeting of the East and the West.

Furthermore, the narrative essay is usually chronological in arrangement. It has a theme or central idea which goes beyond merely "telling a story." It makes use of concrete details, visual description, and, usually, simple and nonliterary language. All these together produce the interest which keeps the reader going and which eventually achieves the desired effect: the communication of the central idea which the writer seeks to put across.

Although a narrative may be described basically as a recital of happenings, it is obvious that there must be something more then mere recapitulation of events. The events must be *about* something, about something worth reading. In other words, there must be a theme, usually either a generalization of a particularization about life. In Orwell's essay, his theme, or the point of view he has reached on the subject of colonialism, is of first importance. Lord Dunsany, in his "A Moral Little Tale," writes a fictional narrative, or tale, which is designed primarily not to entertain but to teach. His theme is the danger inherent in the desire of some people to force everyone else to be just like themselves; his

286

vehicle is a broadly sketched fictional narrative which serves only to publish that theme.

It is hardly necessary to insist upon the large part narration plays in our everyday lives. We all read fiction; we all read the newspapers; we all go to movies and watch television; most of us read biographies and history; we all read and write letters. It is sound practice for the student of writing to study the art of narration—if only to write better, more lively letters home!

SHOOTING AN ELEPHANT
George Orwell

In Moulmein, in Lower Burma, I was hated by large numbers of people—the only time in my life that I have been important enough for this to happen to me. I was sub-divisional police officer of the town, and in an aimless, petty kind of way anti-European feeling was very bitter. No one had the guts to raise a riot, but if a European woman went through the bazaars alone somebody would probably spit betel juice over her dress. As a police officer I was an obvious target and was baited whenever it seemed safe to do so. When a nimble Burman tripped me up on the football field and the referee (another Burman) looked the other way, the crowd yelled with hideous laughter. This happened more than once. In the end the sneering yellow faces of young men that met me everywhere, the insults hooted after me when I was at a safe distance, got badly on my nerves. The young Buddhist priests were the worst of all. There were several thousands of them in the town and none of them seemed to have anything to do except stand on street corners and jeer at Europeans.

1

All this was perplexing and upsetting. For at that time I had already made up my mind that imperialism was an evil thing and the sooner I chucked up my job and got out of it the better. Theoretically—and secretly, of course—I was all for the Burmese and all against their oppressors, the British. As for the job I was doing, I hated it more bitterly than I can perhaps make clear. In a job like that you see the dirty work of Empire at close quarters. The wretched prisoners huddling in the stinking cages of the lock-ups, the grey, cowed faces of the long-term convicts, the scarred buttocks of the men who had been flogged with bamboos—all these oppressed me with an intolerable sense of guilt. But I could get nothing into perspective. I was young and ill-educated and I had had to think out my problems in the utter silence that is imposed on every Englishman in the East. I did not even know that the British Empire is dying, still less did I know that it is a great deal better than the younger empires that are going to supplant it. All I knew was that I was stuck between my hatred of the empire I served and my rage against the evil-spirited little beasts who tried to make my job impossible. With one part of my mind I thought of the British Raj as an unbreakable tyranny, as something clamped down, *in saecula saeculorum,* upon the will of prostrate peoples; with another part I thought that the greatest joy in the world would be to drive a bayonet into a Buddhist priest's guts.

2

Feelings like these are the normal by-products of imperialism; ask any Anglo-Indian offical, if you can catch him off duty.

One day something happened which in a roundabout way was enlightening. It was a tiny incident in itself, but it gave me a better glimpse than I had had before of the real nature of imperialism—the real motives for which despotic governments act. Early one morning the sub-inspector at a police station the other end of the town rang me up on the phone and said that an elephant was ravaging the bazaar. Would I please come and do something about it? I did not know what I could do, but I wanted to see what was happening and I got on to a pony and started out. I took my rifle, an old .44 Winchester and much too small to kill an elephant, but I thought the noise might be useful *in terrorem*. Various Burmans stopped me on the way and told me about the elephant's doings. It was not, of course, a wild elephant, but a tame one which had gone "must." It had been chained up, as tame elephants always are when their attack of "must" is due, but on the previous night it had broken its chain and escaped. Its mahout, the only person who could manage it when it was in that state, had set out in pursuit, but had taken the wrong direction and was now twelve hours' journey away, and in the morning the elephant had suddenly reappeared in the town. The Burmese population had no weapons and were quite helpless against it. It had already destroyed somebody's bamboo hut, killed a cow and raided some fruit-stalls and devourted the stock; also it had met the municipal rubbish van and, when the driver jumped out and took to his heels, had turned the van over and inflicted violences upon it.

3

The Burmese sub-inspector and some Indian constables were waiting for me in the quarter where the elephant had been seen. It was a very poor quarter, a labyrinth of squalid bamboo huts, thatched with palmleaf, winding all over a steep hillside. I remember that it was a cloudy, stuffy morning at the beginning of the rains. We began questioning the people as to where the elephant had gone and, as usual, failed to get any definite information. That is invariably the case in the East; a story always sounds clear enough at a distance, but the nearer you get to the scene of events the vaguer it becomes. Some of the people said that the elephant had gone in one direction, some said that he had gone in another, some professed not even to have heard of any elephant. I had almost made up my mind that the whole story was a pack of lies, when we heard yells a little distance away. There was a loud, scandalized cry of "Go away, child! Go away this instant!" and an old woman with a switch in her hand came round the corner of a hut, violently shooing away a crowd of

naked children. Some more women followed, clicking their tongues and exclaiming; evidently there was something that the children ought not to have seen. I rounded the hut and saw a man's dead   4
body sprawling in the mud. He was an Indian, a black Dravidian coolie, almost naked, and he could not have been dead many minutes. The people said that the elephant had come suddenly upon him round the corner of the hut, caught him with its trunk, put its foot on his back and ground him into the earth. This was the rainy season and the ground was soft, and his face had scored a trench a foot deep and a couple of yards long. He was lying on his belly with arms crucified and head sharply twisted to one side. His face was coated with mud, the eyes wide open, the teeth bared and grinning with an expression of unendurable agony. (Never tell me, by the way, that the dead look peaceful. Most of the corpses I have seen looked devilish.) The friction of the great beast's foot had stripped the skin from his back as neatly as one skins a rabbit. As soon as I saw the dead man I sent an orderly to a friend's house nearby to borrow an elephant rifle. I had already sent back the pony, not wanting it to go mad with fright and throw me if it smelt the elephant.

The orderly came back in a few minutes with a rifle and five cartridges, and meanwhile some Burmans had arrived and told us that the elephant was in the paddy fields below, only a few hundred yards away. As I started forward practically the whole population of the quarter flocked out of the houses and followed me. They had seen the rifle and were all shouting excitedly that I was going to shoot the elephant. They had not shown much interest in the elephant when he was merely ravaging their homes, but it was different now that he was going to be shot. It was a bit of fun to them, as it would be to an English crowd; besides they wanted the meat. It made me vaguely uneasy. I had no intention of shooting the elephant—I had merely   5
sent for the rifle to defend myself if necessary—and it is always unnerving to have a crowd following you. I marched down the hill, looking and feeling a fool, with the rifle over my shoulder and an ever-growing army of people jostling at my heels. At the bottom, when you got away from the huts, there was a metalled road and beyond that a miry waste of paddy fields a thousand yards across, not yet ploughed but soggy from the first rains and dotted with coarse grass. The elephant was standing eight yards from the road, his left side towards us. He took not the slightest notice of the crowd's approach. He was tearing up bunches of grass, beating them against his knees to clean them and stuffing them into his mouth.

I had halted on the road. As soon as I saw the elephant I knew with perfect certainty that I ought not to shoot him. It is a serious matter to shoot a working elephant—it is comparable to destroying a huge and costly piece of machinery—and obviously one ought not to do it if it can possibly be avoided. And at that distance, peacefully eating, the elephant looked no more dangerous than a cow. I thought then and I think now that his attack of "must" was already passing off; in which case he would merely wander harmlessly about until the mahout came back and caught him. Moreover, I did not in the least want to shoot him. I decided that I would watch him for a little while to make sure that he did not turn savage again, and then go home.

But at that moment I glanced round at the crowd that had followed me. It was an immense crowd, two thousand at the least and growing every minute. It blocked the road for a long distance on either side. I looked at the sea of yellow faces above the garish clothes—faces all happy and excited over this bit of fun, all certain that the elephant was going to be shot. They were watching me as they would watch a conjurer about to perform a trick. They did not like me, but with the magical rifle in my hand I was momentarily worth watching. And suddenly I realized that I should have to shoot the elephant after all. The people expected it of me and I had got to do it; I could feel their two thousand wills pressing me forward, irresistibly. And it was at this moment, as I stood there with the rifle in my hands, that I first grasped the hollowness, the futility of the white man's dominion in the East. Here was I, the white man with his gun, standing in front of the unarmed native crowd—seemingly the leading actor of the piece; but in reality I was only an absurd puppet pushed to and fro by the will of those yellow faces behind. I perceived in this moment that when the white man turns tyrant it is his own freedom that he destroys. He becomes a sort of hollow, posing dummy, the conventionalized figure of a sahib. For it is the condition of his rule that he shall spend his life in trying to impress the "natives," and so in every crisis he has got to do what the "natives" expect of him. He wears a mask, and his face grows to fit it. I had got to shoot the elephant. I had committed myself to doing it when I sent for the rifle. A sahib has got to act like a sahib; he has got to appear resolute, to know his own mind and do definite things. To come all that way, rifle in hand, with two thousand people marching at my heels, and then to trail feebly away, having done nothing—no, that was impossible. The crowd would laugh at me. And my whole

6

7

life, every white man's life in the East, was one long struggle not to be laughed at.

But I did not want to shoot the elephant. I watched him beating his bunch of grass against his knees, with that preoccupied grand-motherly air that elephants have. It seemed to me that it would be murder to shoot him. At that age I was not squeamish about killing animals, but I had never shot an elephant and never wanted to. (Somehow it always seems worse to kill a *large* animal.) Besides, there was the beast's owner to be considered. Alive, the elephant was   8 worth at least a hundred pounds; dead, he would only be worth the value of his tusks, five pounds, possibly. But I had got to act quickly. I turned to some experienced-looking Burmans who had been there when we arrived, and asked them how the elephant had been behav-ing. They all said the same thing: he took no notice of you if you left him alone, but he might charge if you went too close to him.

It was perfectly clear to me what I ought to do. I ought to walk up to within, say, twenty-five yards of the elephant and test his behavior. If he charged, I could shoot; if he took no notice of me, it would be safe to leave him until the mahout came back. But also I knew that I was going to do no such thing. I was a poor shot with a rifle and the ground was soft mud into which one would sink at every step. If the elephant charged and I missed him, I should have about as much chance as a toad under a steam-roller. But even then I was not thinking particularly of my own skin, only of the watchful yellow faces behind. For at that moment, with the crowd watching   9 me, I was not afraid in the ordinary sense, as I would have been if I had been alone. A white man mustn't be frightened in front of "natives"; and so, in general, he isn't frightened. The sole thought in my mind was that if anything went wrong those two thousand Bur-mans would see me pursued, caught, trampled on and reduced to a grinning corpse like that Indian up the hill. And if that happened it was quite probable that some of them would laugh. That would never do. There was only one alternative. I shoved the cartridges in the magazine and lay down on the road to get a better aim.

The crowd grew very still, and a deep, low, happy sigh, as of people who see the theatre curtain go up at last, breathed from innumerable throats. They were going to have their bit of fun after all. The rifle was a beautiful German thing with cross-hair sights. I did not then know that in shooting an elephant one would shoot to   10 cut an imaginary bar running from ear-hole to ear-hole. I ought, therefore, as the elephant was sideways on, to have aimed straight at his ear-hole; actually I aimed several inches in front of this, thinking the brain would be further forward.

When I pulled the trigger I did not hear the bang or feel the kick—one never does when a shot goes home—but I heard the devilish roar of glee that went up from the crowd. In that instant, in too short a time, one would have thought, even for the bullet to get there, a mysterious, terrible change had come over the elephant. He neither stirred nor fell, but every line of his body had altered. He looked suddenly stricken, shrunken, immensely old, as though the frightful impact of the bullet had paralysed him without knocking him down. At last, after what seemed a long time—it might have been five seconds, I dare say—he sagged flabbily to his knees. His mouth slobbered. An enormous senility seemed to have settled upon him. 11 One could have imagined him thousands of years old. I fired again into the same spot. At the second shot he did not collapse but climbed with desperate slowness to his feet and stood weakly up-right, with legs sagging and head drooping. I fired a third time. That was the shot that did for him. You could see the agony of it jolt his whole body and knock the last remnant of strength from his legs. But in falling he seemed for a moment to rise, for as his hind legs collapsed beneath him he seemed to tower upward like a huge rock toppling, his trunk reaching skywards like a tree. He trumpeted, for the first and only time. And then down he came, his belly towards me, with a crash that seemed to shake the ground even where I lay.

I got up. The Burmans were already racing past me across the mud. It was obvious that the elephant would never rise again, but he was not dead. He was breathing very rhythmically with long rattling gasps, his great mound of a side painfully rising and falling. His mouth was wide open—I could see far down into caverns of pale pink throat. I waited a long time for him to die, but his breathing did not weaken. Finally I fired my two remaining shots into the spot where I thought his heart must be. The thick blood welled out of him like red velvet, but still he did not die. His body did not even jerk when the shots hit him, the tortured breathing continued without a pause. 12 He was dying, very slowly and in great agony, but in some world remote from me where not even a bullet could damage him further. I felt that I had got to put an end to that dreadful noise. It seemed dreadful to see the great beast lying there, powerless to move and yet powerless to die, and not even to be able to finish him. I sent back for my small rifle and poured shot after shot into his heart and down his throat. They seemed to make no impression. The tortured gasps continued as steadily as the ticking of a clock.

In the end I could not stand it any longer and went away. I heard later that it took him half an hour to die. Burmans were bringing   13 dahs and baskets even before I left, and I was told they had stripped his body almost to the bones by the afternoon.

Afterwards, of course, there were endless discussions about the shooting of the elephant. The owner was furious, but he was only an Indian and could do nothing. Besides, legally I had done the right thing, for a mad elephant has to be killed, like a mad dog, if its owner fails to control it. Among the Europeans opinion was divided. The older men said I was right, the younger men said it was a damn   14 shame to shoot an elephant for killing a coolie, because an elephant was worth more than any damn Coringhee coolie. And afterwards I was very glad that the coolie had been killed; it put me legally in the right and it gave me a sufficient pretext for shooting the elephant. I often wondered whether any of the others grasped that I had done it solely to avoid looking a fool.

QUESTIONS AND PROBLEMS

1. Orwell's "Shooting an Elephant" is an excellent example of a narrative essay, a narrative which makes a point. What is that point?
2. This essay is typical of many of Orwell's in having Burma as its setting. Does he make the setting come alive for his readers? In what ways?
3. If social message is important in this essay, why did not Orwell deliver that message directly? Consider the distinction between the concrete and the abstract in presenting a point of view.
4. Would the message be too subtle for many readers? If not, why not?
5. Comment on the quality of Orwell's prose. How would you characterize his style? Is the style effective in this narrative?
6. Cite examples of effective use of descriptive detail.
7. Comment on this passage (par. 9):

   "A white man musn't be frightened in front of 'natives'; and so, in general, he isn't frightened. The sole thought in my mind was that if anything went wrong those two thousand Burmans would see me pursued, caught, trampled on and reduced to a grinning corpse like that Indian up the hill. And if that happened it was quite probable that some of them would laugh. That would never do."

   What is the subtle comment, what are the implications, of this passage?
8. Sometimes the comments are less subtle, as in the statement (par. 14), "The owner was furious, but he was only an Indian and could do nothing." Is this one equally as effective as that in par. 9?
9. Does the experience narrated by Orwell implicate individuals, a class, or an entire way of life?

SUGGESTIONS FOR WRITING

1. Through a narrative of your first days on the campus of your college give an impression of the kind of school you found and the kinds of students you found yourself associated with.
2. Write a narrative of an experience you have had with people of a foreign country. Present it in such a way that a social or a political message may be inferred.
3. Write a narrative of how you spend a typical day at college. Make sure that the reader gets a "message" about college life.
4. Use the narrative of a return trip you have made to your old home town as the basis for an essay on the changing attitudes one has toward former associates.
5. Write a "travelogue" of a trip—perhaps as if it were a commentary to be delivered with the showing of color slides. Present it in such a way that by the time he has come to the end the reader knows far more about the narrator than appears on the surface.
6. Write a paper on the economic motives of establishing one of the original thirteen colonies.
7. Write an extended definition of colonialism, using illustrations.

SUGGESTIONS FOR FURTHER READING

Alan C. Burns, *In Defence of Colonies* (Lawrence Verry)
R. Delavignette, *Christianity and Colonialism* (Hawthorn)
Stewart C. Easton, *Rise and Fall of Western Colonialism* (Praeger)
J.S. Furnivall, *Colonial Policy and Practice: A Comparative Study of Burma and Netherlands India* (New York Univ.)
William L. Langer, *The Diplomacy of Imperialism* (Knopf)
Barbara Ward, *Five Ideas that Change the World* (Norton)
Harrison M. Wright, ed., *The New Imperialism* (Heath)

THE BLACK HILLS
Francis Parkman

We travelled eastward for two days, and then the gloomy ridges of the Black Hills rose up before us. The village passed along for some miles beneath their declivities, trailing out to a great length over the arid prairie, or winding among small detached hills of distorted shapes. Turning sharply to the left, we entered a wide defile of the mountains, down the bottom of which a brook came winding, lined with tall grass and dense copses, amid which were hidden many beaver dams and lodges. We passed along between two lines of high precipices and rocks piled in disorder one upon another, with scarce-   1
ly a tree, a bush, or a clump of grass. The restless Indian boys wandered along their edges and clambered up and down their rugged sides, and sometimes a group of them would stand on the verge of a cliff and look down on the procession as it passed beneath. As we advanced, the passage grew more narrow; then it suddenly expanded into a round grassy meadow, completely encompassed by mountains; and here the families stopped as they came up in turn, and the camp rose like magic.

The lodges were hardly pitched when, with their usual precipitation, the Indians set about accomplishing the object that had brought them there; that is, obtaining poles for their new lodges. Half the population—men, women, and boys—mounted their horses and set out for the depths of the mountains. It was a strange cavalcade, as they rode at full gallop over the shingly rocks and into the dark opening of the defile beyond. We passed between precipices, sharp and splintering at the tops, their sides beetling over the defile or descending in abrupt declivities, bristling with fir-trees. On our left they rose close to us like a wall, but on the right a winding brook with a narrow strip of marshy soil intervened. The stream was clogged with old beaver-dams, and spread frequently into wide pools. There were thick bushes and many dead and blasted trees along its   2
course, though frequently nothing remained but stumps cut close to the ground by the beaver, and marked with the sharp chisel-like teeth of those indefatigable laborers. Sometimes we dived among trees, and then emerged upon open spots, over which, Indian-like, all galloped at full speed. As Pauline bounded over the rocks I felt her saddle-girth slipping, and alighted to draw it tighter; when the whole cavalcade swept past me in a moment, the women with their gaudy ornaments tinkling as they rode, the men whooping, laughing, and lashing forward their horses. Two black-tailed deer bounded away among the

rocks; Raymond shot at them from horseback; the sharp report of his rifle was answered by another equally sharp from the opposing cliffs, and then the echoes, leaping in rapid succession from side to side, died away rattling far amid the mountains.

After having ridden in this manner six or eight miles, the scene changed, and all the declivities were covered with forests of tall, slender spruce-trees. The Indians began to fall off to the right and left, dispersing with their hatchets and knives to cut the poles which ⟨3⟩ they had come to seek. I was soon left almost alone; but in the stillness of those lonely mountains, the stroke of hatchets and the sound of voices might be heard from far and near.

Reynal, who imitated the Indians in their habits as well as the worst features of their character, had killed buffalo enough to make a lodge for himself and his squaw, and now he was eager to get the poles necessary to complete it. He asked me to let Raymond go with him, and assist in the work. I assented, and the two men immediately entered the thickest part of the wood. Having left my horse in Raymond's keeping, I began to climb the mountain. I was weak and weary, and made slow progress, often pausing to rest, but after an ⟨4⟩ hour, I gained a height whence the little valley out of which I had climbed seemed like a deep, dark gulf, though the inaccessible peak of the mountain was still towering to a much greater distance above. Objects familiar from childhood surrounded me: crags and rocks, a black and sullen brook that gurgled with a hollow voice deep among the crevices, a wood of mossy distorted trees and prostrate trunks flung down by age and storms, scattered among the rocks, or damming the foaming waters of the brook.

Wild as they were, these mountains were thickly peopled. As I climbed farther, I found the broad dusty paths made by the elk, as they filed across the mountain-side. The grass on all the terraces was trampled down by deer; there were numerous tracks of wolves, and in some of the rougher and more precipitous parts of the ascent, I found footprints different from any that I had ever seen, and which I took to be those of the Rocky Mountain sheep. I sat down upon a rock; there was a perfect stillness. No wind was stirring, and not even an insect could be heard. I remembered the danger of becoming lost in such a place, and fixed my eye upon one of the tallest pinnacles of the opposite mountain. It rose sheer upright from the woods below, ⟨5⟩ and, by an extraordinary freak of nature, sustained aloft on its very summit a large loose rock. Such a landmark could never be mistaken, and, feeling once more secure, I began again to move forward. A white wolf jumped up from among some bushes, and leaped clumsily away; but he stopped for a moment, and turned back his keen eye and grim bristling muzzle. I longed to take his scalp and carry it back with me, as a trophy of the Black Hills, but before I could fire, he was gone among the rocks. Soon after I heard a rustling sound, with a cracking of twigs at a little distance, and saw moving above the tall bushes the branching antlers of an elk. I was in the midst of a hunter's paradise.

Such are the Black Hills, as I found them in July; but they wear a different garb when winter sets in, when the broad boughs of the fir-trees are bent to the ground by the load of snow, and the dark mountains are white with it. At that season the trappers, returned from their autumn expeditions, often build their cabins in the midst of these solitudes, and live in abundance and luxury on the game that harbors there. I have heard them tell, how with their tawny mis-   6
tresses, and perhaps a few young Indian companions, they had spent months in total seclusion. They would dig pitfalls, and set traps for the white wolves, sables, and martens, and though through the whole night the awful chorus of the wolves would resound from the frozen mountains around them, yet within their massive walls of logs they would lie in careless ease before the blazing fire, and in the morning shoot the elk and deer from their very door.

QUESTIONS AND PROBLEMS

1. What are the distinguishing features of Parkman's prose? Are there elements of diction and style which date it as a work of the nineteenth century?
2. Do such passages as the following (from par. 4) remind you of the writing of any American literary figure of the same period?

   "Objects familiar from childhood surrounded me: crags and rocks, a black and sullen brook that gurgled with a hollow voice deep among the crevices, a wood of mossy distorted trees and prostrate trunks flung down by age and storms, scattered among the rocks, or damning the foaming waters of the brook."

   Try to find a similar example from a nineteenth-century writer.
3. Compare Parkman's prose with Orwell's, in the preceding essay. Point out similarities and dissimilarities.
4. There is in Parkman's narrative no such clear message as is found in Orwell's essay. Are there, however, overtones which suggest something more than a mere recital of the facts of a trip? Explain.
5. Parkman in the opening sentence of the narrative refers to the "gloomy ridges of the Black Hills." By the time you conclude this narrative what impression do you have of the feeling he has for the Black Hills?

SUGGESTIONS FOR WRITING

1. Write an essay on the motives which took men westward.
2. Do a researched article on the discovery of gold in California.

3. Make a study of the means of transportation to the Far West up to the completion of the first transcontinental railroad.
4. If you have lived in the West, give an account of the founding of your town and its early social and political character.
5. Write a narrative of your own travels in the West in imitation of the early accounts of Lewis and Clark, John Fremont, Francis Parkman, and others.
6. Write a humorous account of your travels to another part of the country or to another country.

SUGGESTIONS FOR FURTHER READING

Jesse Applegate, *"A Day with the Cow Column in 1843"* (*Oregon Historical Society Quarterly,* December, 1900)

Bernard de Voto, *Year of Decision; Course of Empire; Across the Wide Missouri; Journals of Lewis and Clark* (Houghton Mifflin)

John Charles Fremont, *Report of the Exploring Expedition to the Rocky Mountains in the Year 1842 and to Oregon and North California in the Years 1843-44* (U.S. Congress: House Doc. No. 166)

Jacob R. Gregg, *History of the Oregon Trail, Santa Fe Trail and Other Trails* (Binfords & Mort)

D. Geneva Lent, *West of the Mountains: James Sinclair and the Hudson Bay Company* (Univ. of Washington)

Meriwether Lewis and William Clark, *Original Journals of the Lewis and Clark Expedition,* ed. Reuben G. Thwaites (Dodd, Mead)

A MORAL LITTLE TALE
Lord Dunsany

There was once an earnest Puritan who held it wrong to dance. And for his principles he labored hard; his was a zealous life. And there loved him all of those who hated the dance; and those that 1 loved the dance respected him too; they said, "He is a pure, good man and acts according to his lights."

He did much to discourage dancing and helped to close several Sunday entertainments. Some kinds of poetry, he said, he liked, but 2 not the fanciful kind, as that might corrupt the thoughts of the very young. He always dressed in black.

He was interested in morality and was quite sincere, and there grew to be much respect on Earth for his honest face and his flowing 3 pure-white beard.

One night the Devil appeared unto him in a dream and said, "Well done."

"Avaunt," said that earnest man.   4

"No, no, friend," said the Devil.

"Dare not to call me 'friend,' " he answered bravely.

"Come, come, friend," said the Devil. "Have you not done my work? Have you not put apart the couples that would dance? Have you not checked their laughter and their accursed mirth? Have you not worn my livery of black? O friend, friend, you do not know 5 what a detestable thing it is to sit in hell and hear people being happy, and singing in theatres, and singing in the fields, and whispering after dances under the moon," and he fell to cursing fearfully.

"It is you," said the Puritan, "that put into their hearts the evil 6 desire to dance; and black is God's own livery, not yours."

And the Devil laughed contemptuously and spoke.

"He only made the silly colors," he said, "and useless dawns on hill-slopes facing South, and butterflies flapping along them as soon 7 as the sun rose high, and foolish maidens coming out to dance, and the warm mad West wind, and worst of all that pernicious influence Love."

And when the Devil said that God made Love that earnest man 8 sat up in bed and shouted, "Blasphemy! Blasphemy!"

"It's true," said the Devil. "It isn't I that sends the village fools muttering and whispering two by two in the woods when the harvest 9 moon is high. It's as much as I can bear even to see them dancing."

"Then," said the man, "I have mistaken right for wrong; but as 10 soon as I wake I will fight you yet."

"O, no you don't," said the Devil. "You don't wake up out of 11
this sleep."

And somewhere far away Hell's black steel doors were opened,
and arm in arm those two were drawn within, and the doors shut
behind them, and still they went arm in arm, trudging further and 12
further into the deeps of Hell. And it was that Puritan's punishment
to know that those that he cared for on Earth would do evil as he
had done.

QUESTIONS AND PROBLEMS

1. Discuss Dunsany's narrative method. What descriptive adjectives would you
   apply to it? Cite examples from the essay.
2. Dunsany calls this piece a "tale," and he includes it in a volume entitled
   Fifty-One Tales.
   a. Comment on the relationship between the tale and the essay.
   b. May this narrative be correctly called an essay? Why?
3. Why is the Puritan not given a name? What is the effect of his being nameless
   in this narrative?
4. Comment on the character of the Devil in the narrative. Compare him with
   other devil characters you know from your reading.
5. What is Dunsany's theme or central idea? Frame it in a single sentence. How
   does the theme apply to contemporary life?

SUGGESTIONS FOR WRITING

1. Investigate Victorian mores in regard to literature, social life, interior decoration, or some related subject. Write an essay on some part of your findings.
2. Write a narrative of some aspect or aspects of college life. Entitle it "A Moral
   Little College Tale."
3. Contrast social mores of your parents' youth with the mores of college men
   and women today.
4. Dunsany's tale is a satire. Write an extended definition of satire and explain
   the uses to which satire may be put today.
5. Parody the methods and manner of the Victorian novel in a brief narrative
   based on contemporary life.
6. Write a satire which points out a moral about college youth today.

SUGGESTIONS FOR FURTHER READING

Crane Brinton, *The History of Western Morals* (Harcourt, Brace & World)
Léon Cristiani, *Evidence of Satan in the Modern World,* tr. Cynthia Rowland
   (Macmillan)
Jonathan Edwards, *The Nature of True Virtue* (Univ. of Michigan)
Peter Fryer, *Mrs. Grundy: Studies in English Prudery* (London House & Max-
   well)

Christopher Marlow, *Dr. Faustus* (various publishers)
Mario Praz, *The Romantic Agony* (Meridian)
Maximilian J. Rudwin, *The Devil in Legend and Literature* (Open Court)

PART II

SOME
TYPES
OF
ESSAYS

THE LITERARY ESSAY

The literary essay is a type because of its subject matter; yet it also has certain characteristics of manner, diction, and style which make it a distinct kind. First of all, it deals with writers, books, poems—anything within the sphere of what we call literature. Its manner is usually formal rather than colloquial, and as a consequence its diction is usually studied rather than easy. It has something to communicate—something about literature—and it sets out forth-rightly to communicate.

The subject of the literary essay, not the writer, is of prime importance. Usually the writer reveals little of himself, and seldom does he write in the first person. Wright Morris' essay is on the prose style of Ernest Hemingway. Although it was written by Wright Morris and very likely could not have been written by anyone but this accomplished writer, Wright Morris as a person is not revealed. His *ideas,* of course, are revealed, but as far as the ordinary reader is concerned they are the ideas of *the writer* rather than the ideas of a person known as Wright Morris. His subject is Ernest Hemingway, not himself. Compare this style with that of the writer of essays in what we call the "familiar" style, with those of Charles Lamb, for example. Such a well-known essay of Lamb's as "Dream Children" we find to have as its real subject Charles Lamb, and not the dream children at all. The subject is the writer. But in the literary essay the subject is explicitly stated.

Again, Lauriat Lane, Jr., writes with conviction about *Huckleberry Finn.* He deals with the meaning and the importance of the novel; he communicates ideas about it, not about himself.

Literary essays vary greatly in degree of technicality because they are usually written for specific audiences. Some are very technical and are intended for scholars in a particular literary field. Seymour Chatman writes learnedly and well on "Milton's Participial Style" for the scholarly journal *PMLA* (Publications of the Modern Language Association of America). He uses a lot of footnotes. His essay is intended for students and scholars interested in John Milton. Roger Cox, in an essay in *The Yale Review* entitled "Tragedy and the Gospels," demonstrates with keen insight the unsoundness of the notion that "no genuinely Christian tragedy can exist." He writes for adults with some knowledge of theology and with an understanding of Greek and Shakespearean tragedy. Wright Morris deals technically with Hemingway's style for readers whose interest in novels goes beyond mere storytelling. Lauriat Lane, Jr., writes about *Huckleberry Finn* primarily for college students—for students who know the novel and who will welcome his defense of it as one of the great novels of the world.

We have, then, two important considerations for the writer of the literary essay: he must stick to his declared subject, and he must write for a predetermined audience. There are literary essays for Everyman as well as for the dedicated and specialized few. A third consideration, equally important, is that the writer of the literary essay must, by what he says and how he says it, convince the reader that he knows his subject and that he is worth listening to.

THE FUNCTION OF STYLE: ERNEST HEMINGWAY
Wright Morris

> Before I go on with this short history, let me make a general ob-
> servation—the test of a first-rate intelligence is the ability to hold two
> opposed ideas in the mind at the same time, and still retain the ability
> to function. One should, for example, be able to see that things are
> hopeless and yet be determined to make them otherwise.
>
> —F. Scott Fitzgerald, *The Crack-up*

"All modern literature," Hemingway stated in *The Green Hills of
Africa,* "comes from one book by Mark Twain called *Huckleberry
Finn.*" In such a comment there is an uncanny amount of truth, but
it is a characteristically revealing, oversimplified observation. What   1
the master is saying is, "I began with Huckleberry Finn." It was
perhaps inspired in order to settle the dust on that tiresome quarrel
with Gertrude Stein—who claimed that she gave birth to Ernest—but,
as he indicates, it was Twain who got in the first, and the *last* lick.

In the essentials, Ernest Hemingway, born in Illinois, is a latter-
day Huckleberry Finn. His "Big Two-Hearted River" is a latter-day
retreat into the wilderness. The differences are precisely those that
time would have made, what time would have done to both Huck
and the territory ahead. He would have learned, at a very early age,   2
that there was no such animal. His life would have begun with disenchantment rather than enchantment: he would be the first of that
new breed of young men who knew too much, who knew more than
their fathers would admit to knowing.

The boy who witnessed the death in the Michigan woods came
out of the woods a man no longer subject to change. He had had it.
But it took time to learn *what* he had had. The nature of this disenchantment is described with classic finality in the stories and
sketches of *In Our Time.* The man who emerged lived and wrote by
the values forged in his fiction. Both the writer and his work, that is,
resisted change. A process of "seasoning," rather than development,   3
links the disillusion of *In Our Time* with the resolution of *The Old
Man and the Sea.* The facts are the same. You can't win. In the long
run, life will beat you. First the big fish eat the little ones, then the
little fish eat the big ones. But a brave and simple man can win a bit
of the laurel, nevertheless. In never giving up, win or lose, he enjoys a
final triumph over death itself.

With this wisdom, dramatized in a tale that is a lucid model of his
craft, few modern men will care to argue. It seems true to life, and
we know it is true to Hemingway. It is what he has been saying, and

how he has been living, since he stepped, just forty years ago, to the edge of the wilderness and did not like at all what he saw. To that shock of recognition he has been consistent. In his life and his art he has been his own man. His craft has cast a spell that both inspires and takes a yearly toll. In attempting to come to terms with this man—or, as I choose to believe, this *style*—we are essentially concerned with coming to terms with his age, with the fact that he is largely responsible for it. His style—like the clear water that flows at the heart of all of his fiction—sounds the note of enchantment to the very disenchantment it anticipates. The reader grasps, immediately, that this man is not so tough as he looks. Quite the contrary, he looks and sounds so tough because his heart is so soft. Behind the armor of his prose, the shell of his exile, lurks our old friend Huck Finn, American dreamer, the cleancut boy who just wishes Aunt Sally would leave him alone, who wants nothing more, nor less, than a clearing of his own in the wilderness. The dream itself he left unchanged, he merely moved to a smaller river, but he brought to it a style that revealed the dream to itself. There was no need to cry "O lost, lost—lost!" in the voice of Tom Wolfe, since the style had absorbed the state of disenchantment: the style was it. It was not merely the man, nor a handful of crafty exiles, but the age itself, the old moon of enchantment with the new moon of disenchantment in its arms.

When the young man Hemingway came to the edge of the clearing, when he saw what man had left in the place of nature, he found it something more than an unpleasant shock. He found it unacceptable. In that early judgment he has never wavered. It is expressed with finality in his exile. In this feeling, and in his exile, he is not alone, but being an artist he has been able to give his judgment a singular permanence. As the style of Faulkner grew out of his rage—out of the impotence of his rage—the style of Hemingway grew out of the depth and nuance of his disenchantment. Only a man who had believed, with a child's purity of faith, in some haunting dream of life, in its vistas of promise, is capable of forging his disillusion into a work of art. It is love of life that Hemingway's judgment of life reveals. Between the lines of his prose, between the passage and the reader, there is often that far sound of running water, a pine-scented breeze that blows from a cleaner and finer world. It is this air that makes the sight of so many corpses bearable. Invariably it is there—a higher order than the one we see before us in operation—as if the legend of the past were stamped, like a signature, on his brow. We have never had a more resolute moralist. A dream of the good life haunts the scene of all the bad life he so memorably observes, and

4

5

when under his spell it is the dream of the good life that we possess. For such an artist, should there be anything but praise? Could there by anything conceivably impotent about such a style? It is when we come to brood on his consistency—on the man who does not change, or seem aware of it—that we see that the author, as well as the reader, has been under a spell, the same spell—the spell of a style. The consistency lies in what the style will permit him to think, to feel, and to say.

Every writer who is sufficiently self-aware to know what he is doing, and how he does it, sooner or later is confronted with the *dictates* of style. If he *has* a style, it is the style that dictates what he says. *What* he says, of course, is *how* he says it, and when we say that the style is the man we have testified to this property. The writer who develops, as a man and a writer, cannot be self-contained in a style, however memorable and charming, that has served its purpose. The style must change, or the writer must adapt himself to it. This is notably true of the writers whose style is the most highly personalized, and distinctive: the most distinctive stylist of this order in our time is Hemingway. He *is* a style. He has never departed from it. Tentative departures—in *For Whom the Bell Tolls,* for example—have appeared as flaws in the marble, rather than as symptoms of development. It is the nature of Hemingway's style to prohibit development. When he remains within it, he sounds *like himself.* When he attempts to escape, we do not know what he sounds like. Neither does he. It is a lesson he has taken to heart. *The Old Man and the Sea* is a two-way fable, that of an old man who has mastered a fish, and that of an aging writer who bows to the mastery of his style. Within these stylistic commitments he sounds all right. He does *not* sound, however, like he did more than thirty years earlier, when this style, and these commitments, were being forged. *The Old Man and the Sea* is an act of will; within the terms of this will it is a moving achievement, but as an act of the imagination it is dead. The style, not the creative mind, dictates the range and nature of the experience, selects the cast, and determines what is permissible. Here again the Spanish language—the simplifying agent—is used to reduce the complexities, in the manner of that memorable night of love and conversation in the sleeping bag. This technique, on occasion, leads to revelation, but as a rule it is merely reduction. The apparent simplicity lies in the style, rather than in the nature of the material, but Hemingway takes pains to build up a consistently simple scene. Man, fish, and Joe DiMaggio are attuned to the demands of the simple epic; complexities, human complexities, are reduced to a minimum. Complicated types enter Hemingway's world only to lose their complications. Man must appear simple, subject to simple corruptions, so that NATURE, writ large, will appear complex. The restoration of Nature—the Nature undefiled of the "Big Two-Hearted River"— would seem to be the passion behind Hemingway's reduction of man. It is why his disillusion, limited to man, is still grained with hope. Man is a mess, but Nature will prevail. It is the sea that triumphs, the sea and the sky against which man's puny drama is enacted, but they are not used, as in Hardy, to dwarf man to insignificance; rather, they remind him, in the complex way Hemingway will not permit his characters, of the paradise lost that might still be regained, that green breast of the world Huck Finn preserved in the territory ahead.

This scale of values—Man finitely simple, and Nature infinitely complex—is the Hemingway palette and the key to the scale of his style. He is never reduced to tampering with personalities. A Cézanne-like simplicity of scene is built up with the touches of a master, and the great effects are achieved with a sublime economy. 7 At these moments style and substance are of one piece, each growing from the other, and one cannot imagine that life could exist except as described. We think only of what is there, and not, as in the less successful moments, of all of the elements of experience that are not.

The Hemingway economy, his sublime economy, is one thing when dictated by the imagination, but another when merely by the mechanical blue pencil of his style. These two slices of life, superficially, will look the same. Both will have the authority of his craft. There is no litmus test that the reader can apply to distinguish between the prose, the economy of the prose, of *The Sun Also Rises* and *Across the River and into the Trees.* Both books are *written.* But only one has been creatively imagined. In the absence of the shaping imagination Hemingway can always rely on his *craft,* and he is one of the great craftsmen of the age. The proof of this, ironically enough, 8 is less in the books that were intensely imagined than in the books that were primarily an act of will. Here it is craft, and craft alone, that sustains both the reader and the writer, and it is what we mean, what we feel to be true, in observing that the author has fallen under his own spell. Indeed he has. And the spell is almost enough. The response of a new generation to *The Old Man and the Sea* was evidence of how much an artist might achieve through pure technique.

This technique, this celebrated style, was born full-fledged—whatever the line of descent—and in nearly forty years it has undergone no visible change. Neither has the life it portrays, since the style and the slice of life are the same. In the interests of this style things remain as they are, they do not change. It is a lens of the finest precision; it records, accurately, the author's field of vision, but the price of the performance is that the *field* must remain the same. Time—in the sense of development—must stand still. The timeless quality of the Hemingway snapshot is truly timeless—growth and change have been removed. The illusion of things as they are is raised 9 to a point that has seldom been equaled; a frieze-like sense of permanence enshrines the Big Two-Hearted River and its world-wide tributaries. This woodland stream, symbolic of all that is undefiled in both man and nature, rises at the source of Hemingway's young manhood and flows through his life and his work to the sea. Clear water, clear fast-moving water, links the exile, on a weekend in Spain, with the Big Two-Hearted River back in Michigan. From different streams the fisherman pulls the same trout. Good fish and running water serve him as the means of coming to terms with life.

As Thoreau went to Walden for the *facts,* Hemingway went to the Michigan woods and the bullfight. In the grain of both men was a passionate desire for reality—be it life or death. Both men feared only one thing: being cheated of life. The *big* cheat, for both men, was the world of Aunt Sally, and only in the woods could one see life cleanly, in the wilderness of nature, or, for Hemingway, in the *nature* of war. But one began in the wilderness. 10

> He sat on the logs, smoking, drying in the sun, the sun warm on his back, the river shallow ahead entering the woods, curving into the woods, shallows, light glittering, big water-smooth rocks, cedars along the bank and white birches, the logs warm in the sun, smooth to sit on, without bark, gray to the touch; slowly the feeling of disappointment left him. It went away slowly, the feeling of disappointment that came sharply after the thrill that made his shoulders ache. It was all right now.

Any man who has ever tried to write will feel in this passage the line-taut passion of a man who would die rather than cheat you with a cliché. It is *this* that is moving—rather than what he tells us. We feel, in this prose, the man's passion for the truth. We hang on every 11 word, as he intends, secure in the feeling that the word will support us. There is no thin ice in this style. We have our hands on experience. We are in possession of the facts.

On the Big Two-Hearted River the artist cut his teeth, but it is not till his exile that he clamps down with them. He waits, appropriately, till his exiles do a little fishing. It is in Spain, that the trout in the Big Two-Hearted River get their bite.

> While I had him on, several trout had jumped at the falls. As soon as
> I baited up and dropped in again I hooked another and brought him in   12
> the same way. In a little while I had six. They were all about the same
> size. I laid them out, side by side, all their heads pointing the same way,
> and looked at them. They were beautifully colored and firm and hard
> from the cold water. It was a hot day, so I slit them all and shucked out
> the insides, gills and all, and tossed them over across the river. I took
> the trout ashore, washed them in the cold, smoothly heavy water above
> the dam, and then picked some ferns and packed them all in the bag,
> three trout on a layer of ferns, then another layer of ferns, then three
> more trout, and then covered them with ferns. They looked nice in the
> ferns, and now the bag was bulky, and I put it in the shade of the tree.

This is like a summing up and a prophecy. After the sad goings
on of the lost generation, we have plunged, in this stream, back to
clean reality, beautifully colored and firm and hard, like the trout.   13
That is nature. That is the nature of life. Bulls are sometimes good,
sometimes bad, but only man is vile. In returning to nature it is
possible for man to cleanse himself.

It is in keeping with this style that man should undergo a progressive brutalization, and nature a progressive refinement and serenity; that man, who should speak for himself, fails to do so, and
that nature, who cannot, should become articulate. The river that
flows through *The Sun Also Rises,* reflecting what is lost in the lost
generation, is a clearer and more incorruptible stream than the one   14
that flows through *In Our Time.* The Spanish stream has been *tested.*
The trout are firm immortal trout. They lie before our eyes, all their
heads pointing in the same direction, like the timeless fish in one of
the paintings of Braque. Technique has snatched them from the river
of life and made them into art.

The flowering of Hemingway's conception of life—and let us
make no mistake, it is a conception—achieves its fullest expression in
Death in the Afternoon. Although death is its subject, it is a book
that teems with life. But all of this life, with the exception of the
eating and the drinking, is life downgraded, reduced in scale to the
elementary plane. The effect, however, is monumental—like the figures in the drawings of Goya. Deprived of all refinements, they loom
with the starkness of some demonic force. It is nature that speaks,
not the man himself. We are in a scene virtually crammed with young   15
men who are nothing if not "eggheads"—but when this fact appears
in their thinking it is laughed out of court. In the opening paragraph,
that remarkable dictum that so well describes the healthy bird of
prey is given the power and the sanction of Hemingway's style.

> So far, about morals, I know only that what is moral is what you
> feel good after and what is immoral is what you feel bad after and

judged by these moral standards, which I do not defend, the bullfight is very moral to me because I feel very fine while it is going on and have a feeling of life and death and mortality and immortality and after it is over I feel very sad but fine.

We need not concern ourselves with this as philosophy. It is a remarkably accurate statement—with its built-in escape clause—of a profoundly primitive state of being, less human than subhuman, a voice of *laissez faire* from the well of the past that would have frightened Neanderthal man. It is the first cry of that man who did not *want* to be a man. He wanted his simple uncomplicated feelings, his simple uncomplicated gratifications, and he did not want them troubled, at the time or later, by a lot of probing into *what* they were. He liked to eat, since after eating he felt good. He liked to make love—but not when it started getting complicated. He didn't mean to go so far as to say this was a good thing, since he liked it, but he did mean to say that at least he knew what he liked.

16

Now this statement grows, in my opinion, from the style more than it does from the man. It is the style that dictated the turn of the thought, and the style that gives it the ring of truth. Anything, in our time, *any*thing that cuts through the morass of talk and complications—that cuts through and gives light—understandably appeals to us. This sort of plain talk from the shoulder, when the shoulder is a good one, wins our attention. The frank admission and the manly qualification have been sorely abused since Hemingway set the fashion, but it is a fashion that is singularly American. In this voice, if not in these accents, speaks the spirit of Thoreau, Whitman, and Mark Twain. The American grain calls for plain talk, for the unvarnished truth. Better to err a little in the cause of bluntness than soften the mind with congenial drivel. Better a challenging half-truth than a discredited cliché.

17

The moralist in Heminway, kept off stage in his fiction, comes to the footlights in *Death in the Afternoon* to shock the Old Lady with his "immoral" observations on life. What we have here is Huck Finn, grown a little older but not grown *up,* getting in a final lick, a last sassy word, on the subject of Aunt Sally. The style, here, serves him less well: it is the weapon of a bully rather than of an artist, wielded in the manner of his pronouncements on women, big-game hunting, and the press. However telling these pronouncements often are, they are chips from the rocks along the Big Two-Hearted River, and evidence that the man within the artist has not changed. He is still, like his master Mark Twain, a boy at heart. While we pause to read what he has to say he is already off for the territory ahead before the world, or Aunt Sally, tries to civilize him. He can't stand it.

18

WHY *HUCKLEBERRY FINN* IS A GREAT WORLD NOVEL
Lauriat Lane, Jr.

Of all forms of literature, the novel is in many ways the hardest to describe with any precision. Its relative newness as a form and its varied and complex nature combine to make this so. Whenever we try to view such a full and living book as *The Adventures of Huckleberry Finn,* some of it always escapes our gaze. In fact, apart from its mere physical presence, paper, ink, glue, covers, and so forth, it is often easiest to assume that the novel does not exist at all, but only the experience of reading it. Each time we read *Huckleberry Finn* we read a certain book, and each time we read it we read a different book. No one of these books is the real *Huckleberry Finn;* in a sense, they all are.

At the heart of *Huckleberry Finn* lies a story about real human figures with genuine moral and ethical problems and decisions, figures placed in a society which we recognize as having everywhere in it the flavor of authenticity—the whole combination treated, for the most part, as directly and realistically as possible. I would like to move beyond this primary description or definition of *Huckleberry Finn,* however, and suggest that the novel may contain other elements equally important to a full appreciation. I would like to extend the novel in three directions, in space, in time, and in degree: in space, by considering some of the ways in which the book extends beyond its position as one of the masterworks of American fiction and becomes, if the term be allowed, a world novel; in time, by considering how much *Huckleberry Finn* resembles a literary form much older than the novel, the epic poem; and in degree, by considering just how much *Huckleberry Finn* transcends its position as a realistic novel and takes on the forms and qualities of allegory.

I

A world novel may be defined as that kind of novel whose importance in its own literature is so great, and whose impact on its readers is so profound and far-reaching, that it has achieved worldwide distinction. In the total picture of world literature, such a novel stands out as a work always to be reckoned with. The world novel, however, achieves its position not only through its importance but also because of its essential nature. And in discussing *Huckleberry Finn* as a world novel I shall deal not so much with this importance, as measured by permanent popularity and influence, as with the special qualities *Huckleberry Finn* has in common with certain other world novels.

The first real novel and the first world novel is, by almost universal consent, Cervantes' *The Adventures of Don Quixote*. The most important thing which *Don Quixote* has bequeathed to the novels after it (apart of course from the all-important fact of there being such a thing as a novel at all) is the theme which is central to *Don Quixote* and to almost every great novel since, the theme of appearance versus reality. This theme is also central to *Huckleberry Finn*.   2

Even on the simplest plot level the world of *Huckleberry Finn* is one of deception. The very existence of Huck at all is a continual deception—he is supposed to be dead. This falseness in his relations with the world at large merely reflects the difference between his standards and those of the outside world. Huck's truth and the truth of the world are diametrically opposed. Throughout the novel his   3 truth is always cutting through the surfaces of the world's appearance and learning the contrary reality beneath. At the climax Huck tells himself, "You can't pray a lie—I found that out." That is to say, the lie of appearance is always far different from the truth of reality, and to the truly heroic and individual conscience no amount of self-delusion can ever bridge the gap lying between.

In the final section of the book, the theme of appearance versus reality reaches almost philosophical proportions. Both because of the way in which Jim's escape is carried out and because of the underlying fact of there being no need for him to escape at all, the situation is one of total dramatic and moral irony. At the end, however, Twain relaxes the tone, straightens out the plot complications, and lets the moral issue fade away. He avoids, in fact, the logical conclusion to the kind of disorder he has introduced into his world-in-fiction, a world in which the distinction between appearance and reality has, from the reader's point of view, been lost forever. For if   4 we cannot tell appearance from reality, if the two do become totally confused and impossible to distinguish, the only answer can be the one Twain eventually came to in his most pessimistic work, *The Mysterious Stranger;* that all is illusion, and nothing really exists. In *Huckleberry Finn,* Twain does not yet reach this point of despair. By centering his action within the essentially balanced mind of the boy, Huck, he keeps his hold on reality and manages to convey this hold to the reader. But the main issue of the novel, between the way things seem and the way they are, is nevertheless one that trembles in the balance almost up to the final page.

Huckleberry Finn also gains its place as a world novel by its treatment of one of the most important events of life, the passage from youth into maturity. The novel is a novel of education. Its school is the school of life rather than of books, but Huck's educa-   5 tion is all the more complete for that reason. Huck, like so many other great heroes of fiction—Candide, Tom Jones, Stephen Dedalus, to mention only a few—goes forth into life that he may learn. One of the central patterns of the novel is the progress of his learning.

Yet another theme which *Huckleberry Finn* shares with most of the world's great novels is that of man's obsession with the symbols of material wealth. The book opens with an account of the six thousand dollars Huck got from the robber's hoard and ends on the same note. Throughout the intervening pages gold is shown to be not only   6 the mainspring of most human action, but usually the only remedy mankind can offer to atone for the many hurts they are forever inflicting on one another. And as Mr. Lionel Trilling has remarked, in a certain sense all fiction is ultimately about money.

The world novel may also convey a total vision of the nation or people from which it takes its origin. It not only addresses the world in a language which is uniquely the language of that nation or people, but it brings before the view of the world at large many character types which are especially national. In *Huckleberry Finn* we recog-   7 nize in Jim, in the Duke and the Dauphin, in Aunt Sally, and in Huck himself, typically American figures whom Twain has presented for inspection by the world's eye. *Huckleberry Finn* gains much of its justification as a world novel from the fact that it is an intensely American novel as well.

II

In his essay on "The Poetic Principle" Poe remarks that "no very long poem will ever be popular again." In part, no doubt, Poe bases this remark on his own special definition of poetry. But he is also recognizing that during the eighteenth and nineteenth centuries the epic poem was gradually dying out as a literary form. Or, to be more precise, it was gradually merging with another form, the novel. Much of the poetic form of the epic came from the requirements of oral   1 rendition; with the invention of printing, these requirements vanished. More and more writers gradually turned to prose fiction as the appropriate form to accomplish what had once been accomplished in the epic poem. Some novelists, such as Fielding or Scott, drew quite consciously on epic tradition; other novelists and novels, by a more

indirect drawing on tradition, took over some of the qualities originally associated with epic poetry.

One quality of the epic poem is simply scope. Some novels confine themselves to treating exhaustively and analytically a limited
segment of life. But others seem to be constantly trying to gather all
life into their pages and to say, within a single story, all the important things that need to be said. Such novels derive much of their
strength from the epic tradition, and *Huckleberry Finn* is such a
novel. It has geographical scope. It ranges down the length of the   2
great river and cuts through the center of a whole nation. As it does
so, it gains further scope by embracing all levels of society, from the
lowest to the highest. And it has the added scope of its own varying
qualities, ranging from high comedy to low farce, from the poetic
tranquility of life on the raft to the mob violence and human deprav-
ity always waiting on the shore.

Epic poetry gives literary form to the national destiny of the
people for whom it is written. *Huckleberry Finn* gives literary form
to many aspects of the national destiny of the American people. The
theme of travel and adventure is characteristically American, and in
Twain's day it was still a reality of everyday life. The country was
still very much on the move, and during the novel Huck is moving
with it. Huck's movements also embody a desire to escape from the
constrictions of civilized society. Such a desire is of course not
uniquely American, but during the nineteenth century Americans
took it and made it their own. The American of that time could
always say, as did Huck at the very end of the story, "I reckon I got   3
to light out for the territory ahead of the rest, because Aunt Sally
she's going to adopt me and sivilize me, and I can't stand it. I been
there before." Another specially American theme is that of the
Negro, and Huck is faced with this problem throughout the story.
Starting with the typically American prejudices and easy generalizations about Jim, he is gradually shocked into an increasingly complex
awareness of Jim as a human being. And although Huck's relations
with Jim do not so much embody a national attitude as suggest how
the nation may purge itself of one, the theme of the Negro is still one
which achieves epic stature in *Huckleberry Finn.*

The epic hero is usually an embodiment of some virtue or virtues
valued highly by the society from which he has sprung. Huck has
many such virtues. He holds a vast store of practical knowledge
which makes itself felt everywhere in the story. He knows the river
and how to deal with it; and he knows mankind and how to deal
with it. And he has the supreme American virtue of never being at a

loss for words. In fact Huck, though he still keeps some of the   4
innocence and naiveté of youth, has much in common with one of
the greatest epic heroes, Odysseus, the practical man. Jim also has
some of the qualities of an epic hero. He has strength and courage,
and he possesses the supreme virtue of epic poetry, loyalty. It is part
of Twain's irony that in Huck and Jim we have, in one sense, the two
halves of an epic hero. In Huck, the skill and canniness; in Jim, the
strength and simple loyalty.

In the society along the shore we see traces of other epic values,
values which have survived from a more primitive world. The
Grangerford-Shepherdson feud strikes the modern reader as a senseless mess, but as Buck says, "There ain't a coward amongst them
Sheperdsons—not a one. And there ain't no cowards amongst the
Grangerfords either." Huck sees the essential folly behind this cour-   5
age, but the reader, one degree further removed from the harsh reality, is allowed the luxury of a double vision. Similarly, Colonel
Sherburn, destroying a lynching mob merely by the courage of his
presence, illustrates another epic theme, the bravery of one against
many.

One final quality which *Huckleberry Finn* derives from its epic
ancestry is its poetry. The novel is full of poetry. Not just the passages of lyric description, which mark a pause between the main
actions and give a heightened and more literary tone just as they often did in the traditional epic, but also the many similes and turns of   6
speech Huck uses, which, if they are not quite Homeric, are certainly
unforgettable. And much of the exaggerated language of the frontier
world, one not far removed in kind from that of the primitive migra-
tions, is also a natural part of the epic style.

III

Allegory may be defined simply as the representation of one
thing in the form of another. A second definition, more germane to
literature, is that allegory is a process by which the spiritual is embodied in the physical. To go one step further, the main purpose of
allegory is somehow to embody a spiritual action in a physical action. By making a suitable physical object stand for some meta-   1
physical one, or at least for one which cannot be contained in the
terms of normal, everyday life, the writer carries out one of the main
purposes of all art, which is to bring to its audience, through the
representation of real objects, an awareness and knowledge which
transcend the limitations of such reality. Allegory, that is, deals primarily with matters of the spirit.

This assumption helps to explain why the great allegories deal either with a physical journey or a physical conflict or both. For a spiritual change, when embodied allegorically, will take the form of a meaningful physical journey through symbolic space. And a spiritual conflict, when embodied allegorically, will take the form of a real physical conflict between significant forces, each of them representing some metaphysical quality.

Although all novels are in a certain sense descended from *Don Quixote,* it is also true that in another sense all novels, and especially English ones, are descended from Bunyan's *Pilgrim's Progress.* The main difference between the allegorical novel as we know it today and Bunyan's narrative of the human soul is that whereas in *Pilgrim's Progress* we have an allegory that tends to turn into a novel, in most modern instances we have a novel that tends to turn into an allegory. As the author, whether he be Melville or Mann or Twain, develops and elaborates his original materials, he may become aware of certain meaningful connections which are tending to establish themselves between the physical objects and the physical narrative he is describing and the related spiritual values and conflicts. Drawing on a tradition which has existed for a long time in literature and which is a natural part of the artistic process in any form, the author finds himself writing allegory. And this is what happened to Mark Twain. Writing as he was a great novel, his masterpiece in fact, he organized and related certain physical materials to certain metaphysical conditions so that their relationship became meaningful in a special way— became, in short, allegory.

Huckleberry Finn is the story of a journey, a real journey. If we are to find any meaning in Huck's journey beyond the literal level, we must seek it first in the medium through which Huck journeys, in the great river down which he drifts during much of the story. And Huck's movements take on at least the external form of a basic symbolic pattern, one seen in such poems as Shelley's *Alastor,* Arnold's *The Future,* and Rimbaud's *Bateau Ivre,* a pattern stated most directly in *Prometheus Unbound,* "My soul is an enchanted boat." Implicit in this pattern is the suggestion that the river journey can have a distinctly metaphysical quality, that it can be, in fact, a journey of the soul as well as of the body. This suggestion is not at all arbitrary. Of all forms of physical progression, that of drifting downstream in a boat, or on a raft, is the most passive one possible. The mind under such conditions is lulled, as Huck's mind is, into the illusion that it has lost all contact with reality and is drifting bodilessly through a world of sleep and of dreams. Thus the nakedness of

Huck and Jim when they are alone on the raft becomes a symbol of
how they have shucked off the excrescences of the real world, their
clothes, and have come as close as possible to the world of the spirit.

All journeys, even allegorical ones, must have a goal. What is the
goal of Huck's journey? We find the answer in what happens while
Huck and Jim float down the river. The pattern is, very simply, one
of an ever-increasing engagement of the world of the raft, of the
spirit, with the world of the shore, of reality. As the book progresses,
more and more Huck tells about events that take place on the banks,
and less and less he tells about those that take place out on the river.
No matter how hard Huck and Jim try to escape, the real world is   5
always drawing them back into it. Finally, in the Duke and the
Dauphin, themselves fleeing for the moment from the harsh reality
of the river's shores, the real world invades the world of the raft, and
the latter loses forever the dream-like and idyllic quality it has often
had for the two voyagers. The climax of Huck's lyric praise of the
river comes significantly just before this mood is shattered forever by
the arrival of the Duke and the Dauphin.

Parallel to this pattern of the ever-increasing engagement of the
world of the shore with that of the raft is a pattern which begins
with Huck's pretended death, a death which is actual to all the world
but Huck and Jim. The symbolic fact of his death accomplished,
Huck must find an identity with which he can face the real world.
His assumption of various such identities forms a significant pattern.
The various masks he assumes, starting with that of a girl, as far   6
removed from the reality as possible, gradually draw back nearer the
truth. Huck's final disguise, as Tom Sawyer, is only slightly removed
from his real self. When he is about to reveal this real self and is
instead taken for Tom, Huck almost recognizes the meaning of his
journey. For he says to himself, "But if they was joyful, it warn't
nothing to what I was; for it was like being born again, I was so glad
to find out who I was."

This, then, is the allegory of *Huckleberry Finn.* Dying symbolically almost at the opening of the novel, Huck journeys through
the world of the spirit, ever working out a pattern of increasing
involvement with the world of reality and with his own self, both
cast aside at the beginning of the journey. Only when he is finally
forced to assume this real self in the eyes of the world, through the
sudden arrival of Aunt Polly, is he allowed to learn the all-important   7
truth Jim has kept from him throughout the novel, that his Pap "ain't
comin back no mo." We cannot say that Huck has undergone a total
initiation and is now fully prepared to take on adulthood, but

neither can we doubt that he has undergone a knowledgeful and maturing experience. And at the end of the story he is about to undertake another journey, this time to the west, in search of further experience and further knowledge.

HOW HERMANN HESSE SPEAKS
TO THE COLLEGE GENERATION
Henry S. Resnik

Evidence abounds that the works of Hermann Hesse have replaced Tolkien's *Lord of the Rings* as a literary fad on the American
campus. According to an informal survey, Hesse is far and away the
best seller in college bookstores. Hesse, the Hesse fans boast, is the
writer students most want to read when they aren't reading writers
they *have* to read. A coffee house in Berkeley is named Steppenwolf,   1
after the novel that seems to be everybody's favorite, and so is a
popular rock group. Moreover, the fad is only in its early stages; until
the last few years inexpensive paperback editions of Hesse were
rare—now they are beginning to appear with the regularity of doughnuts. And, like doughnuts, the German novelist, who died in 1962, is
becoming a big business.

There is nothing quite so annoying these days as generalizations
about where the college generation (whatever that may be) is at.
Nevertheless, if the college generation—or the youth market, or whatever—is anything more than a fantasy of the mass media, whole   2
passages of Hesse's novels strike resoundingly sympathetic chords in
what one must assume to be that generation's consciousness and
culture.

The Steppenwolf, we learn in Hesse's introduction to the novel,
was "brought up by devoted but severe and very pious parents and
teachers in accordance with that doctrine that makes the breaking of
the will the cornerstone of education and upbringing." Every frustrated youth in groovy America must feel the truth of that observation. Or, also in *Steppenwolf:* "For what I always hated and detested   3
and cursed above all things was this contentment, this healthiness
and comfort, this carefully preserved optimism of the middle classes,
this fat and prosperous brood of mediocrity." What nice suburban
kid with half a brain can read these passages and fail to recognize his
own condition? No wonder *Steppenwolf* is the favorite.

Never mind mere passages. Hesse's lugubrious jibes at the establishment, at the whole complacent snivilized Western world, are
merely an eccentricity of style compared with the appeal of his
dominant theme. More patently than most novelists, Hesse was writing the same story over and over again: well-behaved, middle-class
boy (Steppenwolf; Sinclair, in *Demian;* Siddartha; Narcissus, in *Narcissus and Goldmund*) encounters mysteriously tempting outside influences (SDS, "non-students," Demian, Buddha, Goldmund),   4

opposes the established order, takes either an actual or imaginary spiritual journey, and Grows Up. Now a whole generation of rebels can identify with Sinclair and believe that the mark of Cain might just be a stigma imposed by an uptight society; a whole so-called generation can journey to the East and smoke pot with Buddha; a whole what-you-call-it can freak out in the Magic Theater with old buddy Steppenwolf.

Hesse's overriding anti-intellectualism must be just as attractive as his themes and plots. Whether it be the sensual Goldmund, the drug-happy Pablo in *Steppenwolf,* or the ferryman in *Siddartha,* Hesse determinedly contrasts the more cerebral, conventional culture with another culture that is essentially mystical, spiritual, inarticulate, or magical. The appeal of this juxtaposition to the children of McLuhan   5 must be vast. And, as any Madison Avenue executive worth his salt can tell you, the youth market these days is leaning irrepressibly East-ward. Hesse, youth's hero, has been there and back; while still, like them, basically of the West, Hesse digs the good vibrations from the quiet people who tune in to a higher Unity—He Will Always Have a Place in His Heart for That Wonderful Far-off Land.

But here's the rub: Simply by being the object of a super-cult, Hesse has almost degenerated to the level of pop religion. The insights of *Siddartha* or *Demian,* or even of the far superior *Steppenwolf,* echo in disturbingly predictable places—in slick magazines, in euphorically dumb underground newspapers, wherever weekend hippies play. Hesse's novels have suffered the inevitable cheapening   6 effect of any literary fad, exacerbated by the nasty symbiosis of American popular culture, which eventually drains the life out of anything it touches. Some Hesse-philes say that we should rejoice to see "youth" reading such inspiring literature, but Hesse himself would probably have hated the kind of adulation his novels have received.

The fad is a distinct reality, though, and we will have to wait a long time to see whether Hesse's writings will outlive it. At the moment the plots seem a little too obvious and stereotyped, the style a little too bland and pseudo-lyrical, the entire opus not quite great enough to survive the current popularity. If anything of Hesse's endures, however, it won't be *Peter Camenzind,* the first novel, almost   7 certainly the worst, which Farrar, Straus, and Giroux is publishing here for the first time as part of its extensive Hesse series. And if anything of Hesse's is truly a masterpiece, it is unquestionably his 1946 Nobel Prize-winner, *Das Glasperlenspiel,* which, in the new

Holt translation, has been retitled *The Glass Bead Game* and which was known, in the only previous English translation, as *Magister Ludi.*

When a fad reaches the proportions the Hesse fad has reached by now, followers will read anything at all that appears under their hero's name. *Peter Camenzind,* which Hesse published in 1904 at the age of twenty-seven, is not utterly devoid of reward. Like so many of Hesse's novels, it is the tale of one man's journey through life and his discovery of new worlds beyond the narrow confines of the one into which he was born. After leaving his native village in the Swiss Alps, Camenzind lives in Paris, Florence, and Basel, among other places, **8** and becomes a successful newspaper writer and a drunkard. Plagued by melancholy—at these times so vividly a precursor of Harry Haller, the Steppenwolf—he is continually frustrated in love, but he finds happiness in the wonders of nature that pleased his beloved Saint Francis. Finally Camenzind even finds love, nursing to health and contentment an old hunchback named Boppi, who nevertheless dies, leaving Camenzind little choice but to return to his Alp and reunite with nature.

The book has a few good scenes. There is a tantalizing flirtation with a girl who paints and who finally rejects Camenzind in a row-boat on a lake. The chapters set in Italy have a distinct charm, and throughout there is Hesse's characteristically compelling understated **9** intensity. In Germany before the First World War this book launched Hesse as a successful and popular writer; in America, in 1969, it probably ought to be taken with a pinch of pot.

It is difficult to envision teenyboppers or sub-verbal hippies or sorority sisters ploughing through *The Glass Bead Game,* for this is really a most challenging book, a triumph of imaginative power reminiscent in tone of late Conrad and just as hard to penetrate. Moreover, *The Glass Bead Game* is of a quality that will probably **10** elevate it far above any fad that might touch it. Although the good old "younger generation" may buy it by the thousands when it comes out again in paperback (as it will sometime next year), *The Glass Bead Game* is likely to be the kind of book most camp followers carry around just for show.

The story of *The Glass Bead Game* has much in common with the most popular of the earlier novels. In the Utopian country of Castalia, founded entirely to perpetuate the life of the Mind, one can easily see traces of such rigidly idealized settings as the monastery in *Narcissus and Goldmund.* In the friendship of Joseph Knecht, the Master of the Glass Bead Game and protagonist of the novel, and **11** Plinio Designori, a skeptic from the world outside Castalia who leads

Knecht to question everything he believes, there are echoes of all the other polarized relationships that dominate Hesse's work. And in Knecht's resignation from office there is the inevitable identity crisis that heightens Hesse's appeal to youthful readers.

But *The Glass Bead Game* is in a league of its own. Here Hesse transcends his bitterness towards the corruption of the West and regards the whole tragedy of twentieth-century life with wisdom and humor. The novel is set in a distant future when the Century of Wars—our own—and the Age of the Feuilleton, which can be roughly described as the Age of the Mass Media and Useless Information Overkill, have long since passed. Hesse's descriptions of the Feuille-tonistic Age are all the more devastatingly satirical for their tone of detachment—gentle, wistful, slightly patronizing as if to say, "Things were horrible then—poor little people." To quote at random from Knecht's letter to the Board of Educators of the Order of Castalia, in which he explains his dissatisfaction with his office and traces the history of the Order to the Age of the Feuilleton:

> . . . the anti-intellectuality and brutality of that period are all too visible to us. . . . Everywhere lines of battle formed; everywhere bitter enmity sprang up between old and young, between fatherland and humanity, between Red and White. . . . Fighting, killing, and destroying went on everywhere, and everywhere both sides believed they were fighting for God against the devil. . . . Others put up a struggle as long as it was possible to do so in a reasonably safe fashion, and published protests. A world-famous author of the time—so we read in Ziegenhalss—in a single year signed more than two hundred such protests, warnings, appeals to reason and so on—probably more than he had actually read. . . . Those [intellectuals] who entered the service of the rulers and devised slogans for them had jobs and livelihoods, but they suffered the contempt of the best among their fellows, and most of them surely suffered pangs of conscience also. . . . Scientific research that did not directly serve the needs of power and warfare rapidly sank into decadence. The same was true for the whole educational system. . . .

12

Thus, we see ourselves—perhaps with greater clarity than when the novel was published in 1943—in Hesse's ironic mirror and easily realize that the conception of *The Glass Bead Game* is more powerful by far than anything Hesse had previously attempted.

In fact, Joseph Knecht, more than any of Hesse's other protagonists, is truly relevant to contemporary intellectuals—old or young—and truly a revolutionary. Devoted to the cultivation of the Glass Bead Game, the highest achievement—like some kind of holy Mass, or childish idiocy—of the Castalian Order, Knecht can still have the courage to foresee the collapse of the world as he knows it, just as

Hesse's young readers anticipate several different kinds of revolutions   13
today. Knecht is, once again, the middle class kid who grew up a
straight arrow and rose to the top of his field, only to renounce
everything, but his revolutionary gesture has a monumental, doom-
defying quality: *he* is the Magister Ludi, the Master of the Glass Bead
Game. To some readers of the "college generation" he could just as
well be the president of a huge advertising company quitting to live
in a New Mexico commune.

"I don't want to be a prudent reveler taking a bit of a look at the
world," Knecht tells the President of the Order as he resigns his
office and refuses the option to return if he should change his mind.
"On the contrary, I crave risk, difficulty, and danger; I am hungry   14
for reality, for tasks and deeds, and also for deprivations and suffering." Every college student who knows that his degree qualifies him
for a lifetime job with IBM must want to say these very words at
some point in his life.

It is invidious to associate *The Glass Bead Game* with a specific
time or generation, however. The novel's landscape is vast and suggestive, its tone all-encompassing, its themes resonant with overtones,
its passages of poetry—the confrontations of will and idelology between Knecht and others, the hauntingly beautiful death scene—of a
magnificence unequaled in the earlier novels. Richard and Clara   15
Winston, widely recognized translators of German into English, have
given the novel a liveliness distinctly lacking in the first English translation, by Mervyn Savill, and if theirs can be taken as an accurate
rendering of the original, Hesse was just beginning, in *The Glass Bead
Game,* to shake off the piousness and gloom that he had made the
hallmark of his style.

Perhaps the "younger generation" will be reading *The Glass Bead
Game,* when it reappears in paperback, as avidly as they have taken
to *Steppenwolf, Demian,* and the rest. Perhaps the ones who man the
barricades and occupy the buildings have already read it. There is
little cause for optimism, however: *The Glass Bead Game* belongs to
a literary culture; the other books, for the most part, are easy reading
and offer what is essentially a non-literary pleasure—a pleasure of
identification with an in-group mystique, with a complex of cues and   16
signals, catch-sentences, and ideas flattened by familiarity. "There is
always a large number of strong and wild natures who share the life
of the fold," Hesse tells us in *Steppenwolf.* "The vital force of the
bourgeoise resides by no means in the qualities of its normal members, but in those of its extremely numerous 'outsiders' who by
virtue of the extensiveness and elasticity of its ideals it can embrace."
Solace indeed to captive rebels—sweet medicine!

THE BOOK REVIEW

The book review is a critical essay in which the writer appraises and evaluates
the book before him. Although some book reviews may stress only the content
and the outstanding qualities of the book, the valuable and helpful review attempts a just evaluation of the work. The book review as a true essay form is an
appraisal, not a summary. It does not content itself with a description of the
contents of the book; it analyzes those contents and relates them to the larger
field of subject matter of which the book is a part.

To write a really good book review, then, requires both special knowledge of
the subject matter of the book and an extensive literary background. The reviewer assumes a judicial role; he sits in judgment upon the book. To do so
effectively he must not only convince the reader of his qualifications to act the
judge (sometimes, of course, his very name and reputation bring that conviction), but he must also present his case for and/or against the book with the
decorum we associate with a judge whose pronouncements we receive with
respect. Even so, reviewers of reputation—Kenneth Rexroth, the poet and critic,
for example, or Vance Bourjaily the novelist—constantly reinforce that reputation in their critical reviews.

Of the reviews reprinted here, Vance Bourjaily's is an example of the "standard" review of a newly published book—although the result is far greater than
"standard." He describes the book; he communicates something of the quality
of the book; he judges the book. Kenneth Rexroth's review is a critical essay on
one of the "classics" of literature, a book everyone knows or at least knows
about. He gives, in his brief essay, a "thumb-nail sketch" of the importance and
value of the book. Roger D. Masters, in reviewing a recent work on Karl Marx,
uses the book to reinforce his analysis of the appeal of Marx's philosophy for
those who seek radical changes in the established order of society. All three
reviewers write with evident understanding of their subject; all three write with
conviction; all three communicate valuable ideas to the reader.

The student writing a book review cannot be expected to bring to his task
the background, the extensive knowledge of the subject matter, and the literary

sophistication of the reviewers represented here. But the student can write a respectable review if he has read the book with care, if he has acquired some information on the author and on the subject field (the wise student will review a book in a field which has interested him for more than a few days), and if he remembers that he is reviewing a book and not undergoing psychoanalysis. A mere factual report on author, title, publisher, date, and contents will not be a book review; it will be an answered questionnaire. And a purely subjective response to the book—"What the book means to me"—will not be a review unless the reviewer understands and projects the author's point of view and is able to reach a balanced judgment. The reviewer must remember that both excessive enthusiasm and immoderate censure raise more questions about his competence than about the competence of the book reviewed. Above all, the reviewer must be honest, never pretending to be what he is not. The student reviewer is just that: he is not a judge but is learning to be a judge. Through careful writing he can communicate the purpose of the book, detail something of its contents, and appraise, with carefully presented evidence, the degree of attainment of the author's purpose.

WHAT IN MARX SPEAKS
TO TODAY'S YOUNG ICONOCLASTS?

Roger D. Masters

Whether in Paris or Prague, whether in the S.D.S. on an American campus or among the F.L.N. in the Mekong Delta, the ideas of Karl Marx continue to inspire those who seek radical changes in the established order. Why should this be so? The reasons for Marx's persisting influence are not, after all, self-evident.   1

Capitalist development has not led, "with iron necessity," to the inevitable revolution that Marx apparently foresaw in Western Europe; ironically, revolutionary movements have been most successful in backward peasant societies rather than advanced industrial ones. Compared with Tocqueville, whose famous prediction of a confrontation between Russia and the United States has been so dramatically fulfilled, Marx seems to have been a rather poor prophet. Or, as Shlomo Avineri puts it in his brilliant study, *The Social and Political Thought of Karl Marx* (Cambridge), "the more concrete predictions Marx attempted . . . grew out of his ordinary sociopolitical intuition, which did not prove to be much superior to that of his contemporaries."   2

Nor can the lasting fascination with Marx's principles be entirely explained by the rise of communist governments in Russia, Eastern Europe, China, and Cuba. On the contrary, today's radicals are primarily interested in Marx's analysis of alienation, which has been used to attack communist as well as capitalist regimes on the grounds that both produce "one-dimensional man" (to use Herbert Marcuse's phrase).   3

If S.D.S. leaders praise Cuba or Maoist China, it is not so much for their communism as for their proclaimed hostility to a bureaucratized industrialization that leaves the individual alienated in the midst of material wealth. Far from being part of a world-wide communist conspiracy, the Marxian concept of alienation has been used within Eastern Europe to oppose the orthodox party line.   4

Back in 1923 it was a Hungarian communist—George Lukacs—who first insisted on the importance of this concept in Marx's theory; then, as more recently, the party leadership attacked a defensible interpretation of Marx as politically subversive. Hence Czech demands for liberalization are more than an imitation of Western liberal democracy, for they can be defended in terms of the writings of Karl Marx.   5

This pervasive influence of Marx's concept of alienation justifies careful restudy of his writings. Avineri's *The Social and Political Thought of Karl Marx* is therefore particularly welcome. It is a difficult work, presupposing philosophical acquaintance with Hegel. But the book is also one of the most comprehensive and coherent restatements of Marx's theoretical position ever written, and it will doubtless greatly influence future studies of Marxian political thought.   6

Avineri explicitly confronts the difficulties posed by the discovery of Marx's early writings (notably the *Economic and Philosophic Manuscripts of 1844*), which were largely unpublished until half a century after his death. In these works, unknown to Lenin and the Russian revolutionaries of 1917, Marx developed his most extensive critique of human alienation in capitalist, industrialized society.   7

The problem raised by the *1844 Manuscripts* and other early writings is rather simple. Before they were published, Marx's analysis of the inevitable overthrow of capitalism—commonly described as historical or dialectical materialism—was considered the essence of his theory; for readers of the *Communist Manifesto* and *Das Kapital,* Marx's main point was that the proletariat would necessarily revolt against its oppressors and create a classless communist society in which the State would "wither away." The resulting theory has frequently been viewed as an extreme form of economic determinism, justifying revolutionary violence and sharply at odds with Western humanitarian values.   8

To many, Marx's early writings seemed to contradict this conventional description of Marxism; the *1844 Manuscripts* deny that communism is "itself the goal of human development" and define that aim as "the emancipation and rehabilitation of man." How could Marx have been a simple materialist if he flatly asserted that his method should be called "consistent naturalism or humanism" and claimed that it "is distinguished from both idealism and materialism, and at the same time constitutes their unifying truth"?   9

For those who abhorred Stalinist Russia, here were Marxian texts that could be used to attack the brutalities committed by so-called Marxist-Leninists. It became fashionable to argue that Lenin's revolutionary zeal reflected the principles of the mature Marx, whereas a young Marx—the author of the *1844 Manuscripts*—had been a humanist rebelling against alienation.   10

Avineri's wide-ranging study questions this attempt to divide Marx's thought into an early, humanist phase and a later, more determinist one. Citing familiar texts, hitherto largely ignored writings, and correspondence, Avineri, who is senior lecturer on policial theory at Hebrew University in Jerusalem, gives considerable evidence that Marx's theoretical approach was essentially unchanged throughout his career, and that it can best be understood as a "transformation" of Hegelian philosophy.

Rather than distinguish between the young Marx and the old, Avineri asserts that the appropriate distinction should be between Marx's subtler, more philosophic thought and the rather mechanistic determinism of Engels. Leninism and the conventional interpretation of dialectical materialism could then be traced to Engels's vulgarization of Marx rather than to Marx's own intention.

It will be said that Marx and Engels essentially shared the same position, that Avineri's attempt to reconcile Marx's mature writings with his youthful critique of Hegel forces the meaning of the texts, and that this approach understates Marx's devotion to violent revolution and a "dictatorship of the proletariat." Doubtless the specialists will continue to debate these issues. But for the general reader the principal point lies elsewhere.

By focusing on the Hegelian roots of Marx's concept of alienation, Avineri makes it easier to understand today's radicals. For Marx, as for more recent critics, modern economic life transforms human beings into objects of an impersonal system in which freedom and self-fulfillment are impossible. Although a proletarian revolution seems highly unlikely in affluent industrial societies, transformation of the intrinsic worth of all things into monetary value is more than ever vulnerable to Marx's criticism.

It is precisely on this point that radical students, often coming from middle-class families and wondering why they are at college, sense the fundamental truth of Marx's theory as expressed in the *1844 Manuscripts:* "If I have a *vocation* for study but no money for it, then I have *no* vocation, i.e., no *effective,* genuine vocation. Conversely, if I really have *no* vocation for study, but have money and the urge for it, then I have an *effective* vocation. . . . In this respect, therefore, money is the general inversion of *individualities,* turning them into their opposites."

It takes but little reflection to see that this aspect of Marxian analysis is as true today as it was 125 years ago. When speculators in Zurich can create a crisis in the value of the dollar or the franc—without reference to the actual day-to-day activities of American or French citizens—surely the human creation known as money has come to control human beings themselves. When economists define a developed society in terms of Gross National Product, measured in dollars, rather than by the quality of individual and social life, can it not be said that we make a fetish of money and commodities?

Still, were it merely an accurate criticism of modern society, Marx's thought would hardly have its widespread appeal; Rousseau, not to mention Shakespeare, also warned against replacing human qualities and virtues by the artificial standard of money. The ultimate appeal of Marx is his call to activism, on the grounds that only   17 through practice can a theory demonstrate its objective truth: "Man," he wrote in *Theses on Feuerbach*, "must prove the truth, i.e. the reality and power . . . of his thinking in practice. . . . The philosophers have only *interpreted* the world differently, the point is, to *change* it."

Here above all is what the radicals of today seek. Not merely a critique, but a call to action. However, activism for its own sake can be self-defeating, as Marx emphasized in his studies of the French   18 revolutions of 1848 and 1870; only when the time was ripe, so he argued, would the contradictions of the capitalist system by transcended by the creation of a truly humanized society.

Marx himself was somewhat cautious in politics, but the fusion of theory and practice that he desired might merely lead to foredoomed confrontations with the established order, which do little more than express subjective frustrations. This outcome seems par-   19 ticularly likely in modern industrial societies, where students and intellectuals could be said to have replaced the proletariat of the 1840s as "a class *in* civil society" but not "a class *of* civil society."

Just as supposedly proletarian revolutions have only succeeded with the support of a pre-industrial peasantry (notably in Russia, China, and Cuba), the intellectuals and students can only trigger widespread discontent in alliance with other disaffected classes (workers in France, black activists in the United States). But insofar   20 as the vast majority in an industrial society usually supports the status quo, viewing radical change as a threat to acquired affluence, direct political action intended to overcome alienation may be self-defeating.

The lesson for contemporary radicals is not that they are condemned in advance because of the vagueness of their goals. Rather, it is the disproportion between the intellectual's vision and the recalcitrance of actual human societies. As Avineri aptly puts it, Marx   21 turned "the possibility of human redemption into an historical phenomenon about to be realized here and now." And, at least to date, this attempt to realize the Hegelian synthesis has proved impossible.

That the intellectual sees contradictions in the existing order of things need not prove that these contradictions can be overcome by what Marx called "revolutionary practice." On the contrary, the radical critic may inevitably exaggerate the potential for fundamental change whenever he transforms his analysis of society, however correct, into a program for action.

This danger is, oddly enough, especially obvious where it might least be expected in Marx's writings. Unknown to many, Marx was a London correspondent for the New York *Daily Tribune* during the 1850s and early 1860s. His remarkable dispatches on developments in India, China, and other colonial areas have been collected in one volume by Avineri, under the title *Karl Marx on Colonialism and Modernization* (Doubleday).

This excellent collection has many merits, not the least of which is that it vividly reconstructs for us the mid-nineteenth century. Moreover, it shows the tremendous range of Marx's knowledge of economics, politics, and history; whereas his more famous writings emphasize England, France, and Germany, here he analyzes the consequences of the expansion of European control over backward societies.

Marx saw clearly how guerrilla warfare—or, as he put it, "a national war"—could be a less-developed society's response to attack by an industrialized power. He also understood the immense difficulties of economic development in countries like India and China, and the extent to which the injustice and brutality of colonialism might be a necessary precondition for progress. Finally, surprising as this may seem, Marx was aware that the revolution might break out first in a backward society undergoing modernization, rather than in a highly developed European one.

Nevertheless, despite these insightful analyses, which stand up rather well, Marx clearly seems to have exaggerated the speed and extent of revolutionary change. Commenting in the New York *Tribune,* June 14, 1853, on how British policies in China would inevitably destroy the traditional social structure and pave the way for an overthrow of the Chinese empire, Marx stated, "It may safely be augured that the Chinese revolution will throw the spark into the overloaded mine of the present industrial system and cause the explosion of the long-prepared general crisis, which, spreading abroad, will be closely followed by political revolutions on the Continent."

Twenty-five years later Marx was predicting in a letter to Sorge (September 27, 1877) that a Russian revolution was imminent—and

that it would be the trigger for the revolution in Europe. Forty years   27
after this the revolution did break out in a backward, if modernizing
society, but not in industrialized Western Europe.

Could it be that the very acuteness of Marx's analysis led him to
underestimate the resilience of the capitalist system? Did his philosophic belief in transcending alienation through historical change   28
lead him to exaggerate the possibility of revolution, if only because
denial of this possibility would mean that alienation is inevitable in
industrial society?

The dilemma of the activist intellectual or student is nowhere
posed more clearly than in Marx's own case. He desperately wanted
the revolution to occur, lest man lose forever the chance to control   29
his own fate. But he could neither accurately predict when this revolution would take place, nor assure that it would have the desired
effects.

The danger of Marx's thought lay in the ease with which it could
be vulgarized into a Leninist system. Whereas Marx himself resisted
attempts to set up a rigidly centralized communist party as the van-
guard of the proletariat, and feared, as he observed in *Theses on*   30
Feuerbach, any doctrine that would "divide society into two parts,
one of which is superior to society," Lenin and Stalin could subvert
Marx's subtle dialectics into a mechanistic materialism and a "crude
communism" whose insufficiencies Marx foresaw in 1844.

Avineri's analysis is particularly useful, for he shows not only the
difference between Marxism and Marxism-Leninism, but also why
the former was so effectively converted to the latter. It could well
be, as Avineri concludes, that attempts to realize Marx's insights in   31
practice necessarily destroy Marxism itself, so that "Marx's theory
may thus be denied by the very historical processes he foresaw." If
so, the "Cunning of Reason," which Hegel saw as the ultimate meaning of history, may indeed have taken revenge on Marx.

HEMINGWAY ON TRIAL, JUDGE BAKER PRESIDING
Vance Bourjaily

Judge Carlos Baker calls his court to order, and the trial of Ernest Hemingway begins. More than 200 witnesses will be called. Five times that number of documentary exhibits will be culled, condensed, paraphrased and put in evidence. It is a long trial, and the transcript runs to 697 pages. "If Ernest Hemingway is to be made to live again," says Mr. Baker, professor of English at Princeton, "it must be by virtue of a thousand pictures, both still and moving, a thousand scenes in which he was involved, a thousand instances in which he wrote or spoke both publicly and privately of those matters which most concerned him."

That is the biographer's promise to the reader, and it is generously kept. We follow Hemingway—Hemingstein, Wemedge, Broken Doll, Wax Puppy, Tatie, Mountain, Mister Papa, etc.—from his boyhood summers in Michigan to his final alias. George Saviers, the name borrowed from his doctor in Ketchum, Idaho, under which he registered at the Mayo Clinic to begin treatment for his final illness in November, 1960.

We learn the names of the various people who appeared, disguised, in Hemingway's fiction, and something of the roles they played in his life. We learn about his finances, his marriages and affairs, his friendships and quarrels, and the almost unbelievable string of injuries and illnesses which followed and finally caught up with him. (In fact, one of the chief revelations of the book is the extent to which he led a life of physical pain.)

Most fascinating to me is to learn of the nature and extent of the several thousand pages of unpublished fiction that Hemingway left, all of it conscientiously described so that one knows at last what it is and why it is unpublished.

Judge Baker's trial is thorough, fair—and moves very slowly. Be certain, before you start, that your interest in the prisoner is both lively and enduring; he is accused of having become a legend, and the demythologizing is a process of breaking down into ordinary detail episodes that, if told whole, might seem exciting or even glamorous. Or scandalous.

Follow, for example, the development that led to the celebrated fight with Max Eastman in Maxwell Perkins's office. On page 89 the two men meet in Genoa, and like one another. Between pages 241 and 244, Eastman writes a negative review of "Death in the Afternoon" which includes the famous accusation: "a literary style . . . of wearing false hair on the chest." Hemingway is angry and writes "an open letter in his best (or worst) humorous-sinister manner."

It is a good enough index to the reviewer's sensibilities that I find the letter funny, as I guess Mr. Baker does not. Saying that probably obligates me to quote it so that the reader may make his own estimate. All right:

"Sirs:

"Would it not be possible for you to have Mr. Max Eastman elaborate   7
his nostalgic speculations on my sexual incapacity? Here [in Havana—
Mr. Baker's brackets] it would be read (aloud) with much enjoyment.
Our amusements are simple and I would be glad to furnish illustrations
to brighten Mr. Eastman's prose if you consider this advisable. Mr.
Alexander Woollcott and the middle-aged Mr. Eastman having both
published hopeful doubts as to my potency is it too much to expect
that we might hear soon from Mr. Stark Young?"

Hemingway goes off marlin-fishing, hooks a 750-pounder, fights
it for an hour and a half, and though the rod breaks and he loses the   8
fish, Mr. Baker imagines Hemingway thumbing his nose at Eastman
after this demonstration of strength.

On page 247 a letter of Hemingway's to Clifton Fadiman is paraphrased: "Every two years he would break one 'lousy critic's jaw,'   9
starting with Eastman and drawing his other victims by lot."

It is not until page 317 that the actual fight takes place, such as it
was: "But Ernest, his face contorted with rising anger, smacked Eastman in the face with the open book. Eastman instantly rushed at
him, and Perkins, fearing that Eastman might be badly hurt, ran over
to grab Ernest's arm. Just as he came around the corner of the desk,   10
the adversaries grappled and fell. Perkins grasped the shoulders of the
man on top, certain that it must be Hemingway. Instead he found
himself looking down into Ernest's upturned face. He was flat on the
floor and grinning broadly, having regained his temper almost at
once."

What happens is that by separating cause from effect—and since
the book is doggedly chronological this can be justified by the four-   11
year interval—de-emphasis occurs. Focus, in narrative writing, is
generally achieved by keeping related things in sequence.

For me, after exposure to 564 pages of Mr. Baker's deliberately
flat prose, and 101 of excellent notes, the subject had still not been
"made to live again." This is partly a result of the unfocusing effect
of rigid chronology but even more, I think, a product of the biogra-   12
pher's impartiality. The real middle ground between friendliness and
hostility is indifference. To be judicial is to adopt, if not a fully
hostile attitude, at least one of constant, mild disparagement.

For example: "Ernest was notably truculent whenever he squired Ada [MacLeish] to prizefights or bike races. If anyone even remotely jostled her, he would be invited to stand up and be slugged. Ada was amused to notice that these were nearly all little men, seldom more than five feet tall." Reliability of the witness here is simply assumed, without discussion.

"Ernest developed a sore throat and took to his bed in rue Ferou, convinced, as always, that it might turn into pneumonia or worse." Why "or worse," Your Honor? Wasn't pneumonia bad enough, in those preantibiotic days, to substantiate the implication of hypochondria?

These are very trivial illustrations. Let me try a more substantial one: Mr. Baker's seventh chapter is called "Soldier's Home," the title, of course, of one of Hemingway's stories that has been particularly influential on other writers. The chapter describes how Hemingway returned, as a wounded veteran, to Oak Park and his family. He found himself a celebrity, gave interviews, accepted hero worship, missed Italy, and was lonely because most of his former friends were away or at work. He drank a little, wrote letters, gave a talk at the Y, was jilted, by mail, by the nurse he had loved in Italy. "He presently began to assure his friends that he had 'cauterized' the memory of Agnes with a course of 'booze and other women.' As usual he was exaggerating."

Nowhere are we offered any sort of interpretation of the emotional quality of Hemingway's homecoming which would show us how it could have become the material for a deeply felt and very moving short story.

Here then is the difficulty with Mr. Baker's method of presenting thousands of factual details: it substitutes work, and extremely difficult work it must have been, for the creative risk of interpretation. It gives us the whole substance of a life, but little of its quality.

It seemed to me, particularly during the account of the breakup of Hemingway's first marriage and his second marriage to Pauline Pfeiffer, that I could find more than ony hint that Mr. Baker disapproved Hemingway's conduct. It might be preferrable if the disapproval were more open. One can express disapproval without seeming to fail in sympathy. I think of a literary biography I love very well, Andrew Turnbull's "F. Scott Fitzgerald," and realize how openly partisan Turnbull can be without necessarily approving everything his subject did and said. And I realize, I think, that it is precisely this partisanship that brings a subject to life, no less in biography than in fiction.

It is as simple as this: Judge Turnbull loved his sinner. If Judge   19
Baker did, he is a little too careful about not letting it show.

Let me try to be fair: to me, Hemingway seems a tragic figure.
To Mr. Baker, he seems a genius, but a badly behaved and not altogether pleasant man. The point is that we might both be right, and   20
the biographer himself, a courteous and disarming man when his
judge's wig is off, says in his Foreword: "it will be after the year
2000 before anything like a definitive work can be undertaken."

If this is not a definitive work, it is certainly an exhaustive one,
which will be indispensable to anyone with any degree of special
interest in Hemingway. Whatever its faults of movement, tone and
focus, it seems very nearly complete and absolutely trustworthy as a   21
record. "An enormous fund of misinformation about him is already
in print," as Mr. Baker says in the Foreword, and I feel no insecurity
at all in believing that in "Ernest Hemingway, A Life Story," "all
that is false has been expunged."

Thus, for scholars, the book is bedrock; on it will rest all future
Hemingway studies, except for the purely critical which will con-   22
tinue to derive from Philip Young's "Ernest Hemingway, A Recon-
sideration."

Perhaps it is not a fair test of biography to feel that one should
be able to say: "The book is interesting, even if you know and care
very little about its subject to begin with." If the test is fair, "Ernest   23
Hemingway, A Life Story" seems to me to fail it. I cannot recommend it for general reading.

But where interest in the subject does exist, Mr. Baker's book
replaces all others. For myself I can say that I believe it; that I honor   24
the seven years of patient and intelligent work it represents. I would
not be without it; it's only that I can't quite say I like it.

UNCLE TOM'S CABIN
Kenneth Rexroth

In the first half of the nineteenth century, American writing made its first large-scale appearance on the stage of world literature. Benjamin Franklin, Thomas Jefferson, and others like them had been international writers or thinkers with considerable influence abroad, but they were essentially Physiocrats or Girondins or Jacobins—in other terms, radical Whigs. The sources of their inspiration were in France and secondarily in England, even though in those countries they were accepted, not as bright provincials, but as full equals in the international community of the Enlightenment that stretched from the court of Catherine the Great to the discussion clubs of Philadelphia. Two or three generations later, American writers were playing a determinative if minor role in international literature.

Harriet Beecher Stowe made the moral horror of slavery visible to all the world, but she also made the Negro, slave or free, visible as an essential member of American society, and she made the full humanity of the Negro visible to all, black or white, all over the world. It is possible to disagree with her idea of what a fully human being should be, but she did the best according to her lights. Her lights were, as a matter of fact, just as illuminating as any that have been lit in a more cynical and rationalistic age by writers with a different kind of sentimentality.

Uncle Tom's Cabin, like Mark Twain's weather, is talked about by millions who do nothing about it; that is, "Uncle Tom" is a term of contempt used by everybody today, yet hardly anybody bothers to read the book anymore. The picture of the humble and obedient slave is derived not from the novel but from the "Tom Shows" that toured America for a generation before the First War. Uncle Tom is in no sense an "Uncle Tom." He is by far the strongest person in the book. Although he is whipped to death by the psychotic Simon Legree, his end is not only a tragedy in Aristotle's sense—the doom of a great man brought low by a kind of holy hubris—but, like Samson, he destroys his destroyer.

Is Hariet Beecher Stowe sentimental? And rhetorical? Indeed she is. So is Norman Mailer, or for that matter much greater writers, Thomas Hardy or D.H. Lawrence. It is true that we must adjust to changes of fashion when we read her novel. The early nineteenth-century rhetoric of Harriet Beecher Stowe takes a little getting used to, but it survives the test of the first twenty pages. Once the reader has accepted it, it soon becomes unnoticeable. The sentimental

scenes in the novel, almost the only ones that survived in the Tom 4
Show—Eliza on the ice, the death of Augustine St. Clare, the death
of Little Eva—are deliberate devices to hold and shock the popular
audience of the time. They drive home, to sentimental readers who
give at least lip service to an evangelical Christianity, the overwhelming reality of the rest of the book. How real, how convincing,
this huge cast is—as large as that in any novel of Balzac's or
Dostoyevsky's.

True, the Negroes are seen from the point of view of a white
person, but any attempt to "think black" would have been a falsifi-
cation. Mrs. Stowe simply tries to think human. And human they all
are, even at their most Dickensian. Little Eva is not a plaster statue
of The Little Flower. The evangelical early nineteenth century produced plenty of saintly little girls just like her. They occur in all the
novels of the time, though not in such abnormal circumstances as the
Little Missie-devoted slave relationship. When they appear in Dickens 5
they are usually less believable. Mrs. Stowe's sentimentality lacks the
subtle lewdness that invalidates Little Nell and other girls of Dickens,
because Mrs. Stowe was a far more emancipated and radical person
than Dickens, politically and sexually. Tom, of course, does not
function as a slave but literally as an "uncle" to Eva. He takes the
place of her neurotic and inadequate father, as he substitutes for so
many others who are inadequate, and finally atones for all.

Simon Legree may be a monster but he is a human monster,
more human for instance than Dickens's Fagin or even Mr. Micawber.
No one in *Uncle Tom's Cabin* is completely a villain. Even at their
worst Mrs. Stowe's characters are battlegrounds of conflicting mo- 6
tives, of Beelzebub and Michael. Simon Legree is not a devil. Devils
and angels struggle within him. The slave trader Haley knows the
good, but to him it is reduced to the cash nexus. Uncle Tom in his
eyes is worth more money than an "ornery" slave.

Uncle Tom's Cabin is not only an attack on slavery, the greatest
and most effective ever written; it is a book of considerable philosophical or religious and social importance. Its immense popularity
was a significant factor in the change in the dominant American
philosophy, dominant in the sense of "shared by most ordinary
people." Mrs. Stowe came out of Puritan New England. In her immediate background was the rigid predestination of strict Calvinism
and the literal interpretation of Scripture. *Uncle Tom's Cabin* is far
more tendentious in its constant insistence on a kind of secularized
evangelical deism than in its forthright, realistic portrayal of the 7
horror of slavery. The book says, "Slavery denies the integrity of the

person of the slave; in doing so it cripples the integrity of the person of the master, but it cannot destroy the humanity of either master or slave." This is, or should be, self-evidently true, and it is presented by a dramatic narrative that is convincing as a marshaling of fact. The philosophy of the good life as expounded by Mrs. Stowe through her various spokesmen and spokeswomen in the novel is disputable, but there is no denying that it was the faith by which most of white Protestant America, and most of black, lived until recently.

It is absurd that in American universities there are countless courses in rhetorical, sentimental, and unreal novelists like James Fenimore Cooper or worse, and that this book, which played no small role in changing the history of the world, is passed over and misrepresented. Hawthorne, Cooper, Washington Irving ignore the reality of slavery. Yet slavery was the great fact of American life. 8 Harriet Beecher Stowe alone of the major novelists faced that fact and worked out its consequences in the humanity of those involved in it—master or slave or remote beneficiary. She knew that her New England was almost as dependent on the "peculiar institution" as any plantation owner.

And what were the final consequences? They are not yet. Of the immediate ones President Lincoln said when he received her: "So you're the little lady who started this great war." As for her literary influence, it is one of the best kept secrets of criticism. Most of the characters of William Faulkner and Tennessee Williams, and many of their situations, can be found at least in embryo in *Uncle Tom's* 9 *Cabin,* and the old rhetoric is still theirs. It seems to be necessary in describing Southern life. As for Uncle Tom, he was assassinated in Memphis, and has been before, and will be again, until something like Mrs. Stowe's secular, evangelical humanism wins out at last—or the Republic perishes.

BIOGRAPHY

The biographical essay may be described as biography that makes a point. In other words, it is biography which goes beyond the mere recital of facts relating to a person's life. In this sense all good biography is biographical essay. One of the objectives of an essayist on a life, whether it be his own or the life of another person, is to emphasize those experiences which shaped the course of that life or which serve as objective examples of life. He is both an interpreter of *a life* and an interpreter of *life*.

In expository biography and autobiography we are given facts, the very facts, perhaps, which might be found in such accounts as those in *Who's Who in America*. Written with skill, such an account may be interesting as well as informative. But, other things being equal, it is the interpretative biography which fascinates the reader. The interpretative biographer examines the events of a life in the light of dominant traits. He searches for motives. He sifts the complex and often meaningless details of a life in order to bare motivating forces and explain actions. He deals, to put the matter simply, with cause and effect. He reveals the emotional forces and the motivating philosophy of a life. He analyzes a life so that we as readers will know life better.

The writer of biography has an advantage over the writer of fiction: his readers have a deep interest in the lives and characters of other men and women, an interest which is reinforced by such other media as the motion picture and television. But beyond this advantage he faces the same problems the writer of fiction has. He must do an interesting and competent job of narrative and descriptive writing if he is to succeed. He must choose examples with care, examples which reveal the man. He must emphasize the cause-and-effect relationship of the incidents of the life he is revealing.

The biographer is engaged in a search for *self*. Often his guiding principle is the belief that the essential clue to selfhood is to be found not so much in the society outside as in the child within. Although it has become fashionable to credit environment for all problems of personality, the biographical essayist, conditioned perhaps by Freudian teachings on the shaping force of infancy, does not neglect the importance of the early, the formative, years of a life. Mark Twain, in *Life on the Mississippi,* dwells on boyhood and likewise derived the inspiration for his best novels from his own boyhood. E.E. Cummings, in an essay which follows, stresses self-discovery. Dylan Thomas, in "Holiday Memory," which appears in the section on description, evokes childhood so poignantly that his essay becomes in effect a search for the lost self of the child.

Biographical writing, and autobiography in particular, is a valuable learning device for the student writer, for he can grasp fundamentals which are of value in any type of writing: concreteness, logical sequence, proportion, the establishment of cause and effect. The student writer can undertake autobiography with special confidence because, it may be assumed, he knows his subject. Rather than spending time on research, he can devote his attention to those elements which make for successful biographical writing: to selection, to proportion, to expression.

THE BOYS' AMBITION

Samuel L. Clemens

When I was a boy, there was but one permanent ambition among
my comrades in our village* on the west bank of the Mississippi
River. That was to be a steamboatman. We had transient ambitions
of other sorts, but they were only transient. When a circus came and
went, it left us all burning to become clowns; the first negro minstrel   1
show that ever came to our section left us all suffering to try that
kind of life; now and then we had a hope that, if we lived and were
good, God would permit us to be pirates. These ambitions faded out,
each in its turn; but the ambition to be a steamboatman always
remained.

Once a day a cheap, gaudy packet arrived upward from St. Louis,
and another downward from Keokuk. Before these events, the day
was glorious with expectancy; after them, the day was a dead and
empty thing. Not only the boys, but the whole village, felt this. After
all these years I can picture that old time to myself now, just as it
was then: the white town drowsing in the sunshine of a summer's
morning; the streets empty, or pretty nearly so; one or two clerks
sitting in front of the Water Street stores, with their splint-bottomed
chairs tilted back against the walls, chins on breasts, hats slouched
over their faces, asleep—with shingle-shavings enough around to show
what broke them down; a sow and a litter of pigs loafing along the
sidewalk, doing a good business in watermelon rinds and seeds; two
or three lonely little freight piles scattered about the "levee"; a pile
of "skids" on the slope of the stone-paved wharf, and the fragrant
town drunkard asleep in the shadow of them; two or three wood
flats at the head of the wharf, but nobody to listen to the peaceful
lapping of the wavelets against them; the great Mississippi, the
majestic, the magnificent Mississippi, rolling its mile-wide tide along,
shining in the sun; the dense forest away on the other side; the
"point" above the town, and the "point" below, bounding the river-
glimpse and turning it into a sort of sea, and withal a very still and
brilliant and lonely one. Presently a film of dark smoke appears
above one of those remote "points"; instantly a negro drayman,
famous for his quick eye and prodigious voice, lifts up the cry,
"S-t-e-a-m-boat a-comin'!" and the scene changes! The town drunkard stirs, the clerks wake up, a furious clatter of drays follows, every
house and store pours out a human contribution, and all in a twin-

---

*Hannibal, Missouri.

kling the dead town is alive and moving. Drays, carts, men, boys, all 2
go hurrying from many quarters to a common center, the wharf.
Assembled there, the people fasten their eyes upon the coming boat
as upon a wonder they are seeing for the first time. And the boat *is*
rather a handsome sight, too. She is long and sharp and trim and
pretty; she has two tall, fancy-topped chimneys, with a gilded device
of some kind swung between them; a fanciful pilot-house, all glass
and "gingerbread," perched on top of the "texas" deck behind them;
the paddle-boxes are gorgeous with a picture or with gilded rays
above the boat's name; the boiler-deck, the hurricane-deck, and the
texas deck are fenced and ornamented with clean white railings;
there is a flag gallantly flying from the jack-staff; the furnace doors
are open and the fires glaring bravely; the upper decks are black with
passengers; the captain stands by the big bell, calm, imposing, the
envy of all; great volumes of the blackest smoke are rolling and
tumbling out of the chimneys—a husbanded grandeur created with a
bit of pitch-pine just before arriving at a town; the crew are grouped
on the forecastle; the broad stage is run far out over the port bow,
and an envied deck-hand stands picturesquely on the end of it with a
coil of rope in his hand; the pent steam is screaming through the
gauge-cocks; the captain lifts his hand, a bell rings, the wheels stop;
then they turn back, churning the water to foam, and the steamer is
at rest. Then such a scramble as there is to get aboard, and to get
ashore, and to take in freight and to discharge freight, all at one and
the same time; and such a yelling and cursing as the mates facilitate it
all with! Ten minutes later the steamer is under way again, with no
flag on the jack-staff and no black smoke issuing from the chimneys.
After ten more minutes the town is dead again, and the town drunkard asleep by the skids once more.

My father was a justice of the peace, and I supposed he possessed
the power of life and death over all men, and could hang anybody
that offended him. This was distinction enough for me as a general
thing; but the desire to be a steamboatman kept intruding, nevertheless. I first wanted to be a cabin-boy, so that I could come out
with a white apron on and shake a table-cloth over the side, where all
my old comrades could see me; later I thought I would rather be the
deck-hand who stood on the end of the stage-plank with the coil of
rope in his hand, because he was particularly conspicuous. But these
were only day-dreams—they were too heavenly to be contemplated
as real possibilities. By and by one of our boys went away. He was
not heard of for a long time. At last he turned up as apprentice
engineer or "striker" on a steamboat. This thing shook the bottom

out of all my Sunday-school teachings. That boy had been notoriously worldly, and I just the reverse; yet he was exalted to this eminence, and I left in obscurity and misery. There was nothing generous about this fellow in his greatness. He would always manage to have a rusty bolt to scrub while his boat tarried at our town, and he would sit on the inside guard and scrub it, where we all could see him and envy him and loathe him. And whenever his boat was laid up he would come home and swell around the town in his blackest and greasiest clothes, so that nobody could help remembering that he was a steamboatman; and he used all sorts of steamboat technicalities   3 in his talk, as if he were so used to them that he forgot common people could not understand them. He would speak of the "labboard" side of a horse in any easy, natural way that would make one wish he was dead. And he was always talking about "St. Looy" like an old citizen; he would refer casually to occasions when he was "coming down Fourth Street," or when he was "passing by the Planter's House," or when there was a fire and he took a turn on the brakes of "the old Big Missouri"; and then he would go on and lie about how many towns the size of ours were burned down there that day. Two or three of the boys had long been persons of consideration among us because they had been to St. Louis once and had a vague general knowledge of its wonders, but the day of their glory was over now. They lapsed into a humble silence, and learned to disappear when the ruthless "cub"-engineer approached. This fellow had money, too, and hair-oil. Also an ignorant silver watch and a showy brass watch-chain. He wore a leather belt and used no suspenders. If ever a youth was cordially admired and hated by his comrades, this one was. No girl could withstand his charms. He "cut out" every boy in the village. When his boat blew up at last, it diffused a tranquil contentment among us such as we had not known for months. But when he came home the next week, alive, renowned, and appeared in church all battered up and bandaged, a shining hero, stared at and wondered over by everybody, it seemed to us that the partiality of Providence for an undeserving reptile had reached a point where it was open to criticism.

This creature's career could produce but one result, and it speedily followed. Boy after boy managed to get on the river. The minister's son became an engineer. The doctor's and the postmaster's sons became "mud clerks"; the wholesale liquor dealer's son became a barkeeper on a boat; four sons of the chief merchant, and two sons of the county judge, became pilots. Pilot was the grandest position of   4 all. The pilot, even in those days of trivial wages, had a princely salary—from a hundred and fifty to two hundred and fifty dollars a month, and no board to pay. Two months of his wages would pay a preacher's salary for a year. Now some of us were left disconsolate. We could not get on the river—at least our parents would not let us.

So, by and by, I ran away. I said I would never come home again till I was a pilot and could come in glory. But somehow I could not manage it. I went meekly aboard a few of the boats that lay packed together like sardines at the long St. Louis wharf, and humbly inquired for the pilots, but got only a cold shoulder and short words 5 from mates and clerks. I had to make the best of this sort of treatment for the time being, but I had comforting day-dreams of a future when I should be a great and honored pilot, with plenty of money, and could kill some of these mates and clerks and pay for them.

I & SELFDISCOVERY

E. E. Cummings

In the course of my first nonlecture,* I affirmed that—for me—
personality is a mystery; that mysteries alone are significant; and that
love is the mystery-of-mysteries who creates them all. During my
second outspokenness, I contrasted the collective behaviour of un-
children with the mystery of individuality; and gave (or attempted to   1
give) you one particular child's earliest glimpse of a mystery called
nature. Now I shall try to communicate—clumsily, no doubt, but
honestly—certain attitudes and reactions surrounding the mystery of
transition from which emerged a poet and painter named EE
Cummings.

As it was my miraculous fortune to have a true father and a true
mother, and a home which the truth of their love made joyous,
so—in reaching outward from this love and this joy—I was marvel-
lously lucky to touch and seize a rising and striving world; a reckless
world, filled with the curiosity of life herself; a vivid and violent
world welcoming every challenge; a world worth hating and adoring
and fighting and forgiving: in brief, a world which was a world. This
inwardly immortal world of my adolescence recoils to its very roots
whenever, nowadays, I see people who've been endowed with legs
crawling on their chins after quote security unquote. "Security?" I
marvel to myself "what is that? Something negative, undead, sus-
picious and suspecting; an avarice and an avoidance; a self-surrender-
ing meanness of withdrawal; a numerable complacency and an
innumerable cowardice. Who would be 'secure'? Every and any slave.   2
No free spirit ever dreamed of 'security'—or, if he did, he laughed;
and lived to shame his dream. No whole sinless sinful sleeping waking
breathing human creature ever was (or could be) bought by, and sold
for, 'security.' How monstrous and how feeble seems some unworld
which would rather have its too than eat its cake!"

Jehovah buried,Satan dead,
do fearers worship Much & Quick;
badness not being felt as bad,
itself thinks goodness what is meek;
obey says toc,submit says tic,
Eternity's a Five Year Plan:
if Joy with Pain shall hang in hock
who dares to call himself a man?

---

*The Charles Eliot Norton Lectures at Harvard University, 1952-1953.

For the benefit of any heretical members of my audience who do not regard manhood as a barbarous myth propagated by sinister powers envisaging the subjugation of womankind, let me (at this point) cheerfully risk a pair of perhaps not boring anecdotes.

Back in the days of dog-eat-dog—my first anecdote begins—there lived a playboy; whose father could easily have owned the original superskyscraper-de-luxe: a selfstyled Cathedral Of Commerce, endowed with every impetus to relaxation; not excluding ultraelevators which (on the laudable assumption that even machinery occasionally makes mistakes) were regularly tested. Testing an ultraelevator meant that its car was brought clean up, deprived of safety devices, and dropped. As the car hurtled downward, a column of air confined by the elevator shaft became more and more compressed; until (assuming that nothing untoward happened) it broke the car's fall completely—or so I was told by somebody who should know. At any rate, young Mr X was in the habit not only of attending these salubrious ceremonies, but of entering each about-to-be-dropped car, and of dropping with it as far and as long as the laws of a preEinsteinian universe permitted. Eventually, of course, somebody who shouldn't know telephoned a newspaper; which sent a reporter: who (after scarcely believing his senses) asked the transcender of Adam pointblank why he fell so often. Our playful protagonist shrugged his well-tailored shoulders—"for fun" he said simply; adding (in a strictly confidential undertone) "and it's wonderful for a hangover."

Here, I feel, we have the male American stance of my adolescence; or (if you prefer) the adolescent American male stance of what some wit once nicknamed a "lost generation": whereof—let me hastily append—the present speaker considers himself no worthy specimen. My point, however, isn't that many of us were even slightly heroic; and is that few of us declined a gamble. I don't think we enjoyed courting disaster. I do feel we liked being born.

And now let me give you my second anecdote: which concerns (appropriately enough) not a single human being whose name I forget, but a millionary mishmash termed The Public.

Rather recently—in New York City—an old college chum, whom I hadn't beheld for decades, appeared out of nowhere to tell me he was through with civilization. It seems that ever since Harvard he'd been making (despite all sorts of panics and panaceas) big money as an advertising writer; and this remarkable feat unutterably depressed him. After profound meditation, he concluded that America, and the world which she increasingly dominated, couldn't really be as bad as she and it looked through an advertising writer's eyes; and he

promptly determined to seek another view—a larger view; in fact, the
largest view obtainable. Bent on obtaining this largest obtainable
view of America and America's world, my logical expal wangled an
appointment with a subsubeditor of a magazine (if magazine it may
be called) possessing the largest circulation on earth: a periodical
whose each emanation appears simultaneously in almost every existing human language. Our intrepid explorer then straightened his tie,
took six deep breaths, cleared his throat, swam right up, presented
his credentials, and was politely requested to sit down. He sat down.
"Now listen" the subsubeditor suggested "if you're thinking of working with us, you'd better know The Three Rules." "And what" my
friend cheerfully inquired "are The Three Rules?" "The Three
Rules" explained his mentor "are: first, eight to eighty; second, anybody can do it; and third, makes you feel better." "I don't quite
understand" my friend confessed. "Perfectly simple" his interlocutor
assured him. "Our first Rule means that every article we publish
must appeal to anybody, man woman or child, between the ages of
eight and eighty years—is that clear?" My friend said it was indeed
clear. "Second" his enlightener continued "every article we publish   7
must convince any reader of the article that he or she could do
whatever was done by the person about whom the article was written. Suppose (for instance) you were writing about Lindbergh, who
had just flown the Atlantic ocean for the first time in history, with
nothing but unlimited nerve and a couple of chicken (or ham was it?)
sandwiches—do you follow me? "I'm ahead of you" my friend
murmured. "Remembering Rule number two" the subsub went on
"you'd impress upon your readers' minds, over and over again, the
fact that (after all) there wouldn't have been anything extraordinary
about Lindbergh if he hadn't been just a human being like every
single one of them. See?" "I see" said my friend grimly. "Third" the
subsub intoned "we'll imagine you're describing a record-breaking
Chinese flood—millions of poor unfortunate men and women and
little children and helpless babies drowning and drowned; millions
more perishing of slow starvation: suffering inconceivable, untold
agonies, and so forth—well, any reader of this article must feel definitely and distinctly better, when she or he finishes the article, than
when he or she began it." "Sounds a trifle difficult" my friend
hazarded. "Don't be silly" the oracle admonished. "All you've got to
do, when you're through with your horrors, is to close by saying: but
(thanks to an all-merciful Providence) we Americans, with our high
standard of living and our Christian ideals, will never be subjected to
such inhuman conditions; as long as the Stars and Stripes tri-

umphantly float over one nation indivisible, with liberty and justice for all—get me?" "I get you" said my disillusioned friend. "Good bye."

So ends the second anecdote. You may believe it or not, as you wish. As far as I'm concerned, it's the unbelievable—but also un-questionable—selfportrait of a one hundred and one percent pseudo-world: in which truth has become televisionary, in which goodness means not hurting people, and in which beauty is shoppe. Just (or unjust) how any species of authentic individualism could stem from such a collective quagmire, I don't—as always—know; but here are four lines of a poem which didn't:

8

(While you and i have lips and voices which
are for kissing and to sing with
who cares if some oneeyed son of a bitch
invents an instrument to measure Spring with?

As regards my own self-finding, I have to thank first of all that institution whose intitial I flaunted unknowingly during my very earliest days. Officially, Harvard presented me with a smattering of languages and sciences; with a glimpse of Homer, a more than glimpse of Aeschylus Sophocles Euripides and Aristophanes, and a deep glance at Dante and Shakespeare. Unofficially, she gave me my first taste of independence: and the truest friends any man will ever enjoy. The taste of independence came during my senior year, when I was so lucky as to receive a room by myself in the Yard—for living in the Yard was then an honour, not a compulsion; and this honour very properly reserved itself for seniors, who might conceivably ap-preciate it. Hitherto I had ostensibly lived at home; which meant that intimate contacts with the surrounding world were somewhat pericu-lous. Now I could roam that surrounding world sans peur, if not sans reproche: and I lost no time in doing so. A town called Boston, thus observed, impressed my unsophisticated spirit as the mecca of all human endeavors—and be it added that, in this remote era, Boston had her points. Well do I recall how our far from hero (backed by the most physically imposing of his acquaintances) dared a stifling dump near Howard Street, denominated Mother Shannon's; and how we stopped short, to avoid treading on several spreadeagled sailors; and how my backer, with irreproachable nonchalance, exchanged a brace of dollar bills for two tumblers of something even viler than honest Jack Delaney served during soi-disant prohibition; and finally how, having merely sampled our nonbeverages, we successfully attained Scollay Square—to be greeted by the dispassionate drone of a pint-

size pimp, conspicuously stationed on the populous sidewalk under a
blaze of movie bulbs and openly advertising two kinds of love for
twenty-five cents each. Moreover that distant Boston comprised such
authentic incarnations of genius as Bernhardt, whose each intonation
propitiated demons and angels; Pavlova, who danced a ditty called
Nix On The Glowworm into the most absolute piece of aristocracy
since Ming; and a lady of parts (around whose waist any man's hand
immediately dreamed it could go three times) named Polaire. Those
were the days (and nights) of The Turkey Trot and The Bunny Hug;
of Everybody's Doing It, Alexander's Ragtime Band, Has Anybody
Here Seen Kelly, There's A Little Bit Of Bad In Every Good Little
Girl, On The Banks Of The Saskatchewan, and Here Comes My
Daddy Now (O Pop, O Pop, O Pop, O Pop). Nothing could exceed
the artistry of Washington Street bartenders, who positively enjoyed   9
constructing impeccable Pousse-Cafes in the midst of Ward Eights
and Hop Toads; nor could anything approach the courtesy of Wood-
cock waiters, who never obeyed any ring but your own and always
knocked twice before entering. I am further indebted to Boston
town for making me acquainted (and in no uncertain manner) with
the sinister splendors of censorship. One evening, The Old Howard
would be As Is; the next, you guessed you were embracing a funeral.
When Miss Gertrude Hoffman brought her lissome self and her
willowy girls to Boston, they and she were violently immersed in
wrist-and-ankle-length underwear. A local tobacconist drew jail for
selling a box of cigars adorned with the usual gauzily apparelled but
unmistakably symbolic females—and vainly did an outraged lawyer
object that his client was happily married. Meanwhile, watching-and-
warding Mr Sumner's matchless collection of indecent items consti-
tuted a favorite topic of conversation with high and low alike. But if
the predations of puritanism astonished me nearly forty years ago, I
was recently more than amazed to learn that you cannot now show a
woman's entire breast in any American moviehouse unless she isn't
(to coin a plagiarism) white. Verily, democracy unquote is a strange
disease: nor (I submit) can any human being help sympathizing, in
his or her heart of hearts, with the bad bald poet who sings

        come(all you mischief-
    hatchers hatch
mischief)all you

    guilty
        scamper(you bastards throw dynamite)
            let knowings magic
        with bright credos each divisible fool

        (life imitate gossip fear unlife
mean
    -ness,and
        to succeed in not
            dying)
        Is will still occur;birds disappear
    becomingly:a thunderbolt compose poems
not because harm symmetry
    earthquakes starfish(but
        because nobody
            can sell the Moon to The)moon

Let us now consider friendship.

Through Harvard, I met Scofield Thayer; and at Harvard, Sibley Watson—two men who subsequently transformed a dogooding periodical called The Dial into a firstrate magazine of the fine arts; and together fought the eternal fight of selfhood against mobism, the immortal battle of beauty against ugliness. It would not even slightly surprise me to learn that most of you have remained, till now, quite unaware of the existence of these literally heroic individuals and of their actually unparalleled achievement. Never have I seen courage and courtesy, taste and intelligence, prodigious patience and incredible generosity, quite so jealously mistrusted or so basely misprized or so savagely detested as by The Dial's detractors. Even today, more than twenty years after this true and noble adventure's culmination, the adventurers' chastisement continues—through such a conspiracy of silence on the part of America's intellectual gangsters as would be ludicrous if it were not abominable; nor will that chastisement begin to diminish while general good outflanks minute particulars and spiritual treachery is the order of the unday.

At Harvard (moreover) I met Stewart Mitchell, who soon became editor-in-chief of our university's only serious undergraduate magazine—The Monthly—and was subsequently managing editor of The Dial; John Dos Passos, through whose devoted efforts a dangerous compilation known as Eight Harvard Poets appeared; and S Foster Damon, who opened my eyes and ears not merely to Domenico Theotocopuli and William Blake, but to all ultra (at that moment) modern music and poetry and painting. Nor can or do I forget Theodore Miller; who gladly brought me such treasures as the exquisite

10

lugete, o Veneres Cupidinesque
et quantumst hominum venustiorum

of Catullus; the sublime

labuntur anni; nec pietas moram
rugis et instanti senectae,   11
adferet, indomitaeque morti

of Horace; and Sappho's magically luminous invocation

ποικ ιλόθ ρον᾽, ἀθ άνατ᾽ ᾽Αφρόδιτα

but the token of whose most memorable kindness was a volume
combining poems and letters by that glorious human being who confessed

I am certain of nothing but of the holiness of the
Heart's affections, and the truth of Imagination.

Whereupon—deep in those heights of psychic sky which had greeted
my boyish escape from moralism—an unknown and unknowable bird
began singing.
        After Harverd, I thank (for selfdiscovery) a phenomenon and a
miracle. The phenomenon was a telemicroscopic chimera, born of
the satanic rape of matter by mind; a phallic female phantasm,
clothed in thunderous anonymity and adorned with colossally floating spiderwebs of traffic; a stark irresistibly stupendous newness,
mercifully harboring among its pitilessly premeditated spontaneities
immemorial races and nations

by god i want above fourteenth

fifth's deep purring biceps, the mystic screetch
of Broadway, the trivial stink of rich

frail firm asinine life
                    (i pant

                                                                          12
for what's below. the singer. Wall. i want
the perpendicular lips the insane teeth
the vertical grin

                        give me the Square in spring,
the little barbarous Greenwich perfumed fake

and most, the futile fooling labyrinth
where noisy colors stroll . . . and the Baboon

sniggering insipidities while. i sit, sipping
singular anisettes as. One opaque
big girl jiggles thickly hips to the canoun

but Hassan chuckles seeing the Greeks breathe)

in New York I also breathed: and as if for the first time.

The truly first of first times was (however) still to come. It
arrived with a socalled war. Being neither warrior nor conscientious-
objector, saint nor hero, I embarked for France as an ambulance-
driver. And as my earliest taste of independence had been excelled
by the banquet which I later sampled among Manhattan's sky-
scrapers, so was that banquet surpassed by the freedom which I now
tasted:

Paris: this April sunset completely utters
utters serenely silently a cathedral

before whose upward lean magnificent face
the streets turn young with rain,

two realms, elsewhere innately hostile, here cordially coexisted—each
(by its very distinctness) intensifying the other—nor could I possibly
have imagined either a loveliness so fearlessly of the moment or so
nobly beautiful a timelessness. Three thousand oceanic miles away
and some terrestrial years before, a son of New England had observed
those realms bitterly struggling for dominion: then, as a guest of
verticality, our impuritan had attended the overwhelming triumph of   13
the temporal realm. Now, I participated in an actual marriage of
material with immaterial things; I celebrated an immediate reconciling of spirit and flesh, forever and now, heaven and earth. Paris
was for me precisely and complexly this homogeneous duality: this
accepting transcendence; this living and dying more than death or
life. Whereas—by the very act of becoming its improbably gigantic
self—New York had reduced mankind to a tribe of pygmies, Paris (in
each shape and gesture and avenue and cranny of her being) was
continuously expressing the humanness of humanity. Everywhere I
sensed a miraculous presence, not of mere children and women and
men, but of living human beings; and the fact that I could scarcely
understand their language seemed irrelevant, since the truth of our
momentarily mutual aliveness created an imperishable communion.
While (at the hating touch of some madness called La Guerre) a once
rising and striving world toppled into withering hideously smither-

eens, love rose in my heart like a sun and beauty blossomed in my
life like a star. Now, finally and first, I was myself: a temporal citizen
of eternity; one with all human beings born and unborn.

Thus through an alma mater whose scholastic bounty appeared
the smallest of her blessings—and by way of those even more munifi-
cent institutions of learning, New York and Paris—our ignoramus
reaches his supreme indebtedness. Last but most, I thank for my 14
self-finding certain beautiful givers of illimitable gladness

whose any mystery makes every man's
flesh put space on;and his mind take off time

and so we turn to poetry.

THOREAU AT WALDEN
Van Wyck Brooks

Henry Thoreau had built a hut at Walden. In March, 1845, he had borrowed Alcott's axe,—which he took pains to return with a sharper edge,—and cut down some tall, arrowy pines for the timbers, studs and rafters. For the boards he bought a shanty from one of the Irish labourers on the railroad. The hut was ten feet by fifteen, shingled and plastered, with a garret and closet, a trap-door below, a brick fireplace, windows at the sides and a door facing the cove. The cost, all told, was $28.12½,—less than the annual rent of a student's room in Cambridge. There was a bean-field, close by, with a patch of potatoes, corn, peas and turnips. As a quasi-Pythagorean, Thoreau seldom indulged in beans. He exchanged his crop for rice in the village. Rice was the proper diet for one who loved so well the writings of the Oriental sages. 1

He had long cherished the notion of a forest-life. Ellery Channing had built himself a hut on the prairie in Illinois, and Henry's college class-mate, Stearns Wheeler, who had just died in Leipzig, had also built a rough woodland cabin, over at Flint's Pond, where he had lived for a year to save money, to buy Greek books and pay his way to Germany to study. Henry had spent six weeks in Wheeler's cabin, sharing one of his bunks of straw. There was nothing new in his own adventure, and he could not understand why his friends thought it was so peculiar. Some of them spoke as if he had gone to the woods in order to starve or freeze. Emerson had bought land on both sides of the pond, intending to build a summer-house, and Henry had carried out the project. Alcott, who liked to tinker at rustic architecture, helped him with his saw and hammer, along with the young Brook Farmer, George William Curtis of New York, who was boarding at Edmund Hosmer's in the village and working as a farm-hand. Henry felt at home in his sylvan dwelling. It made him think of some of those mountain-houses he had seen on his inland excursions, high-placed, airy, fragrant, with a fresh, auroral atmosphere about them. It was quiet, clean and cool, fit to entertain a traveling god. For company, birds flitted through his chamber, red squirrels raced over the roof, chickadees perched on the armfuls of wood he carried. There were moles living in the cellar. He had occasional visits from a hare. As he sat at his door in the evening, he remembered that he was descended from the Greeks of old. He was a wanderer, too, one of the crew of Ulysses. The shore of the cove was another Ithaca. 2

There was nothing about his "experiment," as his friends liked to call it, to arouse such curiosity and contempt. It was a common-sensible undertaking, and only a slight departure from Henry's usual mode of living. His average weekly outlay, for necessaries he could not supply himself, was twenty-seven cents. A few days at manual labour, building a boat or a fence, planting, grafting or surveying,— six weeks of work out of the year, when he had grown extravagant and had to have a microscope,—gave him an ample surplus. Why should anyone live by the sweat of his brow and bore his fellowmen by talking about it? Why should not everyone live with an ample margin?—as anyone could do, provided he followed the path of simplification, logically and ruthlessly enough. The mass of men led lives of quiet desperation. Why, if not to maintain a "standard of living" that every law of the universe controverted? Did they not know that the wisest had always lived, with respect to comforts and luxuries, a life more simple and meagre than the poor? Had all the philosophers, Hindu, Greek and Persian, lived and taught in vain? Had anyone measured man's capacities? Was it fair to judge by prece-dents, when so very little had been attempted? Who could say that if a man advanced, boldly, in the direction of his dreams, endeavouring to live the life he had imagined, he would not meet with a success that he had never expected in common hours? Henry believed, and wished to prove, that the more one simplified one's life the less complex the laws of life would seem. Why all this pother about possessions? He liked to think of the ancient Mexicans, who burned all their goods every fifty years. Hawthorne, in one of his stories, had pictured a similar holocaust; and this was the kind of reform that Henry thought was worth considering. He meant to have his furni-ture, actual and symbolic, as simple as an Indian's or an Arab's. There were three bits of limestone on his table. They had to be dusted every day, while the furniture of his mind was still undusted. Out of the window, quick!

If he had had the wealth of Crœsus, Henry's mode of living would not have been different. Space, air, time, a few tools, a note-book, a pen, a copy of Homer, what could he wish more than these? A bath in the pond at sunrise, a little Spartan sweeping and cleaning, then a bath for the intellect, perhaps in the Bhagavad-Gita, the pure water of Walden mingling in his mind with the sacred water of the Ganges. The day was his, for any wild adventure. Sometimes, on a summer morning, he would sit for hours in his sunny doorway, amid the pines and hickories and sumachs, in undisturbed solitude and stillness. The birds flitted noiselessly about him. He could feel him-

3

self growing like the corn. He knew what the Orientals meant by
contemplation and the forsaking of works. He was a Yogi, too, a
forest-seer, who might have composed the Upanishads. His Reality
was also Brahma, not the actualities of the world but its potentialities. What did he care for temporal interests? It was his vocation to
discover God. His days were no longer days of the week, bearing the
names of pagan deities, nor were they minced into hours or fretted
by the ticking of a clock. He felt like a Puri Indian or a Mexican. If
you had put a watch in his hand and asked him what the hour was,
he might have looked at the dial and said, "Quien sabe?" The sounds
of the railway rose and died in his ears like the distant drumming of a
partridge.

His life here seemed to flow in its proper channels. It followed its
own fresh currents, and he felt himself lurking in crystalline thought
as the trout lurked under the verdurous banks. Not so much as a
bubble rose to the surface. At sunset, he jumped into his boat and
paddled to the middle of the pond. There he played on his flute,
while the charmed perch hovered about the stern, and the moon
travelled over the floor of the pond, strewn with the wrecks of the
forest. The wildest imagination could not conceive the manner of life
he was living, for the Concord nights were as strange as Arabian
nights. He struck the side of the boat with his paddle, filling the
woods with a circle of sound. What a pleasant mission it would be to
go about the country in search of echoes! He knew where to find the
prophetic places, the vocal, resounding, sonorous, hollow places,
where oracles might be established, sites for oracles, sacred ears of
Nature.

What could he say to a man who feared the woods, who shud-
dered at their solitude and darkness? What salvation was there for
such a man? Did he not know that God was mysterious and silent?
Henry could never have wearied of the woods, as long as he could
visit a nighthawk on her nest. He could hardly believe his eyes when
he stood within seven feet of her. There she was, sitting on her eggs,
so sphinx-like, so Saturnian, so one with the earth, a relic of the reign
of Saturn that Jupiter had failed to destroy, a riddle that might cause
a man to go and dash his head against a stone. No living creature,
surely, far less a winged creature of the air. A figure in stone or
bronze, like a gryphon or a phœnix. With its flat, greyish, weather-
beaten crown, its eyes were all but closed with stony cunning; and
yet all the time this sculptured image, motionless as the earth, was
watching with intense anxiety, through those narrow slits in its eye-
lids. Wonderful creature, sitting on its eggs, on the bare, exposed hill,

through pelting storms of rain or hail, as if it were a part of the earth itself, the outside of the globe, with its eyes shut and its wings folded. It was enough to fill a man with awe. Henry thought for a moment that he had strayed into the Caucasus, and that around the hill, on the other slope, he would find Prometheus chained to the rock.

Round and round the pond, Henry followed the footpath worn by the feet of Indian hunters, old as the race of men in Massachusetts. The critics and poets were always complaining that there were no American antiquities, no ruins to remind one of the past, yet the wind could hardly blow away the surface anywhere, exposing the spotless sand, but one found the fragments of some Indian pot or the little chips of flint left by some aboriginal arrow-maker. When winter came, and the scent of the gale wafted over the naked ground, Henry tramped through the snow a dozen miles to keep an appointment with a beech-tree, or a yellow birch perhaps, or some old acquaintance among the pines. He ranged like a grey moose, winding his way through the shrub-oak patches, bending the twigs aside, guiding himself by the sun, over hills and plains and valleys, resting in the clear grassy spaces. He liked the wholesome colour of the shrub-oak leaves, well-tanned, seasoned by the sun, the colour of the cow and the deer, silvery-downy underneath, over the bleached and russet fields. He loved the shrub-oak, with its scanty raiment, rising above the snow, lowly whispering to him, akin to winter, the covert which the hare and the partridge sought. It was one of his own cousins, 7 rigid as iron, clean as the atmosphere, hardy as all virtue, tenacious of its leaves, leaves that did not shrivel but kept their wintry life, firm shields, painted in fast colours. It loved the earth, which it overspread, tough to support the snow, indigenous, robust. The squirrel and the rabbit knew it well, and Henry could understand why the deer-mouse had its hole in the snow by the shrub-oak's stem. Winter was his own chosen season. When, for all variety in his walks, he had only a rustling oak-leaf or the faint metallic cheep of a tree-sparrow, his life felt continent and sweet as the kernel of a nut. Alone in the distant woods or fields, in the unpretending sprout-lands or pastures tracked by rabbits, on a bleak and, to most, a cheerless day, when a villager would be thinking of his fire, he came to himself and felt himself grandly related. Cold and solitude were his dearest friends. Better a single shrub-oak leaf at the end of a wintry glade, rustling a welcome at his approach, than a ship-load of stars and garters from the kings of the earth. By poverty, if one chose to use the word, monotony, simplicity, he felt solidified and crystallized, as water and vapour are crystallized by cold.

All praise to winter, then, was Henry's feeling. Let others have their sultry luxuries. How full of creative genius was the air in which these snow-crystals were generated. He could hardly have marvelled more if real stars had fallen and lodged on his coat. What a world to live in, where myriads of these little discs, so beautiful to the most prying eye, were whirled down on every traveller's coat, on the rest-less squirrel's fur and on the far-stretching fields and forests, the wooded dells and mountain-tops,—these glorious spangles, the sweep-ings of heaven's floor. He watched the men cutting the ice on the pond. Some of this ice, stowed in the holds of ships, was going over to India; and many a seeker of Brahma in Calcutta was destined to drink from his own Walden well. If winter drove one in-doors, all the better. It compelled one to try new fields and resources. Days of merry snow-storms and cheerful winter evenings by the fire. Evenings for books of natural history, Audubon, for one. It was pleasant to read about the Florida Keys, the flowering magnolia, the warm spice-breezes, while the wind beat the snow against one's window. Days to sit at home over one's journal, in one's own nest, perhaps on a single egg, though it might prove to be an egg of chalk.

These were the days for writing, days to speak like a man in a waking moment to others in their waking moments. For Henry was hard at work. He was writing articles, which Horace Greeley placed for him. He had begun to write a book, and he wished to pay his tribute to Carlyle, who had liberated the English language, cutting away the fetters imposed upon it by the pedantic writers of the British reviews. The frigid *North American* was even worse, a vener-able cobweb that had escaped the broom. He liked to think of Carlyle, on his vacations, riding on his horse "Yankee," bought from the American sale of his books. His own book, rewritten from his journal, was the *Week on the Concord and Merrimac Rivers,* the story of the journey with his brother, never to be forgotten, when they had doubled so many capes and run before the wind and brought back news of far-away men. He did not propose to crowd his day with work, even if the book had to be written. A writer, he thought, should saunter to his task surrounded by a halo of ease and leisure, and the labour of his hands should remove from his style all trace of sentimentality and palaver. One did not dance idly at one's writing when one had wood to cut and cord. As the strokes rang cheerily through the wood, so the stroke of the pen should ring on the reader's ear. Was the voyage an old story, eight or nine years old, and only a week at that? It represented a lifetime's memories. No boy who had grown up on the Mississippi recalled those floating

enchantments, the river-boats, and the fabulous river-men, with more
of a thrill than Henry felt, remembering the canal-boats of his childhood. The news had spread through Concord that one of these boats
was stealing through the meadows, silent as a cloud, with its crew of
"foreigners" from New Hampshire, and all the village boys had
flocked to see it. Henry wished to write a book that would be saturated with his thought and reading, yet one that would not smell so
much of the study, even the poet's cabin, as of the fields and woods.
He dreamed of an unroofed book, lying open under the ether, a book
that could hardly be forced to lie on a shelf.

He was not by nature a hermit. He might have frequented the
bar-rooms, he thought, if he had had any business that called him
thither. Almost every day he walked to the village, to trade his beans
for rice, to get a boot repaired, to collect the news of the family.
Sometimes he returned late at night, with a bag of rye or Indian
meal, sailing back under the moon to his harbour in the woods. It
was only that he was wary of gossip. He did not wish to lumber his
mind with the rubbish that most men seemed to rejoice in, the
details, for example, of some case in court. One day he was arrested
in the village for refusing to pay his poll-tax. He felt as Alcott felt.
The government supported slavery, the government was backing the
Mexican War; well, he would not support the government. He did not
wish to trace the course of his dollar until it bought a man, or bought
a gun to shoot a Mexican. He spent the night in jail,—a fruitful night.
It inspired his essay on *Civil Disobedience.* He wished to establish a   10
principle, that one man locked up in jail for refusing to countenance
slavery would be the end of slavery, or, to express it on a broader
basis, "If the alternative is to keep all just men in prison, or give up
war and slavery, the State will not hesitate which to choose." A
foolish notion, many people thought, but some of them changed
their minds, in later years, when one of Henry's Hindu readers,
Gandhi, acting on the principle, disturbed the British Empire for
several months. The next morning, Henry, released from jail,
gathered some of the boys and girls for a huckleberry party, on a hill,
whence the State was nowhere to be seen. He never fastened his door
at Walden, though sometimes, in his absence, he had unwelcome
visitors. How did Mrs. X happen to know that his sheets were not as
clean as hers? But nothing was ever stolen, except his copy of
Homer. One had to keep one's eye on bookish people.

He had other guests, especially in April, when all the world
seemed to be on the move. A runaway slave appeared, the Alek
Therien, the French-Canadian wood-chopper, a true Homeric peasant

who had learned a little Greek from his priest in the north, then Hugh Quoil, an Irish soldier, who had fought at the Battle of Waterloo. Old Quoil, with his wife and his jug, was patiently waiting for death in a hut in the woods. The shanty-Irish folk along the railroad sometimes came to see him. Henry thought them shiftless enough, with their women washing under the trees and the pigs poking about among the tubs. He eyed them with a vague hostility, as the red men had eyed the first settlers, and with as much reason; for were they not the first wave of the sea that was to sweep away so many landmarks? Among the little ragamuffins that swarmed about these cabins, there were some in whom the prophetic eye might have seen the masters of the future, the lords of Greater Boston, mayors, governors, captains of police, even, perhaps, a cardinal. Henry had one good friend among them, little Johnny Riordan, with his quaint "old worthy" face, behind the sober visor of his cap, plodding to school through the snow in his next-to-nothing, facing and routing it like a Persian army. A great sight, Johnny, in his rags, beside the well-fed villagers, waddling about in their furs and finery. Emerson also came, of course. Henry read aloud to him some pages from his book, while they sat under an oak beside the pond. Alcott arrived one night, struggling through the snow. Ellery Channing spent a fortnight with him. When the poets and sages came, he was glad that his dwelling was so spacious. As the conversation assumed a grander and loftier tone, they shoved their chairs further and further apart, until they touched the walls in opposite corners. This left plenty of neutral ground for their sentences to deploy in martial order.

Once Henry left his house for a fortnight's excursion. He had cousins in Bangor, Maine, one of them in the lumber-trade, a good excuse to visit the northern woods. He wished to study the Indians in their forest wilderness, and he wished to climb Mount Ktaadn. He never travelled without prayer and fasting, for he did not wish to dissipate his mind. With all the industry of a busy life, how could one hope to know, really know, an area more than six miles square? Isaac Hecker had asked him to go to Rome, the two of them together, Hecker to pay the expenses, for Hecker, who had tried Brook Farm and Fruitlands, was boarding with Mrs. Thoreau for a taste of Concord. He hoped to carry Henry over to Rome, in more than one fashion. Later, another friend, an Englishman, invited him for a visit in England. In both cases, Henry said, No. If Europe was much in his mind, and became more and more to him, Concord might become less and less; and what sort of bargain would that be? He did not wish his life to lose its homely savour. If the fields and streams and

woods that he loved so well, and the simple occupations of his
townsmen, ever ceased to interest and surprise him, what culture or
wealth could ever atone for the loss? He did not wish to go to   12
Europe, nor did he wish to go—like the farmers—west. What could he
think of this foolish American habit, going east or west to a "better
land," without lifting an honest finger to till and redeem one's own
New England soil? As for the rush to California, it was a disgrace to
humankind,—digging gold, the merest lottery, a kind of toil, if it
deserved the name, in no sense beneficial to the world. A startling
development, this, of the ethics of trade and all the modes of getting
a living. It filled Henry with a cold scorn. For the rest, he had his
own western horizon, towards which he was always moving, pitching
his tent each day nearer the Golden Gate. But the really fertile soils
and luxuriant prairies lay on one's own side of the Alleghanies,
wherever a man minded his own business. Were not all the essentials
of life to be found in Concord, ten times found if one properly
valued them?—which a man could only do if he stood his ground.
Henry had something to say to the men in the covered wagons, who
were running away from something besides the rocks. If the men in
the covered wagons had no ears for Henry, he would be glad to wait
for a few generations. The great-great-grandsons of the covered
wagons would be ready to listen to him.

Nobody knew the riches of Concord. As for natural history, he
had found some of the Arctic phenomena there, red snow and one or
two Labrador plants. Still, a little travel now and then was not so bad
to give one's mind an airing, especially if it offered him a chance to
observe the ways of the Indians. For the Indians had a special charm
for Henry; they suggested a simpler mode of life and a greater near-
ness to the earth. Were there not two eternities, one behind him,
which the Indians represented, as well as one before? Wherever he
went, he trod in their tracks, yet only a few poets remembered them.
Here and there, one saw their lonely wigwams, on the banks of some
quiet stream, like the cabins of the muskrats in the meadows,—an old
squaw, perhaps, living in her solitary hut, with her dog, her only
companion, making baskets and picking berries, insulted by the
village boys and girls. Henry dreamed of writing a book about them;*   13
for their memory seemed to him to harmonize with the russet hue of
autumn that he loved. A race that had exhausted the secrets of
nature, a race tanned with age, while the young, fair Anglo-Saxon
slip, on whom the sun had shone for so short a time, was only just

---

*Thoreau left eleven manuscript volumes, about 3000 pages, filled with notes about the
Indians for the book he had hoped to write.

beginning its career. As sportsmen went in pursuit of ducks, and scholars of rare books, and all men went in pursuit of money, Henry went in search of arrowheads, when the proper season came round again. He often spent whole afternoons, especially in the spring, when the rains had washed the ground bare, pacing back and forth over a sandy field, looking for these relics. It might have rained arrow-heads. They lay all over the surface of the country, sometimes mingled with arrow-headiferous soil, ash-coloured, left by Indian fires. They were like so many fossil thoughts to Henry, forever recalling the far-away mind that shaped them.

To Maine, then!—where the Indians grew with the moose. A fortnight in the forest, the home of the bear and the caribou, the wolf, the beaver and the Penobscot redskins, where the wild fir flourished and the spruce-tops, seen from an elevation, were like the odour of cake in a schoolboy's nostrils. Hemlocks and cedars, silver and yellow birches, watery maples, damp and moss-grown rocks, real woods, these, wild and bearded. One caught the whistle of ducks on solitary streams, the flicker of the darting chickadee, the loon's desolate laugh. Sometimes, through the moss-clad aisles, one heard a dull, dry, rustling sound, as if smothered under the fungus-covered forest, the falling of a tree, like the shutting of a door in some distant entry of the dark and shaggy wilderness. There one could feel at home, shooting the rapids in one's birch canoe, like a bait bobbing for some river monster, darting from side to side of the stream, then gliding swift and smoothly. This was the place to sing the "Canadian boat-song," or to play on one's flute, at night, under the stars, while the wolves howled about, in the darkness of the continent. Henry watched Joe Polis, the Indian guide, glued to the bank on his stomach, talking to the muskrats in their sylvan language. Sometimes, by the fireside, Joe Polis also sang, a mild and simple nasal chant, like the dawn of civilization over the woods. The white man's brow was clear and distinct, but over the brow of the Indian lingered a haze or mist. For the Indian, the white man's noon was four o'clock in the morning. 14

A journey like this was only a foretaste, too rewarding not to be repeated. Henry was writing about his travels, and one of the magazines was glad to print his essay on Ktaadn. Later, on two occasions, he went to Maine again. He wished to visit Chesuncook, the Allegash and the East Branch. He was in his element in the woods, as Richard Henry Dana on the sea, as an old French-Canadian *coureur de bois.* Was he not a Frenchman as well as a Yankee, who might have run wild with Du Lhut and harried the woods for beavers? In the mean-

time, he had left his Walden cabin. Why? For as good a reason as he
had gone there. He had other lives to live, and he had no more time
to spare for this one. He wanted a change, he did not wish to stag-
nate. About two o'clock in the afternoon, he had felt the world's
axle creaking a little, as if it needed greasing, as if the oxen laboured
with the wain and could hardly get their load over the ridge of the
day. Who would accept heaven on terms like this?—and a ticket for
heaven had to include, for Henry, tickets for hell and purgatory also.
Walden was only a bivouac in his campaign. He had other journeys in
mind, to Cape Cod, for instance, with Ellery Channing, and later a
jaunt to Canada, Quebec and Montreal. (Total expense, two guide-
books included, $12.75.) Ellery was not a man for camping out,—
that was an art one had to acquire slowly; but he shared Henry's
taste for a simple equipment. And Henry would no more have
thought of dressing,—dressing for a journey!—than he would have
blacked his boots for fishing. Honest traveling was dirty work. A pair
of overalls was the proper costume, a grey sack, corduroys perhaps;   15
and as for this blacking of boots, he despised it on all occasions. In
this, he was like some of the Harvard professors, who, as Mrs. Story
was shocked to note, on one of her visits from Italy, did not have
their boots blacked even for Commencement. Henry, who always
carried a piece of tallow, in order to keep the water out of the
leather, looked like a woodchuck or a musquash. This was his desire,
at least,—the more like a quadruped the better, tawny, russet, yellow-
brown, the colour of the sands. Vermont grey was not so bad; and
once he had had the perfect suit, a skilful mixture of browns, with
light and dark cleverly proportioned, and a few threads of green. He
had looked like a corner of a pasture, with patches of sweet-fern and
lechea. He had been able to glide over the fields, as unperceived from
the farmer's windows as a painted cruiser through a spyglass. The
wild animals thought he was one of them. Ellery, who was not so
systematic, shared Henry's feeling in the matter of hats. His own hat
was old and weather-beaten and had plenty of holes around the brim.
It was as rare and high as a good Stilton cheese. As for the rest of
Henry's outfit, a handkerchief served for a bag, or a firm, stout sheet
of brown paper, well tied up. What else? An umbrella, of course, a
knapsack, with partitions for books and papers, a music-book for
pressing flowers, a field-glass and a measuring-tape. A fish-line, spoon
and dipper, a little salt and sugar, tea, Indian meal and a slice of
fruit-cake. If anyone asked him along the way to do a little tinkering,
that was a tribute to his common sense.

So Henry tramped to Provincetown. Having seen the woods, he wished to see the ocean, and Cape Cod was surely the place to see it. There, on the stretches of sand blown clean by the wind, he could forget the towns, where he felt so unspeakably mean and disgraced. He could forget the bar-rooms of Massachusetts, where the full-grown were not weaned from their savage and filthy habits, sucking cigars and guzzling whiskey-punch. On the Cape, one saw wholesome faces, well preserved by the salty air, faces bleached like old sails, hanging cliffs of weather-beaten flesh. The Cape Cod boys leaped from their leading-strings into the shrouds; it was only a bound from their mother's laps to the masthead. The boxed the compass in their infant day-dreams. They could hand, reef and steer by the time they flew a kite. This was a country almost as thrilling as Maine. Henry had three books more or less on the stocks: *The Maine Woods,* full of the scents of the forest, *Cape Cod,* redolent of the sea, even *A Yankee in Canada.* The well-known publishers, Time & Co., could be trusted to see that they were safely printed. One of his neighbours wrote about Human Culture. Why should he not write about Cape Cod, another name for the same thing, and hardly a sandier phase of it? Or Canada, for that matter? He wrote an opening paragraph, with both hands clenched: "Read my book if you dare!"

SATIRE AND HUMOR

The terms *satire* and *humor* are difficult to define; indeed, perhaps no adequate definition has been made for either. It is clear that they are closely related, yet it is equally clear that not all humor is satire and that not all satire is humorous. Both the humorist and the satirist are keenly aware of the follies and imperfections of men; both show the incompatibility between the moral standards and conventions to which men subscribe, consciously or unconsciously, and actual ways of living. The difference between the two, satirist and humorist, may well lie in the fact that the humorist accepts that incompatibility, whereas the satirist reacts against it. The humorist is much more the detached observer of the human scene; he makes no moral issue of the fact that men depart from or simply ignore the conventions they themselves have set up. What he sees, then, becomes comic, ludicrous, or farcical. The satirist, on the other hand, does not accept, does not tolerate. The incompatibility he sees, the same incompatibility observed by the humorist, moves him to protest. The protest may be bitter, even brutal. When it is so it is often called Juvenalian, after Juvenal, the old Roman who in his verses was moved to indignation and who evokes contempt and moral indignation at the vices and corruptions of men. The Juvenalian satirist may see the follies of men as ludicrous or ridiculous and thus move us to laughter, but he nevertheless presents these follies as present dangers. Jonathan Swift among English writers gives us a good example of the indignant satirist. On the other hand, the satirist's protest may be light—even gentle and good-natured. The writer who gave his name to satire which is genial, playful, and yet persuasive is the Roman Horace, who said he wanted "to tell the truth laughing." In Horatian satire the line between humor and satire becomes much less distinct. The Horatian satirist is the tolerant man of the world who evokes smiles at the foibles of other men. Although he is not moved to forceful expression of moral indignation, he nevertheless suggests that the world would be better off without the spectacle he has reported. Whereas the humorist suggests that the follies—and even evils—he portrays are innate in humanity, the Horatian satirist affirms that they can be eradicated. He is not detached; he gives us warning examples.

Both satire and humor deal with the contrast between reality and pretense. La Rochefoucauld, the French writer of aphorisms, illustrated this contrast when he said, "We all have sufficient strength to bear up under the misfortunes of others." Yet his statement is not merely amusing, or perhaps not amusing at all; it is a witty and wise observation which moves us not so much to laughter as to wonder at man's unhumanity to man. The humorist Robert Benchley, in "What College Did to Me," does not attack the college curriculum or view the college student with scorn. In fact, he does not suggest that he wants any change at all. La Rochefoucauld, on the other hand, gives us the uneasy feeling that reform is in order.

Both the satirist and the humorist are, in some sense, unfair because they *select* and they *exaggerate* (like the caricaturist). They select what supports their position, reject what does not. Yet they select with great care from the available truth, because out-and-out falsehood, if recognized by their audience, would destroy their position. The humorist exaggerates to develop the element of the comic or the ludicrous in a person or a situation; the satirist exaggerates because he faces formidable opposition in his readers, who are not anxious to hear unpleasant truths and who frequently have been taught that these unpleasant truths do not actually exist.

So both the humorist and the satirist observe the dissimulation, the pretense, the hypocrisy of individuals and institutions. The humorist accepts these as natural; he reports them, perhaps even with love. The satirist reacts against them: there is indeed something rotten in Denmark. One of his chief weapons is irony, for by its very nature irony presents values which the reader will eventually, if not immediately, find unacceptable. It is again the contrast between people and things as they are and as we pretend they are. Presented with sympathy, the report is likely to be humorous; presented as a searchlight on reality, as a dispeller of illusion, it will have satiric intent.

SEX IS DEAD!

Earl H. Brill

Sex is dead. Nobody seems to have noticed its passing, what with the distraction caused by recent reports of the death of God, the death of Self, the death of the City, the death of Tragedy, and all the other cultural obituaries of that past few years. Yet it is a fact: sex is dead and we must begin to learn how to live in a world in which that is an incontrovertible fact.   1

There are numerous signs of the death of sex, particularly on the college campus. In recent years there has been a marked decline in the traditional preoccupation of college students with sex. Sex used to be the favorite topic of campus discussions, the chief bone of contention between students and administrators. But in the past decade its place has been usurped: first by the civil rights movement,   2
then by the student "freedom movement," the drive for participatory democracy on the campus. This year, war—or rather antiwar—seems to be the chief topic on the campus agenda. In any case, sex as a central concern of the "college student" has been running a poor third at best.

Look for example at the way college girls dress. The short short skirt made the springtime campus blossom into a veritable skin show (at least by the standards of my own youth). You might suppose that   3
this indicates an increasing sex-consciousness, but you would be quite mistaken: it means the very opposite.

For in fact the creeping nudity of female fashions goes quite unnoticed by the young men. To most of them it doesn't occur to give a second look at a well-turned thigh. Not so with their elders. I have been conducting a little poll among my colleagues and it seems that they (let's be honest—*we*) are the overage beneficiaries of the   4
new landscape. We were brought up in the sexual age and we still keep the faith. But the young men fail to appreciate the aesthetic delights of their environment. It is all quite meaningless to them, because sex is dead.

"But ah," you say, "every spring, every fall, whenever the air is balmy and wherever the grass is soft, the campus boys and girls pair off for the same old sensuous wrestling matches. Every year, in fact, the lovers seem to get bolder and bolder." You are quite right, of course. A senior administrator of my acquaintance, a few years ago,   5
was forced to suspend a young man who had been observed studying female anatomy, apparently by the Braille system, on the grass just in front of the administration building. "I wasn't trying to interfere

with his love life," the dean explained. "I just got tired of intruding into this seduction scene every time I turned toward my window."

Yet a curious paradox emerges upon inspection of the apparent increase in such uninhibited behavior. There was a time when the campus idol and the campus sweetheart—the aggressive and the lovely, the healthy and the attractive—were the lovers-on-the-lawn. Lately, though, it is rather the homely and the odd who do the biological wrestling: scrawny, pimply-faced boys—the kind Holden Caulfield would have called "hard-up guys"—and fat and frowsy girls   6 who need have no fear of walking across the campus alone at midnight. They create a picture not of two healthy, lusty animals reveling in their sexuality and their freedom but of two scared and unhappy young people leaning on each other, compulsively clawing at each other as if to say to themselves, to each other and to the world: "See! We know the game! We can play too." The rituals go on, but they have lost any conviction because sex is dead.

It doesn't take a profound social analyst to demonstrate the basic asexuality of the world of fashion. Flip through *Vogue* or even the fashion pages of your local newspaper and you will see sample after sample of square, shapeless, angular dresses that resolutely deny that they cover warm, soft, curvy female flesh. Look at the with-it haircuts that make women appear ascetic and severe and the man look   7 wan and languid. It's not enough to counter that fashion merely reflects the commercial demand for rapid and dramatic change that will sell new wardrobes every year. The question is, Why should this kind of fashion become the rage at this point in our history? The answer? Sex is dead.

Certainly pop music and the style of dancing that goes with it testify to the death of sex. Whatever else you say about the insistent beat, the strident voices, the primitive tonal patterns, you cannot   8 contend that they add up to sexy music. It is intense music, to be sure, but for all its vigor it is a music without real passion. It may arouse the adrenalin but not the libido.

As numerous observers have pointed out, pop music accompanies a style of dancing that is just as astringent as the music. The movements, like the women's fashions in *Vogue,* are all angles—jerks and twists. This dancing is athletic but hardly suggestive. It keeps people apart rather than wrapping them up in each other. A cartoon many years ago showed a proper Englishman watching an American dance   9 floor where one of the particularly erotic routines of the day was being performed. The visitor was saying: "And after this, I presume they get married?" You can't imagine a foreigner responding in quite

that way even to the most enthusiastic performance of the disco-
theque set.

Perhaps the most convincing illustration of the death of sex
comes out of an insight of Marshall McLuhan, who has been teaching
us new ways to look at our environment. McLuhan, speaking of the
relationship of technology to culture, points out that every new   10
technology creates a new environment which translates the old environment into an art form. Once the old environment no longer
surrounds us totally, it becomes visible. That's why we put Model-T
Fords into museums.

Now just stretch this observation over a wider area of culture and
apply it to sex. When sex was truly a total preoccupation, our major
concern was to become free so that we could express ourselves sexu-   11
ally. We tried to fight repressions, inhibitions and conventional restrictions.

But in recent years, sex has become an art form. We buy quanti-
ties of how-to-do-it books; we construct models of Adequate Sexual
Behavior and try desperately to conform to the images we have
constructed. The development of sex as art form probably reached
its culmination with the recent publication of *The Human Sexual
Response,* by William H. Masters and Virginia E. Johnson (Little,
Brown), which describes in meticulous detail how the sexual act is
carried out, how the body temperature changes, the pulse rate increases, the muscles tense. Imaginative writers have frequently de-   12
scribed the accompaniment to heterosexual genital activity with such
phrases as "her pulses quickened" or "he was sweating like a stal-
lion." Now we are given chapter and verse, number and sequence.
Now, perhaps, we can construct from the data the Perfect Sex Act
and get it preserved for all time in silver at the National Bureau of
Standards. Or perhaps, if it is to be generally accepted as a true art
form, the model ought to be exhibited in the Museum of Modern
Art.

I consider the case for the death of sex as proved, though of
course I concede that there is still a lot of sex around. Babies are
born every day, not all of them conceived by artificial insemination.
People still claim to fall in love and young men and women still take
sexual problems to their pastors. Plays and novels are still expected
to include a predictable amount of good clean sex. Movie ads con-   13
tinue to feature busty chicks in various stages of dishabille, whether
or not the film delivers what it promises. Indeed, much of today's
advertising is still predicated on the question that Philip Wylie (re-

member him?) ascribed to it years ago: "Madam, are you a good lay?" If sex is dead, it is a very lively corpse, as the saying goes.

This line of argument might be more convincing had it not already been effectively answered in another context: by the death-of-God theologians. How can God be dead when there is so much activity in the churches? Easy. Church activity is merely a substitute for an absent God. What we see is not deep religion but shallow religiosity. Religiosity is not faith but only the continuation of a pattern of activity that once, perhaps, had significance but is now merely formal and conventional, routine observance on the part of people who just haven't yet heard that God is dead. 14

The same with sex. What seems to flourish is only a set of activities that once meant the presence of sex but does so no longer. We might call it "sexiosity": the perpetuation of routine sexual activities which lack conviction and meaning. Sexiosity is characteristic of people out of another era, people who are not in the know, people who have not heard that sex is dead. 15

Note the way that sex is normally used in the novel, in the theater, in the movies today. Entertainment sexiosity is neither lusty nor joyful. It is a Big Problem. It gets out of hand. It makes people unhappy. Looking back through the years, you find that every new breakthrough in the treatment of sex in literature or drama has soon produced boredom and indifference. Hence writers have had to resort to more and more exotic forms of sex to keep interest alive. Fornication gave way to adultery, which was followed in quick succession by homosexuality, incest, rape and sado-masochism. And once Tennessee Williams had treated us to the spectacle of cannibalism, it was pretty hard to find a topper. 16

What does all this prove? I ask you. If sex were alive and vital, wouldn't the portrayal of ordinary, normal, healthy sexuality be attractive enough to keep people coming back for more without the need to probe constantly into increasingly esoteric perversions? Doesn't the need to range so far afield in the search for kicks indicate that there's nothing there, at the center of concern? Doesn't it suggest that our so-called preoccupation with sex is a great big myth? I think it does. 17

Well then, what about *Playboy*, the bible of sex-culture? Sells pretty well, doesn't it? What about those pages and pages of big, bare-breasted beauties in glorious living color? Are the boys buying *Playboy* for the interviews? 18

Good question, but too easy, really. *Playboy* is simply the house organ of the fundamentalists of sexiosity. It shouts, "Sex is alive! It is! It is!" It shouts so loud that you wonder whether it believes itself. Hugh Hefner figures as the Billy Graham of sexiosity. He is trying to preserve the remnants of an irrelevant and dying faith. He won't   19 succeed, of course, but meantime there is a buck to be made. People whose faith has been shaken are well known to be generous in rewarding the master who makes an energetic attempt to support them in what they want to believe.

Remember the old *Esquire* magazine, the *Playboy* of a generation ago? *Esquire* was hairy enough to get into trouble with the post office department during the Truman administration. Then it decided to acquire class. It hired a few first-rate writers and journalists to do its material, and what happened? Within a few years people were reading the articles instead of looking at the pictures. Today you can hardly find a decent filthy picture in the whole magazine. I predict that *Playboy* will follow the same route. Already people are   20 actually beginning to read some of the material that Hefner puts in for padding. Of course, Hefner won't take the girls out of the pages of *Playboy;* he's too old. But the next generation will. By the time the present college generation has reached the age of ancients like Hefner and me, the death of sex will be an acknowledged fact and no magazine editor in his right mind will waste money on models posing in the buff. That kind of thing won't sell—except of course to a handful of diehard sexiosity fundamentalists.

What does it mean for us to recognize that sex is dead? What difference it will make? I confess I don't know. I suspect that as we demythologize sex, we will find that we have lost a lot of our anxiety. Maybe then parents and preachers will come to realize that they have been fighting a shadow. Maybe young people will discover the ephemeral nature of the will-o'-the-wisp they have been taught to   21 pursue. Maybe Madison Avenue will disappear in a puff of smoke. Maybe creative writers will go back to writing creatively about creative things. Maybe all the sexologists will go back to earning an honest living. Maybe we will begin to see what are the really live issues of our time.

But a lot of us in the plus-30 category will have to admit that we feel a sense of loss. Sex may have been a big bugaboo, it may have   22 brought problems, anxieties, frustrations and controversy, but it was a lot of fun while it lasted.

WHAT COLLEGE DID TO ME
An Outline of Education
Robert Benchley

My college education was no haphazard affair. My courses were all selected with a very definite aim in view, with a serious purpose in mind—no classes before eleven in the morning or after two-thirty in the afternoon, and nothing on Saturday at all. That was my slogan. On that rock was my education built.

As what is known as the Classical Course involved practically no afternoon laboratory work, whereas in the Scientific Course a man's time was never his own until four p. m. anyway, I went in for the classic. But only such classics as allowed for a good sleep in the morning. A man has his health to think of. There is such a thing as being a studying fool.

In my days (I was a classmate of the founder of the college) a student could elect to take any courses in the catalogue, provided no two of his choices came at the same hour. The only things he was not supposed to mix were Scotch and gin. This was known as the Elective System. Now I understand that the boys have to have, during the four years, at least three courses beginning with the same letter. This probably makes it very awkward for those who like to get away of a Friday afternoon for the week-end.

Under the Elective System my schedule was somwhat as follows:

Mondays, Wednesdays and Fridays at 11:00:
    Botany 2a (The History of Flowers and Their Meaning)
Tuesdays and Thursdays at 11:00:
    English 26 (The Social Life of the Minor Sixteenth Century Poets)
Mondays, Wednesdays and Fridays at 12:00:
    Music 9 (History and Appreciation of the Clavichord)
Tuesdays and Thursdays at 12:00:
    German 12b (Early Minnesingers—Walter von Vogelweider, Ulric Glannsdorf and Freimann von Stremhofen, Their Songs and Times)
Mondays, Wednesdays and Fridays at 1:30:
    Fine Arts 6 (Doric Columns: Their Uses, History and Various Heights)
Tuesdays and Thursdays at 1:30:
    French Ic (Exceptions to the verb *être*)

This was, of course, just one year's work. The next year I followed these courses up with supplementary courses in the history of lace-making, Russian taxation systems before Catharine the Great, North American glacial deposits and Early Renaissance etchers.

This gave me a general idea of the progress of civilization and a certain practical knowledge which has stood me in good stead in thousands of ways since my graduation.

My system of studying was no less strict. In lecture courses I had my notebooks so arranged that one-half of the page could be devoted to drawings of five-pointed stars (exquisitely shaded), girls' heads, and tick-tack-toe. Some of the drawings in my economics notebook in the course on Early English Trade Winds were the finest things I have ever done. One of them was a whole tree (an oak) with every leaf in perfect detail. Several instructors commented on my work in this field.

These notes I would take home after the lecture, together with whatever supplementary reading the course called for. Notes and textbooks would then be placed on a table under a strong lamplight. Next came the sharpening of pencils, which would take perhaps fifteen minutes. I had some of the best sharpened pencils in college. These I placed on the table beside the notes and books.

At this point it was necessary to light a pipe, which involved going to the table where the tobacco was. As it so happened, on the same table was a poker hand, all dealt, lying in front of a vacant chair. Four other chairs were oddly enough occupied by students, also preparing to study. It therefore resolved itself into something of a seminar, or group conference, on the courses under discussion. For example, the first student would say:

"I can't open."

The second student would perhaps say the same thing.

The third student would say: "I'll open for fifty cents."

And the seminar would be on.

At the end of the seminar, I would go back to my desk, pile the notes and books on top of each other, put the light out, and go to bed, tired but happy in the realization that I had not only spent the evening busily but had helped put four of my friends through college.

An inventory of stock acquired at college discloses the following bits of culture and erudition which have nestled in my mind after all these years.

Things I Learned Freshman Year

1. Charlemagne either died or was born or did something with the Holy Roman Empire in 800.

2. By placing one paper bag inside another paper bag you can carry home a milk shake in it.

3. There is a double 1 in the middle of "parallel."

4. Powder rubbed on the chin will take the place of a shave if the room isn't very light.

5. French nouns ending in "aison" are feminine.

6. Almost everything you need to know about a subject is in the encyclopedia.

7. A tasty sandwich can be made by spreading peanut butter on raisin bread.

8. A floating body displaces its own weight in the liquid in which it floats.

9. A sock with a hole in the toe can be worn inside out with comparative comfort.

10. The chances are against filling an inside straight.

11. There is a law in economics called *The Law of Diminishing Returns,* which means that after a certain margin is reached returns begin to diminish. This may not be correctly stated, but there *is* a law by that name.

12. You begin tuning a mandolin with A and tune the other strings from that.

Sophomore Year

1. A good imitation of measles rash can be effected by stabbing the forearm with a stiff whisk-broom.

2. Queen Elizabeth was not above suspicion.

3. In Spanish you pronounce z like th.

4. Nine-tenths of the girls in a girls' college are not pretty.

5. You can sleep undetected in a lecture course by resting the head on the hand as if shading the eyes.

6. Weakness in drawing technique can be hidden by using a wash instead of black and white line.

7. Quite a respectable bun can be acquired by smoking three or four pipefuls of strong tobacco when you have no food in your stomach.

8. The ancient Phœnicians were really Jews, and got as far north as England where they operated tin mines.

9. You can get dressed much quicker in the morning if the night before when you are going to bed you take off your trousers and underdrawers at once, leaving the latter inside the former.

Junior Year

1. Emerson left his pastorate because he had some argument about communion.

2. All women are untrustworthy.

3. Pushing your arms back as far as they will go fifty times each day increases your chest measurement.

4. Marcus Aurelius had a son who turned out to be a bad boy.

5. Eight hours of sleep are not necessary.   14

6. Heraclitus believed that fire was the basis of all life.

7. A good way to keep your trousers pressed is to hang them from the bureau drawer.

8. The chances are that you will never fill an inside straight.

9. The Republicans believe in a centralized government, the Democrats in a de-centralized one.

10. It is not necessarily effeminate to drink tea.

Senior Year

1. A dinner coat looks better than full dress.

2. There is as yet no law determining what constitutes trespass in an airplane.

3. Six hours of sleep are not necessary.

4. Bicarbonate of soda taken before retiring makes you feel better the next day.   15

5. You needn't be fully dressed if you wear a cap and gown to a nine-o'clock recitation.

6. Theater tickets may be charged.

7. Flowers may be charged.

8. May is the shortest month in the year.

The foregoing outline of my education is true enough in its way, and is what people like to think about a college course. It has become quite the cynical thing to admit laughingly that college did one no good. It is part of the American Credo that all that the college   16
student learns is to catch punts and dance. I had to write something

like that to satisfy the editors. As a matter of fact, I learned a great deal in college and have those four years to thank for whatever I know today.

(The above note was written to satisfy those of my instructors and financial backers who may read this. As a matter of fact, the original outline is true, and I had to look up the date about Charlemagne at that.)

17

TWO BY BUCHWALD
Art Buchwald

"I Don't Know"

As student demonstrations on campuses continue, the demands
of the militants keep escalating. Some of the demands are reasonable,
but others have built-in mousetraps. A few that I question have to do
with student demands that universities take in people whether   1
they're qualified or not, that all students who have flunked out be
allowed to return to school, and that professors abolish the system of
grading students for their courses.

I believe that in the liberal arts departments you might not have
to be too much concerned about high standards—you've seen one   2
economics professor, you've seen them all—but it's in the sciences
and professions that you can get a little tensed up.

If our future doctors, lawyers, engineers, and scientists no longer
have to face stiff qualifying examinations, or if the schools refuse to   3
grade them on their abilities, some very weird situations might arise.

A patient goes into a doctor's office.

"What seems to be the trouble?" the doctor asks.

"I have a pain in my side, doctor."

"I don't know anything about pains in the side."

"I thought you were a medical doctor. At least that diploma says
so."

"Are you some kind of a racist?"

"No. I'm a patient."   4

"Well, it so happens I am a medical doctor. I just didn't do very
well in anatomy. Never cared much for it. As a matter of fact, we
locked up the dean of the medical school until he agreed to drop
anatomy as a required course. We got him to do away with biology,
also."

"But if you didn't like anatomy or biology, why did you become
an M.D.?"

"A man has to be something."

Meanwhile, across town, a man was being tried for first-degree
murder and his lawyer and he were listening to the prosecutor.

"I want you, ladies and gentlemen, to send this man to the
chair."

The defendant turns to his lawyer and asks, "Can he do that to
me?"

The lawyer shrugs. "Beats hell out of me."

"But you're my lawyer. Don't you know what the law says?"

"I never told anyone this before, but I never really cared much for law. Matter of fact, all during school I had this girl and she had an apartment and . . . "

"Look, I don't care about your girl. My life is at stake. If I lose, will you at least make an appeal?"

"What's an appeal? You start studying about all this legal mumbo-jumbo in college and you won't have any social life at all."

"But the law says . . . " the defendant cried.

"What does the law say? And don't go too fast because I want to write all this down. I never did take notes in school."

The third scene could take place 20 years from now at the new Mayor John V. Lindsay Bridge connecting Long Island with Connecticut.

The engineer is standing on the platform with the dignitaries.

"Well, Mr. Doubleday, you built a mighty fine bridge."

"That's my job."

"It seems to be sagging at one end. Is that the way it's supposed to be?"

"I'll build the bridges—you cut the ribbon."

"Look, there goes the first truck over the bridge—it's falling. DOUBLEDAY, THE ENTIRE BRIDGE IS FALLING!"

"Sorry about that. I never could figure out how to use a slide rule."

Confrontation is Something a Professor Must Face Up To

Prof. Harvery Yoicks, Wimbledon professor of English studies at Bitter U., said he could only talk to me for a few moments about the new biography of Ernest Hemingway. When I came into his office he apologized.

"I'd love to talk to you about the Hemingway book, but unfortunately I have a confrontation with the students for an Uptight University at 3 o'clock and then another confrontation with the Afro-Polish Society at 4. Then there is a faculty meeting at 6 for the Ad Hoc Committee to Liberate the Dean, which is followed by an anti-war rally I have to attend at 9 to defend the English department's use of Tolstoy's 'War and Peace' as a textbook."

"If you're too busy today," I said, "I'll see you tomorrow."

Prof. Yoicks looked at his calender. "I'm afraid tomorrow doesn't look any better. I have a confrontation at 8 o'clock in the Student Union with the Students Against Tomorrow. And there is a possibility that I will be called upon at noon as a mediator in a dispute over the faculty parking lot which the Radicals for Smaller Cars want abolished. Now, what did you want to ask me about Hemingway?"

"Well, Professor, as one of the outstanding experts on . . . " The phone rang and Yoicks picked it up. I tried not to overhear, but it was impossible not to listen. "Yes, Sir. You want me to attend the confrontation on Thursday with the Students for Lower Grades? I have a class at 3. Well, you see, Sir, I canceled Monday, Tuesday and Wednesday's classes. I thought I might turn up Thursday and lecture,   4 just to keep my hand in. You consider this more important? All right, I'll cancel the class. Yes, Sir." He hung up, and then pushed a buzzer. "Miss Samuels, would you make a note that I have a confrontation on Thursday at 3 o'clock with the Students for Lower Grades."

Miss Samuels' voice came over the speaker. "But, Professor, you have a previous confrontation with the Moderate Radicals for a Restructured Renaissance Studies Program."

"We'll have to postpone that confrontation. The president wants me at the SLG confrontation instead."

Miss Samuels said, "Prof. Barley of the International School wants to know if you're keeping Friday open for the confrontation   5 with the Graduate Instructors Grievance Committee."

"Damn, I forgot about that. What have I got on Friday?"

"You have a confrontation with the Inter-Fraternity Headbusters Organization, the Che Guevara Amnesty Committee and the Ho Chi Minh Revolutionary Movement."

"Tell Barley I'll try to make part of his confrontation, but I won't be able to stay if there is a sit-in."

Yoicks turned to me. "Sorry about the interruption. Let me see. You wanted to know about Hemingway. I found Hemingway a very   6 interesting character. He probably left more of a mark . . . "

A brick crashed through the window with a note on it. Yoicks went over to pick it up. He read the note and said, "The New Left Anti-Defamation League wants me for a confrontation on Saturday. I was hoping to get some papers marked over the weekend."

"There's always Sunday," I said.   7

"No good. On Sunday I promised to meet with some students who want to abolish the Fourth of July."

"For an English professor, you seem to be quite busy."

"It's all part of the teaching game," he said wearily.

Miss Samuels came in excitedly. "Professor, there is a group of students outside who want an immediate confrontation with you."

"You know I'm all booked up for confrontations. Who are they?"

"They're your students from your English literature course and they demand to know when you're coming back to class."

Prof. Yoicks said, "Inform them that I'll try to be in class a week from Wednesday. In the meantime, tell them to reread 'Twenty-Thousand Leagues Under the Sea.' "

A MODEST PROPOSAL
Jonathan Swift

*For Preventing the Children of Poor People From Bening A Burden to
Their Parents or Country, and for Making Them Beneficial to the Public*

It is a melancholy object to those who walk through this great
town, or travel in the country, when they see the streets, the roads,
and cabin-doors crowded with beggars of the female sex, followed by
three, four, or six children, *all in rags,* and importuning every passen-
ger for an alms. These mothers, instead of being able to work for   1
their honest livelihood, are forced to employ all their time in stroll-
ing, to beg sustenance for their helpless infants, who, as they grow
up, either turn thieves for want of work, or leave their dear Native
Country to fight for the Pretender in Spain, or sell themselves to the
Barbadoes.

I think it is agreed by all parties that this prodigious number of
children, in the arms, or on the backs, or at the heels of their
mothers, and frequently of their fathers, is in the present deplorable
state of the kingdom a very great additional grievance; and therefore   2
whoever could find out a fair, cheap, and easy method of making
these children sound useful members of the commonwealth would
deserve so well of the public as to have his statue set up for a
preserver of the nation.

But my intention is very far from being confined to provide only
for the children of professed beggars; it is of a much greater extent,
and shall take in the whole number of infants at a certain age who   3
are born of parents in effect as little able to support them as those
who demand our charity in the streets.

As to my own part, having turned my thoughts, for many years,
upon this important subject, and maturely weighed the several
schemes of other projectors, I have always found them grossly mistaken in their computation. It is true a child, just dropped from its
dam, may be supported by her milk for a solar year with little other
nourishment, at most not above the value of two shillings, which the   4
mother may certainly get, or the value in scraps, by her lawful occupation of begging, and it is exactly at one year old that I propose to
provide for them, in such a manner as, instead of being a charge upon
their parents, or the parish, or wanting food and raiment for the rest
of their lives, they shall, on the contrary, contribute to the feeding
and partly to the clothing of many thousands.

There is likewise another great advantage in my scheme, that it
will prevent those voluntary abortions, and that horrid practice of

women murdering their bastard children, alas, too frequent among   5
us, sacrificing the poor innocent babes, I doubt, more to avoid the
expense than the shame, which would move tears and pity in the
most savage and inhuman breast.

The number of souls in this kingdom being usually reckoned one
million and a half, of these I calculate there may be about two
hundred thousand couple whose wives are breeders, from which
number I subtract thirty thousand couple who are able to maintain
their own children, although I apprehend there cannot be so many
under the present distresses of the kingdom, but this being granted,
there will remain an hundred and seventy thousand breeders. I again
subtract fifty thousand for those women who miscarry, or whose
children die by accident or disease within the year. There only remain an hundred and twenty thousand children of poor parents
annually born: The question therefore is, how this number shall be
reared, and provided for, which, as I have already said, under the   6
present situation of affairs, is utterly impossible by all the methods
hitherto proposed, for we can neither employ them in handicraft, or
agriculture; we neither build houses (I mean in the country), nor
cultivate land: they can very seldom pick up a livelihood by stealing
till they arrive at six years old, except where they are of towardly
parts, although, I confess they learn the rudiments much earlier,
during which time they can however be properly looked upon only
as *probationers,* as I have been informed by a principal gentleman in
the County of Cavan, who protested to me that he never knew above
one or two instances under the age of six, even in a part of the
kingdom so renowned for the quickest proficiency in that art.

I am assured by our merchants that a boy or a girl, before twelve
years old, is no saleable commodity, and even when they come to
this age, they will not yield above three pounds, or three pounds and   7
half-a-crown at most on the Exchange, which cannot turn to account
either to the parents or the kingdom, the charge of nutriment and
rags having been at least four times that value.

I shall now therefore humbly propose my own thoughts, which I   8
hope will not be liable to the least objection.

I have been assured by a very knowing American of my acquaintance in London, that a young healthy child well nursed is at a year
old a most delicious, nourishing, and wholesome food, whether   9
stewed, roasted, baked, or boiled, and I make no doubt that it will
equally serve in a fricassee, or a ragout.

I do therefore humbly offer it to public consideration, that of
the hundred and twenty thousand children already computed,

twenty thousand may be reserved for breed, whereof only one fourth part to be males, which is more than we allow to sheep, black-cattle, or swine, and my reason is that these children are seldom the fruits of marriage, a circumstance not much regarded by our savages, therefore one male will be sufficient to serve four females. That the remaining hundred thousand may at a year old be offered in sale to the   10 persons of quality, and fortune, through the kingdom, always advising the mother to let them suck plentifully in the last month, so as to render them plump, and fat for a good table. A child will make two dishes at an entertainment for friends, and when the family dines alone, the fore or hind quarter will make a reasonable dish, and seasoned with a little pepper or salt will be very good boiled on the fourth day, especially in winter.

I have reckoned upon a medium, that a child just born will weigh 12 pounds, and in a solar year if tolerably nursed increaseth to 28   11 pounds.

I grant this food will be somewhat dear, and therefore very proper for landlords, who, as they have already devoured most of the   12 parents, seem to have the best title to the children.

Infants' flesh will be in season throughout the year, but more plentiful in March, and a little before and after, for we are told by a grave author, an eminent French physician, that fish being a prolific diet, there are more children born in Roman Catholic countries about nine months after Lent than at any other season; therefore   13 reckoning a year after Lent, the markets will be more glutted than usual, because the number of Popish infants is at least three to one in this kingdom, and therefore it will have one other collateral advantage by lessening the number of Papists among us.

I have already computed the charge of nursing a beggar's child (in which list I reckon all cottagers, labourers, and four-fifths of the farmers) to be about two shillings *per annum,* rags included, and I believe no gentleman would repine to give ten shillings for the carcass of a good fat child, which, as I have said, will make four dishes of   14 excellent nutritive meat, when he hath only some particular friend or his own family to dine with him. Thus the Squire will learn to be a good landlord, and grow popular among his tenants, the mother will have eight shillings net profit, and be fit for work till she produces another child.

Those who are more thrifty (as I must confess the times require) may flay the carcass; the skin of which, artificially dressed, will make   15 admirable gloves for ladies, and summer boots for fine gentlemen.

As to our City of Dublin, shambles may be appointed for this purpose, in the most convenient parts of it, and butchers we may be assured will not be wanting, although I rather recommend buying the children alive, and dressing them hot from the knife, as we do roasting pigs. 16

A very worthy person, a true lover of this country, and whose virtues I highly esteem, was lately pleased, in discoursing on this matter, to offer a refinement upon my scheme. He said that many gentlemen of this kingdom, having of late destroyed their deer, he conceived that the want of venison might be well supplied by the bodies of young lads and maidens, not exceeding fourteen years of age, nor under twelve, so great a number of both sexes in every country being now ready to starve, for want of work and service: and these to be disposed of by their parents if alive, or otherwise by their nearest relations. But with due deference to so excellent a friend, and so deserving a patriot, I cannot be altogether in his sentiments; for as 17
to the males, my American acquaintance assured me from frequent experience that their flesh was generally tough and lean, like that of our schoolboys, by continual exercise, and their taste disagreeable, and to fatten them would not answer the charge. Then as to the females, it would, I think with humble submission, be a loss to the public, because they soon would become breeders themselves: And besides, it is not improbable that some scrupulous people might be apt to censure such a practice (although indeed very unjustly) as a little bordering upon cruelty, which, I confess, hath always been with me the strongest objection against any project, however so well intended.

But in order to justify my friend, he confessed that this expedient was put into his head by the famous Psalmanazar, a native of the island Formosa, who came from thence to London, above twenty years ago, and in conversation told my friend that in his country when any young person happened to be put to death, the executioner sold the carcass to persons of quality, as a prime dainty, and that, in his time, the body of a plump girl of fifteen, who was crucified for an attempt to poison the emperor, was sold to his 18
Imperial Majesty's Prime Minister of State, and other great Mandarins of the Court, in joints from the gibbet, at four hundred crowns. Neither indeed can I deny that if the same use were made of several plump young girls in this town, who, without one single groat to their fortunes, cannot stir abroad without a chair, and appear at the

playhouse, and assemblies in foreign fineries, which they never will pay for, the kingdom would not be the worse.

Some persons of a desponding spirit are in great concern about that vast number of poor people, who are aged, diseased, or maimed, and I have been desired to employ my thoughts what course may be taken to ease the nation of so grievous an encumbrance. But I am not in the least pain upon that matter, because it is very well known that they are every day dying, and rotting, by cold, and famine, and filth, and vermin, as fast as can be reasonably expected. And as to the younger labourers they are now in almost as hopeful a condition. They cannot get work, and consequently pine away for want of nourishment, to a degree, that if at any time they are accidentally hired to common labour, they have not strength to perform it; and thus the country and themselves are happily delivered from the evils to come.

I have too long digressed, and therefore shall return to my subject. I think the advantages by the proposal which I have made are obvious and many, as well as of the highest importance.

For first, as I have already observed, it would greatly lessen the number of Papists, with whom we are yearly over-run, being the principal breeders of the nation, as well as our most dangerous enemies, and who stay at home on purpose with a design to deliver the kingdom to the Pretender, hoping to take their advantage by the absence of so many good Protestants, who have chosen rather to leave their country than stay at home, and pay tithes against their conscience to an Episcopal curate.

Secondly, the poorer tenants will have something valuable of their own, which by law be made liable to distress, and help to pay their landlord's rent, their corn and cattle being already seized, and *money a thing unknown.*

Thirdly, Whereas the maintenance of an hundred thousand children, from two years old, and upwards, cannot be computed at less than ten shillings a piece *per annum,* the nation's stock will be thereby increased fifty thousand pounds *per annum,* besides the profit of a new dish, introduced to the tables of all gentlemen of fortune in the kingdom, who have any refinement in taste, and the money will circulate among ourselves, the goods being entirely of our own growth and manufacture.

Fourthly, The constant breeders, besides the gain of eight shillings sterling *per annum,* by the sale of their children, will be rid of the charge of maintaining them after the first year.

Fifthly, This food would likewise bring great custom to taverns, where the vintners will certainly be so prudent as to procure the best receipts for dressing it to perfection, and consequently have their houses frequented by all the fine gentlemen, who justly value them- 25 selves upon their knowledge in good eating; and a skilful cook, who understands how to oblige his guests, will contrive to make it as expensive as they please.

Sixthly, This would be a great inducement to marriage, which all wise nations have either encouraged by rewards, or enforced by laws and penalties. It would increase the care and tenderness of mothers toward their children, when they were sure of a settlement for life, to the poor babes, provided in some sort by the public to their annual profit instead of expense. We should see an honest emulation 26 among the married women, which of them could bring the fattest child to the market, men would become as fond of their wives, during the time of their pregnancy, as they are now of their mares in foal, their cows in calf, or sows when they are ready to farrow, nor offer to beat or kick them (as it is too frequent a practice) for fear of a miscarriage.

Many other advantages might be enumerated: For instance, the addition of some thousand carcasses in our exportation of barrelled beef; the propagation of swine's flesh, and improvement in the art of making good bacon, so much wanted among us by the great destruc- tion of pigs, too frequent at our tables, which are no way comparable 27 in taste or magnificence to a well-grown, fat yearling child, which roasted whole will make a considerable figure at a Lord Mayor's feast, or any other public entertainment. But this and many others I omit, being studious of brevity.

Supposing that one thousand families in this city would be constant customers for infants' flesh, besides others who might have it at merry-meetings, particularly weddings and christenings, I compute 28 that Dublin would take off annually about twenty thousand carcasses, and the rest of the kingdom (where probably they will be sold somewhat cheaper) the remaining eighty thousand.

I can think of no one objection that will possibly be raised against this proposal, unless it should be urged that the number of people will be thereby much lessened in the kingdom. This I freely own, and was indeed one principal design in offering it to the world. I desire the reader will observe, that I calculate my remedy for this one individual *Kingdom of Ireland, and for no other that ever was, is, or, I think, ever can be upon earth.* Therefore let no man talk to me of other expedients: *Of taxing our absentees at five shillings a pound: Of using neither clothes, nor household furniture, except what is of our own growth and manufacture: Of utterly rejecting the materials and instruments that promote foreign luxury: Of curing the expensiveness of pride, vanity, idleness, and gaming in our women: Of introducing a vein of parsimony, prudence, and temperance: Of* 29 *learning to love our Country, wherein we differ even from* LAP- LANDERS, *and the inhabitants of* TOPINAMBOO: *Of quitting our animosities and factions, nor act any longer like the Jews, who were murdering one another at the very moment their city was taken: Of being a little cautious not to sell our country and consciences for nothing: Of teaching landlords to have at least one degree of mercy toward their tenants. Lastly, of putting a spirit of honesty, industry, and skill into our shopkeepers, who, if a resolution could now be taken to buy only our native goods, would immediately unite to cheat and exact upon us in the price, the measure, and the goodness, nor could ever yet be brought to make one fair proposal of just dealing, though often and earnestly invited to it.*

Therefore I repeat, let no man talk to me of these and the like expedients, till he hath at least some glimpse of hope that there will 30 ever be some hearty and sincere attempt to put them in practice.

But as to myself, having been wearied out for many years with offering vain, idle, visionary thoughts, and at length utterly despairing of success, I fortunately fell upon this proposal, which as it is wholly new, so it hath something solid and real, of no expense and little trouble, full in our own power, and whereby we can incur no 31 danger in *disobliging* ENGLAND. For this kind of commodity will not bear exportation, the flesh being of too tender a consistence to admit a long continuance in salt, *although perhaps I could name a country which would be glad to eat up our whole nation without it.*

After all I am not so violently bent upon my own opinion as to reject any offer, proposed by wise men, which shall be found equally innocent, cheap, easy, and effectual. But before something of that kind shall be advanced in contradiction to my scheme, and offering a better, I desire the author, or authors, will be pleased maturely to consider two points. First, as things now stand, how they will be able to find food and raiment for an hundred thousand useless mouths and backs. And secondly, there being a round million of creatures in human figure, throughout this kingdom, whose whole subsistence put into a common stock would leave them in debt two millions of pounds sterling; adding those, who are beggars by profession, to the bulk of farmers, cottagers, and labourers with their wives and chil- 32 dren, who are beggars in effect. I desire those politicians, who dislike my overture, and may perhaps be so bold to attempt an answer, that they will first ask the parents of these mortals whether they would not at this day think it a great happiness to have been sold for food at a year old, in the manner I prescribe, and thereby have avoided such a perpetual scene of misfortunes as they have since gone through, by the oppression of landlords, the impossibility of paying rent without money or trade, the want of common sustenance, with neither house nor clothes to cover them from the inclemencies of the weather, and the most inevitable prospect of entailing the like, or greater miseries upon their breed for ever.

I profess in the sincerity of my heart that I have not the least personal interest in endeavouring to promote this necessary work, having no other motive than the *public good of my country, by advancing our trade, providing for infants, relieving the poor, and giving some pleasure to the rich.* I have no children by which I can propose to get a single penny; the youngest being nine years old, and my wife past child-bearing.

REPORTING

When we think of reporting we think primarily of the news media: of the newspaper, television, and radio. We think of the communication of objective facts which will increase our knowledge and our awareness of the world about us. But the essay report, as opposed to the standard news story, is more than a listing of *who? what? when? where? why?* and *how?* in the petrified form which is referred to as news-writing. The essay report is a literary, as opposed to a journalistic, presentation of facts. It usually implies research: it depends on background for its meaning. It is generally interpretative: it explains and it clarifies.

All good reporting is accurate. The facts are clearly and concisely presented in language which is denotative (words with explicit meanings, rather than connotative language, something suggested by words). The reporter-essayist is expected to be objective, although he may report subjective approaches to his topic. Even so, the reporter-essayist is not likely to be completely objective, for there is no way of knowing absolute truth in this world. It will be better to expect the reporter to be honest, to deal honestly with the facts before him and their background. On this honesty all good reporting depends.

The essayist who writes to inform must deal not only with the facts but with their significance. He analyzes the facts; he compares them with similar facts; he searches for motives; he considers results. He is not the ordinary reporter of the Labor Day parade but a specialist who has both the ability and the background to interpret the meaning of the facts he presents. The subject of "Spinning the Thread of Life," by John Lear, is complex indeed. The reporter of that subject is a specialist who can make his report vivid and exciting for the layman.

SPINNING THE THREAD OF LIFE

John Lear

I never expected to see the thread of life, the mysterious stuff that poets conjured long ago to explain the passage of the heartbeat from generation to generation across the eons.

1

Yet today the thread lies clearly visible before me, under the lens of an electron microscope, here in the Tennessee hills.

2

To watch the spinning of the thread is still not possible. But I have seen the spindle on which the spinning is done; and the spindle is a gene.

3

I have, in fact, seen not just one spindle but long rows of them, strung at intervals as in a factory. Which is as it should be. For the cells where the spinning is accomplished are mixing and sorting places for the raw makings of man and the less dreamy animals.

4

The photograph marked plate 1 is one of the first ever taken of unequivocally identified genes operating as spindles. The images are necessarily two-dimensional. In three-dimensional reality, the spindles are shaped like yarn spools: broad at one end and pointed at the other.

5

The thread that runs from the base of one spindle to the tip of another is deoxyribonucleic acid (nicknamed DNA), the now familiar carrier of the code of heredity. As the thread passes through the long axis of each spindle, the gene extrudes, at approximate right angles from the thread, about 100 individual fibers arranged in a graduated spiral. These are ribonucleic acid (RNA) fibers intended for construction of sub-factories within the cell: the ribosomes, where the twenty amino acid building blocks of life are strung into different configurations to form the various proteins that make up most of the finished body.

6

Since the ribosomes are in the cytoplasm surrounding the nucleus of the cell, and since the spinning process I am describing occurs within the cell's nucleus, the RNA ribosomal precursor fibers must somehow be moved off the genetic spindle and out through pore-like holes that pock the membrane enclosing the nucleus.

7

I could not witness this movement because the life in the thread and the spindles before me had ceased while the cell fragments containing them were being prepared for the microscope. What I have seen is a thin slice of life that had been stopped like a stilled frame in a motion picture. But my host at the Atomic Energy Commission's Oak Ridge National Laboratory, Dr. Oscar L. Miller, Jr., the man who brought the gene into human view for the first time, had

8

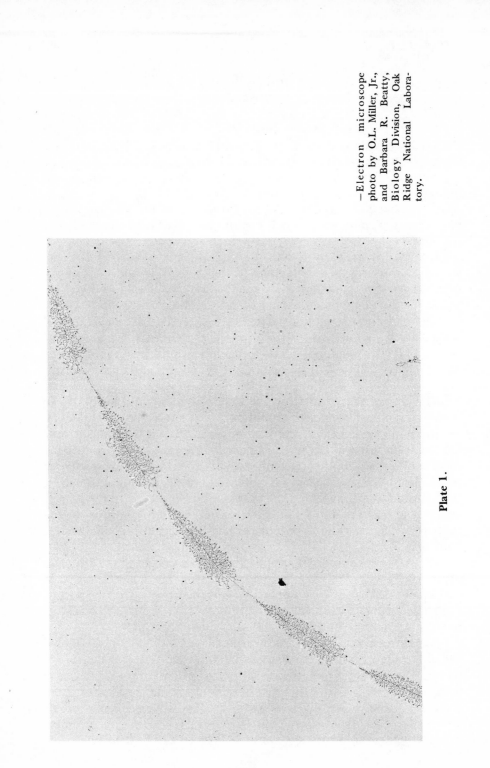

—Electron microscope photo by O.L. Miller, Jr., and Barbara R. Beatty, Biology Division, Oak Ridge National Laboratory.

Plate 1.

checked the fine structure of the cell slice beneath his electron microscope lens against what biochemists, using radioisotope tracers, had determined must be happening in the cell at that same point in time.

According to the biochemical evidence, the opening event in the sequence of the spindle's operation is the extrusion of the RNA fiber from the main thread of DNA. As the extrusion proceeds, the fiber is strung with a protein coat according to coded instructions from the DNA. This process goes on until each fiber reaches a predetermined length (note in the photograph that the maximum length is remarkably uniform), after which that particular RNA fiber separates from the DNA thread like a quill from a porcupine's back. The fibers depart individually after attaining individual maturity. En route they pass under an unidentified biological knife (presumably an enzyme) that chops each fiber into segments. The first segment to be severed   9
is about one-sixth the length of the whole fiber. This segment moves into the cytoplasm very quickly and at once coils into a tiny sphere. The coiling apparently occurs in response to instructions the DNA thread imprinted on the RNA fiber before setting the fiber loose. That part of the fiber that remains in the nucleus is subsequently chopped several times, until the surviving segment is about one-third as long as the original fiber had been. The final segment then moves out through the nuclear membrane into the cytoplasm, finds a tiny sphere formed by an earlier segment of fiber, and coils into a larger sphere alongside the tiny sphere. The two spheres together make a ribosome.

What is the significance of this stepped manufacturing procedure in the cell? This is the question Dr. Miller and his young assistant, Barbara R. Beatty, are now addressing themselves to. Mrs. Beatty is a quiet brunette, thoroughly devoted to her job. He is a serious but good-humored man with the quiet confidence that often accompanies the tall and broad shouldered. Not given to unnecessary verbiage, he has cautioned me to point out that although all genes—   10
those of insects, earthworms, fish, birds, and people alike—are assumed to act in identical fashion, the particular samples of the thread of life and the spindles I have seen here came from one of the eggs of a South African clawed toad. The toad's formal family names is *Xenopus laevis,* but the family is best known to biochemists because of the presence in it of "the Oxford mutant."

Now, a mutant is a genetic freak. Why should a genetic freak be   11
preferred as a source of discovery of the secrets of life?

It might reasonably be supposed that the choice was simply a matter of convenience—that the Oak Ridge National Laboratory is concerned with all aspects of nuclear radiation and that "the Oxford mutant" emerged in a family of ordinary toads because of a radioactive burst of some kind. But this is not true. Dr. Miller, a North Carolinian who has been studying genetics for most of his adult life (first at North Carolina State College, than at the University of Minnesota under Professor J.G. Gall), went to Oak Ridge in 1961 to undertake basic research into cell growth and reproduction. His work was in no sense oriented to the primary mission of the Oak Ridge National Laboratory. He was, instead, concerned with the life of normal cells, which needs to be understood in great detail before it is possible to understand abnormal cells.

"The Oxford mutant" was picked up accidentally by British biologists in 1958. The mutant became an instant scientific celebrity because a piece of its reproductive machinery was missing.

The fate of all living organisms is fixed by the genes, which reside on the chromosomes in the nuclei of cells. Whereas human cells have twenty-three pairs of chromosomes, the cells of *Xenopus laevis* have eighteen pairs. One pair—the sex or germ pair—when observed under an optical microscope is characterized by the presence of two dense globules. The globules are called nucleoli; they are resident sites for genes.

It is at this microscopic level that "the Oxford mutant" departs from the rest of its family. Instead of the two normal nucleoli in the egg cell, the mutant contains only one nucleolus. When the mutant is crossed with other toads, some of the offspring turn up with two nucleoli, some with only one, and some with none at all. The none-at-alls inevitably die before passing out of the tadpole stage.

No one knows how "the Oxford mutant" came to be what it is. The best guess is that eggs of a distant ancestor were struck by cosmic rays. The genealogy does not matter to Dr. Miller, who is content to have access to the massive store of data accumlated by biochemists in their breeding experiments with the mutant.

The great advantage the mutant had for the biochemists was that the mutant's embryo has no nucleolar genes and hence makes no ribosomal RNA. Ribosomal RNA is one of three types of RNA found in the nuclei of normal cells; its volume is much greater than the combined volume of the other two types (messenger RNA and transfer RNA). Consequently, the absence of the ribosomal type simplified observation of the processes that were going on and enabled the scientists to see the DNA clearly. This clarified picture of events in "the Oxford mutant" makes it easier for Dr. Miller to do his work with a normal wild member of the *Xenopus laevis* family.

At his suggestion, Mrs. Beatty showed me how to take an *Xenopus laevis* egg apart. First, she put a cluster of the eggs under an optical microscope. Viewed through the lens, they looked like balls with oppositely tinted hemispheres—one brown, one white. With two jeweler's forceps, she grabbed the membrane covering of one of the balls at two different points and pulled. The membrane burst, spilling the egg yolk into the surrounding liquid. She blew the yolk away from the field of vision with a pipette, leaving the nucleus of the cell suspended almost invisibly on the microscope slide. I thought I could make out a gel-like presence, but I would not have been sure had she not pointed out a cathedral-window effect of pristine light. Each pane of light marked the presence of a nucleolus. Altogether, Dr. Miller said, there were about one thousand nucleoli produced by a multiplier mechanism in the nucleus of the female oöcyte or germ cell.

Again, Mrs. Beatty jabbed with the jeweler's forceps, and now the invisible membrane of the nucleus was gone. All that remained was to lift out one of the nucleoli, drop it into a special preparation Dr. Miller had concocted, and wait for a nucleolus to unwind and reveal the thread of life within it.

Such a study could not possibly be done, at the present stage of knowledge, with a cell from a human or other mammal. Before a mammalian nucleolus could be pried out, so much denaturation would occur that the proteins would be cross-linked before anything could be discovered about how it happened.

A great deal is left to be discovered from the cells of the South African clawed toad. Look at plates 2 and 3 for an example. Notice the blank stretches of central DNA thread that sometimes appear between the spindle shapes of the genes. Usually a blank is about one-third as long as a gene. But some blanks run ten to twenty times the gene's length. Do these long empty stretches denote genes that are being suppressed by the genetic code, in keeping with heredity theory?

Dr. Alvin M. Weinberg, director of ORNL, who gave Dr. Miller's work prominent mention and high praise in ORNL's recently issued *State of the Laboratory—1968* report, thinks they may. Dr. Miller also entertains this possibility, but he wonders whether some of the blanks may not indicate other work the DNA is performing in relation to the chromosomes.

Three rows of spindle-like genes converge in plate 2, taken through the lens of Dr. Oscar Miller's electron microscope at Oak Ridge National Laboratory (AEC) in Tennessee. Note uniformity of graded lengths of RNA fibers being spun on the spindles. Also note long strand of bare thread (DNA) passing out of the field of view midway up the picture's right margin. Such barren stretches are frequent in cell nuclei studied by Dr. Miller. They may signify presence of genes with suppressed activity, as called for by prevailing theories of heredity. Many instances of supposed gene suppression can be seen when plate 3 is closely scrutinized.

—Photo by O.L. Miller, Jr., and Barbara R. Beatty, Biology Division, Oak Ridge National Laboratory

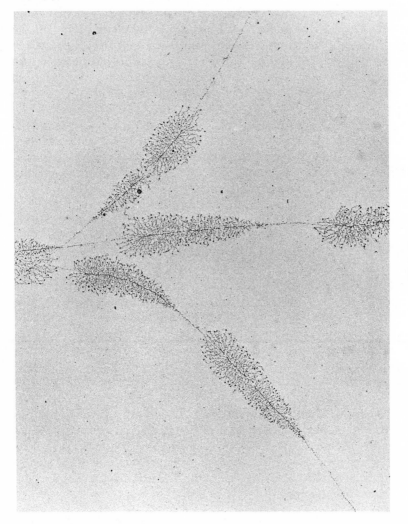

Plate 2.

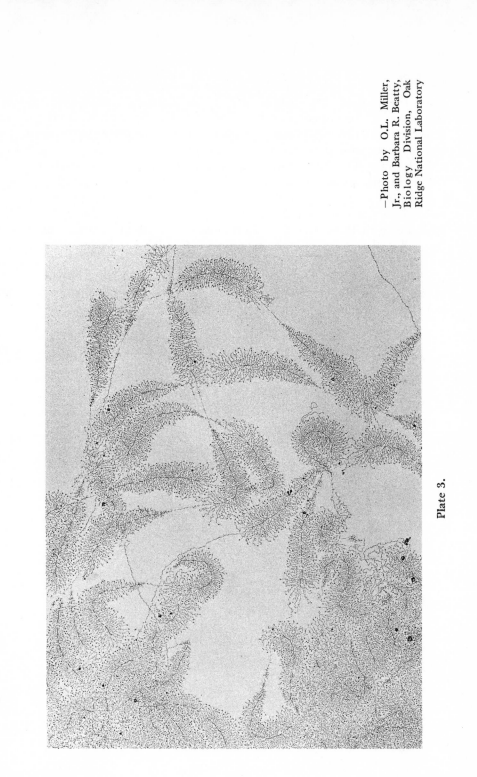

–Photo by O.L. Miller, Jr., and Barbara R. Beatty, Biology Division, Oak Ridge National Laboratory

Plate 3.

A primary mystery that Dr. Miller hopes to approach is the question of how genes are "turned on." There is strong evidence to suggest a period during cell division when the genes are at rest. Do they, 23 at the end of the rest period, go into action all at once? Or do they start to work in sequence, one after another, in a set order?

Although Dr. Miller and Mrs. Beatty are not now directly involved in the specific mission of ORNL's nuclear research, they may in time become so oriented. For in certain types of tumor cells the nucleoli in the cellular manufacturing plant grow to giant size. If the 24 appearance of these giants could be detected in the fine structure of the cell earlier than elsewhere, a new key might be found for the treatment or alleviation of cancer.

That evenatuality is not now in sight. It is enough to exult in man's new ability to see the thread of life and gradually to put 25 together an animated motion picture of its spinning.

THE GREAT TRUFFLE SNUFFLE

The Editors of Newsweek

The truffle is not much to look at—small, dark, wrinkled and warty—but it has a proud history. It was prized for its aromatic pungency by the ancient Greeks, who thought it was sown by the thunder. Pliny the Elder called it "among the most wonderful of all things," and Juvenal praised it in his satires. It acquired a darker reputation during the Middle Ages—the devil's work, people called it, grown from the spit of witches—but with the Renaissance it took on new luster as an aphrodisiac. Mme. de Pompadour fed truffles to Louis XV. Napoleon followed a truffle recipe from Périgord and begot Napoleon II. Even the judicious Brillat-Savarin wrote of the truffle that "it renders women more tender and men more loving." And as a delicacy, Alexandre Dumas called it "the *sacro sacrorum* of gastronomes." | 1

To gastronomes of today the truffle's glory remains undimmed. "The truffle," says Louis Vaudable, owner of Maxim's in Paris, "is irreplaceable." More practically, it also plays a considerable role in the French economy. While the exports of truffles themselves are relatively modest—17.6 tons last year, fetching $400,000—they are a vital ingredient in the luxury foods that are big business in France. "Without truffles," says a Ministry of Agriculture official, "French *charcuterie* would be no different from anyone else's. Even our *foie gras* depends on them for its prestige." With exports of *foie gras* accounting for $3 million last year, no wonder the annual truffle harvest is a matter of concern to France. It is also uncontrollable, unpredictable, and—apparently—unfathomable. | 2

The truffle season drawing to an end last week—it runs from November to February—was one of the best that France has enjoyed since the big freeze of 1956 (which may have upset the truffle's mysterious cycle of reproduction). Total production is estimated at 100 tons, roughly double that of the year before, and with truffles selling at $32 a pound in Paris and $41 in New York, it wasn't a bad showing. Certainly it brought cheer to the truffle hunters of Périgord and Quercy, the traditional truffle-growing regions of the southwest, and to the Vaucluse, Drôme, Gard and Ardèche areas in the southeast, which account for about two-thirds of production. But their cheer about this year's remarkable harvest was tinged with habitual gloom. The current crop was a long way below the bumper harvests of pre-World War I days, when the Périgord area alone produced as much as 300 tons. "It seems sometimes as though the earth | 3 is exhausted," sighs Fernand Henras, a Cahors dealer whose family has been in truffles for a century and a half.

The maddening thing about the truffle—aside from the fact that it grows underground, 3 inches to a foot beneath the surface—is that man has never learned to plant it or cultivate it. "We know neither how it is born, nor how it grows," wrote Brillat-Savarin in 1825. "The cleverest men have studied it. . . . Never has planting been followed by harvest." Even today not much is known about the life of   4
the truffle except that it is usually found around the roots of scrub oak trees. Says André Progent, the Minstry of Agriculture's chief of vegetable production: "There is still as much mystery about how the truffle grows as there is about life on the moon. All we can say is, the more oak trees you plant, the more truffles you are likely to find."

As knowledge of the truffle remains unchanged, so do the methods of tracking it down. From time immemorial, the peasants of Périgord and Quercy have used pigs whose sensitive noses are quick to spot the odor of truffles, and, more recently, specially trained dogs. On a typical truffle hunt last week, in an afternoon of pale sunlight, NEWSWEEK'S Elizabeth Peer accompanied Odette Malgoire, a Quercy farm wife, and a four-month-old pig named Toupière, along a   5
dirt road outside Cahors. "Suddenly Toupière cantered erratically into a clump of scrub oaks, with Mme. Malgoire holding her leash and skidding along behind. Toupière thrust her snout into the loose soil at the foot of an oak and began rooting excitedly. Soon, she unearthed a muddy object, the size of a golf ball, and started to eat it. Mme. Malgoire gave her a quick clout on the rump and snatched it from her jaws."

For the truffle pig it is a frustrating life. Not only is it deprived of savoring what it has scented out, but usually, after one season, it is sent off to market as pork. (Full-grown pigs tend to lose interest, and   6
become hard to handle. Dogs, on the other hand, can be used year after year and also have the advantage of not trying to eat the truffle.)

The selling of truffles also follows traditional patterns. At the goose market in Cahors on Saturday afternoons, peasants appear with baskets of eggs or other commodites—but with no truffles in sight. Only when a would-be buyer has been sharply scrutinized does the peasant dip into his basket, or into a pocket, or even inside his cap, and produce a fistful of truffles to be quickly weighed in a hand   7
scale and exchanged for francs. (He currently gets about $11 a pound, slightly down from last year's price when truffles were scarcer.) This furtive procedure is partly to avoid the attention of the

tax collector, but old truffle hands say it is a matter of native cunning, designed to create the feeling that the delicacy is in short supply.

Certainly the shortage is real enough in terms of demand among the world's gourmets. The French Government, in an effort to prove Brillat-Savarin wrong—that planting *can* be followed by harvest—has been pushing laboratory research into the truffle's habits, but with little success. Some truffle dealers are just as glad. "I hope that science never removes the truffle's veil of mystery," says Jacques Pébeyre, third generation of the country's leading family of truffle merchants. "I don't want to see truffles grown commercially like those pasty white mushrooms. The truffle must keep its mystery and dignity. After all, it isn't a cabbage."

THE PLIGHT OF THE U.S. PATIENT

The Editors of Time

American medicine is the best in the world.

Most Americans take this statement as an article of faith—so long as they are in good health. Even when they have a bout of illness they feel, for the most part, that they are getting excellent care. But growing numbers of patients, the consumers of American medicine, are asking questions that range from mildly nagging to openly angry. 1

When the doctor was first called, why did he refuse to make a house call? Did he take too long in making the right diagnosis? Did he prescribe too many drugs before he knew what the real trouble was? Did he pick the right surgeon to operate? Were all those lab 2 tests necessary? Did the surgeon charge too much? Why does a hospital room cost $60 a day, more than the fanciest resort hotel room? Why doesn't insurance cover more of those bills?

These questions are asked each year by many of the 130 million Americans who pay 500 million visits to the doctor. For them, the doctors write a billion prescriptions for a total drug bill of some $3.5 billion. Each year, 27 million Americans go into a general hospital, where they spend an average of 8.2 days and get a bill of $530, about 3 half of which is covered by insurance. The total cost of U.S. medical care is now $53 billion a year—5.9% of the gross national product, or 7.5% of all personal income. These figures are far higher than those for other Western countries with at least equivalent quality of care.

Is the U.S. citizen getting a fair shake for his money? For an estimated 25% of the population the answer is yes. For another 50% medical care can be described as passable, but it is certainly not as good as it could and should be. For 25% care is either inexcusably bad, given in humiliating circumstances, or nonexistent. The breakdown is not simply by social stratum: the rich do not necessarily get 4 the best care, nor the poor the worst. Says Dr. William H. Stewart, Surgeon General of the U.S. Public Health Service: "If even one American doesn't have access to a reasonable level of care, there's something wrong. And when millions don't, there's obviously something wrong."

As befits a huge industry, U.S. medicine has an impressive plant, and many of its facilities are indeed outstanding. In research and medical technolgoy the U.S. amazes and leads the world. A newborn baby with a defective heart can probably get the best care at Manhattan's Lenox Hill Hospital, which operates an elaborate unit exclusively for pediatric cardiology. For surgery on such a baby's heart,

U.S. surgeons are pre-eminent. So are the surgeons who operate on
older patients' arteries. For trouble in the brain's arteries, researchers   5
at Columbia-Presbyterian Medical Center have helped to develop a
magnetic probe that will swim through the arterial labyrinth and tell
the neurologist what he needs to know. At Harvard, surgeons practice knifeless surgery with a proton gun that destroys overactive
tissue deep inside the skull. At Massachusetts Eye and Ear Infirmary,
ophthalmic surgeons turn patients upside down to let gravity help
them in repositioning a detached retina.

Unhappily, such examples of American medical ingenuity do not
make American medicine the world's best. They are available to only
a few. The U.S. ranks 13th (behind several West European countries
and faraway New Zealand) in infant mortality, and behind most of   6
these countries in maternal mortality and death rates from heart-
artery diseases and cirrhosis of the liver. The U.S. averages are pulled
down largely by the poor health conditions of the blacks, other
minorities, and poor Southern whites.

Other comparisons are equally distressing. One involves dispar-
ities in the quality of medical care within the U.S., within states,
cities, and between cities and rural communities. One man may get
optimum care, while another who lives on the same street and enjoys
the same access to medical facilities may be handled in wretched   7
fashion. The greatest and least defensible gap of all is, in the words of
Dr. Malcolm Peterson, chief of medical services at St. Louis City
Hospital, "the wide disparity between the medicine that we know
how to give and what we actually give. They're miles apart."

Why has American medicine failed to live up to its wondrous
potential? The answer, says Dr. Philip Lee, who was top man for
health in the Department of Health, Education, and Welfare, is that
the U.S. has no system for the delivery of medical care. To talk of   8
the present system is ridiculous, he says, because it is a "non-
system." What the U.S. has, according to Dr. Odin Anderson of the
University of Chicago's Center for Health Administration Studies, is
a "pluralistic system" to match its pluralistic society.

The indirect but basic reason for this is that medicine is the only
big business in which the ultimate consumer has no control over
what he buys. The doctor prescribes the drug, for which the patient
must pay, willy-nilly. He orders a hospital admission, and the patient
rarely has any choice. The patient has no way of knowing whether he
is getting good counsel from his family doctor, good drugs from his
freindly pharmacist, good technical performance from his surgeon.   9
For him there is no Ralph Nader to blow the whistle on unethical

practices. There is no ombudsman to represent him before some impartial tribunal. The tightly organized medical profession fends off any and all attacks from the outside, and in cases of complaints against any of its members, sits as prosecutor, judge, and jury. It is the rare patient who even tries to protest an obviously excessive doctor's bill.*

Most U.S. physicians do not accept this bleak picture and point to the undeniable excellence of medicine in many areas. Yet in many ways the doctors themselves suffer from the lack of more rational organization in American medicine. For the most part dedicated and ingenious, they are usually overworked and harassed. They also have cause to complain of the patient's frequently faulty attitudes toward medical care. Some people, in all social strata, are simply afraid to admit that there is anything wrong with them; they put off seeking care until their disease is far advanced or even incurable. Some, espe- [10] cially among the poor and ill-educated, do not take advantage of care that is available to them. In a single borough of New York City, The Bronx, the infant death rate jumps 100% within five miles, going from north to south. The reason is sad but simple. The southeast Bronx is inhabited mainly by poor blacks and Puerto Ricans. Al- though excellent clinics are open for predelivery and infant care, it takes several hours and several 20¢ bus fares for a woman to avail herself of them, and, lacking a babysitter, she probably has to drag her other children along with her. The northern Bronx is largely white, Jewish, and health-oriented; there women go routinely to their private physicans for the same services.

Most consumers of medical care—again, regardless of status—are "crisis-oriented," as are most of their doctors, virtually all hospitals, and most insurance plans. Not only does this deny the nation the [11] potential benefits of preventive medicine; it also denies the majority of patients orderly access to the care they need when they need it.

Even for the well-to-do and articulate citizen, getting such care involves an obstacle course. He is, in effect, challenged to take out the right kind of insurance, probably in his 20s or 30s, and certain- ly years before he expects to need it. Then he is challenged to find [12] the right doctor. For none of these choices are there any reliable buyers' guides. At successive times in his health history three major components of care—doctors, hospitals, and insurance—will be simul- taneously involved.

---

*In an average year, patients bring 150 complaints of fee gouging against the 7,200 members of the New York County (Manhattan) Medical Society, and 25% of them win remission or reduction of the fee.

Obviously, it is the doctor who should guide the patient through the bewildering health-care maze. Yet not enough U.S. doctors today are qualified to fill this role well, and the organization of the profession discourages it. With the discoveries of new and potent "wonder drugs"—insulin, the sulfas and antibiotics, new hormones and vaccines—each succeeding decade after the 1920s should have been a golden age of medicine. But medicine needed the understanding and compassion for the patient that had marked the old-style, unscientific family doctor. The American Medical Association, long the champion of improved medical practice, lost sight of the patient. It developed certain obsessions, seeing threats to its own and to every doctor's existence or financial well-being on every side. Among A.M.A. fetishes are "free choice of physician" and "fee for service." 13

The first means that the patient must not be locked into a system in which he will have a doctor assigned to him. He must have free choice of all the physicians in his area—if he can find one. There must be no "third party" hiring doctors on salary and then charging patients for their services. For nearly three decades the A.M.A. was almost as strongly opposed to group practice, in which a number of physicians set up shop together and divide the fees collected from all their patients. The A.M.A. feared that this would prove to be a step toward socialized medicine. 14

The second principle does not mean simply that the doctor must be paid for his services, which is his obvious right. Rather, it means that he must be paid for each individual service, on the basis that U.A.W. President Walter Reuther aptly and contemptuously calls "piecework." It means that no doctor should offer lifetime care to a patient for a flat or annual fee, and thus rules out payment by an annual dues system. It means that when a patient goes into a hospital for an operation he must pay the admitting doctor's bill, a separate surgeon's bill, a separate radiologist's bill for X-rays, and a separate anesthesiologist's bill. 15

The A.M.A. has had only moderate success in choking back group practice and prepayment. Group practice is widespread, prepayment plans are growing, and there are numerous third parties in the medical complex. About 2,300 "multiple-specialty and general practice" groups have been formed, comprising 20,000 doctors, some in big cities, some in remote towns, some in hospitals or other large medical centers, some in a simple suite of doctor's offices. 16

By far the biggest and most successful group practice is Minnesota's famous Mayo Clinic, with 500 doctor-members. Most groups, with eight to a dozen members, comprise general practitioners or

internists, pediatricians, obstetrician-gynecologists, a radiologist, a   17
surgeon, an orthopedist, and an ophthalmologist. The mix varies with
local demand, but in each group a family doctor, the patient's first
and continuing contact with the group, steers him to specialists as
needed.

Year after year the U.S. has fewer and fewer family doctors to do
the steering. In 1930, G.P.s outnumbered specialists 70 to 30. Today
the ratio is more than reversed, 21 to 79. The nation's medical   18
schools have been increasingly geared to train specialists, and few
graduates now go from internship into general practice.

Membership in a group practice, whether as G.P. or specialist, is
no ironclad guarantee that a doctor is outstanding. But at least it
ensures that he talks to other doctors regularly and is exposed to
some of the ferment in medicine. The 50 states' licensing laws, and
the attitude of the A.M.A. and most other professional organizations,
offer no such assurance. Theoretically, it would be possible for a man
to have graduated from medical school at 25 in 1934, to have been
licensed after a year's internship, and to have practiced as G.P. ever
since then without having heard a professional word about most of
modern medicine. There is no requirement that he ever read a jour-   19
nal, attend a medical meeting, or even talk to another doctor. In
practice, of course, the doctor's sense of duty and the growing sophistication (or hypochondria) of the public impel him to keep up.
But there is no mandatory continuing education, and there is no
re-examination. There is no law limiting his practice to his competence. A G.P. could legally do a heart transplant, if he were fool-
hardy enough. A license is for life.* Only the American Academy of
General Practice (with 31,000 members among the nation's 72,000
G.P.s) expels members who fail to take required refresher courses.

In most smaller cities and towns virtually every physician is listed
as "on the staff" of one or more local hospitals. This does not mean
that he is paid by the hospital, and it tells nothing about his
qualifications. It does mean that he is a member of the county medical society, has the privilege of admitting his patients to the hospital,
and is basically responsible for overall care thereafter. Many a big-
city patient is denied this continuing contact with his own doctor. In   20
New York City alone, some 5,000 physicans (close to one-third of
the city's total) have no privileges at any voluntary hospital. They

---

*Only 31 states reported revocation of license proceedings for 1967. These states and 469
cases in which 208 licenses were revoked. No fewer than 148 revocations were for nonpay-
ment of license fees. Violation of the narcotics law, including self-addiction, with 13 cases,
and abortion, with ten cases, were the only causes relating to medical practice.

can either surrender their patient to the mercies of interns, residents, and specialists who have never seen him before, or try to get him into a proprietary hospital, which will turn no one away if it has an empty bed.

Good, bad, or indifferent, doctors are doing well financially. Their incomes have skyrocketed and approached escape velocity with the passage of Medicare and, for some states, Medicaid. In 1961 the average doctor, after office and other professional expenses, netted $25,000. By 1965 it was up to $28,000, and last year it reached $34,000. Dr. Martin Cherkasky, the crusading director of New York's Montefiore Hospital, says that doctors have the consumer   21 over a barrel because they are in such short supply and such great demand. The shortage was sedulously fostered by the A.M.A. for 30 years, beginning in the Great Depression and ending only in 1967, when it conceded that something must be done to increase the medical schools' output. "This shortage," Cherkasky says, "makes it impossible for society to deal with the medical profession. You're at their mercy."

The patient is also at the mercy of the hospitals. Which are the good ones? The nearest thing to a criterion, except for university affiliation, is whether a hospital is accredited by the Joint Commission on Accreditation of Hospitals, set up by the A.M.A., the American College of Surgeons, the American College of Physicians, and the American Hospital Association. The U.S. has 5,850 general-care hospitals,*   22 with 645,000 beds for medical and surgical patients, 82,000 for maternity cases. Of the 5,850, only 3,914 have received the cachet of accreditation. Each year there are about 1.5 million admissions to the unaccredited remainder. Worse, in Cherkasky's opinion, accreditation standards are so low as to be meaningless.

Hospitals are big business. Yet according to Jerome Pollack, professor of medical economics at Harvard Medical School, they are a prime example of gross mismanagement. Hospitals are run by boards   23 of trustees, made up mostly of businessmen, who would never dream of running their own corporations the way they try to operate a hospital.

The first objective of most hospitals is to operate in the black. For generations, U.S. hospitals achieved this by paying little or nothing to interns, residents, student nurses, and "nonprofessional"

---

*About 5,100 of them are operated as non-profit institutions and awkwardly called "voluntary"; the rest, concentrated in California, New York, and Texas, are proprietary hospitals, frankly operated for profit. Excluded from these figures are all psychiatric and federally supported institutions.

help. Social justice has caught up with the hospitals and found them totally unprepared. They have to pay interns and residents halfway decent salaries ($9,000 to $12,000 in some areas). What has hit them   24 hardest is the demand of scrubwomen, kitchen help and janitors to be paid what is called a living wage. Most U.S. hospitals are grudgingly raising the pay of this nonprofessional help to $1.60 an hour, though in New York and California the rates are nudging $2.50 an hour.

With the reduction in shift hours and the demands of better care, the ratio of hospital personnel to patients has soared from about 145 employees per 100 patients to 260 per 100 in the past 20 years. With mounting labor costs, up go hospital room rates. Hospital administrators stand aghast at this; yet in all too many ways it is their own fault. Dr. Leona Baumgartner, a former health commissioner of New York City who is now at Harvard, can cite chapter and verse to show how hospitals have consistently lagged behind reality and then reacted in a "Who—me?" way. When the baby boom of the late 1940s   25 was aborning, says Dr. Baumgartner, she got calls early every year asking for her forecast of the prospective birth rate—from diaper services, baby-clothing makers, and baby-food processors. "Would the hospitals call?" she asks rhetorically. "No! The doctors did nothing, and the hospitals did nothing to meet a predictable demand." It was the same, says Dr. Baumgartner, with the mandated wage increases: "They were caught flatfooted when the minimum-wage law was applied to them."

In a Madison Avenue spirit, hospitals play games with words. Blue Cross and most other insurers pay for a semiprivate room. In   26 many hospitals, this may turn out to be a room with four beds, making it a demi-semiprivate room.

Occupancy rates are as important to hospitals as to hotels. Counting the overhead, it may cost the hospital upwards of $40 a day to maintain a semiprivate bed even when it is empty. It costs only about $3 to $5 a day more when the bed is occupied—that being the charge for the patient's meals. But an empty bed earns nothing, while an occupied bed earns dollars. Therefore, while vir-   27 tually no surgery is performed on weekends, it is common practice to admit surgery patients on Friday. That keeps the bed filled, profitably for the hospital, until Sunday, when the patient gets his first dose of medicine to prepare him for Monday's workup in preparation for Tuesday's operation.

Much more that is done to the patient in the hospital is scheduled with no consideration for him. What the medical staff intends as superefficiency seems, by the time it explodes around the patient, merely frenetic, and is highly discomforting. "They woke me up to give me a sleeping pill" may be an apocryphal complaint. But it is still common practice to awaken a patient at 4 a.m. in order to feed him one of his countless, multicolored pills, and perhaps again an hour or two later for a thermometer reading or a hypodermic shot. These universal complaints, though seemingly petty, are symptomatic of the depersonalized atmosphere of too many hospitals. Equally distressing is the noise, which makes sleep or even rest far too difficult.

With rare exceptions, every community hospital is an empire in itself. Its medical and surgical staffs demand—and get—costly equipment and facilities for their exclusive use, regardless of whether another hospital down the block already has them lying idle two-thirds of the time. In Miami, the VA hospital has a $100,000 linear accelerator for the radiation treatment of cancer, but Cedars of Lebanon Hospital is installing its own. Neither will be used at anywhere near capacity. At "hospital corners" in Los Angeles, on North Vermont Avenue and Sunset and Beverly Boulevards, are four cobalt-60 radiation units, also for cancer, where one, or at most two, would do.

Hospital planners have been arguing for years that the crisis-care hospital for the acutely ill patient is only one part of the complex that is needed. There should be, they say, a motel-type unit to which a man can drive his own car when he goes in for a checkup, where he can live like a healthy human being and go to the cafeteria for his meals, merely following his doctor's diet instructions. At the other end of the line, there should be a halfway house for patients not quite ready to go home who still need some, but not 24-hour, nursing care and who can fend for themselves in a dining room. The planners have not proved very persuasive. Hospital administrators give lip service to the idea, but little more.

Countless hospitals have been and still are being built in the wrong places for the wrong reasons. Under the Hill-Burton Act of 1946 any hamlet could raise matching funds to get itself a tiny hospital of 20 to 30 beds—and too many did. These are not only uneconomic but bad for medicine, says New Orleans Surgeon Alton Ochsner: no hospital with fewer than 100 beds is medically viable and he suggests that none should have more than 600.

A basic trouble with today's hospitals is that, like today's doctors, they have been geared to crisis care. In fact, says Palo Alto's grand old man Dr. Russel V. Lee (father of Philip and other M.D.

Lees), 30% of the patients in a hospital at any one time should not
be there. Either they have been admitted for what are really diag-   32
nostic procedures, to gain insurance coverage, or they are past the
acute stage of their illness and should be in some sort of convalescent
or other extended-care facility, in which the costs would be 40% or
50% less.

When the idea of voluntary health insurance for the U.S. germi-
nated in the 1930s, the actuaries insisted that whatever was covered
must be quantifiable, so that it could be priced. They hit upon
hospitalization as a tangible item, and Blue Cross was born. But   33
definitions of hospital costs are so complex that ever since, while it
has expanded into 45 states, Blue Cross has been involved in haggles
with state insurance departments over rates.

What Blue Cross will reimburse varies from state to state, and
within states, according to what plan the subscribing group has
chosen. Some Blue Cross plans in the West cover in-hospital doctor's   34
bills, a function generally reserved in the East for Blue Shield. Whatever its limitations, Blue Cross was such a success that commercial
insurance companies soon tried to emulate it.

The trouble with all the early coverage, by both "the Blues" and
the commercials, was that it was not health insurance, although it
was widely misrepresented as such. It was, and to a great extent
remains, sickness insurance. Far from putting a premium on preventive medicine and the maintenance of good health, it puts a premium on sickness. Until recently, most Blue Cross plans covered no
care outside a hospital and specifically excluded diagnostic procedures. The result has been connivance to defraud the insurers. Often
if a woman needs a diagnostic pelvic examination that might better—
but need not necessarily—be done in a hospital, her doctor enters
some meaningless diagnosis such as leucorrhea or dysmenorrhea
(which practically every woman has now and then) and plunks her in   35
the hospital for two days. The insurance pays virtually all the hospital bill and, if the family has coverage of the Blue Shield type, the
doctor's bill as well. To Mark Berke, director of San Francisco's
Mount Zion Hospital, the system "puts a premium on being a horizontal rather than a vertical patient." Says Surgeon General Stewart:
"For episodic care of the middle-income class, the Blues do a reasonably good job. But there simply aren't enough benefits—for office
visits, for drugs outside the hospital, for a lot of things. Overall, the
Blues still pay only about 35% of an insured's medical expenses.
And for chronic illnesses, even the fully insured subscriber is in
trouble."

However broad the Blues and commercial health-insurance companies may become, they are still likely to suffer by comparison with prepaid group-practice plans on two key issues: hospitalization and surgery. In 1966 the Blues tallied 876 patient days in the hospital per 1,000 subscribers (excluding maternity cases), while the group-practice plans had only 408. Blue Shield subscribers had 73 surgical procedures per 1,000, while the groups' subscribers had 31. For tonsils and adenoids the disparity was still greater: 8.4 *v.* 1.0.

Now both the Blues and the commercials are being crowded by Medicare. Despite the long years of angry controversy that preceded its enactment, Medicare has caused no upheavals in medicine generally. Hospital admissions of oldsters have increased, in most areas, by no more than 5%. True, hospitals that used to do much charity work—and treated their patients as charity cases—are losing these patients to voluntary hospitals. For the first time they have a choice.

Less than two years ago the A.M.A.'s then president, Dr. Milford O. Rouse of Dallas, sputtered against what he considered the heresy of regarding medical care as a right rather than a privilege. "Today," says Walter McNerney, president of the national Blue Cross Association, "it is firmly accepted that no one is going to be without care who needs it. That battle is over." The questions then are: How shall it be delivered? How will it be paid for? And how good will it be?

There is a growing consensus that the best method for delivery is "the satellite system." At the center of each system would be a university medical school with its affiliated hospitals, or some medical center like the Mayo Clinic, which may not be part of a medical school but has equal standing. The first ring of satellites would be community hospitals. The second ring would be community health centers, some along the lines of the Office of Economic Opportunity centers now operating in such disparate places as Boston, Mass., and Mound Bayou, Miss. These centers could have their own satellites; in areas where distances are great and people are few they might be manned by a "physician's assistant," a new breed of paramedical personnel with skills and training equivalent to those of medical corpsmen in the Armed Forces.

To get satellite systems into their proper orbits, regional planning is a necessity. A few areas have voluntarily begun such planning. For the rest, says Houston Surgeon Michael E. DeBakey, it may be necessary for the Federal Government to set rules and enforce them. One area plan has been started by the University of Oklahoma without such prodding and will cover the state. Its clinics, like one now operating in Wakita, will have three doctors: a general physician, a pediatrician, and one for obstetrics and gynecology. With three men on duty, one of them can always get away for vacation or refresher courses. They will have ready access to the medical center's battery of specialists. The three doctors agree to stay for a specified number of years. The citizens of Wakita and surrounding Grant County put up $500,000 for a 27-bed clinic and a 24-bed nursing home.

Staffing the satellites remains a problem, and the "physician's assistants" are probably the best solution. These men and women can replace doctors in some areas, and everywhere they can relieve doctors of time-consuming detail work. Much of this work, from filling out case histories to drawing blood specimens, they can actually do   41 better than many a doctor. Duke University is the pioneer in training physician's assistants. It has 31 in its current two-year class and will soon enroll 50. Three other schools have followed suit, and 50 are getting ready to do so. The numbers are still small, but if the experiment works they can be rapidly expanded.

With added personnel, the U.S. annual bill for medical care will continue to go up, but more care will be delivered in return. How to pay for it will remain a problem at all levels. All or virtually all Americans are now medically indigent," says Economist Pollack. "Health insurance for all has become a necessity." Dr. Philip Lee says: "The Federal Government will have to fill in the chinks of the private system. Private insurance does fine during the years when people are employed, but it doesn't do well for the aged or the unemployed. The Government must fill those needs." Before last   42 November's election, Lee's former boss, ex-HEW Secretary Wilbur Cohen, had on his desk a plan to extend Medicare to provide "crisis care" for all Americans. Some suggest extending it to children, to the handicapped, and perhaps to all the indigent (Medicaid having proved to be no more effective than a bread poultice in most states). McNerney is pressing all Blue Cross plans to broaden their coverage. A practical man, he notes that merely shortening the average patient's hospital stay by one day would save well over $1 billion.

U.A.W.'s Reuther, once reviled but now widely lauded for boosting health insurance by building it into union contracts, keeps saying that he will soon announce plans for nationwide health insurance but has offered no details. Senator Edward Kennedy is on record as favoring, in principle, some such proposal. No serious student of the U.S. medical scene believes that the nation is ready for– or would   43 accept in the foreseeable future–a system like the British National Health Service. All current proposals envision the perpetuation of free enterprise in medical care–but a more responsible free enterprise system, with which the Federal Government and the states could enter into mutually profitable partnerships.

The voluntary programs are expected to predominate. There is increasing clamor from consumers for release from their passive, captive role and for an active voice. One who will support them is San Francisco's Berke, president elect of the A.H.A. The association, he says, will soon set up a national consumer forum, and Berke would like to have it include not only representatives of consumer groups like labor unions, but housewives and other individuals who have been through the medical mill as both patient and parent. 44

One of the most hopeful signs of change on the medical-care horizon comes from the young men and women who, three or four years from now, will be supplying much of that care as interns and residents. Across the continent, New York's Cherkasky declares, there is now "a substantial number of medical students who don't put economics above everything else. These young people want to find in their profession a social commitment as well as a decent living. These kids are marvelous. They're even beginning to force changes in the curriculum. They don't think that molecular biology is more important than people." 45

Another promising development was announced last week in Chicago. For years the American Academy of General Practice has been campaigning to have its branch of the profession recognized as a specialty—despite the contradiction in terms. Now, after many commissions and conferences, the A.M.A.'s Council on Medical Education and the Advisory Board for Medical Specialties have granted the G.P.'s plea and agreed to let the generalist become a specialist in "family medicine." The A.A.G.P.'s president, Chicagoan Dr. Maynard Shapiro, made it clear that no G.P. will get the exalted rank without earning it. There will be no grandfather clause for automatic certification of present members. Each G.P. will have to put in at least 300 hours of accredited postgraduate study to earn it. 46

Said Shapiro: "The new family physician will be a family counselor in sickness and in health. He'll be trained in both the art and science of medicine. He'll have training in psychiatry, psychology, sociology, cultural anthropology, and economics in order to deal with all aspects of the patient's problems." Added Shapiro: the family medicine man will bring back "the compassion of the oldtime family doctor." 47

Doctors are given to claiming that medicine is both an art and a science. The fact is that until a half-century ago it was virtually all art with scarcely a modicum of science. Recently it has become virtually all science, and whatever art remains has often been obscured by materialism and poor organization. Today not only disgruntled patients but also a growing body of opinion makers and activists in public life and in medicine itself recognize its short-comings –and   48 know that they can be remedied. It will take time for the emergence of a better-organized system for the delivery of medical care. It will take even more time for the new types of family physicians and medical graduates to make their mark on the nationwide practice of medicine. When they do, U.S. medicine may yet, in fact as well as in cliché, become the world's best.

INDEX

417